Herman B Wells

Herman B Wells

The Promise of the American University

JAMES H. CAPSHEW

INDIANA UNIVERSITY PRESS   *Bloomington & Indianapolis*

INDIANA HISTORICAL SOCIETY PRESS   *Indianapolis*

This book is a co-publication of

INDIANA UNIVERSITY PRESS
601 North Morton Street
Bloomington, Indiana 47404–3797 USA

iupress.indiana.edu

Telephone orders 800-842-6796
Fax orders 812-855-7931

and

INDIANA HISTORICAL SOCIETY PRESS
Eugene and Marilyn Glick Indiana
History Center
450 West Ohio Street
Indianapolis, Indiana 46202-3269 USA

indianahistory.org

♾ The paper used in this publication
meets the minimum requirements of
the American National Standard for
Information Sciences – Permanence of
Paper for Printed Library Materials,
ANSI Z39.48–1992.

*Manufactured in the
United States of America*

*Library of Congress
Cataloging-in-Publication Data*

Capshew, James H.
  Herman B Wells : the promise of the
American university / James H. Capshew.
  p. cm.
  Includes bibliographical references and
index.
  ISBN 978-0-253-35720-5 (cloth : alk.
paper) – ISBN 978-0-253-00569-4
(e-book) 1. Wells, Herman B. 2. Indiana
University – Presidents–Biography.
3. College presidents – Indiana –
Biography. I. Title.
  LD25161938.W44 C38 2012
  378.0092 – dc23
  [B]
                           2011044883

1 2 3 4 5   17 16 15 14 13 12

To the Genius Loci of Indiana University

and

in loving memory of Herman B Wells

Consult the Genius of the Place in all.

Alexander Pope, 1731

We are the children of our landscape; it dictates behaviour and even thought in the measure to which we are responsive to it.

Lawrence Durrell, 1957

The soul of a landscape, the spirits of the elements, the genius of every place will be revealed to a loving view of nature.

Karl Jaspers, 1970

One has to learn what the meaning of local is, for universal purposes. The local is the only thing that is universal.

William Carlos Williams, 1929

To become intimate with your home region, to know the territory as well as you can, to understand your life woven into the local life does not prevent you from recognizing and honoring the diversity of other places, cultures, ways. On the contrary, how can you value other places if you do not have one of your own? If you are not yourself *placed,* then you wander the world like a sightseer, a collector of sensations, with no gauge for measuring what you see. Local knowledge is the grounding for global knowledge.

Scott Russell Sanders, 1993

Contents

Perhaps biography is the flat map
Abstracted from the globe of someone's life.

Maura Stanton, 1984

A Hoosier State of Mind

AS I LEFT OUR FIRST MEETING IN 1977, I knew at once Herman B Wells was an extraordinary human being. Mindfully present to others, he projected a radiant savoir faire. Fortune had smiled on me and given me the opportunity to learn from this remarkable individual. I labored as a lowly houseboy in the Chancellor's residence. In exchange for a few hours of pleasant work every week, I was provided a room, full board, and the complete run of the house. I also started my study of his personal character and his work at Indiana University, trying to fathom the secret to his effectiveness. This volume is one fruit of that continuing study.

I soon figured out that Wells existed at the center of a massive social network revolving around Indiana University. His devotion to its welfare and his inspired leadership were already legendary. His relationship to the institution stretched back to his college days in the early 1920s, and since that time he had enveloped generations in his warm embrace. He drew me inexorably into that network and made me feel that I had special status as a member of what I would later term his elective family.

After two years, when I graduated and left his employ, I was still amazed at his personal beneficence and institutional charisma. Over the next decade I pursued higher education on the East Coast and he reluctantly accepted the process that threatened to turn him into an icon. In 1990, I happily accepted a faculty position at IU, and joined the university that he did so much to build. Instead of letters and the occasional visit, now we could resume our face-to-face meetings, where we talked about nearly everything under the sun. But it always led back to this place, his beloved IU. When I broached the idea of writing about

his life, Wells needled me playfully, "Isn't there something better to do
with your time?" In his last years, he freely made time for my queries and
questions, and wrote a letter of introduction to my research project. That
blessing was all I needed.

Now a decade has passed since his death and I am experiencing a
common reaction among biographers as they complete their studies. My
late colleague, Richard S. Westfall, the preeminent biographer of Isaac
Newton, put it well when he commented that the closer he got to understanding Newton, the more he receded from view. Westfall recognized a
profound truth about all human relationships – at their essence they defy
reduction into anything other than what they are.[1] Nevertheless I offer
an interpretation of Wells's life and career, albeit a necessarily partial
and incomplete one.

Herman Wells organized his life around Indiana University. As a student, he was born again when he discovered the rich cultural landscape
of the Bloomington campus. The unique genius loci of Indiana became a
touchstone that increasingly guided his activities to the time he became
president in 1937, when he made a lifelong commitment to the welfare
of his alma mater. Wells was the major architect for a prominent exemplar of one of our most distinctive modern institutions – the American
research university – by building upon a premodern sensibility of place
and altruistic devotion to others, using the tools he acquired from the
political, bureaucratic, and technological developments of the twentieth century. During the first part of the century Indiana was a decent,
yet provincial, university. Under his leadership it experienced a great
leap forward, competing with its peers in the Big Ten and developing
an impressive reputation in the sciences, the humanities, and the arts
through graduate and professional education as well as international
outreach efforts.

Although he was well known to other educators during his time,
Wells is little treated in the historiography of higher education – in part
because Indiana University does not figure prominently in the rise of
the American research university before World War II.[2] A related cause
is that the Bloomington campus lacks a medical or engineering school,
so the institution is often overlooked in analyses that begin with mea-

sures of research funds or other monetary considerations.[3] Wells himself cultivated humility and modesty about his leadership. He did not write much about the pressing educational issues of the day, so his impact as an author was minor. His very modus operandi – face-to-face meetings, efficiently pushing papers across his desk, thanking others for their contributions, and generally avoiding the limelight – made this most public of men less famous than one might reasonably expect.

But close observers did notice Wells and what he was accomplishing at Indiana. Stephen Graubard, longtime editor of *Dædalus* (proceedings of the American Academy of Arts and Sciences), stated, "I visited the President of Indiana only once, but I knew a great deal about him. As someone interested in higher education in the '60s, it was impossible not to think of him as well as Kerr and others who retained greater reputations."[4] In their study of educational leadership, Howard Gardner and Emma Laskin maintained that "the builders of the large national universities and multiversities of today, such as Herman Wells at Indiana University, John Hannah at Michigan State University, and, above all, Clark Kerr at the University of California" depended upon success at the public articulation of an organizational saga and, at the same time, an ability to remain in the background while fostering a sustainable institutional culture.[5]

American historian Allan Nevins, in his 1962 book, *The State Universities and Democracy,* thought that the "creation of an atmosphere, a tradition, a sense of the past" was a difficult but important task for tax-supported institutions, requiring "time, sustained attention to cultural values, and the special beauties of landscape or architecture." He had the example of Wells at Indiana in mind when he said: "This spiritual grace the state universities cannot quickly acquire, but they have been gaining it."[6]

Historians of higher education have not been completely silent on the subject of Wells. John Thelin asserts that Wells was one of the best illustrations of "an innovative style of presidential leadership" that was "central to the surge of the new American state university."[7] More than thirty years ago, University of Wisconsin historian Merle Curti wrote this of the Wells administration: "No one, of course, can say what would have been accomplished without the leadership, ability, work, and dedication of President (later Chancellor) Herman B Wells. His contributions cannot be easily summarized. . . . He did much to make Indiana proud of its university. Without uprooting the best in its traditions, he did more than any other single person in transforming a parochial campus into a distinguished, cosmopolitan one."[8]

Wells had a holistic sense of the learning process and the academic enterprise. He came to see clearly the genius loci of Indiana University – the place-based dynamic of human activity and historical associations that inhere in the campus environment, both material and moral. Learning was its raison d'être, and it took place through the academic community's pursuit of specialized curricula, educational programs, scholarship, and creative activity. For Wells, the university's place, its people and its programs were interconnected systems and the cultivation of any one would have ramifications for the others. Literally, the "place" designated primarily the Bloomington campus – the flagship of IU – but it took on metaphorical meaning as well by referring to the constellation of IU-related institutions, organizations, and programs around the world.

His is a story of remarkable intelligence and drive, of financial acuity and fiduciary discernment, of tremendous social skill and grace, and of relentless devotion to a single cause – the greatness of Indiana University as a national, and even international, educational institution. The life history of Wells is inextricably intertwined with the organizational saga of Indiana University as he came to be seen as the embodiment of its institutional values and the personification of its community. His brilliant career as an audacious agent for the commonwealth – whether the commonwealth of Indiana University, the state of Indiana, American higher education, or the international sisterhood of universities – demonstrates the integration of American and Midwestern values into the very heart of the definition of scholarly purpose and academic enterprise. Wells built an institution, and became one himself. These pages recount a tale about cultivating the genius loci of Indiana by a devoted son, extraordinary servant, and faithful partner.

Acknowledgments

THE JOURNEY TO THIS BOOK STARTED A LONG TIME AGO. In the 1950s and 1960s, I grew up in the shadow of Indiana University, utterly unaware of its chief modern architect. I became an IU undergraduate in the 1970s, and worked as a residential houseboy to Chancellor Wells from 1977 to 1979. Since 1990, I have served on the IU faculty. In 1999, agents of IU Press – director John Gallman and sponsoring editor Robert J. Sloan – took a chance on an embryonic project and offered me a book contract. Soon after, I was lucky enough to employ librarian and archivist Faye E. Mark as my research assistant for the Wells Biography Project.

I owe a special debt to Faye. She combines an extraordinary knowledge of IU history and folklore with a truly remarkable ability to ferret obscure records. The project's factotum, she was equally adept in researching sources or conversing about interpretations. Her skill at finding documents and her insightful suggestions were invaluable, and this book would not have existed without her superb effort.

The staff at the IU Archives – Philip C. Bantin, Dina M. Kellams, Bradley D. Cook, Carrie L. Schwier, Kathleen A. Cruikshank, Ryan K. Lee, and Kristen Walker – have been highly effective at managing university records and have been wonderfully supportive colleagues.

Other individuals, including librarians and archivists, who provided assistance were Bridget L. Edwards (Wylie House Museum); Wesley W. Wilson and John R. Riggs (DePauw University); Clifford T. Muse, Jr., and Raymond J. Smith (Howard University); Thomas Mason and Ray E. Boomhower (Indiana Historical Society); and Jamey Hickson (Lebanon Public Library).

Several people provided valuable information in interviews: Philip A. Amerson, Jean L. Anderson, Eugene Brancolini, Dorothy Collins, Marge Counsilman, Jean Creek, James Elliott, Mary Gaither, Paul H. Gebhard, Donald J. Gray, Lee H. Hamilton, Esther Heady, Helen Heady, Guy R. Loftman, Robert M. O'Neil, John Plew, Rudy Pozzatti, John W. Ryan, Denis Sinor, George Taliaferro, Orlando L. Taylor, and LaVerta L. Terry.

While drafting the book I spent a transcendent May in New Mexico at the adobe guesthouse of one of my oldest friends, Andrew R. Campbell. One of my favorite companions, Trena Depel, was always ready to talk about Wells, whether on the phone or in Bloomington, San Francisco, and places in between. Brian J. Kearney has been an indispensible comrade in the mission to bring the Wells legacy to light.

I was fortunate to have many colleagues and friends, at IU and elsewhere, who lent their ears, contributed opinions and insights, told stories, and supplied encouragement in various ways: Malcolm Abrams, Debbie and Fred Albert, John Bancroft, Eric Bartheld, Douglas E. Bauder, Kenneth Beckley, Domenico Bertoloni Meli, Devin Blankenship, Marjorie S. Blewett, David J. Bodenhamer, John E. Bodnar, Sharrel and Joseph Boike, Elizabeth Boling, Bill Breeden, Nan Brewer, Pauline Brin, Ann Bristow, Lisa Brower, Charlene Brown, Linda Bucklin, George Bull, Marcia Busch-Jones, Beverly Byl, Alejandra Laszlo Capshew, David Carrico, Barbara Coffman, Kyla Cox, Wayne O. Craig, Terri L. Crouch, Kate Dacy, Betty Denger, Marvant Duhon, Bonnita Farmer, Hussain M. Farzad, Leo Faye, Harry Ford, Charles R. Forker, Kathleen A. Foster, Lawrence J. Friedman, Michael Friesel, Deborah Galyan, Leah Garlotte, Jonathan Gathorne-Hardy, Roger L. Geiger, Thomas F. Gieryn, Sander Gliboff, Michael Gosman, Kelly Grant, E. Catherine Gray, Carol Gross, Allen Gurevitz, Matthew P. Guterl, Arnell Hammond, Tom Hargis, Barbara A. Hawkins, Hugh Hawkins, Ivona Hedin, Peter Hegarty, Elizabeth Capshew Hert, Nancy R. Hiller, David W. Hohnke, W. Peter Hood, Matilda Hopkins, Maria E. Howard, Lissa Hunt, John Hurt, Peter Jacobi, Owen V. Johnson, Anne Kibbler, Erika Knudson, Noretta Koertge, Stepanka Korytova, Joe Lee, Virginia Capshew Leonard, Frederick W. Lieber, Nancy Lightfoot, Kathryn Lofton, J. Timothy Londergan, Mary Jo Chandler Longstreet, David Lyman, B. Edward McClellan, Mary Ann Macklin, James H. Madison, Donald Maxwell, Mark Meiss, Perry Metz, Christopher M. Meyer, Miah Michaelson, Breon Mitchell, Susan A. Moke, Letha Morgenstern, Beth Moses, R. Paul Musgrave, Ted Najam, William R. Newman, Loretta Nixon, Catherine Norris, Randy Norris, Tracy M. O'Dea, Theresa A. Ochoa, Patrick O'Meara, Alexander Rabinowitch, Henry H. H. Remak, Eric Rensberger, Peggy Roberts, Heather Roinestad, Sherry Rouse, Bill Russell, Scott R. Sanders, Steve Sanders, Edith Sarra, Raymond E. Schaefer, Lynn A. Schoch, Cynthia Schultz, Deneise Self, Robert H. Shaffer, Bill Shaw, Jeremy Shere, Winston Shindell, Jan Shipps, Joel Silver, Lois H. Silverman, W. Raymond Smith, Jayne H. Spencer, Michael M. Sokal, John H. Stanfield, Patricia A. Steele, Jack H. Y. Su, Suzanne Thorin, Mique K. Van Vooren, Helena M. Walsh, Andrea Walton, Michael N. Wilkerson, and Becky Wood.

As the manuscript was taking shape, I was blessed with a raft of excellent readers. Foremost among them was Donald J. Gray, who kept with me, chapter by chapter, offering comments on substance and style as well as unwavering encouragement. I learned much from the suggestions of others who read substantial parts of the draft manuscript: John C. Burnham, Roberta Diehl, Paul John Eakin, Paula Gordon, Kenneth R. R. Gros Louis, Kelly A. Kish, Marianne Mitchell, Michael C. Nelson, Laura Plummer, Eric T. Sandweiss, and John R. Thelin.

I thank the staff of Indiana University Press for seeing the book to completion: Janet Rabinowitch, Robert Sloan, Sarah Wyatt Swanson, June B. Silay, and especially Dawn Ollila, my outstanding copyeditor. Peter-John Leone was responsible for the copublication agreement with the Indiana Historical Society.

I appreciate the generous funding that made this project possible. Curtis R. Simic and James P. Perin of the IU Foundation provided essential seed money at the beginning. Under the administration of IU President Myles Brand, I won a President's Arts and Humanities Fellowship, and received a grant facilitated by Sharon S. Brehm from the Bloomington Chancellor's office. The project obtained a Clio grant from the Indiana Historical Society, and a grant from IU's College Arts & Humanities Institute. Uninterrupted blocks of time for planning, researching, and writing were obtained from periods of sabbatical leave, for which I am grateful.

Although my beloved parents, Ruth and Bob, never saw the dawn of the twenty-first century, their nurturing spirit is with me. They inculcated the domestic virtues while never suppressing my wilder daimons. Their gift of siblings – sister Liz and brothers Ted, Tom, and Bob, Jr. – has been of immeasurable benefit. I remain tremendously inspired by my progeny – Samantha, Bryna, and Andrew – who were fortunate to have met Chancellor Wells when they were children. Perhaps this book will tell them why.

Abbreviations

BL   Herman B Wells, *Being Lucky: Reminiscences and Reflections* (Bloomington: Indiana University Press, 1980)

HBW   Herman B Wells

HWS   John Gallman, Rosann Green, Jim Weigand, and Doug Wilson, eds., *Herman Wells Stories* (Bloomington: Indiana University Press, 1992)

IDS   *Indiana Daily Student*

IUA   Indiana University Archives

IUMP   Thomas D. Clark, *Indiana University, Midwestern Pioneer,* vol. 3, *Years of Fulfillment* (Bloomington: Indiana University Press, 1977)

NAII   National Archives at College Park

OLW   Ora L. Wildermuth

WBP   Wells Biography Project

WLB   William Lowe Bryan

Herman B Wells

Nearly everyone who has ever attended Indiana University will tell you there is no place in the world like Indiana. They sometimes attempt to explain that statement but they cannot. When they ejaculate that there is no place in all the world like Indiana, they are thinking about something else. They are thinking about spring days when the campus is bursting with fragrance, vivid with color of blossoms and new leaves, and then the moon is bright – it is undeniable that spring is nowhere in the world as it is at Indiana. They are thinking about autumn evenings when dusk has settled. . . . They are thinking about hundreds of wholesome, pleasant people, who were their friends. They are thinking something about Indiana which none of them could ever express in words. These persons who make such broad unqualified statements about Indiana say that they have since tried living in many other places but that somehow the tang is missing.

Ernie Pyle, 1922

Campus Centennial

PRESIDENTIAL TIMBER STOOD TALL on the ground at the verdant campus of Indiana University in June 1920 as the university celebrated its centennial. The university had endured fire and drought, a wholesale move to a different campus, ten presidents, and nearly ninety commencements. All of the living former IU presidents – David Starr Jordan, John M. Coulter, and Joseph Swain – had come. Each one had served on the Indiana faculty before his selection as president, and both Coulter and Swain were alumni. The current president, William Lowe Bryan, was also an alumnus and Indiana faculty member before becoming president in 1902. In fact, so many other college and university presidents were drawn from the ranks of Indiana alumni and faculty beginning in the 1890s that IU possessed a growing reputation as the "Mother of College Presidents."[1]

Indiana was not a particularly large, prestigious, or wealthy university. Located in the smallest state beyond the eastern seaboard, it had the distinction of being the oldest state university west of the Allegheny Mountains.[2] Founded four years after Indiana statehood, pioneer Hoosiers made provision for higher education in the Indiana constitution, but that dream had been caught in the thickets of Indiana politics ever since. Opened as the Indiana State Seminary in 1825, the first building, located on a few acres of cleared forest near Bloomington's town center, resembled a schoolhouse, and the first class was composed of ten young men, instructed by a lone professor teaching classics. In 1829 the faculty expanded to three individuals, including Andrew Wylie, who served also as president. Wylie, a minister of the Presbyterian faith, eventually trans-

ferred his allegiance to the Episcopal Church. All of his presidential successors were Protestant clergymen as well, even though the university
was nonsectarian. For its first several decades, Indiana was among the
small and poor colleges struggling on the western frontier of settlement.

By the early 1880s, the original campus, now nestled up to busy railroad tracks, boasted two large buildings, a dozen faculty members, and
a coeducational student body of about 135.[3] In 1883, disaster struck in
the form of a raging fire that destroyed the ten-year-old Science Hall,
and a pungent administrative scandal erupted in the following year that
caused the resignation of President Lemuel Moss, a Baptist preacher.
In short order, the board of trustees decided to move the campus to a
twenty-acre plot five blocks east of the courthouse purchased from the
Dunn family, and to appoint David Starr Jordan, a biology professor, as
president in 1885, thus ending more than a half century of leadership by
members of the clergy. These two events – the move to a new campus and
the selection of a new president – contained the seeds of the university's
rebirth.[4]

REBORN UNIVERSITY

The new campus arose like a phoenix on the old Dunn farm. Two buildings, Wylie Hall and Owen Hall, were rapidly constructed of bricks that
were salvaged from the ruins of Science Hall or produced on site. Substantial limestone buildings followed later. Upon being named president,
Jordan forthrightly announced, "I believe our University is the most
valuable of Indiana's possessions. It is not yet a great University, it is not
yet a University at all, but it is the germ of one and its growth is as certain
as the progress of the seasons."[5]

Shaped by his scientific training at Cornell University and a disciple of the educational ideas of its president, Andrew D. White, Jordan
revised the curriculum beyond the classics, to include science and modern languages, and emphasized specialization by instituting the "major"
course of study for students. Among the professoriate, advanced training
and an earned doctorate became standard. An apostle of the research
ideal, Jordan declared, "The highest function of the real University is
that of instruction by investigation, and a man who cannot and does not

investigate cannot train investigators."[6] He practiced what he preached, energetically pursuing taxonomic ichthyology and inspiring promising students to commit to careers in scientific or scholarly research.

Preoccupied with improving the faculty in the face of limited financial resources, Jordan experimented with another innovation. "Next to freeing the University from its self-imposed educational fetters," Jordan explained,

> [M]y next important move was to bring trained and loyal alumni into the faculty. Up to that time vacancies had often been filled by professors released for one reason or another from Eastern institutions. Among my own early selections were a few young teachers from the seaboard universities, but most of them failed to adapt themselves, appearing to feel that coming so far West was a form of banishment. Indeed, as a whole, they seemed more eager to get back East than to build up a reputation in Indiana. Moreover, I found among the recent graduates several of remarkable ability; to them, therefore, I promised professorships when they had secured the requisite advanced training in the East or in Europe.[7]

Among the many alumni he inspired to become Indiana faculty stalwarts were Joseph Swain, William Lowe Bryan, Carl Eigenmann, James A. Woodburn, David Mottier, and William A. Rawles.[8] Indiana was without endowed wealth or accumulated prestige, so Jordan took a page from Hoosier agricultural heritage and populated the faculty with homegrown talent.

In 1891, Jordan was lured to Leland Stanford Junior University to become its first president. He left with warm feelings for IU, having spent twelve years – nearly a third of his life – in its service, first as a professor and then as a president, making strenuous efforts "to put Bloomington on the map."[9] The IU Board of Trustees basked in the reflected honor, and asked Jordan to name his successor. Jordan suggested his colleague in botany, John M. Coulter. The trustees were probably less pleased that he convinced six other IU faculty members to accompany him to Stanford to provide a nucleus for the new university, but Jordan found replacements before he departed. Local Bloomington wits – with a combination of pride and chagrin – referred to Stanford as the western branch of Indiana.

President Coulter left after two years in office, and the Indiana trustees again turned to Jordan for advice. He recommended mathematician Joseph Swain, who was one of the six IU men that accompanied Jordan to

Stanford two years before. Swain, a Quaker, served for nine years before he was called to lead Swarthmore College. Again, counsel was sought from Jordan, and he recommended another alumni and faculty member, William Bryan, whose research in experimental psychology was well known in the discipline.

As the Bryan administration began, the campus had grown into its new site. An arc of five substantial buildings was arrayed on the border of Dunn's Woods. In contrast to the old campus, where the land was cleared of trees, now the forest served as an amenity and source of identification with the natural world and the pioneer past. Enrollments had increased to nearly eight hundred students, who were supervised by sixty-seven faculty members.

During its first two decades under Bryan, IU experienced unprecedented growth and programmatic diversification. The student population nearly tripled during this period, with a corresponding increase in faculty numbers. IU responded to the state's need for physicians by opening the School of Medicine in Indianapolis in 1903, and new professional schools for nurses and for dentists followed later. On the Bloomington campus, the Graduate School was organized in 1904, although viable Ph.D. programs were slow in coming, and specialized professional schools were created for education (1908), commerce and finance (1920), and music (1921). Statewide general education was addressed by the formation of the Extension Division in 1912. Thus, in its first hundred years, IU had expanded beyond the liberal arts to encompass many categories of training for the professions.

In the space of a century, Indiana University had evolved from humble beginnings to a more diverse coeducational institution, in step with national trends of increasing disciplinary specialization, functional differentiation, and extracurricular offerings. It was an overwhelmingly white school, with a few African Americans in the student body.[10] In its two decades under the Bryan administration, the university labored mightily to modernize its academic profile, creating professional schools and outreach programs to serve Indiana citizens while operating under frugal state appropriations. In contrast, some of its sister schools – the Universities of Michigan, Wisconsin, and Illinois – had emerged as national leaders in research and service, using their increasing enrollments and more generous public support to make gains in scope, influence, and quality. Indiana remained a decent, if provincial, university.

THE OLD SCHOOL TIE

Without the advantages conferred by status or affluence, Indiana did possess an unusually extensive network of educational leaders, much of it traceable to Jordan. As president, he realized that IU could not compete for faculty against an emerging elite of American research universities, among them Johns Hopkins, Clark, Chicago, Harvard, and Michigan. Thrown back on the university's human resources, Jordan began developing local talent for future IU faculty. Preaching the gospel of specialized research, the charismatic Jordan gathered promising undergraduate alumni and assured them faculty positions after further "study in the East or Europe."[11] Both Swain and Bryan were members of Jordan's "Specialist's Club," as were several other faculty who spent their careers at Indiana.

Among the faculty members Jordan took with him to Stanford were mathematician Swain and geologist John C. Branner, whom he had met when they were students at Cornell in the early 1870s. In 1913, Branner succeeded Jordan as Stanford president. When Swain was IU president (1893–1902) and Bryan a department head in the 1890s, three future presidents got their undergraduate training in Bryan's department – Elmer B. Bryan (no relation to William; Franklin College, Colgate University, Ohio University), Ernest H. Lindley (University of Idaho, University of Kansas), and Edward Conradi (Florida State College for Women).[12] Another disciple of Jordan, alumnus Robert J. Aley, became head of mathematics at Indiana before serving as president of the University of Maine and, subsequently, Butler College. Swain, who served as president of Swarthmore College from 1902 to 1920, was succeeded by Indiana alumnus Frank Aydelotte. Aydelotte, IU's first Rhodes Scholar, graduated in 1900 and taught in the IU English Department from 1908 to 1915. Many other alumni graduates from the 1880s and 1890s were presidents of normal schools and colleges, and several former faculty members became presidents of other U.S. universities, including Walter A. Jessup (University of Iowa).[13]

This dense web of academic ties, fostered mainly by necessity, kept Indiana from falling off of the map of the Big Ten. It also opened a channel from the Midwest to California and the emergence of Stanford. Undergraduate alumni such as psychologist Lewis M. Terman found faculty employment there.[14] In 1922, the editor of the *Indiana University Alumni Quarterly* noted that Indiana was supplying educational leaders in colleges and universities across the United States: "Their fellow alumni rejoice in their progress and advancement in the educational world, but feel regret that the University and the state of Indiana must be deprived of their leadership."[15]

INDIANA'S GENIUS LOCI

At the centennial commencement, former president Swain spoke of nostalgia for the Indiana campus, although he had been at the head of a different institution for nearly twenty years: "There are memories that cluster about the spirit of the place."[16] For one hundred years, Indiana was alma mater for generations of students, and faculty and students alike felt loyalty and a sense of kinship with the small Bloomington institution. With the move to a new locale in 1885 and increasing enrollments, the woodland campus exerted its charms of natural beauty in combination with changeable weather conditions and the parade of distinctive seasons. The Indiana milieu operated as a "cultural glue" to attract and fix the allegiances of its academic community and served as a social setting where university norms, rituals, and customs were enacted. The campus had been "culturally instructive," introducing generation after generation to the "rich set of information, values, principles, and experiences which art, landscape architecture, and architecture are capable of embodying."[17]

As a unique place, the campus remained a repository of psychic energies and cultural associations. It had an ongoing history as a physical entity as well as a nonmaterial life as a stimulus and witness to human action and memory, summed up in the phrase genius loci. Typically translated as "spirit of place," genius loci has played a special role in the development of American higher education and its institutions. Campuses have been set apart and deliberately cultivated to reflect the status of learning as well as to enhance the process of education.[18] The Indiana campus at Dunn's Woods, only thirty-five years old in 1920, was already rich in architectural symbols and woodland beauty, and had a century of university history to draw upon as the institution looked ahead to the future.

PART ONE

The Shaping of a Fiduciary, 1902–1937

Upon John grew that affection which no one can escape who walks long under campus trees; that naïve and sentimental fondness at once fatuous and deep, that clings to a man long afterward, and that has been known, of mention of Alma Mater, to show up soft in gnarled citizens otherwise hard-shelled as the devil himself. To a peculiar degree the Indiana milieu was created to inspire love. It has the unspoiled generosity, the frankness, the toil, the taciturn courage and the exasperating ineptness of natural man himself. One listens to the winds sighing through beeches, or plods through autumnal drizzle with gaze divided between the cracks of the Board Walk and that miraculous personal vision that for no two people is produced alike, whether it be conjured from books, or from inner song, or from liquor, or from a co-ed's smile or from all together. Because of this one berates Indiana and loves her doggedly.

George Shively, 1925

ONE

In the Land of Jordan

IN APRIL 1921 THE INDIANA UNIVERSITY REGISTRAR'S OFFICE received a letter of inquiry from a potential transfer student from the University of Illinois. The student, Herman Wells, was completing his first year and wanted to know whether he could transfer his credits and enroll at IU. He enumerated the courses he took, grades received the first semester (an 89 percent average) and anticipated for the second (the same), and asked for full transfer credit. He received a short, impersonal reply from the registrar stating that Indiana would grant full credit for the Illinois coursework, and "We shall be glad to welcome you as a student at the beginning of next semester."[1]

Wells was from Boone County, located west of Indianapolis, and he had graduated from Lebanon High School in 1920. He had gone to Illinois because it had a good business school and had a direct rail connection to his hometown. Although some of his classmates had gone to Indiana, its business school was just getting started, and Bloomington, although closer than Champaign, lacked good rail connections. But after a disappointing year at Illinois, Wells was ready to try something different.

Wells, who was an only child, had high hopes for college. They were inculcated nearly since his birth by his parents, Granville and Bernice, both former schoolteachers. Neither was a college graduate, although his father had taken classes at Indiana State Normal School in Terre Haute. Granville worked as a cashier at Lebanon's First National Bank and served as the Treasurer of Boone County. Bernice helped out at the county treasurer's office and kept the household running smoothly – and, importantly, soothed her depressed and anxious husband.

Arriving at Illinois in September 1920, Wells soon made his way to the College of Commerce, headquartered in an expansive building dedicated only seven years before, and registered for classes.[2] Like other public universities of the time, the Illinois campus lacked dormitories, so Wells roomed with a friend from Lebanon in a private family residence. Like many freshman, he was intimidated by the size and impersonality of the campus. Although he made some friends, social life on the sprawling campus was dominated by wealthy students from Chicago, and revolved around the Greek system and athletics. Wells felt like an outsider, both as an out-of-state student and because of his marginal social role on campus. A studious freshman but not a grind, he was quite aware of his parents' aspiration to provide a college education for him, and especially his father's expectations of success. Wells, away from the comfortable confines of Boone County and cut off from daily family support, was sometimes "wretchedly homesick."[3]

As a beginning student, Wells was well prepared. He had obtained thirteen hours of entrance credit for his studies at Lebanon High School, and during his first year as a general business student, he took courses in economics, accounting, rhetoric, Spanish, and concert band.[4] Wells served on the staff of the student newspaper, the *Daily Illini,* as head of the advertising desk. He went regularly to the Methodist church and participated in its extensive Wesley Foundation program for young people.

Wells persevered through classes that held five hundred fellow students and his feelings of alienation and displacement. By midyear, he was invited to pledge a fraternity, but he had already decided to leave Illinois and transfer to Indiana University. Granville strenuously objected, arguing that Illinois's business school was much better established than IU's fledging School of Commerce and Finance, which was still in its first year, and Herman was getting good grades as a freshman. The younger Wells pointed out that since he expected to make his career in Indiana, his Indiana connections would be more useful. He also had many friends going to school in Bloomington. Wells was a dutiful and respectful son, but bent on his new course.[5] Granville finally relented, giving his increasingly independent son his blessing.

Wells was back in Lebanon for the summer of 1921, living at his parents' home and working again at his father's bank. Starting at age thirteen, he had worked there after school and on vacations, and had learned to appreciate the vital services it provided to the small town and the rural area surrounding it. Among other tasks, young Wells had learned to operate the county's first Burroughs posting machine at the bank, and, by high school, became so proficient on it that he trained bookkeepers at other local banks.[6] After high school graduation in 1920, Wells was hired as bank manager for a small country bank in nearby Whitestown, recently organized as a competitor to the established bank, and earned a sizable amount of money for college.[7]

Banking served to bond Granville Wells and his son, Herman. Granville maintained a stoic and competent persona as a bank officer, financial adviser, and public servant, but was often withdrawn and morose at home. Herman had to grow up quickly to cope with his father's mood disorder, and Bernice relied increasingly upon him as a confidant and ally in managing Granville. Early on he discovered that assisting at the bank pleased his father immensely, and the bright boy took it all in, from the technical details of banking operations to the human drama connected to financial transactions.[8]

Back in Lebanon after a year away, everything seemed pretty much the same, including the daily routines of the family. Still the dutiful and busy son, during the week he approached his summer job with a confident air born of experience, and, on Sundays, went to the Methodist church with his mother and, upon occasion, his father. For fun he would socialize with his many friends or go to movies.[9] Continuing a pattern from high school, he never dated or had a romantic attachment, due perhaps to persistent groin pain.[10] Yet Wells had changed, discovering new sources of strength in himself and renewed determination to become a "college man" on his own terms.

THE SPIRIT OF INDIANA

Herman Wells was a busy young man in Fall 1921 when he started walking under campus trees, becoming immersed in the genius loci of Indiana. He came to Bloomington for the first time and enrolled for classes as an Indiana University sophomore. Adjusting quickly to the southern Indiana environment, Wells responded strongly to the attractive campus.[11]

The town of Bloomington had 13,000 residents and boasted a strong manufacturing base in the Showers Brothers Furniture factory, which was advertised as the largest maker of wood furniture in the world. The university, with its 2,500-member student body, was also an important economic mainstay, providing jobs for residents and customers for local commerce. Although yearly state appropriations to IU were often meager, Bloomington residents had developed an understated pride in "their" university, often sending their sons and daughters there. In fact, students from Monroe County were the largest group from any locale. The state of Indiana was the home of over 95 percent of the student body. Of the 105 out-of-state students, 83 hailed from twenty other states, and twenty-two were from eight foreign countries.[12]

Another new arrival, mathematics professor Harold Davis, sought to orient himself to the campus milieu in the early 1920s and discovered clear signs of the influence of David Starr Jordan, a biology professor and president in the 1880s. Famous among students for his abolition of in loco parentis rules and regulations, he replaced them with two tongue-in-cheek commandments: do not shoot the professors and do not burn campus buildings. With the same liberating impulse, Jordan encouraged each faculty member to follow and "explore those paths into which his own interest and his own imagination may direct him."[13] By example and exhortation, Jordan led IU to get in step with the new national trend toward university research before leaving in 1891 to become the first president of the nascent Leland Stanford Junior University.[14] Before he left, Jordan oversaw the move from the original campus, crowded up against the railroad tracks at Second Street and College Avenue, to some undeveloped land east of the courthouse optimistically christened "University Park." Commenting on the atmosphere and traditions that he encountered in the 1920s, Davis quipped, "It is altogether fitting and proper, therefore, to characterize this institution as the 'Land of Jordan.'"[15]

In September 1921, Wells got his first taste of IU's traditions of academic pomp and circumstance on the opening day of classes when he attended the freshman induction ceremony. At 7:30 in the morning, administrative officers and some of the faculty of the university assembled on the steps of the Student Building underneath the clock tower. They were joined by a student draped in white folds representing the Spirit of

Indiana, who welcomed the crowd with a prepared speech. Exhorting the crowd, she said,

> The spirit that is Indiana knows no limitations of age, color, creed, doctrine, social, political, or economic bounds. . . . It includes all those who have come for the purpose of seeking truth and intellectual freedom. . . . The spirit that greets you here is the rich heritage of a glorious past made possible by students, who, like yourselves upon entering the university, felt strangely far from home and intimate friends, but who soon adapted themselves to their new environment. . . . As rich as is the heritage which you find here, it should be and must be made richer and better because of your having been here.[16]

Then William Lowe Bryan took the stage and offered the "President's Charge," reminding the crowd of the "University's basic purpose: The intellectual development of her sons and daughters." He performed the induction by having the freshman repeat the university pledge. The ceremony concluded with the band playing and the assembled group singing "Indiana, Our Indiana."[17]

The nineteen-year-old Wells threw himself into collegiate life with gusto. Eager to know and to be known, he lost no time getting involved. He took his classes seriously, marveling at his professors' facility in academic discourse, and he was soon absorbed in several student organizations. The most important of these was his fraternity, Sigma Nu. Wells had hopes of joining a fraternity since his freshman year at Illinois, and took the opportunity to pledge at Indiana shortly after his arrival. With its own chapter house, Sigma Nu provided not only a physical home for Wells but also an extensive brotherhood of friends, which was especially satisfying to an only child who had grown up in a family of adults.[18]

Indiana, like many other colleges and universities, was the home of many Greek-letter social fraternities. Dating from the beginnings of American higher education, with the establishment of Phi Beta Kappa at the College of William and Mary in 1776, fraternities and sororities had evolved during the nineteenth century from associations recognizing academic achievement into philanthropic organizations designed to serve the social needs of their members and the wider community. Perhaps their most important practical role in the first half of the twentieth century was to provide living accommodations to college students in an age when university dormitories were rare.

As a new pledge, Wells learned the story of the college fraternity movement as well as the history of Sigma Nu. The fraternity got its start at Virginia Military Institute in 1869, begun by an ex-Confederate soldier who opposed the hazing practices of existing fraternities. Honor was its guiding principal. At Indiana, the Beta Eta chapter of Sigma Nu was founded in 1892 and had grown into one of the larger fraternities on campus, boasting about forty members in 1921. The chapter house was a converted and expanded former private residence two blocks east of campus, at the corner of Kirkwood Avenue and Grant Street.[19] Sigma Nu took over the house at 322 East Kirkwood Avenue (the home of the Phi Psi fraternity until 1911) and called it "Kirkwood Castle."[20] As a pledge, Wells relished his introduction to fraternal ideals and practices. It eased his way into campus social life and provided a ready circle of friends.

THE KLAN IN BLOOMINGTON

Wells had barely settled in his new fraternal home on Kirkwood before the town was in an uproar over the Ku Klux Klan's announcement of a rally in Bloomington. In early November 1921, flyers were circulated to promote membership in the nativist, racist organization, and the *Bloomington World-Telephone* announced that a Klan parade was being planned for downtown Bloomington. The organization revived following World War I and this incarnation was populist and middle class, centered in the newly urbanized areas of the upper Midwest. The Klan stood for white, Anglo-Saxon, Protestant supremacy and was hostile to ethnic immigrants, African Americans, Jews, Catholics, atheists, and others who did not meet their definition of "100 percent white American." Indianapolis was the headquarters of the Klavern of Indiana, the largest state organization in the U.S. Historians have estimated that up to one quarter of the adult white male Hoosier population at the time were members.[21]

Against this backdrop of KKK resurgence, every locale of any size was targeted for a public display. The parade in Bloomington was held on November 6. With full regalia, including white robes and hoods, Klan members assembled in a field about a mile south of the courthouse, and then marched up Lincoln Street to the stately building. They were led by three masked horseman followed by a drum corps of university students, who remained unmasked. Others carried a banner reading: "We stand for Old Glory and the Constitution."[22] Among the crowd of hundreds who turned out to watch the spectacle was Wells. He remembered the parade as a "silent, eerie, frightening kind of thing." Wells had grown up in an area with few blacks but his egalitarian sympathies, nurtured by his family and his church upbringing, were aroused, and he bristled at the ugly display. Reflecting further on its meaning, he said, "It was designed to show the enormous strength of the Klan in a community and to silence the voices of those who had been criticizing the Klan and stood for the things which the Klan opposed."[23]

Wells was no stranger to the Klan's scare tactics. During his boyhood, his father had a confrontation with the Boone County chapter of the secret society. As a member of the Lebanon school board, Granville Wells got a visit from some local Klan members who were upset with a teacher who talked with his students about the League of Nations and internationalism. They branded him a socialist and demanded that he be fired. Granville asserted that if the teacher were competent he would take no such action. Upon hearing Granville's defense of the teacher, the Klansmen threatened to spread rumors and start a run on the local bank. Despite the potential harm to the bank and to his reputation as a bank officer, Wells's father stood firm.[24]

In Bloomington, things returned to normal once the Klan parade was over. But the memory would stay with Wells. Plunging into his first year on campus, the sophomore took a full load of five courses each semester, and began to fill his social life to overflowing. He started going to the First Methodist Church, a prosperous congregation, located on the next block over from the Sigma Nu house. He joined the Young Men's Christian Association (YMCA), a popular group that provided various forms of social welfare for students and another venue for socializing. Among other activities, the group published the popular IU *Red Book,* a directory of student names and addresses.

Lebanon High School had prepared Wells well for college classes. With a solid foundation of book knowledge, he had developed good study habits and was able to apply himself to school work when necessary. During his freshman year at Illinois, he was able to take classes in the School of Commerce, but at Indiana, one had to have junior standing to enter the school, so Wells found himself in pre-business courses during his first year.

In the academic year 1921–22, Wells took 17.5 hours of coursework per semester. In his favorite class, Economics 1 (Political Economy), he garnered a solid B each semester. He received a B in Introduction to Journalism, which slid to a B– in the second semester, when he worked on the *Indiana Daily Student* staff. In his first semester course on Inorganic Chemistry, he received a B; in the second semester, Qualitative Analysis, he squeaked by with a C–. Wells received Cs in two semesters of French. As a male student, he was required to take 1.5 hours of Military Science each semester; in that course he earned his only A grade that year. Wells had an overall average of B–, slightly lower than his B average during his freshman year at Illinois.

Despite his decent grades and a full social life with his Sigma Nu brothers, Wells was not yet firmly rooted in Bloomington. He had met only one professor, economist James E. Moffat, who had been able to inspire him. His college savings had long run out, and his parents were not in a position to help much financially. At the end of his sophomore year, the bank in Whitestown offered Wells a permanent job. Two summers before, he had worked for this country bank before starting college in Champaign. The starting salary was a generous $200 a month, a sum exceeding the going rate for college graduates. Wells, who had not turned twenty, was extremely tempted. Although he had enjoyed his first year at IU, he was willing to leave the campus and his elective family for the prospect of financial independence. But he ran into steadfast opposition from his father, and eventually turned down the offer.[25]

SCHOOL OF COMMERCE AND FINANCE

When Wells returned to Bloomington for the fall semester in September 1922, he was able to enroll officially in the School of Commerce and Finance. The school, begun in 1920 with a starting enrollment of seventy students, was under the direction of Dean William A. Rawles. Trained in history and economics before the turn of the century, Rawles had previously been assistant dean of the College of Arts and Sciences, and had worked assiduously for over a decade to develop the commercial course curriculum. He was the leading advocate for the creation of a separate school. He had to address both the businessman who was skeptical about the value of university education and the academic who was apprehensive about subverting scholarship with material goals. Arguing that the commercial curriculum was "not only disciplinary but also liberalizing" in its focus on critical analysis and reflection of the problems posed by business, Rawles made the case that it contributed to the cultural enrichment of the future business leaders.[26]

During his junior year, Wells carried a full load of seventeen hours during the first semester. Jumping into his major, he took Econ 6 (Money), two courses in Commerce (Business Organization & Management; Finance), and the yearlong Law 1 (Commercial Law). As electives, he took Elementary Psychology along with Experimental Psychology, and he joined the University Band. His grades were Bs and Cs, except for As in Law and Band. Second semester, Wells took sixteen hours, with three courses in commerce (Principles of Investment; Commercial Correspondence; Foreign Trade), one in journalism (Elementary Advertising), and one in music (Nineteenth-century Opera). He got almost all Bs, with one A in Law and a C+ in Music. Among his professors were Dean Rawles, economist Moffat, and music historian John Geiger.

In April 1923, the new Social Science Building (since renamed Rawles Hall) was dedicated. Located on Third Street, wedged between Science Hall and Biology Hall on the crescent, it was a handsome example of collegiate gothic architecture. It provided a home for the School of Commerce and Finance, in addition to housing other university departments, so it acquired the popular name of Commerce Hall. The *Indianapolis Star* noted, "Commerce Hall typifies the new era of education in its realm to the business world, a physical reminder of the link which binds the modern university to the economic life of the state and nation."[27]

Wells took fifteen hours the first semester of his senior year. For his Commerce major, he took three courses: Economics 3 (Public Finance), Commerce 22 (Marketing), and Commerce 30, a yearlong capstone seminar in business. For electives, a course in American government, a mainstay of the newly organized Department of Political Science, and ethics, in the Department of Psychology and Philosophy. (President Bryan was listed among the instructors of ethics.) University Band rounded out his schedule. Wells's grades declined; the busy senior received all Cs except for an A in band. During his final semester, Wells took two courses in his major, Commerce 15 (Railway Transportation) and Economics 6b (Banking), two courses in English (Fundamentals of Public Speaking; Twentieth-century Drama), and band. He managed to raise his grades to the B level.

Overall, Wells did not distinguish himself academically over his three years of undergraduate course work at Indiana. He had a B– average during his sophomore year, which, over the next two years, declined slightly to a C+ average. But grading scales were different then. An A was given for 95 to 100 percent, a B for 85 to 94, and a C for 75 to 84. Wells completed his freshman year at Illinois with an 89 percent – a solid B average – and his grades declined by approximately 5 percentage points during his undergraduate career at Indiana.[28]

Maintaining his longstanding interest in band, Wells joined the concert band as a baritone player his junior year. By the mid-1920s, the IU Band began receiving national attention with favorable publicity. During a visit to Bloomington, famed director of the Marine Corps Band John Philip Sousa declared the IU Band "one of the snappiest marching and playing bands in the country."[29]

The conductor of the University Band, Archie Warner, asked Wells to become the business manager of the group. He leapt at the chance and soon was spending more time managing the band and less time playing the baritone. "My principal job," he described, "was to try to finagle enough money by one means or another to get us to an out-of-town football game or so, which I did by various economies and money-raising schemes." To save money on transportation costs to out-of-town football games, Wells devised a scheme to stuff extra people beneath the seats on the Monon train. When the train conductor, "wise but sympathetic," came around to collect the fares, he "ignored the teeming spaces beneath the arches of the back-to-back seats."[30]

Wells exercised his entrepreneurial ingenuity by negotiating first-time contracts for band performances at the Indianapolis 500 and the

Kentucky Derby. When the manager of the Indianapolis 500 concluded the arrangements for a return engagement the following year, he said, "with a twinkle in his eye, 'This year don't try to bootleg all your fraternity brothers and friends into the race.'" These special performances were highly prized by his fellow bandmates and provided a welcome contrast to the routine work of playing for university functions and ROTC drills and parades.[31]

Wells's career as a musician ended on a trailing note. In his words,

> In my senior year I played once with the band in a formal concert in old
> Assembly Hall. It was in the springtime toward the end of the academic year.
> I put my baritone back in the wings after the concert, then told a freshman
> brother in the Sigma Nu house to see that it was put in my room at the house and
> promptly forgot all about it. When I next needed the horn it could not be located
> and the loss ended my active musical career.[32]

He was philosophical about the lost horn. His position in the band was secure. It lay not in his musical virtuosity, but in financial management, which was based on his keen discernment of human relations as well as his expertise in money matters.

THE BOOK NOOK

After classes, Wells went occasionally to the Book Nook, a popular campus hangout. Located on Indiana Avenue at the western boundary of the campus, it was a dilapidated structure with sawdust on the floor that sold drinks, sandwiches, and stationery. In an earlier incarnation it sold books, hence the name, but the campus co-op drove that business away. The establishment was owned and operated by three brothers – Peter, George, and Harry Costas, natives of Greece who immigrated to Chicago before moving to Indiana.

The Costas brothers were kind but canny proprietors. After petty thefts of cash receipts and customers leaving unpaid checks for food and beverages, they instituted the practice of writing patrons' names on checks at the time of service. Any that were left unpaid were presented to fraternity brothers and other responsible friends. Of the three brothers, Peter Costas had a reputation for tolerance and sympathy for the students, and was able to spot subtle distinctions between members of different fraternities and sororities. "He was a handsome personable young Spartan with a close-cropped black mustache, willing to repay student abuses and pranks with serious fatherly counseling and pleas for offenders to reform."[33] Costas strove to make the prevailing atmosphere "wholesome and beautiful," and he was proud of the Book Nook's role as a vital center of student activities.[34]

The Book Nook had a jukebox as well as an old piano in the corner, and musicians and music lovers gathered there most nights to hear and play new tunes, mostly jazz. Campus intellectuals, such as student writer and wit William "Monk" Moenkhaus, a music major and faculty brat, added a whimsical flavor of eccentricity to the proceedings with his poems and pronouncements.[35] His friend, law student Hoagland "Hoagy" Carmichael, an aspiring songwriter, often played the piano, trying out new songs. Carmichael, a Bloomington native, enrolled at IU during the fall of its centennial year, joined the Kappa Sigma fraternity, and organized bands with names such as the "Syringe Orchestra" or "Carmichael's Collegians" to make ends meet. He became a regular at the Book Nook.[36] He described the atmosphere thus:

> On Indiana Avenue stood the Book Nook, a randy temple smelling of socks, wet slickers, vanilla flavoring, face powder, and unread books. Its dim lights, its scarred walls, its marked-up booths, unsteady tables, made campus history. It was for us King Arthur's Round Table, a wailing wall, a fortune telling tent. It tried to be a bookstore. It had grown and been added to recklessly until by the time I was a senior in high school it seated a hundred or so Coke-guzzling, book-annoyed, bug-eyed college students. New tunes were heard and praised or thumbed down, lengthy discussions on sex, drama, sport, money, and motor cars were started and never quite finished. The first steps of the toddle, the shimmy, and the strut were taken and fitted to the new rhythms. Dates were made and mad hopes were born.[37]

Bloomington's Book Nook was a significant venue for Carmichael's first flowering as a composer of jazz-inflected popular music.[38]

Moreover, the Book Nook occupied a key niche in the ecology of college life. One could find the spectrum of IU student types, from naïve freshmen to the proverbial BMOC (Big Man On Campus) to self-styled members of the artistic avant-garde. It was an important arena to discover and pursue romance, alcohol, and fashion – defining elements of the undergraduate lifestyle.

The national experiment of alcohol prohibition was begun in 1920, enforced by federal laws banning the production, distribution, sales, and consumption of alcoholic beverages. But college students, like citizens everywhere, found ways to drink. Entrepreneurs produced moonshine and bathtub gin and other substances; speakeasies and homebrew cabins and personal networks distributed the easily available contraband. Drinking "dominated the popular image of campus life," historian John Thelin has asserted. "[H]omecoming celebrations, commencement weekend reunions, proms, year-round fraternity gatherings – all were associated with alcohol."[39]

Although the Book Nook waiters served only soft drinks, patrons surreptitiously laced their Cokes with the contents of hip flasks and small bottles. It was an open secret; as long as it was practiced discreetly, chances of an arrest were negligible. Alcohol intoxication lubricated social relationships and lowered inhibitions, and thus fueled romance. Music, with the associated singing and dancing, performed much the same function of aesthetic enjoyment and emotional liberation, only without chemicals. Music also underlined differences between generations.

Many college students during this time embraced jazz and its improvisational, ironic style. In the wake of World War I, it seemed to address the search for meaning with its incongruous phrasing and cool tones. "Jazz was groping its way through the early twenties as we were groping ours," Carmichael mused. "[I]t said what we wanted to say though what that was we might not know."[40] Jazz provided the soundtrack for college life – at the Book Nook and elsewhere.

LIVING AT SIGMA NU

As much as he enjoyed hanging out at the Book Nook, Wells was a quintessential fraternity man, and he loved the communal eating, sleeping, and rowdiness that living with an elective family brought. He greatly respected the fraternal ideals of service and philanthropy, imbuing daily life with a bright sheen of ethical concern for his fellows. At the Kirkwood fraternity house, Wells was a general factotum, doing any and all kinds of work. Whether serving on various committees, welcoming prospective members, scheming to obtain bootleg alcohol, he was the go-to guy. Fun loving and gregarious, he developed into an effective leader and could garner respect not just from fellow students but also from instructors and administrators.

Wells was not only studying business in class; since his parents were not in a position to provide much financial help, he exercised his entrepreneurial skills to provide college expenses. His "Big Brother" at Sigma Nu, John Leonard, recalled,

> Herman followed his father's profession, banking, by lending sums of money to those of us who were momentarily short of cash. Naturally he'd charge us a small fee, something like a quarter a week for the use of five dollars. We were grateful, Herman made a slight profit, and we learned at that early age the whys and wherefores of negotiating a loan.[41]

Another fraternity brother remembered an even more ingenious scheme. Wells installed a massive armoire in his bedroom at the frat house, purchased a stout lock, and set up shop making small loans to his friends. In exchange for the money, he would hold as collateral their tuxedos. Eventually the armoire would be bulging with formalwear. Payback time occurred as a formal dance approached, when the indebted friend clamored for his tux, and Wells calmly said, "Not until you pay me!"[42]

Among the most pressing issues facing the fraternity brothers was the lack of living space for continued growth in new members. The chapter house had not been remodeled for a decade, and the daily wear and tear from three dozen students was taking its toll. In January 1922, Sigma Nu officers petitioned the IU Board of Trustees for a ninety-nine-year lease of university land to build a new house. They requested a building lot on a parcel of undeveloped land at the southwest corner of the campus, at the corner of Indiana Avenue and Third Street. The "Fijis" (Phi Gamma Delta fraternity) had already built a new house in an adjacent lot, backing up to Dunn's Woods. Members of other fraternities were also beginning to think of moving from dilapidated houses on Kirkwood to East Third Street across from campus to new, specially built fraternity mansions. The nearest university building was the Kirkwood Observatory, about 150 yards away in Dunn's Woods.[43] The letter to the trustees stated that the chapter had sufficient funds to build a new facility, and noted: "An up-to-date fraternity home on this site would in fact be in keeping with the idea of the Memorial Fund drive for buildings and a Greater Indiana University."[44] After the trustees discussed the issue, President Bryan responded "that it was not in accordance with [the Board's] policy at this time to lease sites to fraternities or other University organizations."[45]

STUDENT AFFAIRS

With surging postwar enrollments, increasing wealth, and an educational philosophy concerned with the whole student, Indiana University continued to expand student services beyond academic matters in the 1920s. Students themselves became increasingly organized, not only in the Greek system but also within the student union, a nationwide movement.

In the Fall 1923, during his senior year, Wells joined the powerful Union Board, the student directorate that managed the Student Building's multifaceted programming for students. The Union Board, founded in 1909, was the brainchild of John Whittenberger, a student from Miami County. He welcomed the idea behind the Student Building, completed in 1906, which was for the exclusive use of students and their extracurricular activities, but was disturbed that it did not serve to bring the growing campus together.[46] After a visit to the University of Michigan's new student union, Whittenberger became "almost obsessed with the idea that a union would draw Indiana University students into closer bonds of friendship and purpose."[47] Finding support from President Bryan and some of the faculty, the union grew to five hundred members in its first year. Rooms for reading, pipe smoking, and billiards were set aside for members of the all-male organization, ironically in a structure originally conceived as a women's building.[48] By the 1920s, the union, located in the Student Building, was an established presence at IU.

Not surprisingly, given his natural talent for financial matters and his wide fiduciary experience, Wells was elected treasurer of the Union Board. Among the many activities of the group was fundraising for a new building. Although the existing Student Building was only sixteen years old, it had been planned at the turn of the century, and reflected that era's collegiate values in its hesitant accommodation of coeducation and modest assessment of student recreational needs. The Student Building became the first building constructed on the Indiana campus funded by private donations. Although the university had received gifts from time to time from private sources, it had heretofore relied almost exclusively on state appropriations and student fee income.

At IU, the first-ever general fund drive was started. It came to be known as the Memorial Fund, in honor of those who served in World War I. By 1920, as part of IU's Centennial, the fund's goal was originally set at $250,000. Several pressure groups arose, lobbying for construction of a women's dormitory or a journalism building or an indoor track field, among other proposals. An early IU history noted, "As a result of the Memorial Campaign the alumni were becoming constructively articulate."[49] By spring 1921, the university was involved in two great fundraising campaigns: the James Whitcomb Riley Memorial Association (to build a children's hospital at the IU Medical School) and the Memorial Fund.[50] Both had million dollar goals. The Memorial Fund had three buildings as its manifest goal: a dormitory for women (Memorial Hall), a football stadium and track (Memorial Stadium), and a student union (Indiana Memorial Union). None was an academic hall, but each provided what was thought to be essential support and services to the student body.

The university librarian, William A. Alexander, who had public relations experience, and Bryan were cochairmen of the drive. Addressing the men students, Bryan said,

> I call upon you to marshal yourselves and march to the million dollar goal as you marched thru Argonne. I call upon you to build here a great memorial in honor of those who have fought in all our wars. When you build that you are building a greater thing, a thing whose price is supreme sacrifice, the victorious Indiana spirit.

Alexander delivered a similar message combining patriotism and school pride to the women students.[51]

Although the administration and trustees led the campaign, the movement for "a greater Indiana" involved faculty, current students, and former students. The IU Alumni Association had been a major supporter of the university since its creation in 1854. Edward Von Tress, alumni secretary, took the Memorial Fund campaign around the country, speaking to alumni groups and sending information to individual alumni. The excitement was contagious: "The cause of Indiana University in creating a World War I memorial had now become a national crusade which centered partly around actual campus needs, but largely it symbolized an expression of gratitude of Americans everywhere."[52] Law professor Paul McNutt was active in the Memorial Fund campaign, spending summer and fall 1922 in New York, Washington, and Chicago meeting alumni and prospective donors.[53] Students such as James Adams also proved their mettle as effective fundraisers. Uz McMurtie, president of the 1922 senior class, devised the slogan "Let I.U. and Its Welfare Be Your Hobby!"[54] And students were remarkably generous donors, too, with an average contribution of $200.[55]

ARTIST ON CAMPUS

Among the draws on campus was the studio of the famous Indiana landscape painter T. C. Steele, who was designated "honorary professor of painting" in 1922. Located on the top floor of the University Library, the artist occupied it during the winter months. Steele, the acknowledged leader of the "Indiana group" of artists centered in Brown County, had a long association with the university, dating to the late 1890s when he received commissions to paint portraits of several professors. In 1907 he got to know William Lowe Bryan during the several weeks the IU president sat for his portrait. Steele's fame increased, and in spring 1916, an exhibition of his paintings was held in conjunction with the centennial of Indiana statehood. At commencement, Steele was given an honorary LL.D., a mark of distinction that the university had bestowed only two times in the preceding decade, to James Whitcomb Riley (1907) and David Starr Jordan (1909).

When Steele came to campus in 1922, there were no stipulations save that he would be in residence six months of the year. Bryan's idea was that his very presence would help advance art appreciation on campus, thus contributing to the moral uplift of the student body. Steele rendered his mission to the students in simple terms: "to see the Beautiful in nature and in life."[56]

The artist was modest and unpretentious about his work and was unperturbed by visitors dropping in when the studio was open Thursday,

Friday, and Saturday each week.[57] Sometimes he continued painting; other times he took a break. One student observer commented,

> [W]hen Mr. Steele stops his painting to speak to the students informally in this way, they learn many interesting facts in an entirely painless fashion. During the pleasant days of the spring . . . the artist plans to do most of his painting outside on the campus. The students are not permitted to paint with him, but they may watch his work.[58]

The *Indiana Daily Student* ran a series of articles instructing students in the basics of art appreciation. Authored by English professor Frank Senour, it included advice under the heading of "What Not to Do." One suggestion: "If you visit the studio do not go with a paralyzing reverence nor with a flippant nonchalance. If looking at pictures is a new behavior, do not trust too much to the judgment with which you buy clothes or sell eggs. Admit you have something to learn, and then put yourself in the way of learning."[59]

The series of IDS articles was collected and republished as a pamphlet titled *Art for Your Sake* in April 1924. In a note of introduction, President Bryan wrote, "I believe we need beauty as much as we need truth. I believe that the University needs artists as much as it needs scholars." In his forward, Professor Senour lamented, "[W]e have right here good pictures that for a year and a half have been too little visited." He went on to reiterate why the artist was in residence: "Now the plain fact is that Mr. Steele is not here to teach, or to lecture, except by the grace of good nature, but is here to bring a benefit to us all by merely being present and practicing his art where we can see it."[60]

Senour continued his exposition under headings such as "A Typical Picture," "The Studio," "Lines," "Mass," "Color," and "Composition." Turning from the practicalities, he finished the booklet with discussions of esthetic considerations in "True Seeing," "Some Philosophy," and "Joy." Addressing students directly, he admitted, "I know you can live upon many levels below the good, the true and the beautiful," but he urged them to develop their "higher senses" by looking at Steele's paintings in order to "enlarge the circle of your joys."[61] Senour ended his exhortation by connecting the paintings to the painter:

> I want you to go to the studio that you may see Mr. Steele, and catch his joy – a quiet unobtrusive joy it is – in the artist life. I wish I could tell you about his life

and what it has meant to be faithful to seeing things steadily and seeing them whole. His art is his life, and he, as you meet him and talk to him is the best commentary upon his pictures. He puts into his pictures not only what he sees, but what he believes in. . . . The artist's view of the world is worth while.[62]

The pedagogical message was one of moral uplift and spiritual striving. In the face of increasing secularization and the rapid expansion of commercial culture, Bryan and others argued for the finer, nonmaterial things in life.

For his part, Steele relished being on campus, painting in his studio, or, weather permitting, taking his portable easel outdoors. He took a kindly interest in students, sharing with many a rural Indiana background, and he agreed wholeheartedly with Bryan's credo about needing beauty as much as needing truth.

Wells was one of the many students who observed the artist at work. He would frequent the studio, watching the artist paint and engaging in conversation with Steele.[63] Wells also visited the artist when he painted en plein air on campus, by the Jordan River. Steele left a prolific array of campus scenes, often using the stately limestone buildings to accentuate his trademark interpretations of the natural landscape. In 1923, the Union Board bought six of Steele's paintings, the nucleus for the IMU art collection. Although his original term as honorary professor was meant to last only a year, he happily stayed on until 1926, the year of his death.

FRATERNITY MENTOR

After the road was blocked for a new Sigma Nu chapter house located on campus, renovations to the existing structure on Kirkwood became a more attractive option. Wells, already involved with the chapter's finances, spearheaded a plan to renovate and add on to the house. Discussions were held with the new chapter advisor, IU bookstore manager Ward G. Biddle.

Biddle, a 1916 IU graduate and Sigma Nu brother, had returned to his alma mater in July 1923 to oversee the growing operation of the campus bookstore. Hailing from rural Madison County, he entered IU in 1909 after graduating from Pendleton High School. His academic progress was slowed by work as a teacher to pay for college, and he was graduated from IU in 1916. He spent the following seven years working for small Hoosier banks in Pendleton, Anderson, and Middletown. But his heart lay in educational administration and finance. The bookstore, founded as a student co-op in 1890, had grown into an auxiliary enterprise of the university by 1910. No stranger to the bookstore's operations, Biddle's senior thesis was titled "'The Indiana University Book Store,' a Study of the Local Store and a Comparative Study of Similar Stores in Other Institutions."[64]

In his role as chapter advisor, Biddle reluctantly approved of the expansion and remodeling plans. Noting that Sigma Nu alumni lacked interest in a building program and that the treasury was bare, Biddle cautioned the enthusiastic active members that they would have to raise the needed funds themselves. The brothers turned to brother Wells, the resident financial expert, and elected him "Eminent Commander" (that is, president) at the end of his junior year.[65]

Wells forged a special relationship with Biddle. They possessed a natural affinity and common interests in educational affairs, the banking industry, and the Democratic Party. The younger Wells eagerly learned from his older fraternity brother, and Biddle appreciated the energy of the young dynamo who was leading Sigma Nu. They consulted regularly and mapped out a strategy to appeal to alumni of the chapter.

Relying on personal visits to alumni located in Indiana, Wells crisscrossed the state in summer 1923 trying to convince Sigma Nus to open their wallets. Wholeheartedly believing in the worth of the project, Wells used his natural charm to persuade. Explaining the need for enhancements to the existing facility, he argued that it would improve the long-term health and vitality of the organization. He called upon the rosy memories of college life that were held by some Sigma Nus, appealed to the pragmatic connections forged by fraternity membership, or invoked the high ideals found in its charter – whatever it took to persuade them to write a check.

Wells found the experience a great challenge – but also highly rewarding as the young man cultivated his public relations skills and business acumen at a new level. It was also the first time he traveled extensively, which gave him an "introduction to the highways and byways" of Hoosierdom. Exhilarated by movement, his horizons were noticeably expanded. The appeal was moderately successful, but the funds collected did not meet the costs of the new addition. With the assurance of an experienced banker, Wells took the lead in arranging a loan to cover the unmet remainder. The new addition, particularly the modern bathroom, was a strong selling point to prospective members during rush.[66]

CLASS OF 1924 GRADUATION

On May 7, 1924, the university celebrated another centennial: the opening of its doors to students in 1824.[67] A tablet was laid on the old seminary campus on College Avenue marking the site of the first building, and John W. Cravens, secretary of the University, gave an address on "The First Building." Students and faculty performed a pageant depicting the founding of Indiana University, both literally, with reference to historical events, and symbolically, using figures from the Western classical tradition.[68]

President Bryan, presiding over the commemoration, was in his element. Taking as his subject "the complete university" ideal, he referred to the instruction in Latin that IU started with and asserted "we had not here then a complete university":

> The complete university, which all the universities in the world unite to make, cannot stop with one tongue living or dead. The complete university must deal with everything in a world where nothing is useless and where nothing is common or unclean. The complete university must teach those things which seem utterly useless – if necessary, in glorious defiance of the ignorant, and must teach those things which seem basely utilitarian, if necessary, in defiance of the learned. The University can put no bound to its interests narrower than those of the poet whose word has become a proverb quoted in the dictionaries: "I am a man and nothing that belongs to a man is alien to me."[69]

The heady concoction of the Western tradition and university ideals flavored with local history was also evident at commencement two months later.

Nearly four hundred students received their bachelor's degrees at the 1924 ceremony, held in the Men's Gymnasium. Wells was one of thirty-eight who received a B.S. in Commerce. In addition to his IU diploma, he received a gold watch charm – a wreath surmounted by a lyre, with "I.U." in relief – for his five hundred hours' service to the University Band.

Professor James A. Woodburn, a member of the class of 1876, gave the commencement speech, entitled "Since the Beginning: A Retrospect." On the verge of retiring from the History Department, which he had served for nearly forty years, he was preparing a new history of IU. "Let us dedicate ourselves again to the University," Woodburn implored,

> But not to this university alone. Beyond the university is our state, beyond the state is our country, beyond our country is the world. The selfish motive, the provincial motive, the party motive, even the national motive is not sufficient. No motive is sufficient short of a motive for truth and humanity. We must be ready to strike with truthfulness and courage for every great cause in America or out of it.

Tying these sentiments together, Woodburn referred to the recent celebrations of the university's beginnings, reminding the audience of the pioneer spirit that overcame "the physical forces of the wilderness." That same vital essence, he said, was needed today:

> a spirit that will lead us into readiness to encounter trial and adventure, to dare the truth to trust and, if need be, in her defense to stand alone. No victory for an advance in a political or moral cause was ever achieved by men who continually glorify the past without understanding how the struggling pioneer spirits of the past have produced the present and press us on toward the future.[70]

The Men's Gym was decorated with an art display. Pride of place went to a large oil painting representing "alma mater" and the fight against ignorance. It was painted by Edwin Howland Blashfield, who was well known as a muralist and for his allegorical, figurative style. Among his other commissions was the dome of the Library of Congress in Washington, D.C. President Bryan titled his commencement remarks, "Alma Mater and the Dark Ages." Despite the glories of the Gothic cathedrals built during the Middle Ages, he said, the Dark Ages are "eternal," located in the hearts and minds of all of us. He went on to describe the painting thus:

> Alma Mater appears as a woman of splendid beauty. In her arms and at her feet are the books which stand for the learning created and cherished by the University. At her feet is a monster devouring the books. The monster is barbarism, the spirit which scorns and tramples under foot what is fine and loves what is base. The monster is the never-dying spirit of the Dark Ages. A flock of angels

strive in comic distress to save the books. A youth with a sword stands ready, we
hope, to fight for the good cause at the command of Alma Mater. When I saw
this youth with the sword, I thought of our boys who chose to spend their money
for the pictures of Theodore Steele.[71]

Noting that the youth "carries the shield of Indiana University," Bryan,
along with his wife, gave the canvas to the university "in the hope that its
beauty and its meaning may help in the good fight far into the future."[72]

Around commencement time, another historic first was noted. Despite the fact that IU had been coeducational for more than fifty years, it
had not had a woman trustee until 1924, when the alumni elected Nellie
Showers Teter. Teter, a member of the wealthy Showers family, was married to Sanford Teter, IU class of 1893, who served as a major administrative officer of the furniture-manufacturing firm.

To provide an answer to repeated entreaties about his college years,
Wells attempted to explain "what it was really like" in a short chapter of
his 1980 autobiography *Being Lucky.* Looking back to a time over fifty
years before, his view was through glasses tinted a deep shade of rose. He
waxes poetic about his friends, his professors, and the heady atmosphere
of hope and ambition that he found on the campus. Making a literary reference, he noted that F. Scott Fitzgerald's 1920 novel, *This Side of Paradise,*
"served to picture much the same world as ours" in its depiction of college life, but without the Ivy League's "expensive decadence." His senses
heightened to the beauty of the campus and the changing seasons, Wells
remembered that it was "a time of response, growth, transformation,
and inspiration" in which his "whole being responded to the stimuli of
collegiate life, in and out of the classroom."[73]

This retrospection, however accurate, minimizes the confusions,
longings, and setbacks that Wells experienced during his college years.
But it does convey deep truths about the indelible mark that his IU undergraduate experience made. Away from his family of origin, he discovered a set of brothers in Sigma Nu that was the start of his construction
of an elective family. Friendship with peers became his preferred mode.
It provided infinite expansion of his circle while avoiding the ups and
downs of romantic entanglements. Wells also found professors, notably James Moffat, who inspired him as well as provided role models.
Perhaps the most consequential relationship he developed during his

undergraduate days was with Ward Biddle, who became a mentor and confidant. Not only did Biddle assist in Wells's effort to lead Sigma Nu, but the bookstore manager also showed by example that education and business could be combined into service on behalf of the university.

Wells was exposed to the ideals of education, of public service, of community and place during his three years as an undergraduate – all part of the tutelary spirit of Indiana, its genius loci. The people he encountered in the IU environment – luminaries such as William Lowe Bryan and T. C. Steele; fraternity mentors like Ward Biddle and James Moffat; charismatic characters such as Hoagy Carmichael, Peter Costas, and William "Monk" Moenkhaus; faculty lights James Woodburn, Jack Geiger, and William Rawles – would resonate with him for a long time.

It is hardly too much to say that the best hope of intelligent and principled progress in economic and social legislation and administration lies in the increasing influence of American universities. By sending out these open-minded experts, by furnishing well-fitted legislators, public leaders and teachers, by graduating successive armies of enlightened citizens accustomed to deal dispassionately with the problems of modern life, able to think for themselves, governed not by ignorance, by prejudice or by impulse, but by knowledge and reason and high-mindedness, the State Universities will safeguard democracy.

Frederick Jackson Turner, 1910

TWO

Betwixt Banking and Social Science

WHEN WELLS RETURNED TO LEBANON after four years away at college, he had matured considerably. He had made his parents proud that he accomplished what they could not achieve for themselves – a college degree. For a dutiful and respectful son, it was but the latest in his efforts to please them. Although he was still the affectionate boy that he had always been to his family, his behavior was leavened with the knowledge that he was now a young man – a college graduate no less – with all the excitement and incertitude of that state. At college, his horizons had been expanded, both intellectually and socially. Perhaps unconsciously, he had begun assembling an elective family of friends chosen by mutual agreement to augment his family of birth.

Wells realized that college opened a gulf between him and his parents. They, like parents everywhere, could not understand and appreciate how their boy had changed. On the surface, both generations could find some common ground and converse about mundane things. They could speak of what he had learned in classes and of the professors and friends he had met, or university ceremonies or football games. Harder to put into words was Wells's growing sense of himself and his inchoate ambition. Bloomington and Lebanon, separated by only ninety miles on the highway, were worlds apart.

Apparently Wells was comfortable with his decision to move back to Boone County after college. Without a burning urge to pursue graduate study or relocate out of state, the safe bet was to return to Lebanon, where there was a position waiting for him at his father's bank. Wells took a job as assistant cashier for the First National Bank. Moving back in with his parents on Meridian Street, Wells faced mutual adjustments common to any such reunited family. Certain things remained the same, however. His maternal grandmother was still living with Granville and Bernice, and, as his father's father Isaac got up in years, he became more dependent. Wells would experience once again his father's mental illness firsthand instead of hearing about it in letters from his mother.

ASSISTANT BANK CASHIER

At first, everything appeared in a new light. Refracted through his status as a college graduate, old sights had a sheen of newness, backlit by his personal memories. Old family acquaintances would see the new assistant cashier and ask him questions about his experiences at IU. Wells would take the interurban train to Indianapolis to see plays as he did in high school. He stayed in touch with college friends and Sigma Nu brothers, inviting them to Lebanon or going on outings. Within three months of graduation he was even taking college classes again, but in Lebanon, not Bloomington. The IU Extension Division had a standing offer to Hoosier communities that, if sixteen or more members of a community petitioned the university, an instructor would be dispatched to offer lessons on site, either weekly or fortnightly. Perhaps thinking that it might lead to more employment options, Wells took two postgraduate courses in education – Secondary Education, and the History of Education in the United States. He received a B+ in the former, and a B in the latter. A course in Educational Sociology was offered during the summer of 1925, in which Wells earned an A.

But despite varied activities, for Wells Lebanon was not as stimulating as Bloomington, and work in the bank became routine, even as he continued to learn about the art of banking. He also gained firsthand knowledge of the persistent agricultural depression and its effects on economic life in small-town Indiana. As prices for agricultural products began to fall in the early 1920s, farmers fell behind in their payments on land mortgages and farming equipment. Banks were in a tough spot. The situation was exacerbated by loose state banking laws that made it easy for investors to start financial institutions with little capital and even less oversight by the state. The proliferation of small town and country banks in Indiana was astounding: in 1921, there were 1,113 distributed around the state's ninety-two counties.[1]

Severe economic times had devastating effects on farm families. Bank officials were not immune to the entreaties of their farming neighbors when they pleaded for extensions of payments. In the best of times, farming was not an easy or quick way to wealth. As the agricultural depression continued, rural families were reduced to subsistence farming, or, in some cases, dispossession. Bank employees were not only called upon to be good with numbers, but also to demonstrate kindness and compassion to distressed customers, who were more often than not neighbors and acquaintances. By 1927, 34 banks had failed in Indiana since 1920. The problems were not confined to the Hoosier State, however. Nationally, 3,724 banks had failed, nearly 10 percent of the total.[2]

Like his father, Wells excelled at both parts of the job, conveying his ability for the technical details of financial transactions while exhibiting respect and concern for bank clientele. As before, Granville continued to perform his public roles as cashier at the First National Bank and as Boone County treasurer, but at home he presented a different face. He relied on Bernice's help as assistant county treasurer and to keep the office running when he was overwhelmed by work or beset by personal problems. At home, Granville was still subject to black moods and quiet desperation. He regularly visited Martinsville Sanitarium, where he took the waters, rested, and relaxed for two weeks a year.[3]

GRADUATE SCHOOL IN BLOOMINGTON

Over time, Wells's hunger for Bloomington increased. Truly happy in that landscape, he missed the excitement and color of IU, the chance to meet old friends and make new ones, the stimulating presence of hundreds of young people in that oasis of liberal academic culture. His yearning turned to concrete plans to pursue a graduate degree. As always, he talked it over with mother and father, and his parents approved of Wells's plan to return to Indiana University for further education. As before, family finances were thin, and he would have to pay his own way for the most part. Granville assumed that he would study law, a long-standing interest of his and a valuable skill in banking. And so, after two years of small-town banking, Wells enrolled at the university to study for a master's degree in economics, his favorite subject. He took a rented room close to the Sigma Nu chapter house, took some of his meals there, and became a familiar sight to his fraternity brothers. When Wells went home for Christmas, it came out that he was studying economics, not law, contrary to his parents' assumption. Granville was surprised but acquiescent to the wishes of his twenty-four-year-old son.

In the mid-1920s, Bloomington entered a period of sustained growth. One major factor was a solution to the chronic water famines that had plagued the town for the past forty years. Griffy Creek, a deep stream two miles northeast of downtown, was dammed to create a reservoir, for which the city built a waterworks. Progressive forces of town and gown, including the Chamber of Commerce and IU geologists, worked together to defeat politicians and landowners who stood to profit on an alternate site, Leonard Springs, on the karst-riddled west side of town.[4] The subsequent increase in Bloomington's population meant that new neighborhoods and schools were established. The manufacturing sector, anchored by Showers Brothers Furniture Factory, remained strong.[5]

In 1927–28, IU enrollments were also up – to nearly 3,400, an increase of about 800 students since 1921. African American students numbered about 40, slightly more than one in 100, and were subject to severe discrimination. Writing in the campus magazine, *The Vagabond,* one student reported with dismay "an organized, systematic, and relentless effort on the part of the administration and student body to deprive the Negro student of every right except that of attending classes." The university boasted three national African American Greek-letter organizations, yet the local Pan-Hellenic councils did not officially recognize any of them. The ROTC program routinely barred African American students, the university physician refused to grant swimming pool permits, and the university band was off limits. The concerned student writer advocated tolerance among students and efforts by the administration to abolish "the presence of such unwarranted and unjustifiable discrimination."[6] Even though the political power of the Klan was waning in Indiana, the university retained racist attitudes and practices.

As a graduate student, Wells was more academically focused and driven to excel than he had been during his undergraduate years. He was familiar with the Department of Economics and Sociology, and, because his undergraduate degree was in commerce, he could complete the master's degree in a single year with course work and a thesis. In his first semester, Wells took two sociology courses (Principles of Sociology: Social Forces; and Descriptive Sociology: Social Evolution) from Ulysses Weatherly, one in economics from James Moffat (Growth of Economic Thought), plus several hours of the department's graduate seminar. His grades were respectable: one A, one B+, and two Bs. Second semester he continued the graduate seminar, two courses taught by Weatherly in sociology (Descriptive Sociology: Social Assimilation; and Heredity and Eugenics), and two of Moffat's courses in economics (Advanced Economics; and Problems in Advanced Marketing and Foreign Trade). Wells earned two B+s and two Bs.[7]

During the second semester of the 1926–27 academic year, Wells embarked on a study of bank service charges for his master's thesis, under the supervision of department chair Weatherly. Fees for checking accounts and other transactions had been adopted by large, urban banks to recover some of the costs associated with additional bookkeeping and the maintenance of check clearinghouses. But they were not so common among small, rural banks located all over the rural Midwest. These country banks were being squeezed financially because their holdings were composed of many small accounts, yet their servicing costs were comparable to their larger brethren. Indiana was extreme in this regard, because of the large numbers of banks within its borders.

To gather empirical data on current practices and policies, Wells turned to the survey, a standard social science method. He devised a questionnaire to bank officials asking them to provide account data and information on existing or planned service charges. To get bank names and addresses, he contacted the Indiana Bankers Association. The IBA, a trade association serving the banking industry, was formed in the 1890s "to promote the general welfare and usefulness of banks and banking institutions and to secure uniformity of action, together with the practical benefits of personal acquaintance." By 1898, roughly half of Indiana's 300 banks were members; by the mid-1920s, nearly all of the 1,100 banks in the state held membership.[8] In March 1927, Wells made the acquaintance of the IBA secretary, Forba McDaniel, to arrange for the Indiana bank questionnaire. She not only cooperated fully with his request for information, but also offered to send the questionnaire to all of the 1,100 IBA member banks, saving him the not inconsiderable cost of postage.[9]

The scope of his study went beyond the Hoosier state. Wells identified one-, two-, and three-bank towns in Nebraska (eighty total) that had fees for service charges and sent them a similar questionnaire. He added data from recently published studies on bank service charges in North Carolina and South Dakota. Finally, he sent out two hundred personal letters to banks in all parts of the United States "concerning some phase of the problem."[10]

The resulting 117-page thesis, titled "Service Charges for Small or So-called Country Banks," contained a careful review of the literature on bank service charges and an analysis of the empirical data that Wells painstakingly put together. Its conclusion did not offer arcane abstractions, but practical guidance of possible use for bank officers. Because country banks typically held a myriad of small accounts, the thesis argued for the need to institute service charges to avoid running at a loss. "The service charge has been shown to be an effective remedy for unprofitable services and accounts," Wells explained, noting that it had been introduced extensively in larger banks. "Therefore, we may say without fear of refutation that service charges are far more necessary for so-called country or smaller banks, than they are for any other type of bank, are just as feasible, and may be put into operation in such a way as to be received very graciously by the customer."[11]

Wells received his M.A. at the June 1927 commencement. Calling on his new connections to the Indiana Bankers Association, he arranged for the publication of his thesis in *The Hoosier Banker,* a monthly house organ edited by IBA secretary McDaniel. The lengthy manuscript was virtually unchanged when it appeared in two parts in the August and September issues.[12]

WISCONSIN

As Wells was completing his thesis research during the 1927 spring semester, his professors encouraged him to pursue a doctorate in economics. Although the graduate school at IU had existed for years, Indiana had produced very few Ph.D.s in any field, unlike stronger Big Ten institutions. Weatherly and Moffat suggested he go elsewhere – to Cornell, Illinois, or Wisconsin. Wells applied to and got offers of assistantships from all three. By far, Wisconsin had the best reputation overall and a world-renowned social science faculty, especially in economics and sociology. Richard Ely, recently retired, had built up a dominant economics department. Historian Frederick Jackson Turner, famous for the "frontier thesis" of American history, served on its faculty until 1910. The state university was home to the "Wisconsin Idea," the Progressive notion that the university would provide experts and foster research and education that would help the state government to conduct its affairs with efficiency and effectiveness. This service ideal extended to citizens as well: "the university as a kind of teacher-counselor-companion to the people at large."[13]

Wells had no hesitation about accepting the Wisconsin offer made by William H. Kiekhofer, the head of the economics department since 1916 and one of Ely's many former students. The school had a large undergraduate student body, with almost a third from out of state, and a nationally ranked graduate school. Wells thought he was ready to travel farther afield than he ever had before in order to spend a few years immersed in the scholarly study of economics, no matter whether that training would prepare him for an academic occupation or a job in private enterprise or government service. Going to Wisconsin meant movement and excitement and new people, although part of his heart remained in Bloomington. It also precluded a return to Lebanon, at least for a while.

With the successful completion of his thesis, Wells had a well-earned summer vacation. He went to Michigan and stayed for a while at the Terrace Inn in Bay View. The hotel was built in 1911 and operated by W. J. Devol and family. Devol was a prominent banker in Lebanon and a Wells family friend. Out of the blue, on July 21, IBA secretary Mc-Daniel telegraphed Wells:

WOULD YOU BE INTERESTED IN AFFILITATING [SIC] WITH INDIANA BANK-
ERS ASSOCIATION IN CASE OUR PRESENT PLANS MATERIALIZE WHEN
INCREASING ORGANIZATION STOP NEED YOUNG MAN YOUR ABILITY ASSIST

EDITING HOOSIER BANKER DO RESEARCH WORK OUT IN STATE ON COST
ANALYSIS AND OTHER FIELD ACTIVITIES WIRE ME PERSONALY [SIC] NINE
FORTY EAST FORTHIETH [SIC] STREET PLEASE HOLD MATTER CONFIDEN-
TIAL EXCEPT MR DEVOL.

A follow-up telegram from McDaniel asked his salary requirements for
the yet-to-be-created position of IBA "field representative," adding "BE-
LIEVE YOU HAVE QUALIFICATION THAT WE NEED." Wells scribbled
his reply: "NEWNESS AND POSSIBLITIES FOR DEVELOPMENT APPEAL
TO ME STRONGLY." He estimated that he would need at least $2,800 and
traveling expenses.[14]

This unexpected development placed Wells in a quandary. His plans
for graduate school at Wisconsin were well advanced, and he would need
to sign a housing contract shortly. But the banking industry was making its siren call once again. Five years before, at age twenty, he faced a
similar choice – whether to gain more financial stability right away or
to acquire additional training for the future – when presented with the
Whitestown bank job. But now, twenty-five and increasingly independent, he could not rely on his father to come to the rescue and make his
decision for him as he had before. McDaniel followed with a letter the
next day, and Wells responded with his own, saying that he would wait
to arrange his lodging at Wisconsin, but he could not delay indefinitely.
Within a week, McDaniel wrote back with disappointing news: one official at the IBA was holding up the plans for hiring a field secretary, and
she advised him to continue with his doctoral plans.[15]

Wells equably accepted the rescission of the premature job offer. In-
vigorated by the knowledge that his present credentials and skills might
lead somewhere, he gained new optimism about his future and added
this exchange to his private storehouse. With a sigh of relief at avoiding one more complication, however attractive, he went ahead with his
Wisconsin preparations.

Already fond of communal living, Wells found comfortable accommodation at the University Club in Madison, a commodious residence
designed for male instructors and bachelor professors, with ninety bedrooms, dining rooms and recreational facilities, a library, and other modern conveniences. Founded in 1906, it served as "the center of faculty
social life," bringing together scholars and administrators from all across

campus. It provided a myriad of programs, ranging from musical performances to lectures, and was a popular site for transacting university business in informal conferences and formal meetings. The library subscribed to fifty-five magazines, both domestic and foreign, and ten newspapers.[16] Although the basics of communal life were similar to his fraternity in Bloomington, Wells appreciated the refinement and dignity afforded by the club in Madison. Occasionally he joined the campus Sigma Nus for dinner at their chapter house near Lake Mendota.

Wells was keen to know the Wisconsin academic environment. One striking feature was the pronounced class differences among the student body. With an eye honed by years of business study and practical experience in banking, he observed that the university was especially attractive to rich Chicagoans and easterners. Wells described the campus climate thus:

> Sophisticated and from families of social position and wealth, these young men lent an air to student life that was almost Princetonian, and at the same time the campus had a strong La Follette–Progressive political cast. The interaction of these forces, egalitarianism and liberalism on the one hand and elegance and affluence on the other, curiously enough was salutary. Living side by side, tolerating each other, students with these divergent views somehow thrived on the mixture.[17]

Although Wells did not share this upper-class background, he identified politically as a progressive Democrat, which was perhaps more rare in Indiana than in Wisconsin. More significantly, he recognized the value of diversity within the academic culture of aspiration as he continued striving to rise in social status as he rode on the educational escalator.

Wells worked with "Wild Bill" Kiekhofer, who was a renowned teacher and author of a popular economics textbook. "An orator of the old school," he lectured to as many as 1,800 students at a time.[18] His showmanship was grounded in meticulous preparation, which he extended to the training of his teaching assistants, of whom Wells was one. Later known as the father of college economics teachers, Kiekhofer modeled techniques for audience engagement that stood Wells in good stead later.

In addition to training graduate students in teaching, Kiekhofer also directed doctoral dissertations. Wisconsin was a major Ph.D. producer, graduating 112 doctorates in economics from 1908 to 1933. John Commons was by far the most prolific "Doktorvater," supervising nearly a third of the doctoral degree holders. Ely had fourteen during the same period, while Kiekhofer directed six.

In addition to Kiekhofer's devotion to the Economics Department, he was a model academic citizen of the university, serving on a variety of campus committees as well as advocating to the state that the university was a "bulwark for democracy": "His vision was of an expansive, beautiful, and harmonious campus," with the idea of a central library and art gallery that would serve students and visitors alike.[19]

Wells also served as a teaching assistant to William A. Scott, head of the money and banking division of the economics department. This conservative professor, a staunch believer in the gold standard, was a dynamic lecturer. He put Wells in charge of two quiz sections composed of juniors and seniors. The young-looking Wells, only five years older than the bulk of his section students, reasoned that a mustache might enhance his air of authority with the undergraduates, so he grew one.

Wells took three courses his first semester, two for credit and one that he audited. The absent-minded Professor Commons, Wells reported, "would wander into the seminar of forty doctoral students and simply begin thinking aloud about the subject that had been occupying him in his study moments before." In contrast to the complaints of some other students about the unplanned nature of the class, Wells relished "seeing a great mind evolve a whole new theory of value," a central topic of economic theory.[20] Second semester he took a heavy load of five courses, enrolling in three for credit and auditing two. Wells finished a yearlong economics seminar with E. A. Ross, and received a 92. In addition to completing three courses in his major, he took an education course and one in political science.[21] Interestingly, both Ross and Commons had been members of the IU faculty for brief periods in the 1890s.

BACK HOME AGAIN IN INDIANA

After the tantalizing Indiana Bankers Association possibility fell through in the summer, throughout fall 1927 Wells continued to hear from Mc-

Daniel, who dutifully kept the new Wisconsin graduate student apprised of the IBA situation. In October, she wrote that the IBA had appointed a three-person committee to look into the matter of hiring a field secretary.[22] Wells had also befriended one of the committee members, J. Dwight Peterson, a 1919 IU economics graduate, who was a fast-rising bond salesman for City Securities Corporation in Indianapolis. Most likely Wells had advance notice that the committee was tending toward part-time rather than full-time employment for the job of field secretary. In January 1928, at Peterson's suggestion, Wells wrote to the committee chairman, Charles Zigler, cashier at South Bend's First National Bank and past president of the IBA, stating that he desired to change his application for the field representative to part-time. Wells explained that he planned to return to Bloomington at the close of the semester and take up management of a college clothing store again (of which he was part-owner), but he would be available for IBA work on a monthly, weekly, or daily basis. He pointed out that his storefront was located near the university library and the Bureau of Business Research, so he could keep any research projects going.[23] Wells also wrote Peterson a thank-you note, adding, "a college shop, though an excellent earning proposition, leaves one with considerable free time since the hours are not long or confining."[24]

The "college shop" that Wells referred to was Gabriel's, a men's clothing store that his business partner Sam Gabriel had opened up a few months before. Sam was a good friend from Lebanon who had come to IU but had dropped out before finishing his degree. Gabriel's was located adjacent to campus, first on Kirkwood and then on Indiana Avenue, and catered to collegiate fashion. It is not clear whether Wells worked on the retail floor at times, but his role as a trusted advisor and, somewhat later, financial backer, was significant. He was listed as a vice president of the company, with Gabriel serving as president. Wells, in his knowledgeable banker way, had set his friend up in business by providing capital and cosigning a business loan.[25]

Wanting to keep the IBA pot stirring, Wells composed a telegram to McDaniel around the same time. He outlined a possible dissertation plan to investigate the influence of the small bank in social and economic terms in a national context. He concluded his message:

In case I should happen to become Field Representative for two years at least
[I] would probably spend my spare time in Bloomington in conducting this
individual work. . . . In case you care to suggest this to the committee you may do
so, or turn it over to Peterson. In case it sounds too historical and academic [,]
withhold, because although I know my [?] and am not a traditional academic
type, as you know, the committee might think otherwise.[26]

Not neglecting his IU academic connections either, at some point he
sent a similar dissertation prospectus to Weatherly. A twelve-page draft
outlined a study of "The Country Banker: An Appraisal of the Force of
His Influence upon the Social and Economic Life of His Community."
After sections on the internal organization of such banks, the final part
deals with the country bankers' relation to the local community, including their influence on the church, education, civic policies, politics, agriculture, and industry. In a letter accompanying the draft outline, Wells
asked for criticism, saying, "I am not at all satisfied with Part III, that is
the portion that is more strictly sociological. I have so much to say in that
section, yet it does not seem to lend itself very well to organization."[27]
Wells was trying to find a way to integrate his banking background with
his academic ambitions in the hopes of acquiring a useful and interesting livelihood.

In the February 1928 issue of *The Hoosier Banker,* the news that the
association had appropriated $1,500 for a part-time extension worker was
announced.[28] Going slowly, the Indiana Banking Association was feeling its way to address problems that had gained force since farm prices
fell during the early 1920s. That put pressure on the banks that served
farmers and other agricultural workers and businesses, and there was a
growing sense that something had to be done collectively to staunch the
flow of bank failures. Although the IBA membership still included virtually all of Indiana's 1,100 banks, there were no good statistics on their
institutional health and financial prospects. Ideally, extension work by
a field secretary would replace sporadic and anecdotal information with
regular surveys and facts gathered on the ground. It would also facilitate
communication between individual banks and the association in addition to regular state and regional meetings.

In late January, Wells met with IBA president C. O. Holmes, a banker
from the booming steel town of Gary, to talk about the potential job

opening. Holmes had asked the doctoral student to share his ideas of what the job might entail. Wells furnished a written outline of the work of field representative, emphasizing data gathering from meetings with bank officers on their home turf. He did not comment, for example, on the extensive vigilante work to protect banks from robbers, since it was already well organized by the association.[29] He suggested that the field representative should make contacts and host meetings in the county or on a regional level "because experience that I gained a few years ago when I traveled for several months for an organization arousing interest in it, convinced me that men will largely attend any sort of a meeting if they have been urged personally to attend." Although he did not mention his previous fundraising for Sigma Nu by name, that was the source of his experience. In addition to his statewide work, Wells could reach out to neighboring states to check on other "progressive associations" of bankers, such as Wisconsin, Illinois, and Iowa, to compare notes and gain insights. As far as his availability for work, he had arranged his academic schedule so he could work for two weeks in early April, and would be able to start regularly on June 10. Wells reiterated his understanding that Holmes and McDaniel would be pushing for a regular, full-time commitment from the IBA, with at least a $3,000 salary to "maintain my present scale," since he could not afford to turn down his Wisconsin teaching assistantship otherwise, adding that he would deduct $57.50 for each week that he didn't work.[30]

Keeping McDaniel in the loop, Wells wrote to her again: "The only thing that I wish to be certain about is that politics is not allowed to keep the job and myself from a fair trial of six or eight months. After that if I don't deliver, I am willing to take the consequences." He could "sympathize with the caution" about university research that Holmes had expressed, and was quite willing to revise the plan, writing, "May I suggest here also that I always welcome suggestions and criticisms, and true to the fat man tradition, my temper is never ruffled, so never hesitate to let me have your advice." Concerned about his cash flow if the IBA hired him for the two weeks in April, Wells asked McDaniel for a "lift on expenses," explaining that his maintenance was about the same whether he was traveling or not. He concluded his letter thus: "If hard work, all of my energy, enthusiasm, and the little training that I have can make this job a success, it will be one. I certainly appreciate your recommending me for this work, and could do no less than I have suggested in order to justify your confidence in me."[31]

By summertime the Indiana Bankers Association finally made their decision to hire a field secretary, initially on a part-time basis, and Wells obtained the job that he had lobbied so hard to get.[32] Although he was "practically raised in a bank," Wells received a crash course in recent Hoosier banking history. State banking laws were weak, and the industry operated in a laissez-faire environment. The state Department of Banking, created in 1920, had widespread authority over all banks, trust companies, building and loan associations, and the like. But the department had woefully inadequate personnel – just ten examiners – to supervise, much less inspect, financial institutions in the state on a regular basis.

Indiscriminate chartering was a major cause of bank failures. Because organizing a bank was easy, banks proliferated, giving rise to cutthroat competition: "New bank charters were being sought and obtained by church groups, lodge groups or political groups antagonistic to the church group, lodge group or political groups in control of existing institutions." Many villages of 500 people or less had two or more banks operating, and every county in the state had an average of a dozen banks. This era of "spite" banks and bitter competition led directly to banks taking risky loans and desperate measures to stay in business.[33]

Against this backdrop, critical observers, including the membership of the IBA, had come to the realization that the "public interest may not best be served by the addition of new units without economic justification for their existence." Reluctantly, banks were moving from a strict policy of laissez-faire into accepting some state regulation. "It is recognized that although banks are private enterprises," said the IBA, "the public welfare has become so dependent upon their successful operation that they have become to some degree public institutions" and therefore subject to statutory regulations.[34]

The work of the IBA was carried in several administrative divisions: Better Banking Practices, Education, Banker-Farmer Cooperation, Protection, Taxation, Legislation, County Organization, Publications, Research, and Public Relations. The field secretary's position dealt with Research and Public Relations, which were related to all of the rest, so Wells's bailiwick connected to every other IBA division. For the fall meeting in Gary, Wells produced a display of all of the IBA activities.[35]

THE HAPPY TRAVELER

The first step for the IBA field secretary was clear: to gather data from the more than one thousand banks scattered around the state. An automobile was a necessity. Wells admired the Chevrolet coupe that his parents drove to visit him in Madison – their first new car – but he had never learned to drive one. So he acquired a Ford and learned to drive. Country roads, mostly dirt or gravel laid down for horses, buggies, and carts, were gradually being upgraded for automobiles, and were interconnected with an emerging state and federal highway system. For a young man of twenty-six, owning a car and having access to the open road was exhilarating. For Wells, it was doubly exciting. The automobile was a tool for work and it satisfied an itch for freedom and movement. He had started to realize the truth embedded in the saying that "getting there was half the fun," wherever "there" happened to be.

Other than the mandate for extensive contacts with all Hoosier banks, the job description for the field secretary remained remarkably vague. The Indiana Bankers Association was slowly and hesitantly moving toward some form of collective action in an industry that had a tradition of fierce independence. Just about all IBA members agreed that something needed to be done about the poor health of the state's banking system, but that unanimity dissolved once discussion started about exactly what steps might be taken. A major fear was too much government regulation.

Due to his academic training at Indiana and Wisconsin, Wells was ahead of the curve in thinking that banks were more akin to public utilities rather than traditional producers of consumer goods and services. During his two semesters of doctoral study, he observed the social benefits of academic research aligned with and serving state government in Progressive politics in Wisconsin. But he also knew that Indiana differed from Wisconsin in important ways.

Wells did not appear to be worried about the uncertainties of the task. Self-direction and hard work had never worn him down. There was a big mountain of banks to investigate, and it would take sound judgment and excellent people skills to extract sensitive, proprietary information from them. Changes in bank policies would have to wait until empirical data were gathered, summarized, and digested.

Armed with a suitcase, a car, and his new mustache, Wells attacked the field secretary assignment with vigor. He planned his route with military precision, canvassing each bank in a county before moving on to the next. The affable young man would meet the bank officers and employees, explain to them his purpose, and then proceed to examine their account books and records. Keeping good notes, Wells would return to IBA headquarters in Indianapolis periodically to deposit his data and confer with staff.

In the process of visiting every one of Indiana's ninety-two counties, Wells got an education in geographical variation and demographic diversity. Banks and their inhabitants were the main quarry. A collateral benefit was to become further acquainted with the beauty of the state's countryside. When he filled up his belly as well as his automobile gas tank, or when he stopped for the night in cities and hamlets, he encountered many species of Hoosier humanity. Other businessmen, on the road in connection to their job, encountered a similar flood of sense impressions and quotidian human presence. But Wells did more than passively encounter the passing scene. He reveled in it, learned from it, and profited from his investment in people from all walks of life.

As he traveled around the state on IBA business, Wells returned to Bloomington periodically. He kept Indiana University in his thoughts, and his good friend Biddle wrote frequently about campus happenings. The bookstore manager took a keen interest in mentoring Wells by plotting his chances at IU, responding to queries from professors about his activities, and sharing news about Sigma Nu.[36] Both men were intent on finding some position for Wells at the university.

After nine months' employment by the IBA, Wells wrote Biddle a long letter in April 1929, stating his desire to return to the university and outlining a tentative strategy. A major concern was the prospect of an opening in economics and if "the vacancy were filled by a certain type of

man, no vacancy would again be available in my field in a life time probably." Nevertheless, he decided "Bloomington offers certain compensations which would more than offset the advantages in prestige and salary
that might be gained from another institution," adding, "you well know
what I consider those compensations to be." He sketched a strategy to
delicately lobby two of the most powerful men at IU, President William
Lowe Bryan and trustee Ora Wildermuth. He wrote, "I will from time
to time as it appears expedient follow up my little prior contact that I
made with Bryan," and "it runs in my mind also that Wildermuth has
some very active Bank connections and if such is the case I will invent
an excuse to have a conference with him before long in Gary."[37] In fall
1929, Wells was reappointed by the IBA, and secretary Forba McDaniel
reported that he had called on bankers in sixty-eight counties and his
work "has been of inestimable value to the banks of Indiana."[38]

In February 1930, at the urging of editor McDaniel, Wells started
a monthly news column, entitled "Hoosier Highways," for *The Hoosier
Banker*. Underlining the corporate nature of his contribution, the byline
was simply the "Field Secretary" and the column used the editorial "we."
Readers who did not know Wells was the field secretary had no way of
finding out from the text.

Wells penned his monthly pieces with an open, friendly voice, describing his travels over the previous four weeks. Each of these dispatches
from the field was highly specific, containing the names of the banks
visited and of the town or region, plus the names of bank officers or other
staff that met with him. Chatty and cheerful, the author successfully conveyed a wealth of information, observations, and advice to the Hoosier
banking fraternity. Wells began his inaugural column on an autobio-
graphical note:

> It is appropriate that the first account of a trip to appear in this feature should
> be an account of a trip to Boone County. It is our home county. Here nearly
> fourteen years ago we began to learn the intricacies of the Burroughs Posting
> machine. After that first day's experience, we were not at all sure that a banker's
> life was as desirable as it had seemed from the outside. Our first impression did
> not last and since that time we have had some sort of active bank connection
> with banks and bankers nearly all of the time. We are glad we had the chance on
> the first day for it gave us the opportunity for work that has ever since proved to
> be a happy selection.[39]

After detailing his visits to Boone County financial institutions in a series of short notes, Wells talked of his visit to Bloomington to make arrangements for an IBA "Short Course" on banking: "It is a drive we always like to make. It is one of the most beautiful in the state." Calling first on Citizens Trust Company, the field secretary admitted, "[W]hile a student in Bloomington, we carried our unprofitable account there." After calling on two other banks, lack of time precluded a visit to the Bloomington National Bank, "where we as undergraduate carried several treasurer accounts – great banks in Bloomington." After this verbal love-fest, he made a gentle criticism: "It seems peculiar, however, that with such progressive and sound banks they do not organize a clearing house and secure for themselves to the benefits of co-operation through the use of service charges and reciprocal credit information." He reminded readers that the other "Monon Student Towns," where DePauw, Wabash, and Purdue were located, were "100 per cent. on both of these projects."[40]

In his March column, Wells mentioned the great success of the IBA "Short Course" recently held in Bloomington, where "Dean Rawles was able to add a perfectly bewildering array of luncheons, dinners, teas and smokers that the hospitable town and campus wished to give in honor of the bankers." This month's travels took him to the western part of the state. Passing through Jamestown, Wells stopped at the Citizens State Bank, the site of his first job, and visited his father, "who has always been our instructor in the science of banking." Spending several days making calls at various western Indiana banks, one night Wells found himself in Covington. "After the Ford was comfortably stabled at its customary curbstone box stall," he recounted,

> we walked to the Wabash river – watched the sun, as a beautiful red ball of fire, sink behind the river and day dreamed of the days of long ago when the Indians used the river for their canoes, and then its later part in pioneer commerce, when on its bosom each year it bore a burden of whiskey and molasses on the way to New Orleans and the world. And also of the man who made it famous and immortal, Paul Dresser, of his tragic life and of his brother Theodore's biography of him.[41]

The field secretary was developing a distinctive style for "Hoosier High-ways." The main thrust was to communicate news about various Indiana banks through human-interest stories. Written in a style not dissimilar to a society-page column, these telegraphic comments were short and to the point. Leavened with observations on the passing scenery, cultural associations, and food and lodging, Wells was exemplifying the banker as a man of civility and taste, competent to be entrusted not only with money but also with civic leadership.

Heading north in April for a two-week trip, Wells encountered fine spring weather and roads turned into "a bottomless sea of mud." As a consequence, he got the Ford stuck several times, but so far, he joked, he was able to get out without needing "a good team of horses." He raved about Hotel LaFontaine in Huntington and its "unique features," including "one of the finest pools in America," advising bankers to stop there on their way to the IBA convention in Fort Wayne in September. Lauding the Tippecanoe County Bankers Association, centered in Lafayette, for "their practical application of the spirit of co-operation" during "these troublesome times," Wells wrote,

> They have stood shoulder to shoulder, with each and every banker doing his best to protect the reputation of every other banker in the county with the public. Such a concerted co-operation by every county in the state would do a great deal to allay false and dangerous rumors that are apt to arise about the best of banks, due to the public's unstable state of mind.[42]

At the village of Andrews, Wells took some personal time and paid a visit to his "favorite great aunt." Remembering one of his "most pleasant boyhood memories," he recalled "a barefooted trip to her spring house at the bottom of the hill. And from it came fresh raspberries and cold thick cream to be eaten with slices of baked homemade bread, spread thick with yellow butter."[43]

In the May "Hoosier Highways" Wells described stopping in Bloomington to pick up a passenger, Professor William C. Cleveland of the Department of Economics, who had "made so many friends by his able presentation of banking subjects at the Short Course" two months before. Cleveland, an unmarried assistant professor hired in fall 1927 after one year of doctoral work at the University of Chicago, taught banking as well as other subjects. The two men were nearly the same age, born two days apart. Since Wells was awarded his master's degree in June 1927, he first met Cleveland as a departmental alumnus. Their first stop was Nashville, "surrounded by the best of nature's landscapes" in Brown

County. The field secretary thought that the "splendid hospitality of the Nashville House" would provide "an ideal place for a group meeting." The two men traveled for a week through Bartholomew, Decatur, and surrounding counties scrutinizing banks.[44]

Once back in Bloomington, Cleveland thanked Wells for the enjoyable time, and went on to express surprise at learning something Wells failed to disclose on their April journey:

> Since my return from the trip I have learned that you are negotiating with the department with respect to a position. Thus all that I had to say to you on the trip relative to the vacancy here next year was old news to you. However, you fooled me most cleverly, and I must admit that I gained no idea that you were in the process of negotiation. May I wish you luck.[45]

Indeed, Wells had been talking with the senior faculty – since February.

BACK HOME AGAIN *AT* INDIANA

In February, Wells had received an offer for an assistant professorship from Weatherly, his M.A. thesis adviser and chair of the Department of Economics and Sociology, which was part of the School of Liberal Arts. The prospect of teaching at his alma mater was very attractive, but the salary was less than half what he was receiving from the Indiana Bankers Association. That put Wells in a serious quandary: Would he make financial sacrifices to return to his adopted home ground, or continue on his present course, which offered a comfortable living and prospects for advancement, but no guarantee that he would get another shot at the coveted faculty job?

Wells worried himself sick. In despair, he wrote to Biddle, his most trusted confidant. His concerned friend replied,

> I was most happy indeed to see the letter Dr. Weatherly sent you, but extremely disappointed to hear that you seem to have "lost something." Herman, I can't help but feel that maybe you weren't feeling just right when you received it. Perhaps under the proper atmosphere you would react in a different way. Of course, it is hard for anyone to decide for someone else what they should do, but I have always been in hopes that you could link up with Indiana University in some way and preferably, as I have said before, in the Commerce School, – hoping that you might some time become the Dean. Before I turned this down I would give it every possible consideration and from every angle.[46]

Wells was worried about the financial implications of accepting the IU job. He would take a salary cut from his already meager IBA wages. Attempting to allay his friend's black mood, Biddle appealed to Wells's fraternal impulses as he concluded his letter: "Again may I say that I hope you will think about this a long time before you turn it down. I am selfish enough to tell you that I hope you can locate in Bloomington for the inspiration I get from being with you."[47]

Over the next several weeks Wells continued to negotiate with Weatherly, suggesting that he could continue working for the IBA but with reduced hours, while taking on instructional duties at Indiana. The compromise arrangement was acceptable to all parties, and by late March the scheme was sufficiently worked out. "It was good news indeed," his mentor Biddle exulted, "to hear of your definite decision to hibernate yourself with the rest of us down here in the hills. I think it is a wise move, and as the years come and go I think you will get more out of life than you will chasing dyspeptic bankers and doctoring sick banks."[48] True to form, Wells had sought and found a middle ground, shaping the situation from a choice between academe or banking to one that included both.[49]

Just shy of twenty-eight years old, Wells was an IU faculty member, starting on the bottom rung of the university he had graduated from only six years before. Paternal influence had started him down the path of fiduciary management, but after college the path forked. The road of practice was leading to a traditional banking career. The academic fork went to the social science of economics. Wells had sampled both as he grappled with career choices, with diverse experiences as a small town banker, a graduate student, a small business owner, and an applied social scientist. From this welter he was able to extract a wealth of knowledge and understanding that would help him in college teaching and beyond. He was beginning to understand, both intellectually and emotionally, how and why finances were a vital part of the human fabric and the great influence of fiduciary guidance. Perhaps most important, he was now back at home, in Bloomington.

Physical frontiers have been annihilated by reason of the utter fearlessness on the part of the pioneer. There are no longer any physical, geographical frontiers, but there are many frontiers in the field of the social sciences. If our pioneer ancestors did not like a given situation, they set out to change it. We have been too prone the past few years to feel that unfit economic situations could not be solved. Too many of us have lost the pioneer spirit. We need to regain it to use it in fearless experimentation with agencies of social control designed to curb the abuses and the undesirable features of the capitalistic system.

Herman B Wells, c. 1933

THREE

The Politics of Bank Reform

WELLS FELT A SENSE OF RELIEF that the protracted negotiations for his IU instructorship were over. He considered his position as field secretary of the Indiana Bankers Association not only financially necessary, but also an essential lifeline to practical applications of his academic studies. With summer coming on, he could focus again on the field secretary duties, and look forward to his first classes as an IU instructor in Fall 1930. He continued his peripatetic lifestyle, traveling all over the state on business, returning frequently to IBA headquarters in Indianapolis and retiring at night to his bedroom at the Claypool Hotel, a venerable institution on Monument Circle in the heart of the city.

Over the last two years as field secretary, Wells had developed his interpersonal skills. He had proven himself an indefatigable worker, adept at translating arcane theoretical knowledge of economics into practical policies and procedures applied to banking. From rural bankers educated on the job to urban captains of the banking industry, with professors, townspeople, and small business owners, he found genuine pleasure in meeting people, and his winning and cooperative personality added to his effectiveness.

Wells launched into teaching with "great enthusiasm," as he later reported. He wrote to department chair Weatherly during the first semester of the 1930–31 academic year,

> I am delighted with my work. I do not believe that I have ever been happier in my life, and am looking forward to the day when increasing general culture and mastery of my own field will make it possible for me to make my class appearances as satisfactory as I wish them to be. When that day arrives I can think of no happier work in the world than teaching.[1]

59

But Wells also kept in close touch with the IBA, and drove back and forth to Indianapolis several times a week during class terms.

The economic picture in Indiana had been getting darker for some time, with a steady erosion of farm commodity prices and the consequent drop in farmland values. Bank closings were distressingly common, and depositors often lost nearly all of their money if the bank was forced to liquefy, as many did. Moreover, bank owners – typically shareholders – had a double liability; they lost their investment in the bank and they became legally liable for an amount equal to the nominal value of their stock. The effects on Hoosier localities were devastating. If a bank failed, not only would it destroy depositors' assets, but it would also ruin the financial leadership in the community.[2]

Concerned that something be done, the Indiana Bankers Association and the Indiana Savings and Loan League asked the 1931 Indiana General Assembly for help. Acting quickly, the legislature passed a concurrent resolution to create the Study Commission for Indiana Financial Institutions. The body was to investigate bank and savings and loan failures and to propose corrective legislation. Governor Harry Leslie appointed eleven leading Hoosier citizens as members of the study commission. Nearly all were bankers or associated with banking issues in some way. Walter S. Greenough, of the Fletcher Savings and Loan Company in Indianapolis, was chosen as chair.

Wells, who knew Greenough from his work as IBA field secretary, angled for a job with the Study Commission. He knew that the commission would need to base its recommendations on thorough knowledge of banking problems, and he saw that his background and experience was almost ideal. The twenty-eight-year-old Wells sent Greenough a narrative résumé, noting that he had "nearly fifteen years association with various Indiana banks in various capacities from bookkeeper to junior officer" in Lebanon and its environs. In addition to three years of service to the Bankers Association, he stated, "I also have something of the borrower's and depositor's viewpoint through ownership of and contact with various types of businesses, such as a few months as country editor, and at the present time, and for the past five years, as part owner and operator of a clothing store." As an example of scholarly research, Wells included a copy of his master's thesis that was published in *The Hoosier Banker,* adding, "Since I stole this from the University Library, and since it is the only copy now in existence, I would appreciate it if you would take good care of it and I will get it back some time when I see you."[3]

Wells, already known widely in banking circles, was indeed chosen as secretary and research director of the commission in the spring of 1931. Although the commission was state sponsored, it was financed by the Bankers Association and the Savings and Loan League. The commission members were unpaid, and most of the expenses were associated with the small research staff directed by Wells, a paid employee.

Thus, Wells added a third professional activity to his already full plate. Luckily, school was out for the summer, so he could concentrate on banking, doing work both for the new study commission and the IBA field secretary's job. Receiving permission to set up the study commission's research enterprise in the basement of the IU Library, he hired three students and two secretaries, all on a part-time basis.[4] Their charge was to investigate "the history of the development of financial institutions in the state, their numbers, their regulation, their causes of failure, and possible remedies."[5] The research shop under the control of one of IU's youngest faculty members attracted campus attention due to its novelty. Although David Starr Jordan had received outside funds for biological research many years ago, never before had the university housed a social science research project performing sponsored or contract research.[6]

Wells, as the Study Commission's factotum, and Greenough, the chairman, saw eye to eye on many things, and agreed that the study's recommendations, based on exhaustive research, needed to be implemented as state regulations. After eighteen months of arduous work, the Study Commission's report was done. Printed December 31, 1932, the 174-page document was full of dense text bristling with statistical tables and contained "a history of Indiana banking, an overview of current banking regulations, and a diagnosis of problems in Indiana's banking industry." It opened with a long excerpt from Supreme Court Justice Louis Brandeis's opinion in *New State Ice Company v. Liebmann* that was a call for bold experimentation to meet changing social and economic needs. This call for progressive action provided a key motif.[7]

The report echoed Wells's master's thesis in its depiction of banks as akin to public utilities. Competition between banks and internal management problems, rather than economic conditions per se, contributed to the growing problem of bank failures, the report argued. The proposed solution was to replace the old state Banking Department with a new Department of Financial Institutions, to "function flexibly and freely throughout the years to come in the direction of modern trends of control by the public of financial institutions."[8] Wells envisioned a powerful board to oversee the Department of Financial Institutions, with direct representation from the industries involved but removed from the political patronage system.[9]

The report's specific policy reforms included restriction of bank charters to prevent "over-banking" in a community, increased supervision of financial institutions with more bank examiners, confirming the double liability of shareholders, recommending against state bank guaranty (deposit insurance) and branch banking, encouraging Federal Reserve membership among Indiana banks, and simplified bank statements.[10] Although the report was criticized in some quarters, few people plowed through the highly technical analysis. Wells and his expert staff had put together a comprehensive reform package that promised to address the needs of the Hoosier banking industry and restore depositor confidence. The overall message was clear to citizens of the state: experts had proffered their professional opinion; now it was up to the Governor and General Assembly to implement the report's recommendations.

MOCK "COMMENCEMENT" AT THE BOOK NOOK

Wells stayed connected with his undergraduate roots. He regularly took his meals at the Sigma Nu house and interacted with the current brothers. Sporting the narrow mustache he had grown as a graduate student at Wisconsin, he revisited favorite campus haunts such as the Book Nook or made trips to pick up moonshine, as Prohibition was still in force. But now he found himself occupying a curious social status. On the one hand, he was a respectable young adult – a member of the IU teaching staff and a seasoned member of the banking profession. On the other hand, he felt not too far removed from his undergraduate days and, as a bachelor, he had no intimate partners to shape his behavior. As Wells tarried on the threshold of adulthood he pushed against the boundaries a little, giving in to the urge to tweak convention and engage in pranks, but with an ironic twist.

Wells had a chance to express a final "fling of juvenility" when the last of the Book Nook's mock commencement ceremonies was held in June 1931. Held directly across the street from the main entrance to the campus and timed to occur near the official IU commencement, the Book Nook spoof tapped a rich vein of student satire of academic convention. A loose group of Book Nook regulars, naming themselves the "Bent Eagles," conspired with owner Peter Costas to plan the celebration. Since 1927, the party grew to the point where its attendance rivaled that of the regular commencement. Costas later explained its rationale: "Just like the University graduated the seniors for scholastic achievement, I graduated them from a social achievement point of view."[11]

In 1931, Bloomington police blocked off Indiana Avenue between Fourth and Kirkwood to vehicular traffic, leaving the street open in front of the Book Nook for the observance. A parade up Kirkwood Avenue kicked off the festivities. Students wearing bathrobes and funny hats pulled wagons and played musical instruments. Wells, resplendent in a white suit and a straw hat, drove his dignified black Packard slowly in the procession. Around a stage set up outside the doors of the Book Nook, the crowd drank cokes and various illegal concoctions.

Sitting as a member of the platform party, Wells, along with his friend Biddle, listened as Costas was made "president" of the "university." Hoagy Carmichael and his fellow Bent Eagle compatriots were in attendance, and one of their number, Howard "Wad" Allen, gave the commencement address. Holding a live hen under his arm, Allen launched into his remarks, which were full of nonsensical phrases and obscure local references. As he came to the climax of his oration, he held aloft the chicken, the "mystic symbol of the true Bent Eagle," and threw the frightened bird into the crowd.

Costas awarded "earned" and "honorary" degrees on behalf of the campus hangout. Among the diploma recipients was Carmichael, who received a "Doctor of Discord" degree. With due pomp and parody, Wells was awarded the degree of "Doctor of Nookology," with the additional notation "Supervisor of the Faculty Emeritus."[12] Carmichael remembered it as a "session of spiritual rejuvenation in the value of the worthless, a final despairing gesture of rebellion against the world of cold realities that was sweeping us into its grip."[13]

In 1932, Wells moved his Bloomington living quarters again. He rented some rooms at 519 North College Avenue from retired professor James A. Woodburn. Constructed in 1820, the house was one of the oldest in Bloomington, and had been the home of the Woodburn family for generations.[14] Woodburn, whose father was also an IU professor, had been urged by President Jordan to go elsewhere to obtain his doctorate after his IU undergraduate, and then come back to teach at IU. He obtained a Ph.D. from Johns Hopkins University and served on the IU faculty from 1888 to 1924. His area of specialization was American history and government, and he was a noted student of Indiana University history. True to form, young professor Wells mixed business and pleasure, striking up an epistolary friendship with his landlord Woodburn, who lived in Ann Arbor after his retirement.

Three blocks north of the courthouse, the Woodburn House was conveniently located a few blocks from campus on a major artery. Wells could easily check on the progress of his research team in the IU Library, or go to Indianapolis to confer with state officials. The domicile fit with his developing identity as a bachelor faculty member, providing not only a respectable address but also more room to entertain and a place to put his embryonic antique collection and his art collection. Wells roomed with his old buddy Sam Gabriel.

THE INDIANA MEMORIAL UNION

The contours of the Bloomington campus were changing during this period. The university had gradually acquired additional acreage contiguous to Dunn's Woods. The campus footprint's boundaries were Third Street to the south and Tenth Street to the north, Indiana Avenue to the west and Jordan Avenue to the east. The new Men's Residence Center (MRC; now Collins Living-Learning Center) was as far away as possible from the women's dorm – Memorial Hall, located on East Third Street. Memorial Stadium, on Tenth Street near Jordan Avenue, also had been built in the mid-1920s. Both were fruits of the postwar Memorial Fund, as was the Indiana Memorial Union, which opened its doors in 1932. Occupying a space between Kirkwood Avenue and Seventh Street, it served to link the Old Crescent with new facilities on the north, such as the Men's Gymnasium and Fieldhouse and the MRC. The new union building had a large multipurpose room with a stage, dubbed Alumni Hall, ample space for student organization offices, and a commodious University Bookstore. Ward Biddle, retaining his position as bookstore manager, became the first director of the Indiana Memorial Union.

In nine years of careful bookstore management, Biddle accumulated a total of $67,500 toward the new quarters in the Union building. At the dedication of the IMU, President Bryan proudly called it "the most beautiful college bookstore in America." Biddle had a strong hand in designing the three-story space to be aesthetically pleasing and to serve the needs of students efficiently. A broad stairway led to the striking second floor balcony and cozy lounge with a fireplace, where the words of Abraham Lincoln are inscribed: "I will study and get ready, and maybe the chance will come." Above the fireplace hung Blashfield's painting *Alma Mater*, presented at the 1924 commencement ceremony. An "authors' room," which contained photographs and books autographed by authors, and the Woodburn Room rounded out the public areas.[15]

A HOOSIER NEW DEAL

The 1932 election ushered in a new U.S. president, Franklin D. Roosevelt, and a new Indiana governor, Paul V. McNutt. Both were progressive Democrats and both touted a reform agenda, known later as the New Deal, to counter the ongoing economic depression. McNutt, shrewd, ambitious, and strikingly good looking, had parlayed his leadership in the American Legion into a potent political force.[16] An IU alumnus and classmate of Wendell Willkie, he had been a professor and then dean of the IU Law School. Upon his election, the IU Board of Trustees granted him an indeterminate leave of absence to serve as governor.

McNutt was at the head of the Democratic sweep in the Indiana General Assembly. All twelve congressmen were Democrats, as well as ninety-one of one hundred seats in the state House of Representatives and forty-three of fifty in the state Senate. Indiana governors were limited by statute to a single four-year term, and the General Assembly met for a two-month period every two years. With an eye toward a future run at the White House, McNutt quickly went to work on his legislative agenda upon taking office in early January 1933: "McNutt secured his base by ramming through the Executive Reorganization Act of 1933. On the surface, the act was a harmless measure to improve state government's efficiency. It reorganized the decentralized state departments and agencies, all 168 of them, into a more streamlined system."[17] But it gave the governor immense power: he could hire and fire at will any government employee, save six elected officials and their deputies. McNutt, through his lieutenants, consolidated their hold on the Democratic Party by "requesting" each state employee donate two percent of their salary to the party's treasury. As a result of these efforts, patronage (what soon became known as the "Two Percent Club") and state services were rationally restructured.[18]

Nationally, bank failures increased during January and February 1933. In the Hoosier legislature, the main banking reform bill, HB 147, was introduced on January 9. The long draft – Wells estimated that it would cost fifty dollars to type a copy – did not encounter serious opposition on the legislative floor or engender significant amendments, except for an important one affirming the governor's discretionary hiring of personnel. But the Indiana Bankers Association mounted a furious attack, lobbying the legislators with dire predictions of additional bank failures and the dangers of too much government regulation. Ironically, the very organizations that sponsored the Study Commission, the IBA and the Savings and Loan League, were now against it, deriding it as "a theoretical concept that a bunch of kids at the university came up with," as Wells later recalled.[19] Coincidentally, *The Hoosier Banker* masthead that listed Wells as field secretary had disappeared in February 1932.

In the midst of the statehouse debate, Wells received a tempting out-of-state job offer. Harold Stonier, the education director of the American

Institute of Banking, wrote that a position was available in New York doing financial research, with a salary in the range of $4,000 to $5,000, double his IU salary.[20] Interested, Wells wrote back, explaining that his IU position allowed freedom to augment his salary with outside work, and that he had been assured by university authorities that "they would like to take care of me, with a salary sufficient to make it unnecessary for me to readjust my work in any way or to sever the connection with the University." Unfortunately, because of economic conditions, the state had frozen university salaries. "Frankly, therefore, I doubt the adequacy of any provision which the University may make for me in the near future."[21] But the advertised salary for the New York position was still not high enough for Wells to make the leap. Besides, things continued to be interesting in the legislative struggle for bank reform.

Although the *Indianapolis News,* the largest daily in the state, counseled due consideration because of bankers' objections in a February 15 editorial, the public clamored that something needed to be done. The day before, the state of Michigan had suspended all bank activity, starting a nationwide trend of bank moratoria. The Indiana bank reform measure was passed on February 24, in the closing days of the session, and Governor McNutt signed it the same day. Within two weeks, Roosevelt took office. Shortly thereafter, on March 6, the president declared a "bank holiday," temporarily closing every bank in the country.[22]

Forty years later, Wells reminisced,

> I have long had a feeling that the legislature took this, not particularly because they liked it. I don't think they did like it in many respects and as you know many of the bankers didn't like it, they hadn't learned their lesson. Up to the time of the bank closing they were sniping at it. . . . I think they were all ready to tear it to shreds and take all of the guts out of it, except that when they were hit with this body blow by the closing of the banks, then the legislature felt they had to do something about banking.[23]

Once again, timing was everything.

Wells's sense of relief was palpable. He wrote his parents, "You can't realize how I feel. I feel like a boy again with all of the responsibility and strain of the last two years over. I will go to Bloomington with nothing in the world to do but teach school except a few odds and ends such as correspondence, etc., which seem like nothing compared to what I've been accustomed to."[24] Now he could look forward to a time to think more about teaching and to prepare better for his courses, which had been woefully neglected during the feverish activity of the first two months of the McNutt administration. One of his teaching assignments was the economic history of Europe, and he toyed with the idea that a trip to Europe would provide "visual images and perspectives" that would be useful.[25]

After three years of teaching, Wells was still at the rank of instructor. His involvement with Indiana banking research and writing had overshadowed his academic work, dominating his life for the five years since leaving graduate school. At the age of thirty, Wells was widely known in the Hoosier state and respected for his investigative acumen. His parents were demonstrably proud of him. Yet Wells still had a gnawing sense that he needed to do more. What, exactly, he didn't know. Long ago he had made the necessary adjustments to live with his father's perennial melancholy. Perhaps he was trying to live up to the ideal father image he had created in reaction. Whatever the case, Wells reported that the prospect of a renewed focus on teaching was not only a welcome opportunity but also a personal challenge: "My father had had the reputation of being an excellent teacher, and I hoped to discover whether I had the ability to follow in his footsteps."[26] There was more than a little longing in this simple statement. It seemed as if being a respected banker, like his father, was not quite enough.

But his teaching aspirations were soon put on hold as his respite from state banking concerns was brief. In the four-month hiatus between the passage of the reform legislation and its effective date of July 1, Wells was called on to assist the old banking department, which was swamped with work. He had already agreed to become the secretary of the new Commission for Financial Institutions. At an organizational meeting for the Commission in June, he decided to take on the added responsibility of part-time supervisor of the newly created Division of Research and Statistics in the new Department of Financial Institutions. Wells gave up his plan to visit Europe and instead spent the summer at the Indiana State House. By midsummer, the centrality of Wells's unparalleled knowledge and expertise was apparent, and he was asked to take on yet another position, as bank supervisor, in the new Department of Financial Institutions.[27]

Naturally, Wells could not resist putting into practice the reform legislation that he had nurtured and refined for several years. He asked President Bryan for a leave of absence from his university duties. Always interested in finding ways to serve the state, Bryan gave his blessing. His triple position earned Wells a substantial salary, which he was glad to receive, especially after months of penny-pinching and years of enforced frugality. His peripatetic lifestyle, rented rooms in Bloomington and Indianapolis, expensive wardrobe, and expanding appetite for antiques and artworks made the remuneration especially welcome.

VISITING THE CHICAGO WORLD'S FAIR

Wells, based again in Indianapolis, traveled to Chicago for state business on occasion. May 1933 saw the opening of the Chicago World's Fair, a lavish celebration of the city's centenary. Each state of the union had a pavilion displaying the fruits – usually agricultural and industrial – of its region, but Indiana's pavilion was unique. Thomas Hart Benton, a leading regionalist painter, created gigantic murals, 12 feet high and nearly 250 feet long, depicting the "Social History of Indiana" from Native American times to the present.

The selection of Benton, a Missouri native, for the job was controversial; critics wondered why an Indiana painter wasn't chosen for this tax-supported project. Colonel Richard Lieber, father of the Indiana State Park system, took a calculated risk in pushing for a set of murals and in selecting Benton to paint them. Benton received the art commission in fall 1932, and traveled around the state acquainting himself with all things Hoosier and making character sketches of individual people he met. In an almost superhuman effort, he painted feverishly but methodically every day for several months to finish the painting in time for the opening of the fair. The finished product, painted in bright colors and with somber faces on expressive figures, also generated controversy. Some objected to the socialism they saw in its focus on the common, working people. Others caught a whiff of scandal in scenes that featured scantily clad women or the white robes of the Ku Klux

Klan, or were made uncomfortable by several people of color – ranging from dusky Indians to African American steelworkers – that populated the murals.

Wells visited the spacious Indiana pavilion at the World's Fair multiple times, once with his grandmother Ida Belle Harting. The pavilion was designed as a gallery, with the Benton murals arranged high on the walls, explanatory plaques below, and a seating area in the middle. Visitors entered and were confronted with the oversize panels depicting the Indians who gave the state its name. Matched panels, displaying industrial progress and cultural advancement, respectively, marched through time chronologically as visitors wandered through the exhibit. Halfway through one got to the Civil War, with a nine-foot-tall Abraham Lincoln resting on an axe handle while reading a book, while its opposite number presented dead soldiers and burning battlefields. Near the exit, the final panels were titled "Indiana Puts Her Trust in Work" and "Indiana Puts Her Trust in Thought." The former featured trains, trucks, and factory smokestacks in the background, brawny men in the foreground riveting steel and signaling a derrick hauling a block of limestone out of the quarry, and suit-clad men rapping on the closed door of a bank. The latter panel had images of basketball players, automobile racing, architects poring over designs, a chemist with his flasks, and an unemployment line. Governor McNutt points at a big question mark and faded dates – 1933, 1934, 1935 – on a blackboard; behind him are sheets of paper with headlines "State Reorganization," "Banking," and other faded words written on them. On the way out, a big painting of the Indiana sand dunes on Lake Michigan provided a serene coda to the murals' cacophony of images.[28]

Wells described the setting of the Indiana pavilion thus: "Essentially, it was a place for people to sit and look at art." Benton's regional style appealed to him strongly. He enjoyed picking out recognizable faces from the artist's real-life models, and appreciated Benton's exquisite political sensibility that balanced on the edge of caricature. Wells thought the murals were "earthy enough" for "the typical Hoosier" to appreciate, as he did.[29] It was remarkable how closely Benton's vision of Indiana's story recapitulated Wells's family background and personal history. His ancestors' roots as pioneers and homesteaders who became yeoman farmers and small-town citizens could be seen in the early panels of the murals. The last panel, dealing with very recent history, was the artist's rendering of financial catastrophe and the beginning of economic recovery, with which Wells was intimately involved. The young agent of the state of Indiana found his spirit resonating with Benton's Hoosier history.

My door will always be open to you for the discussion of any of your problems. I am sure I may say the same thing for each of the other members of our faculty. Come to us frequently. We wish to know each of you personally, and to share with you your experiences and problems.

Herman B Wells, 1935

FOUR

First Taste of Academic Stewardship

THROUGH THE PROCESS OF JUGGLING THREE JOBS in state government, Wells gained invaluable administrative experience. Work was his life. Endless meetings, telephone conversations, and document preparation left him little time for sleep or leisure. He preferred bachelor quarters, living at the Claypool Hotel or at the Indianapolis Athletic Club, both at the hub of downtown Indianapolis. Bedrooms for sleeping were simple and Spartan, but the public spaces were impressive. Elegant lobbies, dining facilities, meeting rooms, and exercise areas were designed to accommodate the needs of successful and cultured men. Wells found it quite comfortable, and it was a convenient starting point for his frequent business travel to other parts of the state. He was also at ease with the quotidian accoutrements of his job, such as tailored business suits and restaurant food. Occasionally he was able to slip away to Bloomington and visit old friends, or go to French Lick to relax in the grand hotel and gaming establishment. In May 1934, he wrote to his mother about his recent physical examination, saying "I am in perfect condition," but the doctor suggested that Wells lose 50 pounds, do less work and more play, and to get married: "This is rather a peculiar prescription – most of it made in fun, of course." He added that he would be following a diet that evening.[1]

Wells did not have much time to miss teaching. His leave of absence, stretching into a second year, secured his options at IU, at least for a while. During the year prior to his leave he participated actively in a sweeping reorganization of the school. The faculty of the School of Commerce and Finance recommended that freshman be directly admitted to a four-year course in business, to drop foreign language requirements, to add more work in the social sciences, and that its name be changed to the School of Business Administration. All these changes were in line with practices at other members of the American Association of Collegiate Schools of Business, which IU joined in 1921.

During his hiatus from teaching, Wells learned that enrollments at the School of Business Administration had increased sharply. There were 287 students in his last teaching year in 1932-33, but since the four-year program was implemented at the beginning of the 1933-34 academic year, there were 573, and 733 in the following year.[2] William Rawles, the first and only dean of the school since its founding in 1920, was still serving after nearly four decades on the IU faculty. President Bryan, who began his administration in 1902, was even older – in his mid-seventies.

Dean Rawles gave notice to President Bryan that he wanted to retire at the end of the 1934-35 year. The two first met in the 1880s; both were undergraduates during the David Starr Jordan presidency. Bryan joined the faculty shortly afterward, whereas Rawles started teaching in 1894 at the IU Preparatory Department, which functioned as Bloomington's high school. Rawles joined the regular faculty in 1899. In keeping with administrative custom, the longtime president exerted his unquestioned authority to select Rawles's replacement.[3]

CAMPAIGN FOR THE DEANSHIP

Going outside the standing faculty, Bryan selected an individual from a Big Ten rival, the University of Michigan, as a possible dean. Known as "Dr. X" in the record, that individual declined the offer for unspecified reasons in late winter 1934. Word got around to Wells's network of friends, and they started an energetic campaign to recommend him for the position. One of the first to write to Bryan was Hugh Landon, an officer at the Fletcher Trust Company in Indianapolis: "I am wondering whether you are not overlooking a good man close at hand. I mean Herman Wells, whom you have loaned to the Department of Financial Institutions. He has made an excellent impression on everybody who has come in contact with him in that job and I am told that his work in the Department has attracted attention widely outside of this State. . . .

He is young, extremely ambitious and wants to return to his first love, which is teaching."[4] Landon no doubt conspired with his colleague, Walter Greenough, vice president at Fletcher, who forwarded Bryan a copy of an enthusiastic letter that he had sent previously to William Irwin, a trustee of Butler College, about Wells's qualifications to lead the School of Commerce at the Indianapolis school.[5]

Reinforcements arrived soon. On the first of April, Clare Barker, an IU business faculty member, wrote to Bryan nominating Wells for the deanship. Greenough contacted Bryan again, offering to solicit testimony from federal officials about Wells's performance. He asked for Bryan's indulgence: "If I am over zealous in this matter, it is merely because I have deeply at heart the interest of both the University and my friend. I know you will understand."[6] Bryan exercised due diligence and started asking around for testimony from uninterested parties. A raft of recommendations – from Federal bank examiners, Hoosier bankers, and University of Wisconsin economist William H. Kiekhofer – poured into Bryan's office.[7]

F. B. Bernard, a former president of the Indiana Bankers Association who recommended Wells to the Study Commission, wrote to Dean Rawles summarizing his view:

> His services with the Indiana Bankers Association as field secretary took him to all parts of the state and thus afforded him an opportunity to acquire a very intimate knowledge of our state. In fact, I think of no one who has a better first hand conception of a true cross-section of our people than he. It seems to me that he has an extraordinarily pertinent background for such a position, and it is my opinion that his selection would meet with practically the unanimous approval of the quite extensive business acquaintanceship which he has made.[8]

During the several weeks he was under active consideration, Wells made himself scarce, explaining to Weatherly, "I felt if I appeared in Bloomington frequently, the rumor would in all probability be spread that I was making trips to Bloomington for the purpose of waging a campaign for the job."[9] Ever mannerly, Wells sent simple thank-you notes to the many persons writing on his behalf.[10]

In April 1935, Wells got some national publicity through an article he published in *Banking,* a leading journal sponsored by the American Banking Association. In "Top Heavy Bank Supervision," Wells criticized overlapping regulations and called for increased cooperation of state and federal banking agencies. Regulations proliferated during the economic crisis, and the "old-fashioned precept that the least government is the best government" was lost. Reform could be accomplished, he argued, without giving up "the fundamental principle, namely, that the best regulation is that which will assure stability and security with the least possible interference with management." Speaking in the voice of an Indiana banker, Wells enumerated all of the reports that such a banker would have to produce regularly to comply with state and national rules and regulations. He expressed concern over embattled bankers everywhere. Even if the banker survived the Depression, "Nobody loves him, apparently. He is stripped of most of the robes of dignity with which he once was clothed in his community. And he is harassed constantly by legislative threat and public misunderstanding." Wells, as Indiana Bank Supervisor, urged following "the axiom that governmental supervision of the banking business always should strive to allow bank management the greatest possible measure of freedom consistent with public welfare."[11] The financial institutions in the Hoosier state continued to offer a progressive model of reform under the guidance of Wells.

Bryan weighed the outside testimony and talked to Rawles, Weatherly, and other trusted colleagues. Consulting his own internal compass, he decided in favor of Wells. Ability counted more than age in Bryan's view (Wells was not yet thirty-three).[12] Wells's lack of experience in the classroom (only three years as an instructor) was overshadowed by his tremendous record of public service to the state, which coincided with Bryan's conception of the purpose of a state university. On May 18, the IU president sent a telegram to Wells at the State House, congratulating him on his election as Dean of the School of Business Administration, at a salary of $5,000.[13] Earlier in the month, Wells received a message of support from his former Wisconsin doctoral advisor Kiekhofer: "If you are appointed, as I sincerely hope you will be, it will belie the old statement 'a prophet is not without honor save in his own land and in his own house.' Since you have no house of your own as yet, I will say nothing about how high you will rank when you get one."[14]

In his memoir, *Being Lucky*, Wells gave this reconstructed account. He was approached in the spring of 1935 by a group of friends and colleagues who drove up from Bloomington to meet with him at the Athletic Club, where he was rooming. At first Wells resisted the notion, thinking it was "a fanciful idea," but after an hour or more of conversation in the club's library lounge, he relented, on the condition that "if it were the wish of the faculty, the president, and the trustees, I would assume the post."[15] Once he got word that Wells could be persuaded, Bryan then privately offered Wells the post. Flattered yet humble about the responsibility it would entail, Wells delayed giving an answer until after he talked with his current boss, Governor McNutt. The governor, still on a leave of absence from IU himself, tried to dissuade Wells from accepting the job, claiming that the university was in a "moribund state." Besides, McNutt argued, he was needed sorely by the state to continue to implement the new financial policies and practices. For his part, Wells knew that his work on the banking code would survive without his personal involvement, and the offer of a deanship was irresistibly attractive. McNutt finally gave his blessing.[16]

This account, while focused on different events, can be harmonized with the archival record, which inscribed a story filled with politics, positioning, and personal ambition carried out by Wells's dense network of coworkers and supporters. President Bryan played the key role. The aging psychologist, watching generations upon generations of students pass through the university, was a shrewd judge of character and ability. He had kept his eye on Herman Wells for several years, and he decided the young assistant professor deserved a chance to prove himself as dean. In addition, Wells probably improved his chances by being absent from campus during his two-year leave. Had he stayed on campus, he "would have continued to develop a reputation as a good teacher" and to jump "from Assistant Professor of Economics to Dean of the School of Business" would have been extremely unlikely. Instead, he went to the State House and straightened out what was a "horrible mess," proving that he had administrative talent.[17]

DEAN OF THE SCHOOL OF BUSINESS ADMINISTRATION

Thrilled to return to IU as dean, Wells reveled in his new status as a full professor. His friend and mentor Ward Biddle was also happy about his protégé's progress from a B.S. to dean in eleven years.[18] The two men welcomed the set of new challenges presented by the job as well as the larger sphere of action that came with it. There were important things to do to upgrade the business school, and now Wells was in a position to provide leadership.

When the students returned to school in Fall 1935, Wells gave them a warm welcome, assuring the assembled business majors that he as well as the rest of the faculty had an open door policy. Focused on the development of the whole person, Wells had a genuine interest in the welfare of individual students. He wanted to create a climate of acceptance and inclusion, and he realized he was in an influential position as dean to set the school's tone. Universities all around the country were moving from policies of in loco parentis to a focus on the student as consumer of educational services.

The change from a two-year program to a four-year program proved popular with students. Enrollments grew to 879 during the first year of Wells's deanship, increasing to 1,304 and 1,595 in the two succeeding years. Much of the growth was due to the easing of the Depression and the subsequent improvement of the country's economic environment. The value of a college education was also gaining more currency among businessmen.

The growth of faculty lines did not keep pace with growing enrollments, however, and Wells had his hands full dealing with greatly increased teaching loads. His administrative style was cooperative, and depended on freely flowing two-way communication and exchange of information between dean and faculty. Functioning as primus inter pares, Wells consulted with his colleagues frequently and at length about the strengths and weaknesses of the school and surveyed their views on further improvement. Those attitudes and opinions were augmented by an empirical comparative study of IU's "offerings, degree programs, and enrollment with other leading schools of business."[19] Good data and information, Wells had come to believe, provided an essential basis for policy and practice.

Wells discovered the advice of Clare Barker, a senior colleague, exceptionally useful during his first months in office. Barker, popular among students as well as faculty, became the dean's "mentor, friend, and active collaborator" in generating "ideas for the improvement and modernization of the business school."[20]

But Wells was not content with the status quo. At the first business school faculty meeting, he challenged the faculty to prepare a five-year plan for their individual programs of research, teaching, and service. That served a triple purpose. It provided a basis for private conversations between dean and faculty member for further professional development; it was a significant component of the school's master plan for the future; and it afforded a superior rationale for negotiations with the president to increase faculty numbers.

Putting the cooperative ideal in practice, Wells appointed ten standing committees to be responsible for each area of the school's work, from curriculum to facilities, and to public relations with all of the stakeholders. By January 1936, the curriculum committee proposed some revisions and additions of new professional courses and degree programs. Wells successfully lobbied the president and the board of trustees to add new faculty, and saw an increase from ten to twenty-eight full-time, and five part-time, members.

Although Wells had had a heavy speaking schedule while he was a state employee, his speaking engagements as dean were now more extensive than ever and covered a wider geographic area. He continued to be in demand for lectures and panels in his specialty of financial management and related economic topics, as well as addresses connected to education in his new role as business dean.

In his first semester, Wells offered a "Regulation of Financial Institutions" course, open only to seniors and graduate students. It was designed "to review the events of the past two years, both federal and state, in the field of financial institutions, together with a detailed study of the effect of the new federal agencies and of new state laws." Writing to his good friend and supporter Walter Greenough about the course, Wells noted, with more than a hint of pride,

> I believe that I have a very real knowledge of banking psychology, and I believe that I have some skill in securing the acceptance by the banking group of regulatory measures without sacrificing any of their efficacy. I believe also that I know agricultural, industrial, and financial Middle America as few people have had the opportunity to know it. It is a great source of joy to me to be secure in my knowledge of that background regardless of its benefit to me practically.[21]

In this context, "practically" meant personal remuneration – colloquially, fattening his wallet – not the intangibles of prestige and reputation
that he gained. For Wells, it led directly into public service and the non-
monetary rewards of education.[22]

INAUGURATION OF THE PATTEN
FOUNDATION LECTURES

In 1931, Indiana University received the largest single gift in its history
when alumnus William T. Patten willed his entire $100,000 estate "for
the sole purpose of bringing to Indiana University, a succession of persons . . . of high distinction in some field of learning, or art." Patten, who
graduated in 1893 with a degree in history, had a career in real estate
and politics, including service as a county auditor, in the Indianapolis
area. To carry out the bequest, the IU Patten Foundation was established
after Patten's death in 1936 and began inviting one scholar or artist to
campus as a visiting professor for an extended period, during which time
they would give a series of public lectures. The business school, led by
Wells, persuaded the Patten Foundation to invite German scholar Alfred
Manes, an expert in the field of international reinsurance, for the entire
1936–37 academic year. Wells later noted, "He brought an international
dimension and distinction to our faculty that otherwise would have been
unaffordable."[23]

With great anticipation, an audience filled Alumni Hall for the first
Patten Lecture on February 28, 1937. Wells, who was to introduce Manes,
was waiting for the German scholar by the elevator that served the Union
Building tower, where he was staying in one of the hotel rooms. As Wells
described it,

> When the elevator door opened and he stepped out, I was startled to see that he
> was in full dress – white tie, tails, white vest – and that his chest was emblazoned
> with his many decorations and medals. In that era in Europe such dress was
> proper on an occasion of this type and in fact was expected of a distinguished
> scholar. I had an uncomfortable feeling, however, that few in our audience would
> understand his ceremonial dress and that he might even be greeted with some
> laughter, producing an unfortunate though unforgettable beginning for the
> Patten Lectures. Moreover, I felt his style of dress would prejudice the faculty
> at large against him, and we in the business school had already decided that we
> wished to recommend him for a permanent appointment.

Sizing up the situation quickly, and taking account of Manes's sensitive temperament, Wells hesitated only for a moment before kindly explaining the American custom and suggesting that the scholar change into a conservative business suit. Initially disappointed, Manes understood and returned to his room to change. His lecture went on without a hitch, but Wells remembered "more vividly those moments preceding it."[24] In his tactful way, the business dean quietly averted a social faux pas.

REFURBISHING WOODBURN HOUSE

As important as these changes were to refurbish an increasingly important professional school, Wells took other actions as a private citizen that proved consequential. He re-established residence at Woodburn House, persuading his landlord, Professor Emeritus James Woodburn, to rent the entire house instead of a few rooms upstairs. Sam Gabriel, his old roommate, had married and moved on. By now a confirmed bachelor, with no time or interest in romance, Wells realized that his duties as dean would require additional socializing and entertaining.

As Wells ascended the academic ladder, he was able to indulge his taste for the finer things in life. Furnishing his expanded quarters at Woodburn House was a pleasant priority, and he began to buy antiques and artworks on a regular basis. He purchased a massive partners desk, designed for two people working across from one another, and had it installed in his second-floor home office. His bedroom housed a succession of chests of drawers – his favorite article of furniture. The downstairs had the usual dining room table and chairs, a sideboard, a corner china cabinet, and upholstered sofas and chairs. In keeping with his expanded budget and reflecting the ideal of the cultured gentleman, Wells purchased a series of prints of English hunting scenes complete with horses, hounds, and huntsmen.

Without a wife, Wells needed help to establish his first independent household. For nearly a decade he had lived a nomadic existence, living in rented rooms, hotels or clubs, circulating among Bloomington, Indianapolis, and Nashville, with briefer stays in communities across the state.

Located a few blocks from the dry campus, the Woodburn House conferred another advantage: Wells could serve alcoholic beverages if he wished. President Bryan was a notable teetotaler, and Prohibition was zealously enforced on campus. Wells respected custom as well as Bryan's feelings, and he took pains to be discreet about his own occasional consumption when he hosted social events.

EXPLORING THE COLOR LINE

In late September 1935, Wells and Biddle went to a fried chicken luncheon at the local African Methodist Episcopal Church, a regular Friday fundraiser. Wells was always on the lookout for good food, and his ample figure gave silent testimony to his culinary appetites.[25] The prospect of a good meal brought the two white IU administrators through the door, but Wells had more on his mind. He was distressed by the state of race relations at Indiana University, where African American students were still outnumbered by whites almost one hundred to one. Although Indiana was never a slave state and Indiana University had offered its academic programs with no explicit color barriers since its beginnings, the social environment was strictly segregated along the color line. White students "owned" the campus, and had opportunities to participate in a variety of clubs and associations, sports and athletic events, and dances, socials, and other parties. By custom, blacks were relegated to the margins, and had limited or no access to food service, campus housing, and athletic programs.

Life in Bloomington was similarly segregated. Whites owned most of the property, including businesses, homes, and factories. The tiny African American population was economically subordinate. Mostly they found employment as casual laborers, housemaids, and skilled factory workmen. Except for a handful of black schoolteachers and clergymen, the professions were closed off. The presence of a university, however, did provide a measure of educational opportunity, and some local African American families sent their sons and daughters to the institution.

Despite their small number and lack of economic influence, the black community in Bloomington offered something vital to IU's small African American student population: a home away from home. Two churches, some boarding houses, and rooms in private homes offered material comfort to students as well as ministering to their spiritual needs.

In a small way, Wells and Biddle were trying to make changes. The new dean was a member of the Indianapolis Press Club, part of the city's old boy network. A young black waiter, Butler College student John L. Stewart, had come to the attention of some fellow IU alumni who tried to convince him to transfer to Bloomington. The two men assured the young black man that they would help him attend Indiana University, although there was no guarantee of a job. When Stewart paid his first visit to IU in August 1935, Dean Wells took him on an extensive campus tour as well as calling on possible employers in Bloomington, and even gave him a ride in his car back to Indianapolis. Stewart remembered Wells's genuine kindness, but worried about the status of black students at IU – a topic never broached with his new white benefactors until later.

Stewart decided to transfer to Indiana University. He majored in Zoology, pledged Kappa Alpha Psi – a black fraternity that was founded at IU in 1911 – and was elected house manager for 1935–36.[26] His means were limited, so he was obliged to work his way through school. He got a job as a waiter at the Delta Gamma sorority house for his meals, but after the first month, he could not pay his room bill at the fraternity house. Stewart called on Wells, who was interested in how Stewart was getting along. When Wells heard about the financial bind, he granted him a loan. Much relieved by the reassuring conversation and monetary aid, Stewart thanked his benefactor profusely.

Stewart also got assistance from another member of the Wells circle, Walter Greenough, who wrote a recommendation letter for Stewart as part of his application for a job from the National Youth Administration (NYA), a federal work-study program. Stewart received a job assignment at the Second Baptist Church, on Bloomington's Near West Side, working with black youth for $12 a month. For Stewart, that meant a daily walk from the east side to the west side.

But Stewart's income was not sufficient to cover even his normal expenses, and he went without textbooks for some of his courses and scrimped on school supplies. As a consequence, his grades started to suffer. He went to see Wells again. The dean listened patiently and asked Stewart whether he had any ideas to solve the problem. Stewart replied that an account at the IU Bookstore might tide him over until the summer, when he could start paying off the bill. Wells concurred, and scribbled a note to manager Biddle. Stewart expressed his gratitude again, and Wells assured that he would be ready to help again if need be.[27]

Eventually Stewart achieved a precarious financial stability, working full-time during the summer and doing several jobs before and after classes during the academic year. For the 1936–37 academic year, Stewart was elected "polemarch" of Kappa Alpha Psi.[28]

In 1935, black and white students – hoping to ease segregation and promote racial equality – started a new campus organization, the Inter-Racial Commission. One of its founders was Frank O. Beck.[29] An 1895 alumnus, he had a long career as a Methodist minister and social activist in Chicago. One of his friends was Marcellus Neal, the first black graduate of Indiana University. Beck, who hailed from a small Indiana village, had never before had the opportunity to be personally acquainted with an African American. He drew a general lesson from his experience:

> This we often forget or carelessly overlook: Bloomington and Indiana University were to become the stage upon which many, many Hoosier boys and girls were to make their first acquaintance and gain their impression of youth of another color. To hundreds of University students, the first colored person they ever knew by name was, as with me, a fellow schoolmate on the campus at I.U.[30]

After spending his career working for the Methodist church, the Urban League, and other progressive causes in Chicago, he and his wife, Daisy, retired to Bloomington in 1933 and continued their outreach among IU students.

By the end of its first year, the Inter-Racial Commission had gathered documentation on the social life of African American students and acts of racial insensitivity and discrimination. Blacks were a small minority – only about one out of fifty students – but individually and as a group they withstood many instances of humiliation and indignity. The organization was frustrated by the IU administration's lack of official policy on race relations. They appealed to a basic principle:

> If the University is to achieve its greatest good as a free, democratic institution, we feel that it should promote organizations which aid in preparing students to participate more intelligently in democracy. We believe, therefore, that the Administration should assist the Inter-Racial Commission in realizing its aim by granting it full recognition on the campus, by making it possible for

the Inter-Racial Commission to sponsor a Negro speaker for open forum or convocation, thus inaugurating a new program of anti-discrimination on the campus.[31]

There is no record of a university response.

BRYAN'S RESIGNATION

President Bryan attended the first Patten Foundation Lecture, and, as it turned out, his last as president. On March 15, 1937, Bryan dropped a bombshell on the trustees, saying that he wanted to resign. He had led the university for nearly a third of its 117 years and was universally recognized as the chief architect of its twentieth-century incarnation. Bryan was lauded in a front-page editorial in the *Bloomington Evening World*, and university officials boasted, in a fit of hyperbole, that one hundred thousand students had passed through IU during his presidency of 35 years. "I am profoundly moved by the news," Dean Wells commented to the newspaper. "It will seem strange to me to have any one other than Dr. Bryan in the President's chair. From my student days to the present, Indiana University and William Lowe Bryan have, in my mind, been indissolubly one and the same."[32] Bryan's resignation set off a stormy period of transition and an extended search for a successor.

Wells was a protagonist in this struggle for leadership. Two years before, on the eve of Wells's selection as dean, Walter Greenough scrawled to Wells a paraphrasing of Shakespeare, exulting, "There comes a tide in the affairs of men, which, taken at the flood, leads on to victory. I sincerely trust this is the tide, boy!"[33] Gathering momentum was another, even greater tide.

PART TWO

Transforming the University, 1937–1962

I stuttered, "Why Judge [Wildermuth], that's, that – that's a very strange, that's a preposterous idea, it seems to me, because I am just a young dean and a new one at that. I think I might make a pretty good dean of the School of Business eventually, but I don't think I know enough to be president. Far be it from me to tell you what to do, but you should take one of the other men...."

"Well," he said, "to be perfectly frank with you, the reason we don't want to take one of the other men is that we might want him for the president. We know we won't be considering you. We can make you acting president without prejudicing the choice of any of the others."

Herman B Wells, 1980

FIVE

Acting like a President

ON FEBRUARY 23, 1937, the Indiana University Library celebrated the acquisition of its three hundred thousandth volume. IU President William Lowe Bryan, a noted experimental psychologist as well as a scholar of philosophy, had been asked to select one of his books for the distinction. His choice was *Plato the Teacher,* his 1897 compilation of excerpts and commentaries designed to introduce Plato's thought to Indiana high school teachers, which Bryan edited with his wife, Charlotte Lowe Bryan.[1] The book symbolized Bryan's commitment to education, his love for his wife, and his allegiance to a fading era of IU's history. Then in his thirty-fifth year of service as president, Bryan was himself a living symbol – of the aspirations of Indiana's state university. Overseeing steady increases in enrollment throughout the first third of the twentieth century, Bryan sought to balance the university's mission to serve the state with the school's academic priorities, which were national in scope. His kindly but stern moralizing made him a familiar figure to generations of students.

With the exception of Indiana's southern neighbor, Kentucky, its surrounding states had greater populations and provided a ready labor pool for the rise of Midwest manufacturing and industry. Thrift and understatement, two qualities Hoosiers prized as virtues, made support for higher education in Indiana a shadow of that enjoyed by state institutions in Illinois, Michigan, and Ohio. As a result, by the mid-1930s, Indiana University remained a provincial institution.

Although the faculty was competently teaching a growing number of students, nearly all from Indiana, the university's graduate education and research profile had lagged behind its Midwestern peers. Slightly less than half of the faculty had doctorates, a smaller percentage than any other Big Ten institution except for the University of Minnesota.

Indiana was better known nationally for the quality of its undergraduates who pursued doctorates at other institutions and for being "the mother of college presidents."[2] Only ten IU departments were deemed qualified to offer graduate work, as compared with eighteen at Ohio State and fourteen at Wisconsin. Financial statistics reveal a stunning lack of investment for the support of research. According to the biennial survey of the U.S. Department of Education for 1936–37, Indiana University spent a measly 1.7 percent of its annual budget for support of original investigation, compared with a national average for 135 public universities of 10 percent. IU was last in the Big Ten by a wide margin for direct research expenditures, spending $21,108 in 1935–36. All the other schools spent at least $80,000 annually, led by the University of Wisconsin at $146,636.[3] The Graduate School was established in 1904, but IU had produced few doctorates, reaching a rate of ten a year only in 1923–24. The biographical directory *American Men of Science* had "starred" three faculty members since 1907, compared to twenty-two from Illinois, thirty from Michigan, and sixty-eight from Harvard.[4] There was a certain irony in the slow fall of the research enterprise under the Bryan administration, because Bryan himself had made his reputation in experimental psychology in the 1890s and had earned a star by his name in the first edition of *American Men of Science* in 1906. Perhaps even more ominous was the fact that no IU scientists had earned a star in the last two editions published since 1921.

The Bryan administration was running out of steam. Not only was the president himself a septuagenarian, but also the school's department heads and deans – all Bryan appointees – were mostly of the same generation. Because all lines of authority radiated from the president's office, younger deans – including Henry Lester Smith of the School of Education and Herman Wells of the School of Business Administration – sometimes found it difficult to make overdue changes. Some faculty members expressed frustration at the slow pace of change. English professor Lee Norvelle, hired to teach public speaking and serve as debate coach in the 1920s, had an implacable desire to augment the curricular offering in the dramatic arts and theater, but Bryan, who insisted on censoring school plays, would not hear of it.[5] In 1935, Alfred C. Kinsey, a noted entomologist and one of the most productive scholars at Indiana, wrote to a former student and groused about the older men who, he said, were serving only as "caretakers." Kinsey laid the blame for this situation at Bryan's door: "All this goes back to the fact that our President is 75 years old and unwilling to settle any question, large or small. The whole University is in a mess, we get nothing done apart from the ancient routine – I would leave at the first opportunity offering comparable recompense and research opportunities."[6]

Indiana's youthful and reform-minded governor, Democrat Paul V. McNutt, was determined to make IU competitive with other public universities in the Midwest.[7] McNutt, an IU alumnus and dean of its School of Law when elected in the New Deal landslide of 1932,[8] prodded the university administration to augment the state's support by applying for federal funds for the physical plant and student employment. A building boom ensued as the campus acquired new facilities and refurbished old ones.[9] McNutt had statutory authority to appoint five members (out of eight total) to the Indiana University Board of Trustees; the other three members were elected by alumni ballot. The shape of the board changed when, in an unprecedented move, McNutt replaced four trustees, who averaged twenty-three years of service, with his own selections. Critics charged that the governor was turning IU into another bastion of patronage, and started the rumor that he was motivated by a plan to take over the IU presidency when Bryan retired.[10]

In March 1936, speculation about the governor's future plans was fueled by the sudden resignation of longtime IU trustee and board president James W. Fesler, an Indianapolis attorney. First elected by the alumni in 1902, the same year Bryan had taken office, Fesler had worked hand in hand with Bryan for his entire administration and had served since 1919 as board president. Trustee Fesler had complained privately about the business practices of IU Bursar U. H. Smith, and, when the other trustees did not share his concerns, he left the board.[11] The trustees, however, created the new post of university comptroller shortly thereafter, and appointed IMU director Ward Biddle to the position.

Fesler's resignation, said the *Bloomington Telephone* newspaper, paved the way for a successful candidacy for McNutt to become the next IU president because he would now have a majority of votes on the Board of Trustees. Moreover, if McNutt became president, the newspaper specu-lated, all administrators over sixty-five years old would be forced to re-tire, explaining that the state legislature was considering a retirement proposal for the university.[12] Although several department heads had served for decades and about a dozen faculty members were over the age of seventy (Bryan was seventy-six), the lack of a retirement system meant that faculty worked until they dropped.

But the "tall, tan, and terrific" governor had his eyes on another presidency – of the United States.[13] McNutt, limited by Indiana statute to one four-year term as governor, wanted to retain his national visibility as his governorship wound down in the final months of 1936. (McNutt's lieutenant governor, M. Clifford Townsend, was elected his successor in November 1936.) The rumor that he would get the IU job was revived a few days before Christmas when a Chicago radio station announced that he would be named IU's next president. IU officials moved quickly to say that the report was unfounded, and McNutt's office also issued a denial.[14] Despite this, the press and the faculty scrutinized the actions of Bryan and the IU trustees for clues to the university's future course. University historian Thomas Clark noted, "Rumor had it that the only thing which would keep McNutt away from Bloomington would be appointment to the Roosevelt Cabinet, either as Attorney General of the United States or Secretary of War."[15]

Gossip took on a new flavor in February 1937 when President Roo-sevelt appointed McNutt high commissioner of the Philippines. McNutt accepted the position, despite the low federal salary and the alternative offer of a lucrative job as head of the New York Stock Exchange, because it kept him in the public eye. When McNutt asked his close political advisor, Frank McHale, to estimate his chances of being elected U.S. president in the 1940 campaign, McHale said the odds were about 100 to 1 against. Spurning the opportunity to make money, McNutt replied he "would never be happy or satisfied until he had his chance at running for the Presidency."[16] White House advisors to President Roosevelt were also pleased for different reasons, thinking that the distant post would effectively sidetrack the handsome former governor from being a factor in the 1940 race.[17] But local newspaper speculation that McNutt would take over the IU presidency after Bryan stepped down persisted, noting that the two men were good friends as well as former colleagues.[18]

BRYAN'S EXIT

In late February 1937, Bryan greeted townspeople at an open house showing off the recently completed Administration Building at the corner of Indiana and Kirkwood Avenues. Replacing the cramped quarters of old Maxwell Hall, the president's new office was a suite of tastefully appointed rooms on the second floor, with light oak paneling and a limestone fireplace. The board of trustees named the structure William Lowe Bryan Hall, in honor of his lifetime of service to the university, and all of the trustees, save the ailing trustee president George Ball from Muncie, attended the reception.[19]

It was less than a month later, on March 15 at a regular board of trustees meeting, that Bryan dropped a bombshell, announcing that he wished to step down as president. Citing his age and long administrative service, he requested a replacement be found in short order. Other factors included his wife, who was increasingly infirm and required more care. Finally, what tipped the scales in favor of his retirement was the inauguration of a decent retirement plan – the first ever for the university. One could almost hear the collective sigh of relief by faculty and administrative staff when, after approval by the Indiana General Assembly, IU adopted the Carnegie-designed Teachers Insurance Annuity Association retirement scheme in early 1937.

Bryan's imprimatur on IU was everywhere. Not only had he resisted sharing administrative control for thirty-five years, he had won the hearts of generations of students with his obvious interest in their welfare. He had outlasted a series of governors and legislators, and had witnessed a remarkable recent turnover among the trustees. Not surprisingly, Bryan's sudden retirement precipitated an institutional crisis of leadership at Indiana.

The next day, the *Bloomington Evening World* trumpeted the headline "Dr. Bryan to Remain at I.U. Helm Until New President Selected."

The story following said that "it is believed that the next president will be an outstanding educator connected with some other institution and not at present affiliated with the Indiana University faculty." Rumors that Law School dean Bernard Gavit would be acting president were discounted.[20] Professor Kinsey offered practical advice and fired off a letter to the IU Board of Trustees immediately after learning of Bryan's impending retirement. He favored an outsider rather than one of the present faculty and outlined his view of the qualifications of the position: executive ability; scholarly interests obtained through firsthand contact; and "a certain freedom from established traditions of Indiana University."[21]

The eight-member board of trustees was faced with an unprecedented problem in choosing Bryan's successor. For every one of the trustees, the only president they knew was Bryan. Three of the group had served for more than a decade, but five were relatively new, having been selected since 1934. There were no written policies to guide them and very little institutional memory of procedures that were used in the past. Bryan stayed aloof from the process, and expressed his disinclination to be involved in choosing his replacement. He had not cultivated a successor, at least overtly. The trustees soon realized that they were on their own in choosing the next president.

TRUSTEES MOBILIZED

The IU trustees were not without resources, however. As a group, they had wide experience in business and legal matters as well as extensive political connections around the Hoosier state. Their president was George A. Ball, head of the Ball Brothers Corporation in Muncie. A trustee since 1919 and a member of the Republican National Committee since 1932, he served as trustee president after James Fesler's resignation. Fesler's alumni seat was won by John S. Hastings, another Republican, in 1936. Hastings, a Washington, Indiana, attorney, had strong connections to the university, obtaining a law degree in 1924 and serving later as president of the alumni association. The first woman trustee, Nellie Showers Teter, was elected by the alumni in 1924 and had served since then. Part of a prominent Bloomington family, she was a Republican also. Vice president of the board was Ora L. Wildermuth, a Lake County attorney and former city judge of Gary, was also a perennial favorite of the alumni, having been elected every three years since 1925. He voted Democratic.

The other four trustees were all McNutt appointees. Paul L. Feltus, appointed in 1934, was the longtime editor of the *Bloomington Star-Courier* newspaper. An officer in the Indiana National Guard, he was active in Hoosier Democratic politics. Trained as a lawyer, William A. Kunkel, Jr., was a Fort Wayne businessman and banker who took his seat in 1935. The previous year he purchased and became the publisher of the *Fort Wayne Journal-Gazette*. Also picked in 1935 was Val F. Nolan from Evansville, who was serving as the U.S. attorney for the southern district of Indiana. In 1936, the governor appointed Marion County attorney Albert L. Rabb, a Republican, as an acknowledgment of the tradition of political parity on the board. Rabb, educated at Indiana and Harvard, served on the IU Alumni Association Executive Council.

Ball was in ill health, however, so trustees' vice president Wildermuth took the lead in organizing the search.[22] As Wildermuth pondered how to proceed, he wrote for assistance to Walter A. Jessup, former president of the University of Iowa and President of the Carnegie Foundation for the Advancement of Teaching in New York City, lamenting that the Board of Trustees had "for so many years learned to depend upon President Bryan that I am afraid we are quite helpless in this emergency."[23]

Judge Wildermuth took the bull by the horns and convened a meeting of ad hoc advisors in Chicago's tony Palmer House hotel on April 10. Included in this small group were three "fine friends of Indiana" – all IU alumni – who occupied high educational administrative posts: Jessup; Ernest Lindley, recently installed Chancellor of the University of Kansas and former IU faculty member; and Lotus Coffman, president of the University of Minnesota. Also attending was fellow board member Hastings. Jessup, Lindley, and Coffman were aware of IU's tradition of selecting presidents from the ranks of faculty members. Accordingly, Coffman advised to canvass the faculty "to see if there is a possible man there," reminding the group that Harvard University had picked James Bryant Conant from faculty ranks a few years before.[24]

From the discussions at the Palmer House, Wildermuth derived several principles to guide the search. Although the faculty should be consulted, he argued, no faculty search committee should be formed nor a faculty vote taken. Next was the idea that the faculty should be "thoroughly canvassed for available material for the presidency." He then laid out the kind of man he believed should fill the job. "We should not select a very young man because of the grave danger of the errors of youth," Wildermuth contended. "I gathered that a minimum age limit of about 40 should be set." The advisors cautioned that young university presidents had made errors that "in some instances had been fatal and in all instances bad." But on the other hand, an old president would not do. Finally, if an outsider is chosen, then he should have prior experience as a president. Wildermuth concluded his report by mentioning some possible candidates, to be "discussed privately" among the board: President Raymond Kent of the University of Louisville; President Frank Aydelotte of Swarthmore College; and President Raymond Walters of the University of Cincinnati.[25]

Wildermuth wrote Bryan after the meeting, reiterating his wish to profit from his counsel: "I hope you appreciate that I would like to have your opinion as to whom to select to take your place than any other man in the world, but I have understood you preferred not to select your successor, but I am quite sure that sometime before we finish the job, I would like to have the benefit of your judgment."[26] Sidestepping a direct reply, Bryan responded tersely, "May blessings attend your search."[27]

Soon applications and referrals for the position came trickling into the board of trustees office. One writer suggested that the new president should be a scientist to revitalize research at IU. Wildermuth replied, "I agree with that diagnosis but I am not quite sure that it takes a scientist to cure our ills.... [W]e must, of course, always keep in mind the absolute necessity of a good business administration of the general affairs of the University. It would be most disastrous if the business affairs of the University were ever permitted to go bad."[28] And another, less helpful correspondent – an IU faculty member – advised that the president should be a father with lots of children and not a native Hoosier.

Wildermuth gathered information that cast doubt on Bryan's perennially rosy assessment of the state of IU research. No IU scientist had

earned a star in *American Men of Science* since 1921.[29] Loyal alumni working in scientific fields, such as Stanford University psychologist Lewis
Terman, a former student of Bryan's, commented on the weakness of
IU's scientific departments. Brown University biologist Arthur Banta, a
fellow student in the early days of the Bryan presidency, wrote a compas-
sionate but pointed letter to the trustee vice president: "President Bryan
is generally highly regarded among alumni and others as a teacher and
moral leader but it is generally appreciated that under his regime Indiana
University has not made progress comparable with that in other like institutions." Banta thought the erosion was due to the lack of leadership
among department heads. The sole exception to the general pattern of
stagnation, Banta wrote, was the Department of Zoology under Fernandus Payne, former head and current dean of the Graduate School. Banta
believed that a "marked improvement" could be accomplished by a new
president, a scholar in his own right, who could secure the retirement
of "some twelve or fifteen heads of departments and their replacement
by men of competence and energy."[30] After Banta's searching critique,
Wildermuth confided to Hastings that the contents of the letter could
not be shared with Bryan because he had "grown to resist any criticism
of anything that he has done at the University under his regime" in the
last couple of years.[31]

Indeed, Bryan had begun acting erratically. When he resigned in
March, the trustees promised him a continuing salary and the use of
the President's House in his retirement, which he accepted gratefully.
In May, Bryan abruptly declined the retirement pay and the house. He
also suggested to the board to appoint an acting president if a replacement was not found by commencement in June.[32] At the same time, the
local newspaper headline blared: "Report Trustees Cable McNutt Offer
to Take University Presidency." The report was false, but the former
governor was still rumored to be the inside favorite.[33]

WILDERMUTH EXERTS CONTROL

Wildermuth was growing increasingly restive at the slow pace and dis-
organization of the presidential search. Writing to Bryan near the end of
May, Wildermuth suggested that the board of trustees appoint a special

subcommittee to be in charge of the search because to involve the entire board would be unwieldy.[34] Wildermuth also wrote to board president Ball, complaining that most board members were irregular in their attendance at meetings, further hampering the search process.[35] Private misgivings about McNutt were expressed to Wildermuth.[36]

Soon Ball took up Wildermuth's suggestion and appointed a presidential search subcommittee consisting of Wildermuth, and Rabb and Nolan, both recently appointed. Ball had not specified who was to be chairman of the group, so Wildermuth continued his leadership. Bryan's insistence on standing down meant that an acting president would have to be appointed by June 30, so the trustees immediately turned to the ranks of IU deans. Hastings had suggested Fernandus Payne, a Columbia-trained geneticist who had come to IU in 1909 and had been serving as dean of the Graduate School since 1925. Oriented toward research, he had wide contacts among the scientific community, and was considered a fair-minded administrator. Wildermuth thought that H. Lester Smith, dean of the School of Education, had perhaps the widest administrative experience of any man on campus and might be most suitable. Smith had also been at IU since 1909, advancing to the deanship in 1916. But Wildermuth had recently learned that Smith would be going to Japan that summer and would not be available. Bryan suggested that Wells "could be safely trusted with this odd interim appointment."

Wells had been mentioned as a possible successor to Bryan before, and Wildermuth was worried that Wells's many friends might interpret the acting appointment as a "forerunner of a permanent appointment." Bryan thought the situation could be explained to Wells "so that he would understand that the temporary appointment carried with it no commitment, or rather the idea that some other person would eventually be appointed." Wildermuth agreed with Bryan about Wells's probable response, but had doubts about tempering the enthusiastic reaction of some of his friends.[37]

In addition to Payne, Smith, and Wells, the name of Bernard C. Gavit came up in public speculation. Gavit, on the law faculty since 1929, eventually succeeded McNutt as dean in 1933. In another letter, Banta weighed in again. Although he did not know either Wells or Gavit personally, he got the feeling from Wildermuth that neither "quite measures up to the requirements." He was also worried about narrow specialization: "a man generally goes into the special field [business or law] early and does not keep in touch with the whole academic field, as a university president should do."[38]

Wildermuth circulated Banta's letter as well as others to the subcommittee. Nolan wrote to Hastings that he agreed that Payne was "the logical selection for Acting President." Paraphrasing Banta's recent letter, he thought the job should go to "a man whose life, experience, and ambitions are within the academic field." Although Nolan had "great personal regard and admiration" for Wells, he said that "in view of the fact that all of my contacts with Herman Wells have been in fields other than academic, I wonder whether he meets the test."[39]

At the same time, Rabb was inclined to go along with President Bryan's high opinion of Wells, and was confident that, if Wells understood the temporary nature of the appointment, he would be able to halt any meddling by his friends. Hastings had mentioned to Rabb earlier that Wells was of "the promoter type." Rabb continued, "I expect there is some accuracy in that characterization; but on reflection, I think that we may need something of that type for a while." He was convinced that "the business side" of the university was in good hands under comptroller Biddle, and, for the scholarly part of the president's job, "we are taking steps to obtain some recommendations."[40]

The board of trustees was also busy putting the faculty retirement machinery into motion; the annuity plan was scheduled to go into effect on July 1. Faculty and administrators seventy years or older were eligible for retirement. A total of eleven professors, including several longtime departmental heads, and President Bryan would be its first recipients.[41]

The board of trustees met, as was their annual custom, before commencement in Bloomington. The June 1937 meeting was unusually busy. On June 10 the board met in executive session to discuss the state of the presidential search and to formally select the acting president. After deliberation that lasted into the night, the assembled trustees, minus their ailing president, decided to offer the job to Wells.

Wildermuth called Wells at his summer place in Nashville, Indiana, and offered the young dean (only three days past his thirty-fifth birthday) the acting presidency. Wells, trying to make sense of the proposi-

tion, responded that other IU deans had more experience and knowledge for the job. Wildermuth explained the temporary, place-holding
nature of the job. "Under these circumstances," Wells replied, "if you
will promise me that during this period you won't consider me for the
Presidency – I don't want to get involved with that – I'll do it. I'll try to
be a good soldier and do it, if you will let me get back to my dean's job as
soon as possible."[42]

Wells certainly knew he was among the front-runners for the position – his friends were rooting for him and the newspapers had profiled
him as well as other candidates. What he did not know was the depth
of the divisions among the board of trustees regarding his suitability
for the job, and how his public persona as an affable business educator
with wide connections outside of academic life tipped the balance in his
favor as the trustees' pragmatic choice for the role of acting president.

On June 11 the local newspaper declared, "Wells Named Acting
President; Townsend Approves Selection." According to this account,
the official announcement was made at one PM that day. Wells's new
duties were to begin July 1, and he would continue as business dean as
well. Governor Townsend was quoted: "Herman Wells will act very
ably as temporary president." The young dean, after a sleepless night
due to the excitement, said, "I deeply appreciate the recognition which
the Board has given me, but I shall look forward to the day when I can
again devote all of my time to the development of the School of Business
Administration."[43]

Bryan presided over his last commencement ceremony later that
day.[44] The commencement address was delivered by Frank O. Aydelotte.
Governor Townsend was on hand, exhorting the graduates to perform
public service in the future and mentioning his hope that the board of
trustees would name Bryan's permanent successor by September.

In addition to naming Wells acting president, the trustees appointed
an advisory committee "to advise and act with the Acting President at
his request." The members of the committee – Biddle, Payne, Smith, and
librarian Alexander – were old hands in IU administration and well acquainted with Wells.[45] At the same meeting, Biddle was given the additional post of secretary to the board of trustees. Although Wells had
many friends and supporters in the faculty, Biddle served as his most

valued confidant and counselor. The day of his retirement, June 30, Bryan commented to the newspaper, "I gladly resign the responsibilities of office to a man who is an unexcelled executive and a right-hearted man."[46]

DRESS REHEARSAL FOR PRESIDENT

Perhaps the highest priority that the acting president and his advisors faced was the issue of faculty personnel. Although many older faculty were planning to take advantage of the retirement plan instituted earlier that year, some thought that they should be allowed to work as long as they wanted. In his first two weeks as acting president, Wells interviewed every faculty member who was seventy or older. In consultation with the presidential advisory committee, decisions were made about those faculty members who would continue for a semester or year and those who would take immediate retirement.

With the exception of zoology, the science departments would need new leadership. Trustee Rabb, a graduate of Harvard Law School, contacted Harvard president James Conant in early June for advice selecting appropriate department heads for the fields of chemistry, physics, geology, and botany. He responded with a list of senior scholars in those fields who could provide suggestions. Rabb forwarded the list to Wells soon after his elevation to acting president.[47]

Wells carried out this necessary purging of the faculty ranks with impressive diplomatic skill. "Such a procedure involved a great deal of individual discussion, as much tact as possible, and as much kindness and compassion as we could summon, since some of the men who had spent their lives building the university felt that they should be allowed to continue indefinitely," Wells later explained. As a university official during a time of transition, he thought it was his job "to make retirement as palatable as possible for these great and good colleagues and to assist them in every way to move into dignified and happy retirement."[48] The net result was to remove a severe blockage from the IU system.

With practical good sense, Wells attended to the university's routine business as well. Presiding over his first board of trustees meeting in July 1937, the trustees saw a dignified young executive moving through the items on the agenda with deliberate speed: ratifying personnel decisions, approving salaries, letting contracts, and a host of other mundane but necessary judgments. Among the items on the table was whether to buy the Smithwood property, a tract of land running eastward from Jordan Avenue to Rose Avenue and north from Third Street to Seventh Street (currently the site of Read Quadrangle, the Jordan Avenue parking structure, and the School of Education). Trustee president George Ball urged its acquisition, recommending that the university acquire every parcel of land adjacent to the campus as it became available. Wells readily agreed that investment in real estate would yield long-term benefits to the university.[49]

THE SEARCH CONTINUES

In July, Wildermuth followed up with Governor Townsend for his views on the IU presidential search. Although Townsend owed a lot to the Democratic machine built up by McNutt, he reportedly looked askance at McNutt's naked ambitions to run for the U.S. presidency. Speaking of Wells's selection as acting president, Wildermuth reflected, "Personally, I feel that he would make a good president." But he also thought he should finish his job as business school dean and also complete his doctorate – "this important step in his career." Wildermuth believed that a "little seasoning as an acting president" would overcome the "handicap" of his youth. Commenting on the rampant speculation about McNutt and the IU president's job, Wildermuth divulged this: "I have some very well-defined ideas in this connection which I would be perfectly willing to make plain to you, but which I think should not be committed to paper at this time." He also expressed his awareness of Townsend's negative attitude toward McNutt's presidential dreams, which he did not expect the governor "to commit to paper" lest it lead to political embarrassment, but requested "having a line from you on the question of whether or not you really want to urge us to have a new president installed by September 1st." In Wildermuth's judgment, the board "should not undertake to fill the vacancy that soon."[50]

As the summer wore on, the list of possible candidates kept growing, but the trustees' search committee had scheduled no interviews. In August, a few weeks after his appointment, Wells circulated "A Memorandum Concerning a Fact Finding Program for Indiana University" to the deans and the board of trustees. He proposed to form a special committee to perform an internal investigation of Indiana University and its academic programs to identify strengths and weaknesses, and to suggest recommendations accordingly. Wells proposed that the committee's report be ready by the time a new permanent president was selected.[51] In suggesting this course of action, Wells drew on his academic training in empirical social scientific research, which could be usefully applied to the formation of institutional policies. It also demonstrated his sensitivity to the limitations of his current position as well as to the realities of academic politics at IU.

The plan met with general approval by the IU academic community, and the trustees approved the self-study in November. After surveying the faculty for names, Wells chose "three staunch academic yeomen who brought to the committee three widely differing points of view."[52] Occupying a centrist position, Herman T. Briscoe, an IU-trained chemist, had high academic standards but also defended students of average capabilities. The more conservative Wendell W. Wright, a professor in the School of Education, had an independent cast of mind. Rounding out the trio was its chairman, Fowler V. Harper, professor of law since 1929, who was considered liberal. The committee's charge was a broad one, and called on nearly all faculty and administrative staff for assistance and information. At the outset, the committee was guided by the basic assumption that "the principal business of the University is to advance knowledge and to train the minds of its students."[53]

Meanwhile the presidential search committee was continuing its work of compiling nominations. By the end of August there were three dozen names on the search committee's list, including Wells's, having been formally suggested by IU English professor Henry T. Stephenson and two other members of the faculty.[54]

Although the appointment of the acting president had given the trustees some breathing room, Wildermuth was determined to keep the search on track. In early September, Wildermuth reported to the trustees that, out of the total of nearly sixty names gathered, the search committee had narrowed the field down to twenty-one candidates – fourteen external and seven internal. Responding to a letter from Stanford psychologist

Terman, he confided, "As a matter of fact, we have not definitely decided against anybody any more than we have decided in favor of somebody. What the Board wants to do is to get the best man available, and I am sure we think that McNutt is not the best, although we do not want to embarrass him by saying so."[55] Wildermuth wrote a similar letter to Jessup, adding, "[Wells] has great executive ability, and if the date were two or three years later, I would say he would meet our requirements quite nicely."[56] Striking a different tone, the trustees' vice president wrote to the trustees' president Ball about three "most likely" candidates: Chancellor George R. Throop of Washington University, Raymond A. Kent, and Raymond Walters.[57]

VETTING WELLS

Wildermuth remained bullish on Wells. In mid-September he wrote again to Jessup, saying,

> Dean Wells is doing right well as President. He seems to have the ability to get along well and the get things done. He stepped into a rather difficult position in that the Board had ordered a number of older professors retired and some of them were naturally quite bitter about the action. It seems to us that Wells has done a remarkable job in keeping these old men in fairly good humor.[58]

He asked the Carnegie Foundation president to meet with Wells and evaluate his suitability as a candidate for the permanent post. Wildermuth was keeping all of his options open as the search committee started to interview.

Swarthmore president Aydelotte, mentioned as a possibility early on, had turned into a valuable advisor to the trustees. He reminded them that they had a "very tempting offer" to make to candidates: the large number of vacancies to be filled in the ranks of faculty and administrative staff. In his opinion, "this will be worth more to a new college president than money or anything else that the University could possibly offer." Aydelotte met with Wildermuth, urging him to appoint a scholar and giving a list of recommendations. He thought that Wells would never measure up to the criterion of scholarship.[59]

Negative letters from alumni about McNutt's suitability for the IU position reinforced Wildermuth's private view. One fiery letter referred redundantly to the ex-governor as a "machine politician of the McNutt type." Another noted the "distinct cleavage of opinion concerning Col. McNutt" and the "low state of opinion into which the career of 'politics' has fallen," concluding "the presidency of Indiana University should not be made into a whistle-stop on a through-express line of ambition for high *political position*."[60] In late September, the *Chicago Daily News* asked "Two Questions About McNutt": whether his intention was really to seek the White House and whether Indiana University wanted a man with such ambitions.[61]

In early November, Wildermuth received a letter from Jessup reporting on his meeting with Wells in New York. Jessup was "impressed by his intelligence and charm," and he could "readily understand the fact that he has already endeared himself to your Board." Moving to a broader theme of successful university administrators, the past university president said that "the ability to formulate a policy and execute it" was fundamental. In IU's case, with so many vacancies to fill, "it is essential that each appointment and each promotion be made in light of a broad general institutional policy," and that "the next dozen important appointments will determine the academic standing of the University for many years." After saying "I like the way Wells has gone about collecting information concerning the best men available," he qualified it by noting that "naturally, at this distance I am in no position to form an estimate of his ability to formulate and carry through an administrative policy." Jessup was careful to point out the subtle difference between popularity and executive skill: "[W]hile on the one hand it is exceedingly important that the university constituency shall like its president and that he shall be popular on the campus and off, on the other hand it is easy to confuse freedom from criticism with that type of leadership which is willing to run the risk of temporary unpopularity for the sake of formulating and executing sound institutional policy."

Jessup concluded his long letter with a pointed comment "about the undesirability of making an appointment with political implications," adding that Coffman and Lindley would surely concur.[62] Wildermuth knew this was a tacit reference to McNutt. Although he was one of Indiana's best governors, McNutt was now tainted in the eyes of traditionalists in the academy, despite having served earlier with distinction as dean of the IU law school. Privately, George Ball thought that if McNutt were to leave politics and devote himself once again to academics, he would make a fine president.[63]

Jessup's letter was copied to the entire board of trustees, and was added to the growing pile of evidence favorable to Wells. Wildermuth thanked Jessup for his evaluation of Wells, adding, "I confess that I have been rather favorably impressed with his manner of attacking and handling the problems that have arisen."[64] Wildermuth also received advice from Stanford University president Ray Lyman Wilbur, who met with the search committee in late November. When asked about age, academic degrees, and the like for potential college presidents, he replied firmly, "look for a man and not a lot of degrees," urging the trustees "to get a very young man who had promise even though he had not reached the heights academically."[65] The comparative youth of Stanford presidents such as Jordan and Wilbur himself, each of whom had turned forty-one in the year he was selected, lent support to that view.

By early December, Wildermuth was emboldened to share some of the private communications to the search committee with Wells after the acting president paid a visit to Arthur Banta. A canny judge of character, Wildermuth sent Wells copies of his correspondence with Banta with a cover letter explaining that, although there were some unflattering things said, he was "satisfied now that you could read even adverse criticism of yourself and not get mad about it." Wildermuth also paraphrased Wilbur's comments about age.[66]

In the meantime, trustees' president Ball wanted to retire due to poor health. Everyone – including former president Bryan and acting president Wells – was trying to keep him on, but Ball got his wish. When Wildermuth told Townsend of Ball's retirement, he made some suggestions for a replacement and encouraged the governor to maintain the tradition of an even split between Democrats and Republicans. In early January, Townsend announced the choice of J. Dwight Peterson, president of City Securities Corporation in Indianapolis. Peterson was a Republican, thus preserving the longstanding tradition of political balance of four Democrats and four Republicans on the IU board. He was also an old banking friend of Wells's. Wildermuth wondered whether the search committee should recommend the new president, or just leave it to the entire board to decide, which meant that only the dependable trustees would show up.[67]

The December 12 *Indianapolis Sunday Star* carried an article head-lined "McNutt Is 'Not in I.U. Picture,' Trustee Friend Says." An un-named trustee, speaking off the record, said, "a majority [of the board] is not thinking of him" to head the school, despite persistent rumors to the contrary. What sparked this story was the announcement that the IU presidential search committee would be meeting in New York in early January to interview candidates. McNutt, high commissioner of the Philippines, would also be returning for a visit to the States in January, thus giving new legs to the enduring rumor. But the timing was only a coincidence. Nevertheless, the "Hoosier McNutt men" con-tinued to believe that the IU presidency would be a springboard for the 1940 Democratic nomination for the U.S. presidency. In fact, the article reported that the McNutt men thought the reason McNutt was coming back at this time was to confer with President Roosevelt and seek per-mission to accept the presidency of Indiana while continuing his work in the Philippines.[68]

Planning for the search committee's trip to New York yielded fewer candidates to interview than expected – only three accepted the offer to interview. Hastings wrote to Wildermuth about the disappointing rate of favorable replies, ruefully admitting, "[W]e must recognize the fact that not everyone wants to be President of Indiana University."[69] Wildermuth decided that it be too costly to take the entire board to New York, so he appointed a subcommittee of Nolan (a member of the search commit-tee), Hastings, and Feltus.

Prior to the New York journey, Wildermuth corresponded with Henry M. Wriston, president of Brown University, to get his advice on the three candidates to be interviewed: Frederick L. Hisaw, an endocri-nologist at Harvard University; Joseph H. Willits, dean of the Wharton School of Finance at the University of Pennsylvania; and Detlev W. Bronk, a biophysicist at the University of Pennsylvania. Wildermuth noted that Hisaw was being paid $13,000 as a faculty member at Har-vard, whereas the IU presidency would offer $10,000 to $12,000.[70] At the last minute, Hastings was unable to go, and Wildermuth went in his place.

Between Christmas and New Year's Day, Acting President Wells attended the annual meeting of the American Association for the Advancement of Science (AAAS), held in Indianapolis, to interview prospective faculty members. The IU science departments had been hit particularly hard by the wave of faculty retirements in the past academic year, and it was imperative that the university hire good replacements. Dean Payne worked hand in glove with Wells to winnow the possibilities, and the AAAS meeting in Indianapolis was an excellent opportunity to meet face to face with candidates. Wells wrote to Wildermuth shortly after the meeting to report on his experiences interviewing scientists. Wildermuth in turn forwarded that information to Jessup, saying the "letter makes a very favorable impression and confirms your judgment that he is growing rapidly."[71]

After the trustees returned from their New York interviews, there was a flurry of activity. Hastings wrote to Wildermuth that he had attended a reception and dinner at the Indiana Memorial Union a few nights before, where William Cogshall, head of the IU astronomy department, had spoken to him about the faculty's opinion of the ongoing search. He paraphrased the professor: "a very great majority of the faculty were *strongly* in favor of Herman Wells. That they were pleased with the way he had taken hold of things and that he felt sure Wells would be the choice of most of the faculty if they were permitted to express an opinion." Hastings trusted Cogshall and respected his judgment. He went on to express his own opinion, echoing Wildermuth: "I, too, am finding myself more strongly convinced that Herman is the man as each month goes by. If he is the final selection, I still think there is a certain build-up we should consider in order to get the correct reaction from the alumni and the public generally. The movement has already built itself up as far as the faculty and students are concerned."[72]

But Wells's unmarried status continued to be a potentially troublesome issue. Hastings found out about an earlier conversation between Wells and Biddle on the "marriage question." It seems that Wells, returning from a trip down South, remarked on the beauty of women in that region, whereupon Biddle advised him "to spend all of his vacation time in the South and marry one of them." In a chat with George "Dixie" Heighway, the IU Alumni Association secretary, and Alexander, the librarian, Hastings joked, "Maybe we could put a marriage stipulation in his contract to the effect that he marry within a specified period of time or forfeit a certain percentage of his salary each month he remained single after the time limit had expired." Or perhaps, he suggested, Dean of Women Agnes Wells should be consulted for a solution.[73] In reality, there was little the trustees could do.

Wildermuth had asked Claude Rich, the assistant alumni secretary, to make discreet inquiries among the faculty to survey their opinion of presidential possibilities. In early January, Rich reported,

> Directly or indirectly, I have probably gotten the opinions of some 50 or 60 members of the faculty [out of nearly 400] and I have even been surprised at the way he is accepted. Many of them have voluntarily said, although having no relation to our particular conversation, that they hoped Herman Wells would be the next president.
>
> I have found that Deans such as Stout [College], Payne [Graduate], Edmondson [Students], etc., are for Herman. Professors such as Miss Berry [Latin], Miss Hennel [Mathematics] and others of their type think Herman is the man and have been very impressed with what he has done as Acting President.
>
> I believe the faculty as a whole believe that the new man should be a local person and will be a little unhappy at an outside choice. The only other person here I have heard favorably mentioned is Gavit [Law], and of the two, Wells seems to be the preferred one. There are others who have been rated high, of course, but because of their ages have been eliminated as a possible choice in the minds of the faculty members.[74]

Wildermuth now possessed much information and opinion, culled from many sources: candidate interviews, advice from senior educators, faculty opinion and alumni input, and counsel from fellow trustees. In general, they pointed to Wells as the best selection. In a letter to Jessup, he reported on the confidential survey of faculty opinion and sketched a possible scenario. Wildermuth mused, "If he is to be selected, I am rather of the opinion that we should delay his election for a while and perhaps build up a more general public acceptance of him. And, I am becoming more and more of the opinion that Wells is perhaps our best bet, but I am not yet quite sure that he is the best available material."[75]

For his part, Wells remained busy reorienting the university as the temporary position stretched into its seventh month. At the end of January, he addressed the Bloomington Chamber of Commerce on relations between the town and the university. A particular concern was real estate and housing, especially if the university was to grow significantly. He mentioned the need for more undergraduate dormitories built by the university and apartments for graduate students built by the private sector. His roots as a small town Hoosier banker led him to aver, "The genius of an American community finds its highest expression in the ingenuity with which it can and will attack its own economic and social problems." Confident that the intimate relationship between town and gown would continue to grow and flourish, he explained, "I am interested in Bloomington's future because this is my home and I love it, and while I am not a native son of the city or of the community, I hope that circumstances are such that I never have to leave here for residence."[76]

The stage was set for the board of trustees to make its choice. At their meeting on February 8, 1938, Rabb, a McNutt appointment, made a surprise move to elect Paul McNutt to the presidency, angering Wildermuth, the board's president. Four of the eight trustees were in favor of McNutt, but the motion, lacking a majority, did not carry. The four McNutt supporters – Paul Feltus, Albert Rabb, Val Nolan, and William Kunkel – had all been placed on the board during the former governor's administration. Of the opposition, three of the other four trustees – Nellie Teter, John Hastings, and Ora Wildermuth – were elected by alumni. Dwight Peterson, Governor Townsend's appointee, had served for only a month.[77] Wildermuth blasted the action of the McNutt partisans, saying that this "surrender to politics" would have led to his resignation if the motion happened to carry. He turned on Rabb, accusing him of leaking information about the trustees' search to the press, which Rabb denied.[78] Other business was impossible after the McNutt bombshell. The newspapers picked up the story of the trustees' split over McNutt.[79]

For more than two weeks the imbroglio continued, with all eyes focused on the trustees and McNutt. Newspapers across the state talked about the turmoil surrounding the selection of a new IU president. Graduate School dean Payne said he would leave if McNutt prevailed. Acting President Wells was barely mentioned. Ultimately, McNutt ended the controversy by removing himself from further consideration.[80]

DECISION FOR WELLS

Growing tired of the clamor, Governor Townsend pressed the board of trustees to name the new president. Wildermuth wrote to his fellow trustees, "I still think that Herman Wells will make a great president of the University." Calling a special meeting of the board for March 22, Wildermuth sent out telegrams to the trustees four days before. After sending out the telegrams, he became very ill. But Wildermuth made it down to Bloomington for the 10:00 A M meeting and was able to preside over the voting. All of the trustees were there, except for Kunkel, who was traveling in Florida. This time the vote was unanimous for Herman Wells. He would become the president of Indiana University, only the eleventh in its 118-year history.[81]

Wells was called in to the board's executive session and received the news in a formal statement from Wildermuth:

> The Trustees of Indiana University have come to a decision on the most momen-
> tous question that has come before the Board in thirty-five years. We have by
> unanimous ballot elected you President of Indiana University. In so doing we
> have brought very great honor to you. But, we have also given you equally great
> responsibilities.

He invoked the names of Jordan, Swain, and Bryan – "three of the great-est educational administrators of this country" – and claimed that "no university in America ever had three succeeding presidents that stood higher in their fields than these three men." After an extensive search, "from Maine to California," by the trustees, and after intensive inter-views of potential candidate, the Board was "satisfied with your supe-riority." Wildermuth continued, "We have picked one of our own sons, a native Hoosier, in whom we place our trust and hopes." Lest their be any doubt about the unanimity of the trustees, the judge reiterated the Board's total support and cooperation.[82]

Wildermuth glossed over the prolonged contention in the presiden-tial search in his ceremonial recapitulation of this important episode in iu history. Repeatedly emphasizing, almost to the point of exaggeration, the high standing of the presidential predecessors as well as the inten-sity of the search, perhaps Wildermuth was giving voice to unease over

Wells's relative youth and lack of a Ph.D. But by hard work and some luck, Wildermuth successfully guided the selection process to the end he preferred. More than most people knew, the Gary judge had played a crucial role – and would live up to his pledge of support to Wells in the future.

Summoning his strength and dignity on this climatic occasion, Wells replied, "I deeply appreciate the compliment you have paid me," but admitted to being overwhelmed by the magnitude of the task. He had disclosed his fears to Bryan a few hours earlier, and the outgoing president provided reassurance. He concluded his acceptance simply: "There is a great opportunity here. To meet it, I shall need your cooperation very much. I shall do my best – I shall give all my thought and energy to this work. And I pray that will be enough."[83]

Wells and his family, both biological and elective, were jubilant, and mentor Biddle savored the triumph that he hoped and planned for. Now, eight years after Wells had signed a faculty contract, he stepped up and tied the knot with Indiana University, promising full measure of his devotion to its welfare.[84] Later that day, the Trustees issued a press release:

> Herman B Wells is this day elected President of Indiana University. With great expectations, we invite him to great responsibilities. His observed experience, practical wisdom, admirable temperament, and high ideals give conspicuous assurance of enduring achievement. With trust in him, we have confidence in the future.[85]

The next day, Bryan sent a handwritten note to Wildermuth. "Herman ought to go away *soon* for a month," Bryan advised, in order "to build up physically and to be alone so as to take deliberate stock of himself and his job." The other suggestion was to hire a "thoroughly competent and loyal 'assistant to the president'" such as Bryan had enjoyed. He concluded, "I am very happy at the outcome. The best thing has been done."[86] In his reply, Wildermuth exclaimed, "I am so happy at the escape we had," referring to the abortive attempt to resurrect McNutt's candidacy. "It can be said with the greatest of justice," Wildermuth continued, "that at no time during his service as Acting President did he ever do anything to indicate to the Board that he even hoped to be elected President. . . . This may be hard to believe but I am convinced that he is just that unselfish." Wildermuth agreed with Bryan that the new president should take time for rest and rejuvenation, but anticipated "that we will have difficulty in getting him to take any time off."[87]

The University cannot discharge *any* of its obligations to society unless it is first and foremost an institution dedicated to scholarship and scholarly objectives: a place where students learn the slow and arduous processes of mental discipline by which knowledge is acquired and wisdom won; a place where the frontiers of new truth are pushed back by the research explorer and old truth is subjected to critical analysis until it assumes new significance; a place where reason is exalted over emotion and force.

Herman B Wells, 1938

SIX

A Vision for Indiana University

AS NEWS GOT OUT ABOUT WELLS'S SELECTION AS PRESIDENT of Indiana University, congratulatory wishes flowed into his office in the new Administration Building.[1] Completed in 1936, the imposing limestone structure at the corner of Indiana and Kirkwood Avenues was in the collegiate Gothic tradition with a light Art Deco touch. Wells had occupied the suite of presidential offices for nine months as acting president. Now the office was truly his. He basked in the warm good wishes conveyed by post and telegram. His banking friends and acquaintances also sent flowers, to the point that the office was filled to overflowing with fragrant blooms.

Relishing the celebratory atmosphere while it lasted, Wells was characteristically modest about his personal role, but channeled the enthusiastic attention to help him accomplish institutional goals. Some needs were immediate, such as filling the ranks of a depleted faculty; others were more systemic and long term, such as increasing the research profile of the university. The self-study underway would identify more needs and opportunities. All would occupy his agile mind and harness his enormous energy.

Wells had the beginnings of an executive staff, with secretaries and office assistants already in place. Ruth McNutt and Mary Ellen Cook (née Woods), both presidential secretaries under Bryan, continued their service and were joined by Bernita Gwaltney, whom Wells brought over from the Business dean's office. Ruth Correll, and then Mary Craig, served as clerk of the President's File Room, a specially built multi-floor archive to preserve and make accessible the paperwork that flowed unceasingly through the office. Ward Biddle, University comptroller and secretary to the board of trustees, continued as "wise and indispensable counselor," in the president's words, and new business faculty member Edward E. Edwards served as his unofficial administrative assistant.[2] The president's office turned into a beehive of productive activity. Seemingly, the new president was always around – if not in his office, then on campus, and, if not on campus, then somewhere in the state, oftentimes Indianapolis, promoting the interests of the university. The businessman president was always on the job.

The evolving vision that Wells had for the university was predicated on input from its broad constituency. He was careful to align with desires expressed by the academic community in Bloomington – the faculty, students, and staff. He was also responsive to outside stakeholders – alumni and the government and citizens of Indiana – who provided essential moral and monetary support. What was perhaps most unusual was its all-encompassing focus: No aspect of the university's identity, mission, or operation was omitted. Wells maintained a laser-like focus on IU's internal milieu centered in Bloomington. At the same time, he cultivated an ever-widening sphere of external relationships that could benefit the university. The articulation of that vision was months away, in a speech he was preparing for his inauguration. In the meantime, the quotidian work of university administration continued.

Although in this era it was not uncommon for university presidents to be involved in faculty selection and retention, Wells took an unusually proactive approach. He firmly believed that the institution was only as strong as its faculty. Having successfully negotiated the retirement of longtime heads and other faculty members when the university's retirement system went into effect in 1937, he identified faculty hiring as his top priority.

Although he had great appreciation for scholarship, artistic creation, and scientific innovation, Wells realized that he was not a specialist outside his own area of banking and institutional finance. To become educated in other fields, he consulted regularly with senior faculty, and especially with the Graduate School dean, Fernandus Payne. Payne, a Hoosier native who obtained his Ph.D. in genetics in the famed Columbia laboratory of Thomas Hunt Morgan, was a shrewd judge of scholarly horseflesh. He had cultivated wide contacts, especially in the sciences, in his long service at Indiana. He was also aware of the local academic culture and the chronic financial plight of IU.

Since the beginning of the acting presidency, Wells and Payne had embarked on an ambitious plan to replenish faculty ranks with younger, research-oriented people. They relied on *American Men of Science* as a ready biographical reference to identify talent. As a general rule, they wanted candidates for department head to rate a peer-reviewed star by their names. Realizing that IU could not attract those in well-established positions with high salaries, their strategy was to seek "promising young men and provid[e] the working conditions and salaries necessary to attract them" and to keep them with generous promotions and salary increases. Payne wrote hundreds of letters and visited more than a dozen universities in his search for new faculty.[3] In his first year, Wells himself traveled 33,000 miles by automobile, railroad, and airplane to meet prospective faculty at professional meetings and, better yet, at their home institutions, where he could gauge subtle qualities such as community spirit and local reputation. A total of 190 candidates were interviewed.[4]

For prospective faculty, Indiana University did not have much to offer in financial incentives or research support, and it lacked an intellectual student body, so Wells had to sell his vision of a renaissance of learning at IU. Although he could do little to increase directly the quality of the student population or set higher faculty salaries, he was able to promise improved facilities for research and scholarship. Working with existing IU faculty and his financial factotum Biddle, he was able to garner small amounts of research funds and money for library acquisitions through reallocation. His enthusiasm for the renaissance of IU was contagious, and new faculty joined the hopeful enterprise. Wells did not, however, neglect the research faculty that were already in residence, and made special effort to encourage their efforts.

Wells agreed with the self-survey team's preliminary report of April 1938 that called for more active faculty engagement. "This belief," they wrote, "is based upon the conviction that the University can be no stronger than its faculty, and that, in the final analysis, the responsibility for the success of the educational program of the institution rests largely on that body."[5]

KINSEY AND THE BEGINNINGS OF SEX RESEARCH

Shortly after his promotion to the presidency in spring 1938, Wells received a request from zoologist Alfred C. Kinsey. A specialist in the taxonomic biology of gall wasps, the professor had been at the university since 1920,[6] and had amassed an impressive research reputation, culminating in the award of a star in the recent edition of the biographical *American Men of Science.*[7] Kinsey was also a passionate teacher, both in the classroom and in the writing of his 1926 general textbook, *An Introduction to Biology.* Popular in high school and college courses, it endorsed evolution and united zoology and botany, presenting a unified picture of biology. Kinsey was on the verge of a second major publication that would reinforce his national status as a scientific expert on gall wasps and his local reputation as one of the most productive researchers at Indiana.

Wells, in a May radio address celebrating Founders Day to honor the university's birthday, declared that the university is undergoing "a period of experimentation, exploration, and self-analysis in an attempt to discover the basic materials for an adequate future program."[8] Kinsey, acting on a long-delayed impulse, was confident enough to make his first overt move toward the study of human sexual behavior.

Kinsey and the Association of Women Students were laying plans for a course on marriage, including biological, sociological, economic, legal, and ethical aspects. Perhaps figuring that it might stand a better chance of acceptance, the student organization petitioned the Board of Trustees for a noncredit course, taught by a faculty committee headed by Kinsey. When the petition crossed the new president's desk, less than two months after his selection, Wells was in support. The trustees' minutes recorded a terse approval in June. (One trustee was so uncomfortable that he requested to be recorded as "not present" for the vote.)

The marriage course was inaugurated in summer 1938. Although it was taught by a team of eight faculty members, Kinsey presented three of the course's twelve lectures. And he started collecting sexual histories. When students came to him with personal questions, Kinsey asked for their cooperation in filling out a questionnaire. Writing to Wells in September, Kinsey said, "You will be interested to know that the personal case history work bids fair to become one of the most significant parts of our program. The 32 cases handled by the biologists this summer was a startling indication of the need of such work on the campus."[9] Although there was a psychological clinic on campus, its main focus was the educational problems of schoolchildren.[10]

Over the next two years, Kinsey remained in charge of the lectures and found his time increasingly devoted to gathering sexual histories, both in connection with the class as well as on field trips. He made initial forays into homosexual circles in Chicago, as well as conducting so-called emotional clinics after he lectured in small towns around Indiana. Even Wells abetted his collecting mania, and personally intervened with the IU chapter of Sigma Nu to get cooperation. Bill Armstrong, 1939–40 chapter president, recalled, "If Wells had said 'Jump from the roof' we would have done so. Kinsey came – talked – and got the whole fraternity. Even those who had nothing to tell him told him."[11] It became his first 100-percent group sample.

But Wells was coming under increasing fire from Kinsey's critics, particularly from an alliance of Bloomington ministers. The president offered the professor a choice: either the sexual histories or the course, but not both. Naturally, Kinsey exploded, at least to his family and friends, fuming that he was a modern-day Galileo suffering from religious persecution. But Wells had a strategic goal in mind, namely to protect Kinsey's work from critics who might have charged, "he was a propagandist for a particular point of view which he hadn't yet sustained by his research."[12] The actual choice between research and teaching was easy for Kinsey. Now he could devote all of his energy to the mammoth task of data collection.

THOMPSON AND THE DEVELOPMENT OF FOLKLORE

Among the industrious researchers at Indiana at the beginning of the Wells administration was Stith Thompson, who had been a member of the English faculty since 1921. Pioneering in the study of folktales and their motifs, he had done yeoman's work directing the reorganization of freshman composition early in his career. Thompson became increasingly preoccupied with his research, traveling widely to consult with scholars elsewhere in America and in Europe and building up an impressive record of publications. President Bryan had recognized his academic talent and gave him moral support and a modicum of financial assistance.[13]

Thompson was abroad when Wells was appointed acting president. As a teacher in the humanities, Thompson was "somewhat disturbed" that a business school dean was now to run the university. Upon his return from a trip to Ireland, Thompson encountered Wells at a barbershop and they exchanged small talk. They had a subsequent conversation in which Wells outlined his ambitious plans to renew the university, and Thompson was encouraged, feeling "that it would be a privilege to help with its development."[14]

A couple of years later, Thompson had an attractive offer from New York University to head their English department, at a substantial increase in salary. In addition to the faculty position, the offer included a post as secretary-editor of the Modern Language Association. Thompson and his wife made the trip to New York, and looked over some houses in New Jersey. But life in small-town Bloomington, with many friends and colleagues and a busy schedule of social activities, suited the Thompson family well. Promising innovations were happening at IU under the new administration, including the building of a fine auditorium. Their eventual choice was made easier by the strenuous efforts of Wells to retain the distinguished humanist. He matched the offered salary, gave funds for building the library collections in folklore and to create a folklore series of university publications, and promised a sabbatical under a new policy that was in the process of being established. Further gilding the generous retention offer, Wells suggested an addition to his professorial title. Thompson could not resist, and became the first professor of English and folklore in the United States.[15]

HILLEL COMES TO THE UNIVERSITY

Wells's egalitarian philosophy was put into practice as he reached out to students, especially members of minority groups. His administration was built on the foundation of tolerance for racial and ethnic differences. Focused on individual students and their needs, he celebrated diversity, fervently believing that the university had an obligation to be ecumeni-

cal in spirit as well as practice. In May 1938, he negotiated with Abram L.
Sachar, national Hillel director, to establish a chapter of the B'nai B'rith
Hillel Foundation on campus. Sachar described the new president as "a
young, vigorous, forthright executive, with clear conceptions of a well
rounded education," adding, "he was a joy to meet." At the time, the
Bloomington student body was less than 3,000, with about 175 Jewish
students, of whom nearly a third came from the New York area.[16]

After the policies and practices of campus Hillel groups were explained by Sachar, an enthusiastic Wells pointed out that, in addition
to providing Jewish sacred and social services, it would also serve the
Christian denominations through a general strengthening of the spiritual impulse and religious values among all students. Urban Jews, mostly
from the East Coast, would enliven campus intellectual life, he thought.[17]
Replacing the informal Jewish Students Union, the IU Hillel chapter
opened in the fall of 1938, in a house on East Third Street.[18]

In thanking Sachar for his efforts, Wells wrote, "There is a recognized need on this campus for such a foundation to serve the Jewish
students here, and I am sure your efforts will result in greater happiness
and deeper understanding among them."[19] The chapter was the twelfth
university Hillel branch in the nation, joining sister chapters already
established at the Universities of Illinois, Michigan, and Wisconsin.[20]

Just a few years later, the United States was at war with Germany,
and American universities, including Indiana, provided an institutional
refuge for scholars who were fleeing the Nazi regime. Notably, the IU
Hillel Foundation became the first to bring refugee students to an American campus.[21]

A CAPITALIST FOR CULTURE

On February 8, 1938 (the same day the McNutt partisans on the board of
trustees staged their failed coup), a front-page story in the *Indianapolis
Times* appeared under the headline, "Six-Ton, $20,000 Mural History of
State Decaying at Fair Grounds Awaiting Home Big Enough to Hold It."
It described how Thomas Benton's narrative murals of Indiana, painted
for the 1933 World's Fair, were languishing in storage. Wilbur D. Peat, the
director of the John Herron Art Institute, opined, "Certainly art patrons

would like to have this history where it could be seen. But there seems to be no place to put it. Not even the World War Memorial. Looks to me like there'll have to be a building built for these paintings or at least a part of a new building set aside for them."[22]

In a follow-up story the next day, Richard Lieber, director of the state commission originally in charge of the murals, declared that the paintings must be preserved. He had hoped that a proper display could be found somewhere in the planned expansion of the State House complex, but, if not, the state should entrust the mural to the Indianapolis Art Association and pay for a wing to house them at the Herron Art Institute.[23]

When Wells, an avid reader of newspapers since his youth, heard about the uncertain fate of the murals, he was immediately taken back to 1933. He remembered being on leave from his university post, living at the Claypool Hotel in Indianapolis, and working for banking reform under the McNutt administration. He recalled visiting the spacious Indiana pavilion at the World's Fair several times, and marveling at the Benton murals. Now, five years later, he was in charge of the state's flagship university, learning about the responsibilities that serving as an agent of the state entailed. Those enlarged responsibilities came with commensurate opportunities as well, and the acting president, thinking that IU might provide a suitable home for the murals, started making discreet inquiries about the state-owned property. Within the month, Wells talked with Biddle about finding a place in the still-growing Indiana Memorial Union.

In April, a month after being named president, Wells wrote to his friend Ralph Thompson, who was an Indianapolis insurance agent, seeking accurate information about the dimensions of the murals. Under some pretext, Thompson visited Ross Teckemeyer, the state employee who had custody of the murals, and obtained the exact dimensions. "It will take a room 75 × 35 without any openings to hold these canvases. Any room, however, with 220 linear feet of wall space can be made to do the job, providing the ceilings are 18' high," Thompson wrote.[24] In the months following, a search for an appropriate space on campus proved futile. Plans for the new Business and Economics Building (now Woodburn Hall) might accommodate a few panels, but not the whole sequence, without increasing construction costs significantly. By now, the trustees had learned of Wells's determination to obtain the paintings for the university. In early August, Wells received word from fine arts professor Harry Engel that Thomas Hart Benton "would be delighted to see the murals go up at the university." Benton was not completely surprised about the possibility, because a friend pointed out a recent news article referring to the university's interest. Benton concluded his letter to Engel, "Whatever is decided upon for the murals is O.K. with me and I will do what you wish, even to the extent of talking my head off."[25] But the question remained: Where to put the gargantuan canvases?

BUILDING THE IU AUDITORIUM

Facilities were another major item on the new president's priority list. Several buildings planned during the Bryan administration were completed during the first few years of the Wells presidency. Plans had already been advanced for a new physics building (now Swain Hall West) and a home for the School of Business Administration and the Department of Economics (abbreviated "the B & E"; now Woodburn Hall), both completed in 1940 in collegiate Gothic style. The new home for physics was next door to Biology Hall on the Old Crescent, and the B & E was opposite the Men's Gymnasium on Seventh Street.

Although some new buildings were on the drawing board or under construction in 1937, only one classroom building had been built between 1910 and 1930. In the late 1930s, the Hoosier State was still experiencing difficult economic times. To try to address these problems, Governor Clifford Townsend called a special session of the Indiana General Assembly during summer 1938. Only a few months after taking office, Wells reached out to his Purdue University counterpart, Edward Elliott, to talk of university needs on their respective campuses. Both campuses lacked a large, modern auditorium, which could serve not only the student body but also the surrounding community. A plan was devised to make a joint request for auditoriums, and, with the consent of the Indiana and Purdue trustee boards, a request was made to the state legislature.

Elliott, who had been president of Purdue since 1922, had more experience than Wells did with state appropriations for university purposes, but the new Indiana president was familiar with state government and had extensive political connections in the state legislature. And Wells's right-hand man, Biddle, had only recently stepped down from nearly seven years of service in the Indiana assembly, first as a state representative and then as a state senator. After more than a month of strenuous debate, in late July capital funds for the auditorium were cut from the proposed state budget. Through the efforts of George W. Henley, the university's attorney and state representative from Monroe County, and lobbying by Wells and Biddle, funds were restored to the budget.[26] Soon twin appropriations were approved, with further authorization to apply for federal Public Works Administration (PWA) funding that was available and to issue fee bonds (paid off by income from student fees). For IU, the result was $1,100,000 ($300,000 from state appropriations, $450,000 from PWA, and $350,000 from the bond issue) – enough, as Wells said later, "to build one of the outstanding auditoriums in the country."[27]

Wells, mindful of future expansion, supported the placement of the new auditorium at the far eastern edge of the campus, beyond the Men's Gymnasium and Fieldhouse. Seventh Street would have to be extended into vacant land and connected to Jordan Avenue. In the early 1930s, the Old Crescent boundary was breached with the construction of the chemistry building and the Indiana Memorial Union, and new buildings were sprouting up along the East Third Street corridor. During the long Bryan administration, the university's land area had expanded from 50 to nearly 140 acres.

When Wells became president, almost all campus buildings were in a large quadrangle bounded by Indiana and Jordan Avenues and Third and Tenth Streets. Convinced that the campus would expand in a north-easterly direction into undeveloped land, Wells intensified the university's land-buying activities both within and beyond the existing footprint. The president explained, "We tried to place facilities that would be used by the whole campus as close to the center of the campus-to-be as we could then envision it. We picked the site for the Auditorium in 1939 with that thought in mind, and mentally we began to reserve the site north of it for the central library of the future."[28]

Fully appreciating the work of previous architects and landscape designers of Indiana University, including Carlisle Bollenbacher, Robert Frost Daggett, and the Olmsted Brothers, Wells dreamed of a major building program. Eager to exercise his aesthetic judgment and indulge his love of beauty, but with a banker's prudence, he decided to retain a major architectural firm to oversee a campus-wide development plan. Shortly after he assumed the presidency, Wells and Biddle went to New York to consult with leading architectural firms. The work of Otto Eggers, who had been the principal designer for John Russell Pope Associates, caught his eye. Eggers had designed the National Gallery of Art in Washington, an addition to London's Tate Gallery, and many of the buildings on the Yale University campus, including its beautiful gymnasium. After Pope's death in 1937, Eggers and partner Daniel Higgins formed Eggers and Higgins (later Eggers and Higgins Associates). One of their first jobs was the completion of the Pope-designed Jefferson Memorial in Washington.

Eggers and Higgins were interested in the Indiana University building program. They also proved sensitive to the need to have collaboration from Hoosier architects to maintain good relations with the Indiana architectural profession and to supply essential knowledge of local circumstances. Thus Eggers and Higgins would be in general charge of the design, and local architects were to create working drawings. In the case of the auditorium, Eggers and Higgins drew the original design, with A. M. Strauss of Fort Wayne as the associated architect.[29]

WIDENING THE CULTURAL FRONT

Although the chance to build the auditorium was unforeseen, Wells knew at once that it might solve the riddle of providing a home for the Benton murals. As he continued make legal arrangements to transfer the murals to IU's custody in fall 1938, the auditorium architects were drawing plans to incorporate the paintings within the interior of the structure. In September, the Benton murals were formally transmitted to the university by the governor's executive assistant in a brief letter: "Governor Townsend has instructed me to inform Indiana University that it have the World [sic] Fair murals now stored at the State fair grounds for use at the University."[30] Over the next several months, the Hall of Music architects, in consultation with officials from the Wells administration, drew and redrew plans, and consulted with the artist to obtain his approval of the presentation of the murals.

Meanwhile, in October, Wells was contacted by Karl Detzer, a journalist who was hired by the *Reader's Digest* to do a profile of the new president and his efforts to expand cultural opportunities throughout the state. Detzer first contacted a mutual friend, Walter Greenough, to tell him of the assignment: "We're chiefly interested in his theory and plans for extension work, for the spread of culture across the state via these unusual methods he is employing or planning to employ." He added, "Has any of Wells' work gone far enough in this short period to find tangible results?"[31] Wells wrote to the journalist saying he was delighted in his interest in what Greenough called IU's "carrying culture to the crossroads" and thought possibly the work of the Extension Division "would have the widest popular interest, being unique in several respects."[32] Detzer came to the campus for a week in late October, concurrent with a big conference of bankers that Wells helped organize. The new president captivated the journalist with his charm and sold him on IU's ambitious program to support arts and cultural programming in nearly every part of the state.[33]

Detzer's article first appeared in the March 1939 issue of the national *Kiwanis Magazine* (Wells was an active member of the Kiwanis Club of Bloomington) before being reprinted in *Reader's Digest* later that month. Written in a lively, boosterish style, it opened with this description of the unusually young president: "Fat (230 lbs.!), energetic, good-humored, he combines the earthy background of midwest smalltown upbringing with the smart politician's capacity to make and keep friends." The reporter explained Wells's philosophy thus:

> But the *most* unusual thing about him is his belief that a modern state university should not be a cloistered stay-at-home; that it should not only educate those who seek it out, but go out and aggressively carry its message to *all* the people. Through forums, music, drama, movies, radio, he is pushing the university influence to the farthest corners of the state. As a result, not only those seeking academic credits, but thousands of plain Hoosier housewives and workers with no thought of diplomas are dipping into culture.[34]

The story described Indiana University's ambitious plans for extension work around the state, including supporting music and drama groups in various localities or traveling art displays and film rentals.

Conversely, the university also was sponsoring conferences in Bloomington, inviting different groups of businessmen, professionals, and
women for talks by experts and scholars. "The University fulfills its true
purpose," Wells stated publicly, "not only in the classroom, but also by
affording facilities and trained personnel to cooperate with all citizens in
the solution of their particular problems. It is in this spirit that Indiana
University invites you." This comprehensive program was summed up as
service to the state's citizens, supplied with gusto and delivered personally by the president:

> It is this welding of culture and the counting room, business and erudition,
> art and economics, that Indiana believes it is pioneering. Where many other
> schools, working toward the same ideals, reach out cautiously in a few direc-
> tions, Wells is seeking to widen the cultural front until every taxpayer in every
> county gets some intellectual return from his state university.

After recalling some illustrious cultural figures from the Indiana
past, such as James Whitcomb Riley and T. C. Steele, Detzer lamented
that "coal, corn, steel, and gasoline pushed arts and letters into obscurity," thus dimming "the torch of Hoosier culture." "For years," Detzer
maintained, "no cultural leader emerged to guide Indiana to a renaissance. Today many Hoosiers think they have found one. His name is
Herman Wells."[35] Although he did not like the focus on him as an individual, Wells could not have helped being pleased at this positive press
so early in his presidency as he sought to construct an image of the university as a cultural force in service to the state. Detzer's story was exclusively concerned with the centrifugal parts of IU's extension program
taking culture to the crossroads of the Hoosier state. Meanwhile, back
on the flagship campus, Wells continued his resourceful move toward
marrying the Benton murals to an impressive and functional architectural monument.

Not only was IU generating cultural opportunity around the state
under Wells's administration, it was also acquiring cultural attractions
and making capital investments in Bloomington. Acting centripetally,
Indiana University was gaining ground as a capital of culture, bringing
artists, their work, and students together in a fruitful pedagogical relationship. As an agent of the state, Wells clearly saw his role as a leader in
the cultivation of cultural heritage, reframing and incorporating it into

the liberal arts context, and thus making it available for the education of all citizens of the commonwealth.

In late March 1939 – the Detzer article in wide circulation – Wells wrote to Governor Townsend that most of the Benton murals could be placed in the capacious foyer of the Hall of Music, with a few elsewhere in other parts of the structure and in an adjacent building.[36] Perhaps emboldened by his success in bringing culture to campus, Wells unveiled an audacious aspiration to create a new campus precinct devoted to the fine and performing arts in the auditorium's vicinity. University architect Otto Eggers sketched the auditorium as the focus of a future plaza, with a fine arts building on the north and a Greek theatre on the south, built on a natural slope. "His original design called for a centerpiece," Wells wrote, "a fountain it was hoped." A striking rendering of the plaza proposal was used in presentations to prospective donors.[37] Filling in a blank area on the campus map, it became a twentieth-century campus precinct, a counterpart to the nineteenth-century Old Crescent.

IU FOUNDATION

When Wells was named university president, he automatically became president of the board of directors for the Indiana University Foundation, established only two years before. The board was composed of IU trustees and other prominent alumni, including Paul McNutt and Wendell Willkie. Private universities had long relied on charitable gifts from individuals, and the great corporate philanthropies of Rockefeller and Carnegie had focused their attention, too, on private institutions. Indiana was lagging behind other public universities making explicit provision to acquire and administer private monies to enhance the university's mission of teaching, research, and education.

Wells and the board of directors, all busy men, met infrequently. Although the IU Foundation's mission was clear, the board had no strategic plan nor had they hired any personnel to develop one. In June 1938, the university was notified by John Bradford, a Mooresville businessman, that he intended to bequeath his family homestead, nearly eight hundred acres, to the university. Located in Morgan County between Martinsville and Mooresville, the land was a beautiful tract of rambling forests and meadows. Bradford, the last surviving member of a Hoosier pioneer family and a friend of James Whitcomb Riley, envisioned a place where children with disabilities could encounter the healing and life-enhancing properties of the natural world.

Although the gift was the first substantial one handled by Wells, he performed the transaction with his usual decorum, complete with a small ceremony and a group photograph for publicity purposes.[38] Bradford lived for two and a half years beyond his bequest, and the deed was transferred to IU after his death in January 1941.[39] The property, named Bradford Woods, became a center of outdoor education and nature study.

A VISION FOR INDIANA UNIVERSITY

The new IU administration was more than a breath of fresh air; it was an invigorating wind penetrating into every part of the university, full of the promise of new beginnings. Wells was approachable and communicative, and evinced a genuine interest in people. People marveled at his warm charm and palpable common sense, and there was a widespread belief, on campus and around the state, that IU was on the move again. A faculty wife observed, "That he is both energetic and enterprising is an established fact. Nor is his genial smile the mask to a more austere personality. On the contrary, he is as affable and approachable as he appears."[40]

For his part, Wells was an expert reader of community concerns and of the Hoosier milieu. Although he was motivated by an unshakable belief that education was the key to human development, he understood that actions speak louder than words. He therefore focused on the immediate tasks at hand, including planting seeds for the future. Wells would have an opportunity to restate his educational philosophy and objectives at his formal inauguration, set for December 1, 1938, nearly a year and a half after he started leading the university. His open office hours provided a symbol of his accessibility: "And if his visitor feels that he knows the President well enough, whether he be student or otherwise, he may address him familiarly as 'Hermie,' short for Herman, which is the affectionate title by which he is known throughout the state of Indiana."[41]

But the IU academic community had little idea of what a proper inaugural ceremony for a new IU president should be like. Wells's predecessor Bryan was inaugurated in January 1903, coinciding with the dedication of Science Hall (now Lindley Hall) and his administration had outlasted generations of students, two or three sets of trustees, and most of the faculty of his cohort. Wells was alert to messages, both intended and unintended, that official ceremonies conveyed, and insisted on a modest observance, plowing the savings back into the university's research budget.[42] People noticed.

December 1 was sunny and unseasonably warm in Bloomington. On the main campus of Indiana University, classes were cancelled so students could attend the inauguration of IU's eleventh president. A crowd of 3,500, including faculty and dignitaries, was assembled in the Men's Gymnasium and Fieldhouse (now the Wildermuth Center) at 11 AM for the ceremony.[43] The entire ceremony was broadcast and press photographers swarmed. One satiric wit cracked that the professors "have a curiously flattened look, as though they had been slept on, while the leaner members appear to have been squeezed out of a tube. All but the President, who is a shining example of buoyant avoirdupois."[44]

The patrician Bryan, who had recently turned seventy-eight, introduced Wells with a playful nod to their disparate ages. He said, addressing Wells,

> Thirty-six years ago you and I were beginners. I was beginning what was thought to be a difficult and sometimes dangerous enterprise. You were beginning what is known to be a more difficult and more dangerous enterprise. I began with very little experience and very little idea of what I should have to live through. At the same date you had no experience and no idea of what you would have to live through. I took my risk and somehow lived through it. You took your risk and here you are at 36, eleventh president of Indiana University, and more than that, my son, a man.[45]

Wells began his inaugural address with a note of gratitude to Bryan, lauding him for leading the university through its greatest period of "growth in physical and intellectual resources" and thanking him personally for his support.

Reiterating his enthusiasm for the position, which he considered to be the job of a lifetime, Wells marked his inauguration day with a speech that revealed his educational philosophy and academic ideals, coupled with an expansive vision for a greater Indiana University. In ringing tones, he declared the essential scholarly function of the university – to impart what is known and to discover what is not – in fulfilling its important social role. Wells went on to enunciate the role of education in a democracy, quoting John Dewey with approval: "Democracy has to be born anew every generation, and education is the midwife." He harkened back to the origins of Indiana University in 1820 and urged that the university provide leadership as an example of democratic governance: "Authority must be derived from reason, not from position." The speech itself was clear and well constructed, delivered in a plain style with no verbal fireworks. Using the university's rich past as prologue, Wells reiterated institutional goals of broad access to education, superior teaching, innovative research scholarship, and service to the state and nation. He took care to distinguish between vocational preparation and professional training. The tone was humane and resolute, with expressions of hopefulness overcoming worries and obstacles.[46]

The state and national media noted the inauguration of Wells. *Time* magazine profiled the "roly-poly 'Hermie' Wells" and the "youngest president of a State university." The brief story mentioned his work drafting new state banking legislation but claimed "the campus knows him best as a jolly, convivial gourmet, and a Rabelaisian storyteller." Also calling attention to his relative youth, *Newsweek* highlighted his joie de vivre: "Wells is noted for indefatigability – and a habit of regarding anything of his own as the best there is. 'When he carried a paper route,' says his father, 'his paper was the best in the world.' He now applies that attitude to Indiana University." Wells was quoted at the end of the ceremony by the *Indianapolis Star:* "Well, I'm glad it's over – the trouble is, it's just begun!"[47] The ceremony was indeed over, but the president had already been on the job for nearly eighteen months, and signs of progress were already showing.

HEARTH-BUILDING AT THE IMU

In early spring 1939, recently installed President Wells was absent from the Bloomington campus – on another cross-country recruiting trip for new faculty. Accustomed to living out of a suitcase, he found travel an essential part of his job as well as personally rewarding. He relished good food, nice hotels, and interesting conversation on the road. They slaked, at least temporarily, his perpetual need for movement. Musing to himself, he scrawled these notes:

> Nearly a month of steady travel and 10,000 miles lay behind me and Indiana University. Every night a strange hotel and every day another train and plane, with strange people to interview at the end of the journey in an attempt to match my wits against theirs to see whether we wanted them at Indiana University. I was tired, lonely, and homesick. It was a rough trip through the clouds, over the mountains from Seattle to Spokane. At Spokane I expected to find just another drab, dreary hotel. Instead, I found [the Davenport Hotel].[48]

Indeed, this was an unforeseen find for this connoisseur of lodging and cuisine. The Davenport Hotel was reputed to be the finest west of the Mississippi River. Built in 1914 at a cost of $3 million, the hotel was a joint venture between wealthy rail magnates James and Robert Hill, the rich newspaperman W. H. Cowles, and a prominent restaurateur, Louis M. Davenport. It boasted five restaurants and nearly five hundred rooms, and it "contained both a dazzling collection of spaces intended to evoke a magical world of fantasy and the latest in American technology."[49]

The hotel lobby was particularly striking, with Spanish Renaissance architecture and a huge skylight of pale green opalescent glass. Carved griffins and dolphins abounded, symbolizing strength and sociability, respectively. Heraldic crests and medallions were placed throughout the ornamentation, and an Italian marble fountain featured a child grasping a dolphin, from the mouth of which a stream of water flowed. But the dominating feature of the lavish lobby was a massive fireplace. Innkeeper Davenport, who lived in an apartment on site, had decreed at the hotel's opening in 1914 that a fire be kept burning continuously in the fireplace. The fire, still burning after a quarter-century, was a welcome amenity to guests like Wells.

Wells returned to Indiana with extensive notes on several faculty prospects and an idea borrowed from the Davenport Hotel. The day following Thanksgiving in 1939, Wells led a group to light the fire of perpetual hospitality in the south lounge of the Indiana Memorial Union. The occasion was the third biennial reunion of the Union Board, a student organization that was established in 1909. During Wells's student days in the 1920s, he served as Union Board treasurer. When the Union building was opened in 1932, it soon became the living room of the campus, and the fireplace in the general lounge was a natural focal point. The fire, symbolizing hearth and home, kindled "the spirit of friendship which emanates from Indiana University to all who come within its reach."[50] In this Promethean act, Wells participated in one of humankind's oldest rituals – borrowing fire and making it useful to others.

The early years of the Wells administration constituted one of the most important periods in Indiana University history. Not even David Starr Jordan had restructured both the faculty and the aims of the university so thoroughly. New standards had been set for the institution and the blueprint for achieving them was in hand. There continued to be a central emphasis on teaching, and there lingered on some of the traditional folksy provincial spirit which tended to make the campus a snug human island in Hoosier society. The addition of new research-oriented professors, the ending the great national depression, and the increasing tensions of impending worldwide conflict thrust Indiana University not only outward from the campus, but well beyond the confines of Indiana itself.

Thomas D. Clark, 1977

SEVEN

Charting a New Course

THE SELF-STUDY COMMITTEE CONTINUED ITS WORK through 1939 – consulting with faculty, gathering data, and interpreting the findings. Debate and controversy accompanied the release of comprehensive final report in January 1940. The faculty-led committee did not agree on all of its recommendations, so it wasn't surprising that its findings got a mixed public reception. It called for a basic reorganization of the university, with existing schools to be abolished and replaced with functional divisions: Humanities, Music and Fine Arts, Physical Science, Biological Science, Social Science, Education, Business Administration, Law, Medicine, Dentistry, Health and Physical Education, Lower Division, Extension Division, Library Division, and Division of Student Personnel. The undergraduate core was to be the Junior Division, in which students would spend their first two years. At the end of their sophomore year, they would decide on one of the various divisions to complete their baccalaureate degree. The professional divisions such as law, medicine, and dentistry would keep their own entrance requirements and would not accept students directly from the Junior Division.

The committee recommended a wide sharing of functional responsibility at the executive level of administration. In contrast to the steep hierarchy presided over by Bryan, the committee proposed an academic vice president, a financial vice president, and two advisory boards composed of division heads to oversee the educational program. After strenuous debate, the faculty agreed to many of the reforms, but voted down the radical divisional restructuring in March 1940. (The trustees restored provision for the Junior Division in 1942.) The basic administrative structure of schools, set up by Bryan, would remain. Bloomington would have the College of Arts and Sciences, Law School, Business, Education, Music, and the Graduate School; Indianapolis retained the professional Schools of Medicine, Nursing, and Dentistry.[1]

The self-study committee also conducted a frank examination of the IU faculty as a group, comparing them to their regional and national counterparts. "By whatever criteria the committee used, be it the percentage of PhD's, time spent on research, the degree of nepotism on the staff, or how many departments were qualified to offer graduate work, Indiana University was found wanting when compared to similar institutions in the Midwest."[2] By the time the report was made public, Wells had already been busy revitalizing the faculty roster.

The president borrowed from his experience in the banking world as he sought to improve the university's research profile. Within a year of taking office, he requested that each faculty member "suggest concrete needs for a well-defined teaching or research project." Then reallocated funds, although small, were distributed on the basis of merit, giving faculty more incentive to pursue scholarly endeavors. It also proved useful for the administration to have specific faculty research plans as they formulated their annual appeal for funds from the state legislature. Wells knew from his past business dealings that information on "exactly how much money [IU] needed, and how the money would be spent" would increase the chances of support.[3]

Longtime faculty members noted that this policy of providing material incentives to scholarship was a sharp departure from the Bryan administration. Bryan often spoke glowingly of the value of scholarship, but it was difficult "to extract the coin of the realm" for support. Upon seeking funds for research, one professor said Bryan replied rhetorically, "On every campus and in every faculty there are a few men eager to advance knowledge. They will do this whether they are supported or not. They are devoted people whom nothing can stop. Why, then, is it necessary to give them assistance?"[4] This attitude highlighted a clear difference in administrative philosophies. In Bryan's opinion, the university's main mission was to transmit knowledge to the next generation; the research mission was equally important to Wells.

Even if its more radical provisions were not adopted, the self-study charted a progressive, even bold, course for the future, and its broad outlines became a guide to policy changes at the outset of the Wells administration.[5] It represented a clean break with the monarchical system of administration that went before, where power was concentrated in the president's office. Wells believed that university governance should be essentially democratic – government by the people, of the people, and for the people (to paraphrase Abraham Lincoln). The academic community was where free speech reigned and democratic debate was fostered.

The self-study achieved its goal of harvesting innovative ideas about all aspects of the university's operation, and provided a sturdy framework for reform and reorganization. But the process had even more important benefits. It cultivated a common goal and nurtured a sense of solidarity among the faculty and administration in a time of momentous transition. In less than three years, the self-study process affirmed the value of reasoned debate in democratic self-governance, in addition to confirming Wells's talent for engagement. He joked later that the self-study was a safe way for him temporize and avoid controversial actions, especially as an acting executive. In actuality, he exercised his presidential authority from the beginning, behaving always as an executive and not as a caretaker or placeholder.[6]

Among the disturbing findings of the self-study was the low level of student interest in intellectual and cultural activities, despite a wealth of student clubs, organizations, and events. The study's authors were astonished at the student body's general unconcern and "phlegmatic indifference to the highly controversial social problems" of the day, which should have generated serious controversies about what to do about them. The self-study committee studied the coverage in the *Daily Student* newspaper and concluded that censorship had prevented the expression of views at variance with the university's administration or the dominant political party. The report called for making the student newspaper completely independent, with all control over editorial and news policy in the hands of students.

Two recent exceptions to the prevailing apathy and superficiality of student organizations were noted. In 1937, a local chapter of the American Student Union was formed to explore problems of international peace, economic prosperity, and social justice. And, as noted earlier, the Inter-Racial Commission was formed in 1935. Initially, both groups were denied recognition as official student organizations by Dean of Men Clarence Edmondson.[7]

THE RACE PROBLEM AT INDIANA

Among the important problems that had been avoided during the entire history of the university were racial intolerance, discrimination, and hate. Skin color made a difference in how people were treated – in Bloomington, in Indiana, and in the United States. Although policies were unwritten, IU operated under a system of segregation as rigid as any Jim Crow society in the Deep South. Its very invisibility made it even more pernicious.

Influenced by his parents and the Methodist church, Wells had learned egalitarian principles at an early age. Although there were very few blacks in Boone County, in high school Wells made trips to Indianapolis, where there was a growing African American population. He observed and read about the rise of the Ku Klux Klan as a young man, and felt moral repugnance. His banking work in the late 1920s took him around the state, especially to Indianapolis, where the largest Ku Klux Klan branch was located. Like other progressive Hoosiers, he wondered what to do about this cancer on the body politic. Once he became president, he was confronted with decisions about how to turn his high principles into practical action.

As acting president, he overruled Dean of Men Edmondson and granted the Inter-Racial Commission official status. He worked with the advisor to the group, Frank Beck, to create a campus interfaith "Religious Cabinet" in 1937, with Beck as director. In keeping with the historic connection between organized religion and progressive civil rights, the religious cabinet became the official sponsor of the Inter-Racial Commission. This made Beck an ally, harnessed the retired minister's energy for the cause, and provided an effective distance from the president's office to ensure Wells's freedom of action.

The Inter-Racial Commission was a response to deep-seated institutional racism. Although the university's academic program had always been open to African Americans, black students often found prejudice and hostility as they pursued their studies. Their social life was segregated and their extracurricular activities were restricted. They could join one of the few black Greek-letter organizations but they could not live in the university dormitories. They did not have equal access to food service and dining facilities on campus. Their participation in intercollegiate athletics was restricted to sports where sustained skin-to-skin contact was not required. So basketball and wrestling were out, and also swimming because of fears of pollution. And there were no African-American faculty or coaches, and very few professional staff members.

Student research projects in the Sociology Department held up a glimmering light on the plight of local African Americans, both students and non-students. Raytha L. Yokley received her master's degree in Sociology in 1941. Her thesis, entitled "The Negro Community in Bloomington," cited local population statistics from 1910 and 1930 that displayed an overall growth, but the African American population showed a marked percentage decrease, from 4.5 to 2.8 percent. She gave three reasons for the decrease: higher death rates, lower birth rates, and increased migration to larger cities. Yokley reported the common wisdom of her informants that Bloomington blacks used to have a chance at skilled jobs, such as at the Showers Brothers Furniture factory, but Klan-influenced attitudes had taken over among white employers. Despite the presence of overt racism in Bloomington, there were no organized protest groups or civil rights bodies, such as the National Association for the Advancement of Colored People (NAACP) or the Urban League, operating in the city.[8]

Wells continued to be concerned about the plight of African American students, and the larger issue of civil rights, but did not know exactly how to intervene in an effective manner. Quite confident of the power of his office, he was acutely aware that his direct authority stopped at the edge of campus. He was still learning about how to best use his position as a bully pulpit to advocate change.

A VISIT FROM AN OLD CLASSMATE

In the late summer of 1940, working on assignment from the *Indianapolis News*, journalist Ernie Pyle paid an extended visit to Nashville, Indiana, and the artists' colony in Brown County. He ran into Wells, who was renting a cabin for the summer and commuting back and forth each day to his campus office. Wells promptly invited him to dinner. Deftly sketching a verbal portrait of the young president, Pyle later wrote about the big dinner, featuring "a couple of steaks as big as your wrist" cooked on the grill outdoors. He noted that everyone called him "Hermie," including his students and even his Brown County cook, Rosie. Although Pyle had left school before graduation, he was sentimental about Indiana University, and felt bad when he lost his 1923 *Arbutus* yearbook. Wells found a replacement copy and gave it to Pyle.[9]

Pyle was impressed with Wells's humble nature, illustrated by an offhand remark, "This job I've got . . ." made in reference to the presidency. Citing Wells's great love for teaching, Pyle reasoned that Wells was able skillfully handle the transition from the Bryan administration and the retirement of a host of senior professors. "But he has not let his administrative duties deny the pulse of the University," as Pyle observed:

> He sees students constantly by appointment, and one afternoon a week anybody can come to see him. They sit in front of the fireplace in his office, and gab out their hearts. Students bring their troubles to Hermie, their love affairs, their financial troubles, the little jams they're in. I doubt there's another university president in America who wins more little confidences from his charges than Hermie Wells does.[10]

Pyle saw beyond Wells's calm demeanor and recognized his quicksilver mind. Prone to muscle tension and headaches, Wells found relief hunting for antiques. He had his secretaries maintain a list of antique stores within driving distance, so when he needed a break from administrative pressures, he took off for two or three days.[11] "His house is reeking with antique furniture," Pyle reported. It wasn't the mere possession of such objects that Wells cared about, however, "but the routing out, the discovering, the acquiring."[12]

It made no matter whether Wells was in his Bryan Hall office or his Woodburn House residence, he always made time for meetings with students. Eager to learn details about their background and academic plans, he epitomized Hoosier hospitality. Kutsi Beğdeş, a Turkish graduate student in economics, came to IU in the late 1930s and was invited to have coffee with Wells on a Saturday morning. He arrived at the appointed time, engaged in pleasant conversation, and took his leave, at which time Wells said, "Nice to see you; hope to see you again soon." The following Saturday, Beğdeş came back at the same time and knocked on the door. Wells, hiding his surprise at seeing him, ushered him into the house and offered coffee once again. As the student was leaving, Wells said, "Hurry back!" Puzzled by Midwestern customs, Beğdeş was nevertheless pleased about the personal attention he was getting. The next Saturday morning, Beğdeş was getting ready when his American roommate asked him where he was going. In reply, he told about the Woodburn House coffees. The roommate laughed, explaining that such expressions convey courtesy and were not to be taken literally. Beğdeş decided not to go. A few days later he received a phone call from Wells, "Kutsi, are you sick? We haven't seen you for coffee." The Turkish student finished his M.A. in 1940, and, four years later, was the first person to earn the doctorate in economics at Indiana.[13]

PHYSICS REBIRTH

In addition to fostering talented faculty, the Wells administration was interested in rebuilding departments. A case in point was physics, whose head, Arthur L. Foley, was fond of boasting, "There is not an electron in all Indiana!"[14] Taking pride in the classical approach to physics, Foley tried to ignore the rise of nuclear physics and quantum mechanics as he guided the small physics department from 1897 to 1937. He retired as the Bryan regime was swept away, and Dean Payne and President Wells consulted about new faculty.

Nuclear physicist Allan C. G. Mitchell, from New York University, was hired as chairman and an ambitious program of particle physics emerged. The offer to Mitchell, who specialized in the analysis of beta-ray spectra of radioactive substances, was sweetened by the promise to construct a particle accelerator known as a cyclotron because of the circular shape of its beam.[15] E. O. Lawrence, a physicist at the University of California at Berkeley, had pioneered this new instrument (known colloquially as an "atom smasher") that was revolutionizing experimental physics. Lawrence's fame was abetted by his appearance on the cover of *Time* in November 1937.[16]

Mitchell assembled a small staff of nuclear physicists, including Lawrence M. Langer, who was one of his Ph.D. students at NYU, Franz N. Kurie, an instructor from Lawrence's laboratory, L. Jackson Laslett, a recent Berkeley Ph.D., and Emil J. Konopinski, a postdoctoral fellow from Cornell. Kurie and Laslett, aided by a few graduate students, were in charge of building the big machine, measuring forty-five inches between the poles of its gigantic magnets. Sited adjacent to the new building for physics and mathematics and named after Joseph Swain, the fourteen-foot walls of the Cyclotron Room went up after the specially designed concrete foundation was poured and the eighty-ton magnet was maneuvered into place. At the time, it was the third-largest cyclotron in the world.[17]

Swain Hall was dedicated in October 1940 with a two-day colloquium devoted to nuclear physics.[18] Six months later – after sundown on April 10, 1941 – the cyclotron achieved its first successful beam. Wells, still working in his office in Bryan Hall, was called, and he came through Dunn's Woods and joined the physicists in toasting their success with a bottle of champagne.[19]

AUDITORIUM DEDICATION

The first building planned by the Wells administration, the IU Auditorium, slowly took shape on East Seventh Street between 1939 and 1940. The bulk of the Indiana murals were placed in a grand hall that functioned as the auditorium's lobby; two panels were installed in the Business and Economics Building, occupied in 1940; and two in the adjacent Little Theatre (now the IU Cinema), dedicated to student performances. On March 22, 1941, the IU Auditorium was dedicated.[20] Thomas Hart Benton was among the notables who attended. Several days of programming followed, to put the building through its paces. Wells was in his element – officiating at ceremonies, hosting dinner parties, enjoying musical and dramatic performances. "He felt," as IU historian Thomas Clark noted, that the auditorium dedication "was truly the beginning of the fulfillment of a special university obligation to light a spark of creativity in Hoosier youth."[21] In a manner analogous to William Lowe Bryan's presentation of the "alma mater" painting at Wells's graduation seventeen years before, Wells's presiding over the auditorium dedication underscored the role of the arts in the university while at the same time exemplified changing aesthetic tastes. After the ceremony, President Emeritus Bryan made this gnomic comment to a *Daily Student* reporter, "It is with our Hall of Music as with every first-rate thing that men do – it is old *and* new. Builders of genius in Egypt, Babylon, Athens, Canterbury were present within the man who conceived of this home of beauty."[22] For Wells, the opening of this specialized facility was a major step in revolutionizing the role of the arts at Indiana.

TRIP TO LATIN AMERICA

Wells traveled the Hoosier State incessantly as president, and also made longer journeys around the country. Whether meeting legislators in Indianapolis or visiting the extension center in Gary, or recruiting new faculty members on the West Coast, he was often away from Bloomington. Always on the lookout for superior food and comfortable accommodations, Wells found it easy to live out of a suitcase. Of course, travel was an essential part of the education business, but he enjoyed the geographic variety (and the concomitant human diversity) for its own sake.

But he had never traveled outside of North America until 1941. Invited to participate in the Institute for Inter-American Affairs by Hubert Herring, the executive director of the Committee on Cultural Relations with Latin America, Wells joined a small group with representatives from journalism, labor relations, business, religion, and education on a seven-week cultural tour of South America. The continent was considered a backwater, but rumors of Nazi influence brought it into the news. Herring, an authority on Latin America, had extensive contacts with domestic professional and political elites in South America as well as U.S. Foreign Service staff. From late July into mid-September, the group visited Panama, Colombia, Ecuador, Peru, Bolivia, Chile, Argentina, Brazil, Trinidad, and Venezuela. In each country, the group met the U.S.

ambassador and various leaders in government, economic life, education, and cultural affairs.

Over the fifty-day journey, Wells gained a wealth of knowledge and
valuable contacts. In Peru, he met Dr. and Mrs. Virgil DeVault for the
first time. DeVault, a surgeon and a graduate from the IU School of
Medicine, had established a successful British-American hospital in
Lima.[23] In that same country, Wells renewed an acquaintance with
Alberto Arca-Parro, whom he had known as an undergraduate. Arca-
Parro, a social scientist like Wells, had directed the first modern census
of Peru.[24] In Bolivia, students in the American School of La Paz were
assigned to be guides to the Institute group. One particularly talented
fifteen-year-old, Peter Fraenkel, whose father had emigrated from Germany to escape from the Nazis, impressed his teachers so much that
they encouraged Wells to find aid to enable him to attend college in the
United States.[25] Before the trip, Wells had been authorized to grant two
scholarships to deserving South American students. Besieged by eager
students, he succeeded in attracting several more than two. Jokingly,
Herring called Wells a "pied piper" as students followed him back to
Bloomington.[26]

Wells brought back vivid memories of the "incredibly colorful and
picturesque" trip. It brought tangible experience to bear upon his wide
reading of foreign affairs and history, and some of his first international
contacts. Not only was this sojourn personally rewarding, but also it
expanded his vision for the university: "From this venture I gained great
enthusiasm for enlarging the international dimension of Indiana University, a new conception of the strength and values that international
studies might offer us, and a determination to continue encouraging
our foreign-student program, bolstered by the several Latin American
students who came to Indiana University as a result of my contacts during the trip."[27] It also demonstrated the reach of the IU alumni network
as he renewed contact with an old classmate.

Although his first overseas trip opened his eyes to the horizon of
international education, Wells was also getting into national circulation.
That same year he was selected for the board of the Carnegie Foundation
for the Advancement of Teaching, like his predecessor Bryan before him.
Not only did it open many doors, but the selection also reassured IU fac-

ulty that Wells would be able "to represent them properly in the academic world."[28] Only a few months afterward, Japan attacked the United States in Hawaiʻi on December 7, 1941, precipitating American involvement in World War II. The university and its young helmsman would have to face unknown challenges caused by global conflict.

Most of you, therefore, can serve best through devoting extra effort to the matters at hand. Study a little more, use the library a little more, use the laboratory apparatus a little more – learn a little faster – in order that you may achieve more rapidly than you would in peace time the training and maturity which you will need for the tasks ahead.

Herman B Wells, 1941

EIGHT

War Stories

IN THE LATE 1930S AND EARLY 1940S President Wells led significant changes in university policies and practices. The spirit of reform that
suffused the new IU administration was coupled with a general unease
about the war in Europe that had started in fall 1939 with the invasion of
Poland by Nazi Germany. The campus had responded by ramping up the
Reserve Officers Training Corps (ROTC) program in 1940.

Wells was settling comfortably into his role as a university president.
The commonplace tasks of meeting the basic challenges of personnel,
programs, and facilities had intrinsic interest to Wells because of his
overriding concern about human relationships and the development of
human potential. The job kept Wells constantly on the move through
different social groups (students, faculty, trustees, legislators, and staff),
in different venues (residence, office, campus, and statehouse), and for
different purposes (campus planning, financial management, entertainment, and ceremony). Wells had honed his native instincts to sense the
emotional needs of any group of which he was part, articulate and embody those concerns, and then imagine a way forward for the collectivity.
He was able to exercise his large gift for interpersonal problem solving,
whether one on one or with larger assemblies. A natural servant-leader,
Wells found his deepest satisfaction in assisting others to meet their
personal academic goals and thus enabling the progress of the university
as a human institution.

On the evening of Saturday, December 6, 1941, Wells had gone to a
Democratic Party fundraiser. Early the next morning, Japan launched
an air raid on the U.S. Naval Base at Pearl Harbor in Hawai'i. By the af-

ternoon, President Franklin D. Roosevelt announced the United States was at war with Japan. When the news broke, Wells was on campus entertaining foreign students at the Cosmopolitan Club.[1] Later that afternoon, the *Indiana Daily Student* published an "Extra" edition, beating out other papers that were distributed in Bloomington. The two thousand copies sold out within two hours. Wells made this brief statement: "The news of the attack is tragic and terrible. It seems fantastic that Japan would take such a step. Indiana university [*sic*] through the one hundred and twenty years on [*sic*] its history, has always done its full share in every national crisis and may be expected to do so again."[2] Wells called for an emergency meeting with his advisors later that evening at his home.[3]

Once he had gathered his wits, he published "A Message from the President" a couple of days later in the *Daily Student:* "In this crisis, every patriotic American wishes to make a contribution to the defense of the nation and to victory. In keeping with the tradition, established in other wars, the students of the University naturally are eager to do their share." The message went on to briefly mention opportunities for military, civilian, and volunteer duty. "Total war requires a stable, smoothly functioning society," Wells explained, and therefore it was crucial that the supply of persons "with college training be uninterrupted" to maintain the economy "through a long period of productive strain."[4] Counseling the students to maintain their focus on their studies, Wells was attempting to counteract the confusion and incipient panic that the attack on Pearl Harbor generated. For example, San Francisco was blacked out at night, and rumors raised the possibility that even Bloomington might be subject to attack from the air.

Wells had gained the students' attention as never before, and he rose to the challenge of communicating a measured, calm response to the fluid national situation. It was another opportunity to put into practice his eloquent inaugural rhetoric about democracy and social progress. Nine days after the Pearl Harbor attack, Wells spoke to the campus community. Dubbed the "war convo," it attracted one of the largest audiences ever assembled for convocation. The university band, dressed in military uniforms, played martial airs as the crowd filed into the old Assembly Hall. Standing in front of an enormous American flag, the president urged students to keep their heads and avoid hysteria in the present emergency. Attempting to reassure students, he told them that self-discipline

> must start in your own heart and in your own mind. If the war is long continued, it is inevitable, of course, that many of you will have your academic career interrupted. Remember, however, that peace will come some day, and most of you will be fortunate to come back to complete your work. You cannot, therefore, afford to relax in any way your personal standards of conduct or of intellectual performance. Be jealous of the record you are making now. You will need it when you return, and you will need it likewise in the discharge of the heavy responsibilities which you must be prepared to assume during the reconstruction period.[5]

Wells explained that the university would be cooperating with state and federal agencies as the national mobilization proceeded. Military service information would be available through several campus outlets, including the office of the dean of men and the Department of Military Science and Tactics. The university would make provision for the awarding of credit if a student went into the armed forces before the end of the semester. The war convo ended with everyone singing the national anthem.[6]

WARTIME MOBILIZATION

Many academic routines were interrupted as the campus lurched onto a wartime footing. College-aged men were prime fodder for the armed services. Inexorably, state and federal government agencies played a growing role in university affairs. Academic schedules, course offerings, and instructional personnel were altered to accommodate the influx of soldiers needing immediate training.

The university responded by creating the War Planning Council, which first met in early January 1942 to discuss how best to contribute to national defense needs. The council's membership consisted of three administrators, twelve faculty members, and one student. Wells announced on January 17 that IU would adopt a three-semester plan whereby the regular four-year program could be compressed into two and two-thirds years. The war council reasoned that a graduate would be more useful in the war effort, and the plan "would prevent unnecessarily large numbers of young men and women to face the present emergency and the post-war period without the benefits of a college education."[7] Annual faculty workloads (and salaries) were adjusted to two and a half semesters. Perhaps the most momentous change was the formation of the Junior Division, in which all entering freshman were required to enroll.[8] Although other American universities had mobilization plans, Wells claimed that Indiana had the most complete one. "Our society," he said, "is faced with the necessity for a supreme military and productive effort. There is no shortage of manpower. There is a tremendous shortage of trained manpower."[9]

Wartime highlighted the importance of higher education, particularly in training for modern, mechanized warfare. Scientists and engineers and other technical specialists were in high demand. Wells found his enthusiasm for education took on an added meaning as it became coupled with the defense of the democratic way of life. Speaking about the importance of "trained brains" became a familiar refrain in Wells's speeches.

Foreign language instruction at Indiana received a tremendous boost as it met wartime demands. The American Council of Learned Societies (ACLS) coordinated university efforts to train students in foreign languages that were not commonly taught. In August 1942, anthropology professor Charles "Carl" Voegelin taught courses in Turkish, with the help of graduate students from Turkey. So successful was this instruction that the ACLS offered to underwrite courses in Russian as well. In the meantime Voegelin had been appointed head of the recently organized Department of Anthropology as well as a new Division of Eastern European Areas and Languages – IU's first area studies program. In summer 1943, he spoke to the Bloomington Rotary Club about the program – Indiana was one of ten universities in the country engaged in intensive language training – and the recent expansion to include nine Balkan languages. (After the war it was revealed that the focus was on Russian, with about two hundred men trained at the university, of whom one third served overseas.) As many as sixteen highly specialized instructors served the language program at its wartime peak, and linguist Thomas Sebeok joined Voegelin in directing their efforts.[10]

Sebeok, who came to Indiana in 1943 at age twenty-one, headed the Russian language program in the Army Specialized Training Program.

He recalled, "[T]here were absolutely no resources for the teaching of Russian . . . and very few for most of the other languages we had to teach, which included Turkish, Finnish, Hungarian, Polish, Serbo-Croatian, and Greek." No textbooks were available, "so during the days we taught the languages, and every night we wrote the texts and lessons for the following day's classes." Sebeok could teach Hungarian and Finnish, but had to find "informants," or native speakers, for the remainder.[11]

The physics department, newly revitalized with additional personnel and boasting a working cyclotron, was among the units that provided vital services to the war effort. Department head Allan Mitchell obtained funding from the National Defense Research Committee, the federal agency that was responsible for contract research, to perform studies of various radioactive isotopes. That work fed into the federal laboratory located at the University of Chicago, known as the Met Lab (for "metallurgical"), where secret research involving nuclear fission experiments under Enrico Fermi and Karl Compton had begun. The Met Lab was one of the handful of large federal organizations that contributed to the effort to build an atomic bomb, known by its code name, the Manhattan Project.

Other physics faculty contributed to the Manhattan Project. Emil Konopinski contributed to solution of equations to test whether the atmosphere might be ignited by such an atomic blast. Assistant professor of physics Lawrence Langer was called to project headquarters at Los Alamos, New Mexico, and spent the remainder of the war working on atomic bomb development. He was sent to the island of Tinian, where the final assembly of the bomb destined for Hiroshima was to take place. "But when we got to Tinian, we discovered that about 400 planes a day were taking off from the island to bomb Japan, and about 1 percent of those planes crashed on takeoff," Langer recounted. So plans were made to perform the bomb's final assembly in the plane after it was aloft, and a special tool was secured in a toolbox in the plane's bomb bay. The officer in charge of the final assembly was so worried about the tool that Langer decided to stay with the plane, even though it was guarded by military police. In the bomb bay, Langer explained, "I stretched out on top of the bomb, fell asleep and spent the night there. So the tool was in the box when they took off in the morning, and it worked."[12]

SERVING THE U.S. STATE DEPARTMENT

Late in 1942, Paul McNutt, who had become administrator of the Federal Manpower Commission, wrote to Wells requesting the loan of Dean of Faculties Herman T. Briscoe to formulate policies regarding the utilization of colleges and universities in federal training programs. Wells readily acceded to the request, although the expected few weeks turned into several years, as Briscoe eventually became the director of the War Manpower Training Bureau in 1944. Although the university had to deal with Briscoe's intermittent absences from campus, the position gave Briscoe a valuable window on postwar educational planning around the nation.[13]

Wells had already been tapped for various brief war assignments, but he longed for a substantial job helping the war effort. In March 1943, Sumner Welles, the acting secretary of state, offered Wells the post of director-general of economic operations for French North and West Africa, a joint British-American project. The position entailed managing several hundred staff as the American chairman of the North African Economic Board, and would deal with problems of civilian supply and production in war-torn areas, the operation of transportation and communication systems, and the like. Wells would report to Robert Murphy, American minister and chief civil affairs officer under General Dwight Eisenhower.[14] Wells gracefully declined the assignment, probably because it lay beyond his areas of expertise.[15]

By mid-July, Assistant Secretary of State Dean Acheson and his associates were talking with Wells about another assignment. The young IU president, still shy of forty and his appetite for foreign travel whetted by his recent trip to South America, expressed a desire for a post that might involve fieldwork. The previous month, the State Department reorganized some of its activities in response to the rapidly changing military situation, and newly installed Secretary of State Cordell Hull created the Office of Foreign Economic Cooperation. The secretary agreed with Acheson that Wells would be a good choice for deputy director for liberated areas, to oversee and coordinate civilian agencies in conjunction with the armed services. The role would also entail working with the deputy director in charge of plans and organization in dealing with foreign economic policy.

In the offer letter, Acheson said policy for liberated areas "must be framed with a knowledge of and in harmony with similar policy in other areas. It is, as you see, a great undertaking, with great possibilities and great difficulties. After many months of consideration we know of no one else who will bring greater capacities than yourself to this task."[16] Wells was eager to accept the position, but first he needed permission from the IU Board of Trustees.

The trustees were concerned that two top administrators, Wells and Briscoe, would be on assignments that took them away from campus. The governor chimed in when worries were expressed about potential public criticism about paying their salaries when they were absent from the university. Wildermuth, the president of the board of trustees, agreed: "[U]nder no circumstances should the funds of the State be used to provide employees for the Federal Government." In the end, Wells received the trustees' permission to take the State Department assignment, but with the proviso that he spend at least two days a week in Bloomington. In a private aside, Wildermuth expressed his skepticism to Wells as he groused, "[T]here was so much government boondoggling going on that [I] doubt whether any good will come out of either of these positions."[17]

In early August, Wells was shuttling back and forth by airplane between Bloomington and Washington, spending the workweek at the capital city and working weekends back at IU's Administration Building. He savored the days in the beehive of wartime Washington, the nerve center for far-flung American forces, both civilian and military. In his bailiwick of economic affairs, Acheson had assembled a remarkable staff at the State Department. Wells pursued his assignment with gusto, relishing the esprit de corps that came with collaborating on an important national goal.

Wells's working style, refined by a decade and a half of administrative experience, was to set clear goals, devour data omnivorously, and draft sound policies that could be revised as needed. Internal coordination among members of work group was vital, as well as external communication between groups in pursuit of a shared objective. He quickly became a valued member of Acheson's group, with successive assignments bearing increased responsibility. By October, Wells was serving in a new role, as special advisor on liberated areas, to assist Acheson in "dealing with the foreign policy aspects of wartime economic activities in the liberated areas."[18]

UNRRA CONFERENCE

Shortly after Wells was promoted to special advisor in the fall of 1943, he was chosen as a delegate to the organizational meeting of the United Nations Relief and Rehabilitation Administration (UNRRA), one of the precursors of the United Nations. In the midst of the fighting, with the outcome yet in doubt, the Allied countries called for an international conference to plan assistance for war-ravaged nations in the postwar world. Acheson was head of the U.S. delegation, and was made chairman of the conference, which included representatives from forty-four nations. Before the conference, the assistant secretary of state summed up the objectives:

> UNRRA should do those things which will not be done without it and avoid what can be done with existing means. The problems will be so great and the demands so many that UNRRA should adopt something in the nature of an international Jeffersonian principle of doing the least which is necessary to accomplish the result – which is another way of saying that it should center its attention upon the essential problems which cannot be solved without it.[19]

The three-week meeting, held in November at the Claridge Hotel in Atlantic City, was marked by extensive discussion and intense debate as delegates attempted to balance national interests with global goodwill. Wells and others shared the dawning realization that, since it was the first organization designed for the postwar environment, "it would probably furnish precedent and pattern for the others and particularly for the United Nations organization itself, which the allied leadership had already begun to dream of and plan for."[20]

His assignment at the conference was to cover three subcommittees of the so-called First Committee, on "Organization and Administration," and to be the American representative on the subcommittee responsible for constructing a formula to allocate UNRRA's expenses, including costs connected to relief efforts. Wells's economic training and banking experience were put to practical use. After vigorous debate, a formula was devised and accepted by the delegates. (Later, the same formula was incorporated into the administration of the United Nations.) "Although the subject matter was not one of great ideological importance," as Wells wryly understated his role, "I found this diplomatic exercise broadening and interesting, revealing the nuances of international relationships and character as expressed in the representatives' reaction to the obligation of paying for the cost of an international humanitarian relief agency."[21]

The conference provided new international contacts for Wells. His network expanded to new acquaintances throughout the Allied world. Among the people he met, a few were singled out in his reminiscences: Jan Masaryk of Czechoslovakia, Lester Pearson of Canada, Sir Girja Bajpai of India, Edward G. Miller, Jr., one of Acheson's top aides, Jean Monnet of France, Paul-Henry Spaak of Belgium, Carlos Romulo of the Philippines, and Andrei Gromyko of Russia.[22]

Always learning, Wells gained much from the UNRRA conference, including "how things could be accomplished in an international gathering." Wells summed up the conference thus:

> As the conference completes its work, there is agreement on all sides that a practical and comprehensive machinery has been devised. If the executive work is a good as the legislative, the success of UNRRA is assured. Likewise, the essential wisdom of the move becomes evident. A system is provided by which the resources of the entire world are mobilized for most effective use wherever needed, and the burden of sacrifice is distributed. What is even more significant, countries are given an opportunity to work together toward an immediate practical objective and in so doing may learn how easy it is to cooperate in international programs. An organization dealing solely with principles and policy would find it even more difficult to function in the beginning, just as any group finds it more difficult to deal with the abstract than with the concrete and the immediate.[23]

Back in Washington, Acheson thanked Wells for his excellent work at the relief conference.[24]

After spending the entire fall semester shuttling back and forth to Washington, Wells tendered his resignation as special advisor on liberated areas in early January 1944. His original assignment for perhaps three or four months had stretched into nearly six, and his State Department office was organized and relatively stable. An additional reason for leaving was impending modifications in army procurement procedures that would entail changes in the office. But the real motive was to end the "bone-tiring" shuttle schedule and take care of business back in Bloomington. "We have the second largest Army training program in the country in full operation," Wells wrote to Acheson, "and the University is giving more instruction this year than any other year in its history." He also cited Briscoe's absence from campus. As it happened, Wells's tenure at the State Department did not include any work in the field. Ending his resignation letter on a upbeat note, he offered his services again, saying he "would be happy to undertake a mission of a few months abroad if by so doing I could serve the Department and the war effort" once he got IU affairs in good order.[25]

It took a month for Acheson to reply. Meanwhile, the State Department underwent yet another major reorganization because of the fluid wartime environment. Assistant Secretary Acheson was put in charge of the Office of Wartime Economic Affairs, with Wells penciled in as chief of the Liberated Areas Division.[26] In early February, Acheson informed him that the Secretary of State would be writing to thank him officially for his service. But he wanted to add a personal note. He admitted he was uncomfortable when Wells praised him in a public speech earlier, but that he would "treasure" his words nonetheless. He continued,

> All through the Department there is a really sincere regret that you have gone back to your work at the University. I shall miss you perhaps more than anyone else, not only because you went ahead doing things and took the load off of me, but because you combined with a first-rate ability a first-rate sense of humor. That combination is the rarest there is.[27]

Wells's tired bones soon recovered, but the glow of national service remained with him. His personal aspiration to know and be known was expanding to global dimensions.

NATIONAL ASSOCIATION OF STATE UNIVERSITIES

The National Association of State Universities (NASU), an organization composed of state university presidents, counted Wells among its members soon after he was selected for the IU post. "The most clubbish of the major institutional associations," they had lively annual meetings and a tradition of open discussion, allowing the assembled presidents to exchange ideas confidentially with their institutional peers.[28] The war made the organization even more important as a conduit for information as well as an important consulting body to the federal government. But the war also disrupted NASU's internal routines.

In July 1943, Wells was unexpectedly thrust into leading NASU as acting president.[29] This largely ceremonial post had one major requirement: giving a speech at their annual meeting. Adding one more thing to his already heavy load, he attempted to use the occasion to learn more about the history of higher education and reflect on possible future directions. During the summer and early fall, Wells had his IU staff gather all of the NASU presidential addresses, reports, and papers given from 1917 to 1942, as well as similar materials from the other two national associations for higher education, the Association of American Colleges (AAC) and the Association of Land-Grant Colleges (ALGC). Wells plowed through this mountain of documents – twenty-five years' worth – to analyze trends in the content, and spent hours drafting his presidential address.

On October 22, 1943, Wells delivered his speech to the National Association of State Universities. He offered his remarks in the spirit of constructive "self-examination and self-appraisal." He noted that some informal discussion recently compared NASU unfavorably with other national associations, citing the description of the organization presented five years ago by a former NASU president as "a pleasant club offering a congenial place from which to point with pride and to view with alarm." Rather than start with his own point of view, Wells offered the results of his empirical study.

The proceedings of NASU, in Wells's analysis, had been overwhelmingly concerned with the need for increased resources and financial matters, with a puzzling lack of discussion of the role of the state university in a democracy. The main issue under discussion by the Association of American Colleges was the position and responsibility of the college in American life, and the purposes of a liberal education. The Association of Land-Grant Colleges and Universities, devoted primarily to progress in agriculture, engineering, and home economics, had longstanding discussions about the development of graduate research programs and the place of military training in the curriculum.

Wells observed that "there are some strange omissions" in the historical preoccupations of the three organizations, namely in the areas of students and their problems, adult education, and alumni relations. Wells also noted that NASU's budget and operations had remained virtually unchanged over the twenty-five-year period, whereas both the AAC and ALGCU had increased their operating budgets and hired full-time professional staff to support greater activity on the part of committees and members.

Assuming widespread agreement with his claim that "the outstanding feature of the history of higher education during this period has been the emergence of the state university as a dominant educational force," Wells argued for a more active role for NASU in the formation of national educational goals and policies in the coming era of greater federal involvement. He concluded with a call to mobilize the resources of the National Association of State Universities to overcome difficulties ahead and take advantage of "exceptional opportunities."[30]

Institutional inertia hindered efforts to create a comprehensive association representing education after the war, however. The American educational landscape proved too varied and the politics too local – even in the face of increased federal aid to higher education. Not until 1963 did the state-supported institutions embrace their similarities and merge into the National Association of State Universities and Land-Grant Colleges (NASULGC).[31]

PROFESSIONALIZING FUNDRAISING

The prewar gift of Bradford Woods to the university made Wells cognizant of the lack of institutional machinery in the Indiana University Foundation to handle gifts such as these. But with the advent of war mobilization and other pressing concerns, the president let the matter drop. In August 1943, alumni secretary Dixie Heighway sent Wells a forty-page report on how other universities managed alumni funds and a proposal to mount a postwar scholarship fund coordinated by the IU Foundation. Heighway had surveyed nearly one hundred universities and made personal visits to a dozen schools to gather further information. His report began with the history of organized alumni giving, starting with 1890, when the Yale Alumni Fund was established. Harvard, Amherst, Cornell, and Dartmouth soon followed suit, and by 1919, about fifteen alumni funds were in operation. World War I brought financial problems to higher education, and many schools started fund drives in the aftermath, including Indiana University. The Memorial Fund drive at IU concluded in 1926, and raised $1.6 million dollars for new facilities. Heighway noted that Clarence Cook Little, president of the University of Michigan, was critical of such "intensive" campaigns: "we have come to the recognition of the third type of support – steady giving, non-emotional, rational – that is permanent and relatively inexpensive [and is] the one sound, sane type of support, whether it be financial or spiritual, moral, intellectual. Any of the types of support that an alumnus can give is best given on the basis of steady donations."[32]

Heighway went on to note organized giving at other universities. He mentioned, for example, the "Cornellian Council," which started a bequest program in 1924, under the slogan "Cornell – Better Still by Your Will," which was influenced by law school alumni. At Wisconsin, the Alumni Foundation was started to supplement state appropriations; its research arm held the Steenbock patent for a vitamin D discovery. Among state universities, Michigan was probably most successful, with its Michigan Alumni Ten Year Program, begun in 1929. From his survey of other universities Heighway concluded that annual giving was the most successful technique for fundraising and that the alumni network should be closely involved.

He finished his report with a plan for a Post-War Scholarship Fund to raise money for students and increase faculty salaries at Indiana University. The campaign would be directed toward alumni and former students, who numbered about 60,000. A tentative budget included salary for a Director of Fund Raising and direct mail costs.

The IU Foundation board, including President Wells, approved Heighway's plan, and proceeded to hire Lawrence Wheeler as executive director in early 1944. The foundation thus acquired its first professional fundraiser. Wheeler was a 1921 IU alumnus, and had served as a Union Board director as a student.[33] He had a career as a publicist and financial campaigner for various church and civic groups, and was employed by the fundraising firm of Ketchum, Inc., in Pittsburgh prior to his return to Indiana. He was a friend of Ross Bartley, head of the IU News Bureau in the Wells administration.[34]

Friendly and genial, with deep loyalty to the university, Wheeler lost no time in getting to work. He began to give speeches about the university and its needs to alumni, fraternal organizations, and business groups around the state. By April, he drafted a letter for Wells's signature to be sent to all alumni, telling them that the University would have significant postwar needs.[35] In December 1944 he presented a proposal to the board of directors for annual giving program. Wheeler described two categories of gifts: those designated by the donor for specific purposes and those for the "general welfare of the University." Special attempts would be made to organize alumni in New York, Chicago, Boston, Washington, and Detroit. In the state of Indiana, counties with a high proportion of alumni would be targeted as well. Newsletters to all alumni would be used to announce the campaigns.[36]

A solicitation letter was sent to all IU alumni in April 1945, marking the first general appeal since the Memorial Fund drive. The appeals continued after the war finally ended in August 1945, and the IU Foundation reported a total of $159,635 in gifts received by December.[37] Wells was glad to have some competent assistance to help in the increasingly important area of financial development.

AMERICAN COUNCIL ON EDUCATION

Wells's natural gregariousness and the hothouse atmosphere of Washington threw him into contact with the American Council on Education (ACE), the all-inclusive national association for higher education institutions, which was headquartered in Washington. Colleges and universities, like other sectors of American society, were intensively mobilized for the war, and groups such as ACE played an increasingly important role in coordinating with the proliferation of wartime federal agencies. Wells, interested in cooperative work among institutions, was tapped to be a member of the council's new Committee on the Relationships of Higher Education to the Federal Government in 1943. Adding another item to his Washington portfolio, Wells made the committee's work a high priority, and visited federal departments and attended Congressional hearings. Luckily for Wells, his workspace at the ACE headquarters was located within a block of his State Department office.

The committee often dealt with proposed legislation that would affect the shape of higher education, such as manpower policies for scientific and specialized personnel, campus housing for wartime trainees, and the indirect-cost reimbursement by the federal government for university services. Because of the important nature of these issues, George F. Zook, the ACE executive officer, often attended committee meetings, so he and Wells got to know each other well.

Given the international situation, their conversation turned often to the role that education was to play in the postwar world. Zook, having held his position since 1934, had experience dealing with Committee on Intellectual Cooperation, an international body established by the League of Nations following World War I, and had a low opinion of their efforts. As plans gradually took shape for an international conference to devise a more effective successor to the League of Nations, Zook was determined that practical issues would be addressed in the arena of international education. Wells, who was becoming a committed internationalist, learned much from this energetic politician that accorded with his own developing ideas about how universities could help their international counterparts as a way of strengthening themselves.

In 1944, Wells was elected chairman of the American Council on Education for the fiscal year 1944–45, no doubt aided by his friendship with Zook. Modestly assuming that the recognition was in part because he happened to be located in Washington, he nevertheless felt "surprised and gratified" by the top honor.[38] This positioned him, as a representative of the ACE, to attend the historic United Nations Conference on International Organization. The ACE was one of some forty-odd voluntary associations whose official observers advised the U.S. delegation.

Meanwhile, back on the IU campus, President Emeritus Bryan, now eighty-four years old, was enlisting the support of a key alumnus, James S. Adams, president of Standard Brands in New York. Adams, who first enrolled at IU in 1917, was a student caption of the Memorial Fund drive and worked closely with Bryan.[39] In a frank exchange of views in December 1944, Bryan responded to criticism "from those who fear that a banker and economist will lead the University away from cultural ideals to bread studies." Noting that Wells was strongly supporting the professional schools that the Bryan administration established, but that his heart was set on developing an art center to provide "first rate opportunities for the children of Indiana to go as far as they can and will into the life of the artist." To that end, Wells was advancing music, painting, and sculpture with the aid of new faculty and facilities, such as the new auditorium. "I wish to have you know how very heartily I believe in him," Bryan said, adding, "a president needs all sorts of support," ranging from sharp criticism, loyal followers, and individuals who will watch his back.[40]

The foundation for what became the United Nations was a two-month meeting held in San Francisco from late April to late June 1945. A total of fifty Allied nations participated in the creation of a treaty that would supersede older ones and provide a rationale, expressed in the UN Charter, to ensure world peace. Several agencies, such as the United Nations Educational, Scientific, and Cultural Organization (UNESCO), were inaugurated to devise programs and practical procedures for this unprecedented cooperative effort. After the countries in attendance signed the treaty in June, it took effect when the five permanent members of the Security Council (China, France, Russia, the United Kingdom, and the United States) ratified it in October.[41]

Wells attended the conference for the first month, and Zook the second. Wells became friends with William G. Carr, the research director and associate secretary for the National Education Association (NEA), which represented teachers. Despite the fact that Zook and the head of the NEA, Willard Givens (who happened to be an IU alumnus), did not get along, Wells remembered that he and Carr "maintained close working relationships" as they shared a room in the Sir Francis Drake Hotel.[42] Writing home on the second day of the conference, he noted that the observers "are being shown every consideration," including seats immediately behind the official delegation in the newly constructed civic opera house. "The weeks spent in San Francisco were lively and stimulating," Wells said. "[T]here were many meetings to attend, presentations to be made, and personages to be cultivated." In addition to making many new friends, he was not immune to the charms of the Bay Area, including its flowers, seascape, and cosmopolitan life.[43] On May 8, as Victory in Europe Day was announced, Wells took to the streets in San Francisco as millions all across the country celebrated. Soon he would return home, to the campus he loved, pondering how best to help create a new, postwar world for Indiana University.

Now for the first of these: renunciation of color, class, and race prejudice – where? In England? In China or in Palestine? No; we must renounce prejudice of color, class, and race in Bloomington, Monroe County, Indiana. Our renunciation must be personally implemented by deeds. Our actions will the measure of the sincerity of our words.

Herman B Wells, 1944

NINE

Renouncing Prejudice

IN THE EARLY 1940S, as Wells assembled "the broadest war program of any institution in the Nation," with various specialized training programs for nearly all branches of the military, he confronted the sinister legacy of the university's institutional racism against the small minority of African American students. In 1942, a master's student in sociology, Tilman C. Cothran, made a statistical survey of "The Attitude of Negro Students Toward Indiana University." His primary hypothesis was that attitudes of Negro students were related to their degree of involvement with campus activities. Sending a detailed questionnaire to all seventy-nine African American students, he was able to get sixty-three usable responses. He found, "in general, Negro students possess rather unfavorable attitudes toward the University," and "as Negro students advance scholastically, the more unfavorable toward the University they become." Black students were found to be participating in almost all campus organizations and activities, with the exception of ROTC and Concert Choir, although their level of participation was low. The data supported his hypothesis: people with high participation scores had more favorable attitudes.[1]

Cothran empirically verified common wisdom among African American students, alumni, and associates. Students of color had long found a chilly climate on campus. As they progressed from freshman to seniors, their experience of unacknowledged institutional racism led to increased frustration and the effort to band together to generate an alternate social world. Those few black students who had the motivation and drive to participate in white-dominated campus activities had more favorable attitudes, perhaps not surprisingly.

Despite this bleak situation, there were some small, hopeful signs of change. The Inter-Racial Commission had succeeded in organizing a regular program of black guest lecturers. In January 1942, as Cothran was completing his thesis, noted contralto Marian Anderson was invited to perform at the IU Auditorium. Her invitation signaled a new attitude among the IU administration. Quietly, Wells facilitated the appearance. He responded favorably to a request to attend a post-concert reception hosted by black sorority Alpha Kappa Alpha, and threw a small dinner party for Anderson at his Woodburn House home.[2]

Anderson, whose melodic voice was powered by a courageous heart, was no stranger to racial politics. In 1939, she endured with dignity a rescinded invitation to perform at the Grand Hall of the Daughters of the American Revolution in Washington, D.C., when the organizers discovered she was African American. Having a keen sense of public relations, President Roosevelt and his wife Eleanor capitalized on the outrage and made the Lincoln Memorial available for a free public concert. Thousands of people gathered on April 9 – Easter Sunday – to hear her sing on the steps of the famous monument, making her a household name overnight. To underscore his commitment to civil rights, Roosevelt also invited Anderson to the White House, along with the king and queen of England, for a private meeting.[3] Wells knew this history, and he felt that public tolerance could be safely stretched by her appearance at the university. By all accounts, her performance was a rousing artistic and political success.

INTER-RACIAL COMMISSION PETITION

Shortly after Marian Anderson's IU performance, Wells was presented with a petition authored by the Inter-Racial Commission to redress racial discrimination and segregation. The list was extensive. At the Indiana Memorial Union, many privileges were denied to black students, including no admittance to public dances, no service at the Grill, discontinuance of meal tickets in the Commons, and no use of lounges. African American students were not admitted to the University Band, and were barred from baseball, basketball, and swim teams. The use of the swimming pool, whether for physical education classes or recreation, was segregated by race as well as gender. Students of color faced inadequate housing options, discrimination in sites of practice teaching, prejudice among fellow students, and insensitivity from some instructors. The list of grievances closed with a quotation of President Roosevelt: "World events are moving at an almost incredibly rapid pace; it is vital that we keep up with this pace and achieve national unity immediately."[4] Wartime mobilization had disturbed the status quo, giving rise to hope that progress could be made in civil rights.

The communication from the Inter-Racial Commission galvanized Wells into action. Enclosing a copy of the resolution, he sent memos to each of the administrators in charge of organizations or activities that were complained about: Ward Biddle, IMU director; Zora Clevenger, athletics director; Raymond Shoemaker, dean of students; and Lester Smith, dean of education.[5] In the meantime, Wells paid a visit to James Patrick, IMU manager, to look over the situation in the Commons on a deserted afternoon. Certain tables were marked with reserved signs, which was an open code for the African American seating area. "Pat," Wells said, "I want you to remove all those signs. Do it unobtrusively and make no mention of what you've done." A couple of weeks passed before anyone noticed the signs were gone, "and then, of course, the absurdity of the previous situation was apparent," Wells noted matter-of-factly.[6]

Athletics Director Clevenger replied quickly, stating that there were no conference or local rules prohibiting "colored boys" from competing on teams. Swimming, he said, would be permitted under the "Physical Fitness Program as you and I discussed it," so boys would go in when their classes met, the same as other students.[7] What was not mentioned were the unwritten customs that were preventing full participation by students of color.

But recreational swimming remained segregated. To integrate recreational swimming in the Men's Pool, Wells took a novel approach. Realizing that African American football players were welcomed on the IU squad, unlike some other sports, he asked Clevenger who was the most popular black athlete. The athletic director told him he was Chestine "Rooster" Coffee, a well-known football player. Wells instructed Clevenger, "Some afternoon when the pool is quite full, go down on the floor [of the gymnasium], find Rooster, and tell him to strip in the locker room and go jump in the pool." Expressing skepticism, the athletic director asked, "Do you mean it?" to which Wells replied, "Yes, and don't tell anybody, even Rooster, what you're going to do in advance." Clevenger carried out the plan, and Rooster cheerfully complied and swam freely. "He was so cordially greeted," Wells recalled, "I doubt that anyone realized a policy had been changed."[8]

A characteristic pattern was beginning to develop. Wells looked for unobtrusive, inventive ways to combat discrimination, held in place either by policy or custom, which would not lead to confrontation and eventual loss of face for somebody. He was learning to use the persuasive power of his office to redirect institutional practices toward egalitarianism, fair treatment, and compassion for all. Also concerned with keeping lines of communication open, Wells wrote the petition organizers of the Inter-Racial Commission that he would be glad to see them once he had the information from University officials assembled.

A new student group, the Negro Student Council, took another volley in the war against prejudice and discrimination and sought official University recognition. Organizers wanted to create a "bridge" between black students and the administration so that "problems relevant to our group may be attacked intelligently and cooperatively." A Negro Student Mass Meeting was held at the Student Building on April 12, 1942; two thirds of the African American student body endorsed the purposes of the new group. Walter C. Bailey was elected president, and he wrote Wells a lengthy letter outlining the council's goals, "aimed primarily at the reduction of interracial conflicts, frictions, and misunderstandings in this university situation." Bailey continued,

> We realize that you, Mr. President, and other members of the present administration are sincerely interested in the welfare of all campus minority groups including our own. We further realize that you are fighting a "two front battle," so to speak, in that you are attacked on the one hand by the reactionary forces of your own group and on the other by members of the Negro group for not doing enough. The fundamental purpose of this organization, therefore, is one of closer, more intelligent cooperation with the administration and the progressive elimination of racial frictions which program we sincerely believe will prove to be ultimately advantageous to every one concerned.[9]

There was an emerging group consciousness among black students, and with it a newfound sense of responsibility for and pride in their collective behavior. The possibility of real change was in the air.

Wells conferred with his staff, in particular Dean of Women Mueller and Dean of Men Edmondson, and informed the trustees of the new group. A couple of weeks later, Edmondson, writing as chairman of the Student Affairs Committee, informed the Negro Student Council that they had gained official recognition and were eligible for campus privileges.[10]

About the same time, Wells got news of another incident of racial discrimination. Four African Americans from Indianapolis, including Charles Stewart, a science teacher at Crispus Attucks High School in Indianapolis and an IU alumnus, were refused service at the Men's Grill in the IMU. Stewart was surprised, because he had been served there previously. Presenting this case to Wells, Stewart urged, "I have been told that you are an exponent of justice and fair play, and I know that, because of your position, you can do much to alleviate these conditions at the University. Just a hint from you could do much."[11] Wells apologized: "I regret very much the incident to which you refer. As you no doubt know, I have constantly endeavored to eliminate all discriminatory practices at the University, and much has been accomplished in that direction during the past few years."[12] Despite some modest successes, there would be much work ahead.

For example, housing continued to be a vexed issue. The university had provided on-campus housing only since the 1920s, first with the construction of the Men's Residence Center (MRC) at Woodlawn and Tenth, and then the erection of a women's dormitory, Memorial Hall, on Third Street. (Their respective location at opposite borders of campus was no coincidence.) But most students – including black students – lived either in Greek houses or off campus in private residences. Wells called for some data on the subject, and a memo on "Negro Housing, 1941–42" was produced. It listed only fifty African American students living in university housing the first semester, thirty-six the second, and twenty-four the third (the university was on a three-semester schedule during wartime).[13] But the significance of the problem went beyond the small number of affected students.

Living arrangements for African American women students presented a compound problem. Campus dormitories for women had special rules and regulations to protect the virtue of female students. The trustees were willing to try to desegregate male dormitories, but they drew the line at extending integration efforts to female dormitories. The solution was to create a special residence. So all first-year black women had to live at the Elms residence hall, located on Forest Place, the future site of Ballantine Hall. Perhaps not surprisingly, it became "the social center for all negro women, and Director of Residence Halls Alice Nelson thought the students were pleased because it 'was just like having their own little Union Building.'"[14]

After two years of this policy, African American women students began to be admitted into the regular dormitory system. Administrators tried to place members of the same race in the same room, but occasionally they did not have information about the race of students and placed whites and blacks together. According to Nelson, this sometimes would cause "a little problem with poppa and momma because their daughter's got a 'sunburned' roommate." The converse could also be true: "We also get it the other way around too. We've had some 'sunburned' ones that were very much upset because they had a white roommate." But overall, students in the white majority failed to view race or culture as a problem in the residence halls because it affected so few of their number.[15]

A STRATEGIC VISION OF TOLERANCE

With the Inter-Racial Commission and the Negro Student Council respectfully agitating for the IU administration to do the right thing and eliminate campus racial discrimination, Wells was put on notice that they would hold him accountable. The students and Wells were in agreement about the ultimate goal – the end of segregated facilities and activities and an increase in racial tolerance. But they sometimes favored different methods of effecting change. Wells preferred not to confront directly the powerful forces that reinforced the racial status quo, but quietly to sabotage the unthinking assumptions that supported them. Mindful of his position and the power it gave, he practiced what might be described a sociocultural martial art that used the weight of his opponent against him. It depended completely on exacting precision and exquisite timing.

After Marian Anderson thrilled campus audiences, plans were made to invite her back. She was scheduled to sing in the same venue almost exactly a year later, in February 1943. For this appearance, Wells instructed Ross Bartley, head of the IU News Bureau, to send complimentary tickets to music critic Walter Whitworth. Whitworth wrote a glowing review in the *Indianapolis News,* the state's largest-circulation newspaper.[16] The *Arbutus* yearbook enthused, "Marian Anderson, beloved American Negro contralto, recaptured the musical favor she won the previous Series Season with her selection of classical, semiclassical songs and a satisfactory number of Southern spirituals."[17] The university, by inviting black artists for public performances, modeled racial tolerance and ethical behavior to its students. By garnering favorable publicity, that message could be taken to the whole state.

But examples of passive racial discrimination on campus abounded. For instance, the highly visible Convocation Program had never had an African American speaker. The Inter-Racial Commission lobbied the University Committee on Assemblies and managed an invitation to educator and poet Leslie Pinckney Hill, president of Pennsylvania's Cheyney Training School for Teachers (now Cheyney University), the oldest African American institution of higher education in the nation. When questions about his accommodations arose, Wells stated that he should be shown the same hospitality as other Convocation speakers; Hill stayed at the Union Building. On March 26, 1942, Wells joined Hill on the podium and introduced him. Speaking on the subject of "Individual Responsibility," Hill spoke of his belief in universal brotherhood – "the human family is one" – a vision that minimized racial differences "in celebration of transcendent commonalities."[18] Hill had several other speaking engagements on campus, including appearances at Alumni Hall and at the Wesley Foundation of the Methodist Church, where four hundred students were in attendance.[19]

ANTI-DISCRIMINATION STRUGGLE CONTINUED

When Wells returned to campus in spring 1944 after his State Department service, he turned his attention again to student empowerment and removing barriers to African Americans. Student self-government was a perennial issue, made more germane by the growth in the student body over the past several years. Sporadic agitation had been seen since 1938, as different groups of students schemed to overcome perennial student apathy. The president was on record in support of student self-rule, "when the students prove they really want it." In January 1944, Wells, encouraged by a new attempt by students to frame a constitution, stated, "I have long favored student self government and I shall be glad to do anything in my power to aid in the movement."[20] During the war, regular (civilian) enrollment was significantly down, as armed forces training programs were burgeoning. African American enrollment also dropped. In 1943–44, only 75 African American students were enrolled, down from a high of 110 in 1940–41.

On March 5, 1944, Wells took the unusual step of speaking out publicly on civil rights. The venue was "Layman Sunday" at the First Methodist Church, where he first attended as an undergraduate student. The previous year, the church was the site of the keynote address of Negro History Week, sponsoring Edward B. Jourdain, Jr., a prominent African American lawyer from Chicago, who spoke on "The Gifts of Dark America."[21]

President Wells's address, titled "The Church at Its Best," was a remarkably vigorous exhortation on the theme of "the brotherhood of man." His sermon began with a lengthy quotation from Corinthians in which St. Paul makes the analogy between the physical body and the body of Christ: although the body has many members, they are all one body: "And whether one member suffer, all the members suffer with it; or one member be honoured, all the members rejoice with it. Now ye are the body of Christ, and members in particular."[22] He underlined the most important message contained in the scripture above, "namely, the common fatherhood of God with the consequent universal brotherhood of man." He challenged the congregation to think about "the important work of shaping our lives and society in such a way that the Brotherhood of Man may be a reality here and now."

Wells proceeded to offer some direction on how to achieve the brotherhood of man, introducing a recent statement by ninety-three nationally prominent Protestant church leaders, published as the pamphlet

"What We Are Fighting For," who included the following among their admonitions:

> We must prepare to renounce prejudice of color, class, and race, both within our own nation and toward other nations.
>
> We must make ready to assume our responsibility as a nation for the ordered life of a community of nations. National pride and self-sufficiency must no longer be allowed to triumph over our Christian belief in such a world community.

Using a forceful rhetorical style, Wells brought home the import of these lofty aims, challenging his listeners to reject prejudice where they lived – in the local community. As important it was to change people's minds, he told his listeners, it was not enough if they failed to change their discriminatory behavior.

Class conflict, Wells believed, could be eliminated quickly with the application of "Christian brotherhood" among both employers and employees. The bigger obstacle was color and racial prejudice. To his mind, "securing fair treatment for our Negro citizens" would be the chief problem in postwar American society. Wells put the blame squarely on white citizens:

> I would not deny that we have made progress in the past; but none, I suppose, will deny that our progress has been painfully slow. There are those who blame the Negroes for this snail-like pace. And the Negroes are not blameless. But our responsibility for failure dwarfs theirs. We, the white race, are overwhelmingly dominant both as to number and economic position. Let us not forget that the Christian religion imposes an *extra* obligation on the strong for the welfare and protection of the weak. We cannot escape principal responsibility for the racial intolerance, discrimination, and exploitation which blights our society.

Advocating civil rights for Americans of every color was a major move toward the ideal of universal brotherhood. After the clash of nations in war and his first immersion into different cultures a few years before, Wells had become convinced that increased international cooperation would be a necessity in the postwar world. His views were similar to those of IU graduate Wendell Willkie, Roosevelt's Republican opponent in the 1940 election, who was a prominent anti-racism activist and internationalist. Willkie, in response to Detroit's race riots in June 1943, drew an analogy between racism and Fascism: "The desire to deprive some of our citizens of their rights – economic, civic or political – has the same basic motivation as actuates the Fascist mind when it seeks to dominate whole peoples and nations. It is essential that we eliminate it at home as well as abroad."[23] In his 1943 bestseller on the international situation, *One World*, Willkie reflected on his world travels and emphasized what unites the human race, not what divides it. "Freedom is an indivisible word," Willkie said, and to enjoy it, it must be extended to all.

In his lay sermon, Wells scolded isolationist sentiments, using the trope of the shrinking world caused by revolutions in transportation and communication. Now the globe had become a single, interdependent community, necessitating "world Christian brotherhood." Following the prevalent assumption that the war would be won by Allied forces, making the United States "the most important temporal power," Wells wondered whether the nation's "spiritual resources" would measure up. The war scattered American forces all over the world, Wells noted, and they observed "instances of meanness, avarice, and unpleasant conduct" in other peoples, and, regrettably, others found the same qualities in American soldiers.

> Yet, all peoples, regardless of their color, creed, or stage of economic progress, have some who exemplify the noblest qualities of mankind. In a world grown small, lasting peace is possible only when all peoples are willing to look for the good in the other races, and to regard each other in a spirit of toleration and mutual esteem. Let us keep that truth ever before us.

After quoting from John Donne's "Meditation 17," from which came the title of Ernest Hemingway's *For Whom the Bell Tolls*, Wells closed with the following:

> Once our enemies have been defeated and threat of these barriers removed, there must be positive action to take advantage of the opportunity which is then ours. Each of us personally must assume his share. Unless we do, we repudiate our stated war aims and cause a reflection upon their very sincerity. Our victory can have little meaning or significance unless we proclaim our belief in the brotherhood of all men, men of all races, classes, and nations, and personally practice our belief by extending the cordial hand of fellowship to all men.

In so doing, the church can be at its best, Wells argued, ending his sermon with another verse from I Corinthians.[24]

Wells, in the midst of war, was searching for spiritual renewal, and preaching for the cause of civil rights and social justice. In Bloomington and on the IU campus, as well as nationally, organized religion took a leading role in the civil rights movement – and churches, both black and white, were heavily involved. After working behind the scenes for change, Wells went public with this expression of his ecumenical faith in human dignity, much to the approbation of his local fellow workers in the struggle.

By 1945, as the war wound down, the problem of race relations and civil rights garnered public attention. The United State military, whose new policies called for integrated forces, was an unlikely partner in de-segregation.[25] Certain African American units, such the famous Tuske-gee Airmen, met with public celebration for their bravery in combat. The Serviceman's Readjustment Act, known as the GI Bill, promised to swell the student ranks, but the estimates varied widely, and blacks faced pressures that their white counterparts did not.[26]

In February 1945, the Bloomington chapter of the National Asso-ciation for the Advancement of Colored People (NAACP) was formed in response to a black female student's having been put off a local bus the month before. When Wells heard about the new organization, he directed his staff to do some research on nationally prominent people associated with the organization.[27] Responding to rumors in March 1945, Wells stated, "There is no 'negro problem' at Indiana University except in the minds of a few local bigots. They are responsible for the story that the institution is being overrun with negro students and what not." He backed up his contention by citing enrollment statistics to show the tiny minority of African American students at IU.[28] Wells was understand-ably upset that dormitory space precluded the enrollment of 900 quali-fied women, white and black, who would not be able to attend IU in the fall. Stung by criticism from black leaders in Indianapolis, he asserted, "Neither the state nor the university has or can assume total responsi-bility for the housing of students," adding "I am always interested in anything I can do to further the welfare of the Negro students who come to Indiana University."[29]

POSTWAR DEVELOPMENTS

After the war, the fight against discrimination escalated on the Blooming-ton campus, and progressive individuals – from both town and gown –

joined forces. A longstanding social compact prevented black males from getting a haircut or a shave at any local barbershop, notwithstanding a fair number of African American barbers who worked in Bloomington. The excluded customers were forced to visit black barbers after hours and on weekends, sometimes in the barber's home, in order to get haircuts. In late May 1947, a Race Relations Institute was held on campus, and plans were made to send delegations of white and colored students to various businesses in Bloomington that practiced racial discrimination. One was the popular barbershop in the Indiana Memorial Union. When the students asked for service, the barbers refused to cut the hair of, or shave, the African American students. In the resulting turmoil, the IMU barbershop was closed while Wells consulted with its management about serving the needs of all customers.

Wells got his hair cut regularly by the manager of the IMU barbershop, Edgar Correll, who was also the secretary of the local barbers' union. But a big problem remained: apparently no white barber would cut black hair. So the idea was floated to staff the entire barbershop with black barbers. The shop remained closed for most of the summer, much to the consternation of the campus community. Correll finally located a white barber who was willing to cut the hair of blacks. The new employee was John Plew, a Caucasian born in Greene County and a member of the Christadelphian faith. In his mid-twenties, Plew was a conscientious objector during World War II. After the shop reopened, business was good. Since the other Bloomington barbershops continued to not serve African Americans, the IMU shop attracted the patronage of many non-student blacks.[30]

In spring 1947, black student George Taliaferro, a football star, was doing his student teaching at the University School, located on the IU campus. For his one-hour lunch break, he had the habit of running back to his boarding house, eating, and running back to class. One noon hour he decided to pay a visit to President Wells, whom he had met just once before at a social event. Wells, whose door was always open, heard Taliaferro in the reception area and boomed, "Come in, George." The student explained his problem: he had the money to eat lunch in the restaurants contiguous to campus, but he was barred on account of his color. Wells said, "Well, we'll see about that." And then he proceeded to

call the manager of the Gables, who assured him that he was not preju-
diced but feared a drop in business were he to allow blacks to patronize
his restaurant. After more talking, the manager agreed to an experiment: Taliaferro and a date would be welcome for one week to see how
it would go. There was no negative reaction to the presence of the two
African American students. The following week, Taliaferro was invited
to ask another black student couple. Again there was no negative reaction. After that, the Gables was desegregated.[31] But other Bloomington
restaurants resisted opening their doors to African American customers
until 1950, when Wells brokered a behind-the-scenes deal with the owners, threatening to expand campus dining facilities if the restaurants did
not drop their restrictions.

As Taliaferro was integrating the Gables, Wells and the basketball
coach, Branch McCracken, were laying plans to recruit Bill Garrett, a
star African American basketball player. Garrett came to IU as a freshman in 1947, and became the first black starter in Big Ten basketball.[32]

With full consciousness of the fact that what makes a university great is its faculty, President Wells, soon after he took office, began a program as he stated it, "to bring to Indiana the best possible men and give them the means and the freedom to do their work." . . . This policy meant not only appointing scholars whose reputation was well established but also younger men who showed promise of future eminence. As a result, Indiana now boasts a staff which can compare favorably with any in the country. There exists among them an atmosphere of intellectual ferment; men are doing important things, adding to knowledge, with the confidence that they will be encouraged, protected, and forwarded. Recently several of the mature scholars who have been appointed told me that it was this milieu of dynamic optimism which induced them to come here rather than any consideration of salary. . . . Not an artist or a natural scientist himself, by sheer power of sympathetic imagination he has, innumerable times, anticipated the needs of specialists in the pursuit of his goal of making the University great.

Lander MacClintock, 1962

TEN

Postwar World, Home and Abroad

SOBERED BY ALL THE NEWS OF DESTRUCTION and human suffering in the last phases of World War II, Wells looked forward eagerly to peacetime. It was abundantly clear that it would not mark a return to the prewar Indiana University. That was gone forever. Although the shape of postwar IU was still hazy and indistinct, the now veteran president, tempered by the management challenges of running a university during wartime as well as his international travel and national service, knew that it would be bigger, focused on research, and responsive to the needs of the federal government in addition to maintaining its obligations to the state to educate its young people.

World War II marked a watershed in American higher education. Faculty and administrators interrupted their academic routines for defense projects, both on and off campus. They came into contact with new colleagues, shared new goals, and had new tools with which to work. Interdisciplinarity was the order of the day. With national mobilization, the federal government had become a major source of funds of research, training, and education. Massive programs of military research, such as the Manhattan Project, swallowed huge amounts of financial and human resources in centralized facilities. Other programs, like training specialized personnel for civilian agencies, were decentralized and scattered throughout the country. At the close of the war, a consensus emerged that the nation's security was dependent on a continuing supply of research, both basic and applied, and a healthy supply of technical specialists and research workers. To provide a firm base for the expansion of specialized personnel, the schools and universities would have to be strengthened.[1]

After the war, Wells found his attention being drawn to upgrading the Bloomington physical plant in response to burgeoning campus enrollment. Key sectors were under the guidance of dynamic deans and directors, and Wells delegated increasing responsibility to them for recruiting new faculty members. Of course, he was available to meet any prospective faculty, especially stars, whether in genetics or music. Wells was absorbed in the immediate, pressing details of campus construction, and he was able to act swiftly and decisively to take advantage of unexpected opportunities offered by the postwar environment. But he kept his long-range vision firmly in sight, making sure that short-term gains did not close off desirable long-term options. He pushed not only for the construction of adequate classrooms and residential housing, but also for the development of specialized facilities, whether oriented toward a specific discipline or field (such as the B&E Building) or for more general purposes (such as the auditorium).

Wells was aware of the gap between prewar and postwar university, and the different worlds inhabited by older alumni and newer faculty. How to graft the new emphasis on research onto the hallowed traditions of undergraduate education was a challenge. "This is more difficult as we grow in size, although not impossible," Wells mused. "Difficult because of the increased intellectual competitiveness which we have fostered as a necessary prerequisite to increased scholarly productivity."[2] One way to provide coherence between the old and the new was to develop the physical plant, adding new and specialized facilities, but respectfully accommodating the folkways and traditions of IU, including deference to the woodland character of its geographical setting. Expanding the campus organically in a planned and methodical way made the seams connecting the old and the new practically invisible.

Balancing the centripetal focus on building a bigger and better Bloomington campus, Wells found himself drawn inexorably to off-campus educational affairs, which meant time away from the growing campus. His wartime work in the State Department and the American Council on Education raised his profile and strengthened his connections on the national level. Education was a vital part of national security, and became a factor in the Cold War period. For his part, Wells loved working on the bigger canvas that national and international affairs provided, because he saw that it could be another, exciting way to lift the university out of its provincialism.

The GI Bill, signed into law by Roosevelt in June 1944, brought unprecedented aid to U.S. veterans and unparalleled changes to higher education. The act subsidized tuition, fees, and books for veterans attending college and also provided a stipend for living expenses. Veterans were free to attend any institution as long as they met admissions requirements.[3] At Indiana University, administrators were scrambling to meet the coming tsunami of students. The Office of Veterans Affairs boasted that IU was the first university in the country to enroll veterans under the GI Bill, thanks to quick work with an improvised form.[4]

In August 1945, IU added refresher courses in English grammar, mathematics, and reading and study methods for college students whose academic career had been disrupted by wartime service or for new students who had not planned to go to college but for the GI Bill. The program, supervised by the dean of the Junior Division, Wendell W. Wright, included instruction on an individual basis combined with intensive counseling.[5] In the meantime Wells and other administrators were bracing in other ways for the coming influx of students.

The student body had hovered around 5,000 since 1940, but projections estimated that 9,500 students would be enrolled in Fall 1946. Many of the new students would be married veterans who would need family apartments rather than dormitory rooms. Existing housing stock in Bloomington in 1945 had dwindled to about half of its 1930 level, so the university could not turn to the city for student accommodation.[6] Wells and the Board of Trustees met in a special meeting at Camp Brosius in Wisconsin to draft a long-range student housing plan. The plan was built on two propositions: the university would borrow large sums of money for construction, which would be paid back from rent collected; and buildings would be on the university's surplus land contiguous to the existing campus.[7] With a banker's foresight, Wells had quietly purchased parcels next to campus as they came on the market.

No campus administrator was more central to the effort to provide student housing than Alice M. Nelson, director of the Halls of Residence. After earning a Ph.B. in Institutional Economics at the University of Chicago in 1919, she came to IU the following year to "straighten out" Alpha Hall, one of the earliest dormitories. Apparently she did, and her success led to her 1921 appointment as director of the nascent service sector. Nelson was a formidable presence, able to hold her own in the male-dominated world of university administration. Her commitment to the welfare of the student body was total, and the housing emergency brought her skills in management and planning to full expression. Recognizing Nelson's abilities, Wells made her an integral part of the administrative team, relying on her to organize the university's move to provide living quarters for an increasing proportion of the student body.

University administrators combed the country for temporary housing. During summer 1945, Ward Biddle, in a conversation with military officials in Washington who were wondering what to do with surplus house trailers, convinced the government to turn them over to IU. Soon there was sharp competition from other colleges and universities. The unadorned trailers were moved to Bloomington, reconditioned, and repainted a light tan. They were grouped tightly into trailer parks on Jordan Field (Woodlawn and Tenth Streets) and other locations. The spartan living conditions engendered a remarkable esprit de corps among student families.[8] Various colloquial names – "Trailer Town," "Biddle's Buggies," or "the Swamp" – were attached to the three hundred units in the busy area. Students who came to town with their own trailers – about twenty in all – had a park on South Henderson where they could set up their households.[9]

As the magnitude of the coming housing problem became clearer, Wells declared that housing was the university's first priority and put Biddle in charge of procurement. Looking for "almost anything that had a roof and four walls," the trusty vice president and his staff scoured the land for "barracks, trailers, furniture, bedding, tables, and chairs."[10] These surplus buildings and furnishings soon were installed on campus. Recently released veterans found themselves again living in army barracks. "Only Michigan State University had exceeded Indiana in the acquisition of ex-military and warplant housing," noted historian Thomas Clark.[11]

Called away to serve as a member of an international team to observe the Greek elections in February 1946, Wells offered the use of his home, Woodburn House, as temporary student quarters. Three married couples shared the old house. In April, they moved out, remarking, "We were quite anxious about the date of President Wells' return. We felt sorry for the University being minus a President, but the longer he stayed, the longer we stayed."[12]

Headway was made with an estimated 184 new buildings on campus, but once the structures were in place, utilities costs skyrocketed and the small maintenance staff was overwhelmed. By summer 1946, estimates for housing needs were revised upward, to an astounding 500 percent of prewar levels.[13] Construction of a new dormitory (now Wright Quadrangle) began at the corner of Jordan Avenue and Tenth Street.

In a postwar administrative reorganization, the separate positions of dean of men and dean of women were combined into a single job, the dean of students, and Colonel Raymond L. Shoemaker, formerly military head of IU's Army Specialized Training Program, filled the role. Described as a "strong personality," he "exercised finesse" in dealing with the myriad adjustment problems caused by the housing shortage.[14]

In keeping with the university administration's emphasis on public information, Wells's assistant, Fenwick T. Reed, reported to the local Rotary and Kiwanis clubs that seventy buildings were under construction at once and the border of campus would be pushed a half a mile eastward.[15] Unexpected kudos came from an article in the *St. Paul Pioneer Press*, written by IU alumnus Howard Kahn. Lauding IU's response to the housing demand, he suggested that University of Minnesota administrators visit Bloomington. He wrote,

> Indiana University has shocked a lot of public officials by building its trailer village and temporary dormitories on the loveliest sections of its fine campus. . . . Most schools and cities have sacrificed the rights of former G.I.'s on the altar of aesthetics. . . . The policy at Indiana has been revolutionary. It can be stated in these words: "provide a place for veterans to live. Even if the housing consists of unbeautiful trailers, dormitories and barracks, put them into attractive surroundings and beautify them as much as possible."[16]

But the optimism was short lived. President Wells toured construction sites almost daily, talking with contractors, workmen, and university personnel. "He climbed through partially constructed buildings, inquired about schedules, and prayed for good weather, good labor relations, and speed," according to reports.[17] By September 1946, less than three weeks before the start of the fall term, it was clear that the university could not open as scheduled.

After a three-week delay, the university opened the fall semester with over 10,000 students, double the previous year's number. Construction continued at a frenetic pace, with military surplus buildings still coming to campus for conversion to student housing. With literally dozens of new buildings, the campus doubled in area, spreading in a northeasterly direction from Dunn's Woods and the Old Crescent buildings.[18] The variety of living accommodations was staggering. Not only were trailers and army barracks used, but the Canyon Inn at McCormick's Creek State Park, the Student Building, and the Indiana Memorial Union also provided temporary quarters. Perhaps the most dramatic example was the housing of twelve men in Bryan Hall in the board of trustees' meeting room, next to Wells's office. The students were greeted daily by the president as they waited for assignment to another residence center still under construction.[19]

The housing crisis eased after 1947, but enrollment patterns added about 1,000 students a year, so ongoing plans were made to provide residential services. Because of lack of housing stock in Bloomington and the town's relative isolation, combined with Wells's desire to enroll as many students as possible, IU embarked on a comprehensive student housing program during the 1950s, eventually providing "a greater proportion of its student housing than did almost any other major American university with comparable aspirations and objectives."[20]

Wells had kept an eye on the historic Wylie House, home of the first IU president and located on Second and Lincoln Streets near the original campus, with his self-professed interest "in anything that was a living reminder of the antiquity of the University."[21] Professor Amos Hershey, a political scientist, and his wife, Lillian, lived there after they bought the house from the Wylie heirs in 1915. As an assistant professor, Wells had attended dinner parties there. After Hershey died in 1933, his widow opened "Treasure House," an antiques business, in the home. A year or two after the war, Wells used the opportunity of a visit by Governor Ralph Gates to put into motion another ingenious plan. On a tour around campus and the city, Wells and Gates drove by the Wylie House. The governor was suitably impressed and urged Wells to include it on the university's 1947 budget request. The purchase went through, and Mrs. Hershey lived there until her death in 1951, after which it began housing the new Indiana University Press.[22]

President Wells met the challenges of creating a small metropolitan community on campus in characteristic style. Although standard techniques of university administration did not apply, he approached the problem pragmatically, delegated responsibility to trusted associates, and kept both the students and the public informed. He took advantage of increases in state and federal funding and the positive momentum of a larger student body to nurture pride in the growth of the university. Upon this expanded base, Wells was determined to make the academic peaks higher.

FACULTY CULTIVATION

The university's response to unprecedented growth in student numbers was perhaps the most visible challenge immediately following the war, but more consequential was the state of the faculty. President Wells and Dean Payne led a revolution in faculty reorganization beginning in 1937.[23] New department leaders, now called chairmen rather than heads, were supporting new research-oriented faculty while trying to accommodate the instructional needs of an enlarged student body.

Through long experience in managing personnel, Wells knew the vital importance of delegation to trusted colleagues and assistants. He was especially careful to pick academic deans and directors who had drive, vision, and appropriate interpersonal skills. Secure in his leadership role, he was not intimidated by the brains and talent of his administrative subordinates. In fact, he relished surrounding himself with gifted persons.[24] Wells had great success in attracting key individuals who built up important areas of the university. Two wartime hires – Henry Hope (fine arts, in 1941) and Robert Miller (libraries, in 1942) – exemplified his approach of aligning the university's needs and aspirations with the person's career ambitions, redounding to mutual benefit.

A later example was Wilfred Bain, hired in 1947 as dean of the Music School.

Although Wells had largely delegated his functional role in recruitment to deans and department heads, he still met many faculty candidates, especially those of eminent reputation. He imbued his administrative staff with his profoundly held conviction that "the first task of the academic administrator is to try to attract and hold the most talented faculty members, encourage them, support them, and then get out of their way and let them go wherever their talent and energy lead them."[25]

Unlike Bryan, who applauded faculty achievement when it happened, Wells had been actively nurturing faculty careers with incentives such as internal research grants. With his enthusiasm for inquiry and investigation, he "became a patron to his own faculty, a Maecenas, so to speak, of the humanities and the sciences."[26]

With growing numbers and reorientation towards research, augmented by increasing faculty mobility between institutions, there developed strains between faculty generations. As IU historian Clark described it,

> For the returning professors the prosaic daily routine of classes, picking up delayed research projects, and struggling with curricula revisions proved a complex transition. Rapidly expanding enrollments, the in-rush of veterans, and the constant confusion of new campus expansion and construction, and the appearance of new, and for the most part, younger professors brought immediate changes, not only in university procedures, but in the way of life in the Bloomington community. For the first time in Indiana University history there appeared a sharply discernible division between the "Old Guard" and the "Young Turks." The endearing intimacies that had prevailed historically in university relationships became, after 1945, less clearly defined.[27]

The glue that held it all together was the steadying influence of Wells. He was a product of, and had deep appreciation for, the prewar university's proud traditions. His deft handling of the wave of senior faculty retirements in 1937, coupled with President Emeritus Bryan's quiet faith in his abilities, did much to allay the fears of longtime faculty members. Wells's fine working relationships with various senior figures – such as Fernandus Payne, Stith Thompson, and Alfred Kinsey – also contributed to faculty morale.

One way of bridging the generation gap, Wells suggested, was to write departmental histories "to keep the record continuous and green." Focus on shared programmatic purposes and goals might provide a common ground between the new junior colleagues and their elders. Wells fostered an inclusive culture, respecting the Old Guard whose work contributed to the current stature of the university and, at the same time, realizing the Young Turks had "the future in their bones."[28]

Two hires in genetics illustrate the modus operandi of the Wells administration. In 1938, a postdoctoral fellow from Johns Hopkins University, Tracy Sonneborn, was hired as a junior professor. A specialist in cytoplasmic inheritance, he had a promising research program using the *Paramecium* as a model organism. In a bold move, IU hired *Drosophila* specialist Hermann J. Muller in 1945. The researcher, one of Thomas Hunt Morgan's Columbia University laboratory associates, had had a serious flirtation with Marxist ideology and had worked in the Soviet Union in the 1930s. The brilliant and iconoclastic biologist used X-rays to produce genetic mutations in fruit flies, leading to chromosomal maps. After a year at IU, Muller was awarded the Nobel Prize in Physiology or Medicine. After the award ceremony in Stockholm in January 1947, the certificate, gold medal, and other souvenirs were displayed in the lobby of the Indiana Memorial Union, and *Life* published a photojournalistic essay.[29]

IU hired rising star B. F. Skinner to become chair of psychology in 1945. After years of lab work with white rats, he had recently switched to the common pigeon as his organism of choice.[30] His system of operant conditioning of behavior had recently escaped the laboratory and been applied to real-life contexts, notably the diverse contexts of missile guidance, child-rearing, and social philosophy. During the war, Skinner invented a missile guidance device that was controlled by shaping the behavior of pigeons.[31] As a young father, he devised an air-conditioned crib for his younger daughter. It was publicized in *Ladies' Home Journal* in an article with the sensational title "Baby in a Box."[32] Marketed unsuccessfully as the "Heir-Conditioner," Skinner shared blueprints with other Indiana faculty members and several Bloomington babies were reared in this way. *Walden Two*, his foray into social design, was published in 1948.[33] In the genre of scientific utopias, the book presents an account of a fictional community based on the principles of operant conditioning. Skinner oversaw an increase in faculty numbers and research output in the psychology department before Harvard, where he had earned his doctorate, hired him away in 1948.

After a decade of working closely with Wells, Fernandus Payne retired in summer 1947. He could look with pride at the revitalization of several science departments, including biology. Genetics, Payne's own field, was exceptionally strong. Payne's replacement as dean of the Graduate School was internationally recognized folklorist Stith Thompson. Originally hired in the English Department, Thompson built up the study of folklore until it reached departmental status in 1947, the first such department in the country.[34]

A CLASSICAL EDUCATION

Although Wells was piling up the miles around the state and across the country traveling on IU business, he had been overseas only once. In 1946, he was invited by Acting Secretary of State Dean Acheson to join a tripartite commission (of the United States, France, and Great Britain) to monitor democratic elections in Greece after a hiatus of ten years. The Mediterranean country, considered a strategic prize by the Soviet Union, was in political turmoil following Axis occupation. Wells joined the U.S. mission, whose eight members each held the rank of minister – with the exception of its chief, Henry Grady, who served as ambassador. The official instructions called for inspection of "the status of the electoral registers" and reporting on provisions made for election, and to observe "the effectiveness and integrity of the polling" on the day of the election.[35]

Aided by a substantial team of experts, the mission met in Washington, D.C., on January 14 and 15, 1946, to prepare. After intensive briefing sessions, the group met with President Harry Truman. All were expecting a perfunctory well wishing, but the president launched into an hour-long speech, incisively describing what later became known as the Truman Doctrine for the Eastern Mediterranean. The entire party, Wells reported, was amazed at this performance, so at odds with the press's depiction of him "as a petty, impulsive, and weak president."[36]

Wells's anticipation was high as the group departed from Washington a month later on a military transport plane. The plane, a DC-4 model, was commonly known as an "old groaner" because of the odd sound of the motor. The IU president, a novice at international air travel, received some valued advice from Ambassador Grady. To adjust to time zone changes, he advised taking sleeping pills and milk of magnesia. After stopovers in Bermuda and Casablanca, the mission arrived at Naples, Italy, where the group received further orientation for nearly a week. Preparations for Greece continued, but the schedule allowed plenty of time for sightseeing. Despite wartime ravages, the countryside was turning green again, and Wells was thrilled to see the ruins of Pompeii and the venerable sights of Rome:

> On our return from Rome we took another route, via Monte Cassino, where we had a glimpse of the terrible destruction that had occurred when Italy was liberated. The drive back was otherwise a great pleasure because everywhere were little gay carts, horses with tinkling bells, people strolling along the roads, fields green with spring planting at the base of the majestic mountains – an indelible experience.[37]

Wells drank in the sights, sounds, color, and smells of Italy, heightening his already keen appreciation of cultural landscapes.

The mission moved to Greece in late February, setting up headquarters in a fancy hotel in Athens. The country was divided into five districts, and Wells was put in charge of northern Greece at Salonika, which happened to be the region of greatest unrest. "In every village," he wrote, "there are those who hate others until it is almost impossible to weld any village into a cohesive community."[38] Wells was fortunate to have State Department employee Peter W. Topping as his personal assistant. Topping, who was fluent in Greek, had come a month before to organize local arrangements and hire interpreters.

Although he had no prior experience in making ministerial courtesy calls, Wells relied on his innate dignity and charm to fulfill the demands of protocol. In the Greek tradition, the host offers a little cup of the customary strong coffee to his guests. One morning, as Wells called on dignitaries one after the other, he found himself intoxicated by all of the caffeine. Thus elevated, he went back to his office in the afternoon to await the return calls of each person visited that morning. "I assured

each of the privilege we felt in being in Salonika, of our awareness of
the importance of the election, and of our dedication to being impartial
observers and reporters to the world," he wrote later.[39]

Wells had a staff of 1,200 to cover the territory of northern Greece.
Although France and Britain, as well as South Africa, had representatives
stationed in Salonika, they were understaffed and relied on the American field workers. Scholars trained in new techniques of public-opinion
polling by statistical sampling were part of the staff, and sampling teams
spread out over hundreds of villages to check the adequacy of the regis-
tration lists. (Greece was predominantly rural; 80 percent of the population lived in an estimated ten thousand villages.) Over the course of this
data gathering, there were indications that the democratic forces were
gaining ground against the communists. Terrorists struck in the district,
which was mountainous and relatively wild. A week before the March 31
election, the Greek Communist Party announced that the election was
being rigged and urged all Leftists to abstain from voting.

Wells was in regular contact with the mission's headquarters in Athens and traveled by plane to attend weekly staff meetings. For local travel
around mountainous northern Greece, he was assigned a car for urbanized Salonika and had the use of a jeep for the rural countryside as well
as a small plane to visit remote areas. The peripatetic Wells easily added
these conveyances to his expanding locomotor repertoire. Crisscross-
ing northern Greece repeatedly, he eagerly absorbed the local culture.
He visited several Greek islands, including Crete, where he saw some of
the archeological sites. As a courtesy to his friends in the Bloomington
Greek-American colony, Wells took the time to call on members of their
families.

Describing a beautiful drive back from the Aegean seaside town of
Kavalla, Wells waxed poetic:

> Out across the plain, the freshly plowed soil was a chocolate brown, splashed
> with the bright green of new wheat and the pink of blossoming almond trees.
> You could see people with their donkeys silhouetted against the horizon, and
> furnishing a backdrop for it all was the beautiful, snowcapped mountain,
> Mt. Pangaeus, from which Philip of Macedon, father of Alexander the Great,
> obtained the gold to finance his conquests. . . . As you drive along the country
> roads, you can see the shepherd with his flocks, tending those flocks in exactly
> the type of costume his ancestors of two or three thousands years ago wore.

In his autobiography, he overlaid the visual appeal of this "captivating spring scene" with a religious reference: "I was traveling the exact route that St. Paul had followed when he landed at Kavalla and then proceeded to Salonika to bring his gospel to the Philippians."[40] In his characteristic way, Wells was always learning, using his aesthetic sensibility to plumb the depths of human culture, whether archeological, religious, or artistic.

Wells's diplomatic skills were challenged toward the end of his month-long sojourn in Greece. After the Salonika harbor was sufficiently cleared of sunken ships and other debris, the first United Nations Relief and Rehabilitation Administration (UNRRA) freighter docked with a cargo of wheat for the Yugoslavs and the Balkan region. The wheat was reloaded into railroad cars to make its way from Salonika to the Yugoslavian border. The Allied officer in charge invited Wells to join the official party, which filled a combination dinner and parlor car attached to the end of the train. The sumptuous car was a relic of the prewar Orient Express.

When the train stopped at the Greece-Yugoslavia border, a high barbed-wire fence separated milling crowds of Greeks on one side and Yugoslavs on the other. Bands were playing noisily and insults were being tossed back and forth. "Ironically," Wells noted, "traditional rivalries were manifesting themselves in the midst of this dramatic gesture of international cooperation and friendship."[41] When a young Yugoslav colonel entered the train car to check the papers of the official party, he found that Wells had no specific authorization to cross into Yugoslavia, and thus the car could not cross the border where the ceremony and luncheon were to be held.

The State Department personnel were incensed, pointing out that Wells was the highest-ranking American official present, and they were not about to accept an insult to the United States by proxy. Adding to their indignation was the fact that the freight cars were carrying American wheat. To defuse the situation, Wells offered to get off the train so it could proceed across the border, but the rest of the party were adamantly against it. Things remained at an impasse until, as Wells related,

> Our railroad car was pulled across the line, half resting in Yugoslavia and half remaining in Greece. The Yugoslavs sat at one end of the car and the United

Nations personnel, including the Americans, sat at the other. The ceremonial speeches were given, toasts were drunk, and we enjoyed a delicious five-course luncheon. The honor of the United States was upheld, the dignity and authority of the young Yugoslav colonel were preserved, and all was sweetness and light. Afterward, a Yugoslav engine came to pull the wheat into Belgrade, and our engine returned us to Athens. This little incident out at the periphery of diplomatic and strategic events in retrospect still brings a smile.[42]

Despite its relative unimportance in the great scheme of things, Wells added a valuable lesson to his expanding knowledge of the world, renewing his wonder at the infinite cultural adaptations to fundamental aspects of human nature.

On the verge of leaving Greece, Wells was invited to a reception on board the battleship USS *Missouri* (the site of the Japanese surrender in 1945) docked in the Piraeus harbor. As he returned to Athens after dark, floodlights illuminated the Parthenon, standing "silhouetted against the black sky," Wells recalled: "It is perhaps man's most perfect physical expression of all that is good in him, of his eternal search for truth and beauty."[43] Once he returned home to Bloomington, Wells savored his memories of Greece and Italy, later writing that being in the cradle of Western civilization made "a profound impression."[44] Reinforcing a pattern set in his first international travel five years before, his first visit to Europe provided a template for subsequent international journeys. They were cultural events of high purpose, both explicit (observing the elections) and implicit (soaking up new ideas and making connections to people).

After returning from Greece in April 1946, Wells was full of enthusiasm for his experience in the classical world. His high school Latin class and his bookish introduction to Greek and Roman culture did not prepare him well for firsthand contact, but it did give some notion of the history of these ancient lands. Combined with his uncanny powers of observation, Wells was able to put his contemporaneous encounter into a rich geographical and historical context.

Although they were proud of the president's activities on the international stage, the IU trustees were also apprehensive about his absences from campus. It was one thing to serve at the request of the U.S. government on matters of educational import; it was another to be a part of a political mission of U.S. diplomacy. Seeking to deflect the lure of international diplomacy, the board strongly suggested to Wells that he not accept any substantial commitments away from campus unless they were connected to educational affairs.

Wells agreed readily, secure in the belief that, despite his absences, he did not neglect university business during such times. He was careful to delegate authority to other members of the administration to take care of routine business, and to stay in close contact by letter, telegram, and telephone. He continued to exercise his urge to movement on the state and national level, and his two trips overseas expanded his horizons immensely.

INDIANA CONFERENCE OF HIGHER EDUCATION

Cooperation was a basic principle Wells had learned while in the Jamestown Boys' Band. He also understood that institutions working together expand the reach and the power of each one – and the group's efforts would redound to the benefit of Indiana University. The IU Post-War Planning Committee, appointed by Wells in 1943, came to realize that IU's potential problems would be shared by other Hoosier higher education institutions, and that IU, acting independently, could not possibly handle all of the postwar educational needs of the state. So the committee called a conference of all the Indiana colleges and universities "to discuss mutual problems to be faced in the post-war period."[45]

The conference was held March 17 and 18, 1944, at the Columbia Club in Indianapolis. Twenty institutions sent some seventy individuals to represent them. The general topics of discussion were divided into five categories: admission and credit evaluation, counseling and guidance, curricular adjustments, variables outside the control of the colleges, and foreign students and international relations. Wells served as chairman of the general session.[46] The meeting was deemed valuable, and a Second Indiana State Conference on Problems of Post-War Higher Education was held in June. By that time, it became clear that ongoing meetings would provide important assistance to institutions as well as provide a useful clearinghouse for ideas and techniques.

A simple charter was drawn up, and the Indiana Conference of Higher Education (ICHE) was born on June 10, 1944. A voluntary association of Indiana's thirty-three private, church-related, and state-supported colleges and universities, the ICHE had "no legal status or corporate powers" and "no stated purposes, responsibilities, or authority," and it even lacked bylaws to guide its activities.[47] There were two officers. Its first president was M. O. Ross, president of Butler University; the secretary-treasurer was Dean Wendell W. Wright of Indiana University. To keep costs down, Wells suggested that the ICHE office be located at IU, with secretarial services at no cost other than incidental expenses such as postage. The ICHE studied problems of mutual interest among Indiana institutions of higher education, among them student enrollment and migration and faculty compensation, and it encouraged cooperative programs.

In November 1947, Wells talked to the conference about "The Role of the University in a Democratic Society," sharing his thoughts about why it was important to protect academic freedom. He had recently taken the defensive step of incorporating the Institute for Sex Research as a nonprofit entity to provide legal separation from IU as Kinsey's sex research gathered steam and a cloud of criticism.

Wells's logic was based on the premise that "the paramount method of democracy is that of rational problem solving: and this method applied to social problems involves primarily free inquiry and discussion." This academic freedom is "a public trust of colleges and universities," and they "stand as great bulwarks of democratic culture" in a world riven by authoritarian ideologies. Linking democratic culture and truth, the university functions as "the most precious realm of the free, inquiring spirit of man," in Wells's poetic phrasing. "If this be our major role in history," Wells concluded,

> the free universities of this land will play, if not the most spectacular role, certainly a most important and enduring one. For the values of democracy and the method of problem solving through which it progresses rest ultimately on free inquiry and free dissemination of the truth. . . . It therefore behooves thoughtful persons to support the universities when they are unjustly attacked – especially when the freedom they require to carry on their functions is endangered by thoughtless criticism of selfish interests.[48]

In this forum, Wells was refining his concept of academic freedom, and making common cause with other Indiana colleges and universities. IU, as the state's flagship university, served as a lighting rod for criticism.[49] Wells, in his efforts for racial integration and to foster controversial research, had withstood much.

RECONSTRUCTION IN GERMANY

In summer 1947, Wells was approached by a representative of the U.S. Military Government in Germany, headed by General Lucius D. Clay, to head its troubled Education and Cultural Affairs Branch. After Germany surrendered in April 1945, the victorious Allied forces occupied and split the country; the Soviet Union controlled East Germany and a democratic tripartite command (the United States, France, and Britain) was in charge of West Germany. The capital city of Berlin was also split into sectors managed by Soviet, American, French, and British forces.

Around the same time, the U.S. government announced an ambitious European Recovery Plan to aid in the reconstruction of Western Europe and to foster democratic institutions in the hopes of repelling communism. Dubbed the Marshall Plan after General George C. Marshall, the postwar secretary of state, gave a speech at Harvard in June 1947, the plan focused on economic recovery and reestablishing a stable society. In Germany, the Military Government's Education and Cultural Affairs Branch had a wide bailiwick: education at all levels, libraries, museums, fine and performing arts, and the press and other media – as a staff member quipped, "anything that the military didn't want."[50] The cultural affairs advisor had the equivalent rank of a two-star general.

Wells was sorely tempted to take the job, which combined overseas travel and service to the federal government. Both were things he enjoyed. But he remembered his promise to the trustees not to take assignments that would take him away from campus for extended periods. Reasoning that the position was directly involved in educational administration, Wells requested leave and was granted six months.

Berlin and other parts of Germany were in shambles. Buildings and roads and other infrastructure had been bombed and destroyed. Agricultural production was quite low, and German citizens depended on imported food from the occupying forces and were chronically under-nourished. Clothing and household items were in short supply. Wells knew that he was packing for a hardship post, and he made an extensive list of items to purchase and take to Germany. The list ranged from pots and pans to candles, cutlery, and laundry soap. It included over sixty food items: three hams, six jars of pickles, fifteen pounds of sugar, four cans of pineapple, and six cans of lima beans. To satisfy his gourmand's taste, delicacies such as anchovy paste, pâté de foie gras, lamb's tongue, angostura bitters, and rum cake and rum sauce were included. Some extra clothing and miscellaneous articles, among them a sewing kit, photographic film, flashlights, heater, and lamp, rounded out the list. He purchased two books to provide context for developments in Germany: *A Short History of Germany* and *Mein Kampf.*[51]

Wells left Bloomington in November 1947. When he got to Berlin, unfamiliar sights greeted him and a host of problems awaited his atten-tion. Not daunted by either, he quickly set up shop, started reading the files, and began consulting with various people. General Clay made it clear that he would have autonomy to define his priorities within the expansive agenda of the Education and Cultural Affairs Branch and that the general would not attempt to manage the branch's business. Wells was pleased with this working arrangement, and he maintained a cordial relationship with his military superior.

Much of his work was trying to impose administrative order on the branch so it could help more effectively. The U.S. Military Gov-ernment was preoccupied with the overwhelming logistical needs for basic services and the political process of realignment, known as "de-Nazification." Rebuilding the educational system was a low priority, and planning for higher education was almost nonexistent when the Ameri-cans took over in fall 1945. German schools needed to be rebuilt, both organizationally and physically.

The U.S. government considered fostering the spirit of democ-racy through democratic institutions to be its main mission. Although Wells had responsibility for all levels of education from kindergarten up through university, he paid special attention to the problems of higher education. With the partitioning of Berlin into two sectors controlled by the Western powers and the Soviet Union, accidents of geography became vitally important. After failed attempts to establish quadripartite management over the world-class University of Berlin, whose central administration was located in the Soviet sector, the Soviet Union exercised its control and renamed it Humboldt University in 1949. As communication and commerce between East and West sectors became increasingly restricted (culminating in the building of the Berlin Wall in 1961), students living in West Berlin encountered growing difficulty studying at the university.[52]

Wells convinced Peter Fraenkel, whom he met in 1941 on the trip to South America, to accompany him as his assistant. Fraenkel had graduated with honors from IU, and was currently enrolled at Harvard in a master's degree program. He was also fluent in German. Fraenkel joined him in January, and soon after the two were detained by Russian soldiers in Potsdamer Platz after visiting Fraenkel's German nurse, who had cared for him after the early death of his mother. Potsdamer Platz was under Soviet control, but the four-power treaty guaranteed access to personnel from other sectors. Arrested and held at gunpoint for two hours, Wells and Fraenkel were accused of "taking pictures in a manner unfriendly to the Soviet Union" even though they did not possess a camera. Released to American authorities, the Soviets later issued a rare apology for the incident.[53]

Meanwhile, back in Indiana, Wells missed the publication celebration that put Bloomington on the literary map. On January 5, 1948, the immense and hugely important tomes *Sexual Behavior in the Human Male* and *Raintree County* were published. The former was the work of IU zoology professor Alfred Kinsey and his associates; the latter was the creation of Ross Lockridge, Jr., a gifted writer who grew up in Bloomington and had been a brilliant student at the university. The two met just once, although they lived just a few blocks from each other. Kinsey's and Lockridge's books held the top spots on the nonfiction and fiction best seller lists for some months. Tragically, Lockridge took his own life in early March. Former president Bryan, who had known this talented individual, offered consoling words.[54]

Later in March, Wells's work in Germany was interrupted by a suicide in his own family. His father Granville, now seventy-three, had continued to suffer periods of depression and anxiety. Although retired, he maintained his connection to the bank, serving as financial consultant, as well as giving advice when asked by friends and neighbors. Apparently, some fiduciary problem arose that Granville felt responsible for, he ruminated about it, and his morbid thoughts spiraled out of control until he made an attempt on his own life by ingesting a toxic substance.

When his wife Bernice found him and the bottle of poison in the early morning of March 20, she ran to awaken the other occupant in the house, Wells's unmarried cousin Helen Heady, who had lived with her uncle Granville and maternal aunt Bernice for nearly fifteen years. Bernice shouted, "How could he have done this to Herman?!" Granville was taken to Lebanon hospital where he lingered for several hours before expiring.[55]

Wells was notified and soon was on his way back to Boone County on the earliest available flight. He arrived the next day and joined his grief-stricken family. The funeral occurred on March 22 (ten years to the day after Wells was named president), and rural folk joined townspeople to laud the life of an upright man. One obituary referred to an earlier conversation with Granville about his prominent son, asking why he turned out the way he did. Thoughtfully, the elder Wells mused that Herman just followed his own course, finding his own way. He made no mention of his essential role or his wife's in providing the family environment and the support that made it possible, or his son's attempts to emulate him by his choice of career as a banker and a teacher.[56]

Although he did not commit his thoughts to paper, Wells was influenced deeply by his father's passing, with its echo of his paternal grandmother's end when he was twelve. Granville had provided a model for his approach to his own life of fiduciary concern and public service. More problematic, however, was his father's history of depression and the strains it produced in the family, hidden for the most part from public gaze. Marking him in unseen ways, Wells had managed to integrate the sadness of his individual life with the Weltschmerz he sometimes felt surrounding him, adding bitter notes to life's sweetness and making it all the more poignant. At Granville's funeral, Wells's friend and IU trustee John Hastings held his hand in tender concern.[57]

ORIGINS OF THE FREE UNIVERSITY OF BERLIN

But Wells's work was calling him back to Germany, where he had little more than a month to finish up. Soon after his return, the situation in higher education took an unexpected turn and Wells was able to play a crucial role in laying the foundation for a new institution. In mid-April, three students were dismissed from the university in Berlin. The students called for the creation of a new university. Berlin newspapers ran stories; the Eastern Bloc press was critical of the students and their protests whereas the Western press supported the students and their call for a new university. Covering the story, Kendall Foss, an American staff writer for the *Neue Zeitung,* an American-licensed newspaper for the German population, suggested that the students call on officials from the U.S. Military Government to see what their options were.

Taking his own initiative, Foss contacted General Clay to tell him what was afoot. Impressed with the reporter, Clay suggested that the students meet with his cultural advisor, Wells, even though it was a Saturday. Later that day, the student group, accompanied by Foss, found Wells in his apartment and met with him, delineating their appeal for a new university to be located in the Western sector. Wells was always happy to see students take the initiative, and he promised to bring the idea up with Clay. Privately, however, he tempered his enthusiasm with skepticism derived from his experiences with General Clay.[58]

Although Wells had developed a good relationship with Clay, circumstances were such that "support for educational programs had been uneven at best."[59] Other plans to create new universities had come to naught. Various efforts in 1947 and 1948 in Munich, Bremen, and Dahlem (where a concentration of the independent Kaiser Wilhelm Institutes were located) had foundered because of a lack of support by the U.S. Military Government, which was content to have existing universities take up the slack.

When Wells brought the students' plan to Clay, the cultural advisor was pleasantly shocked by the general's wholehearted endorsement. Clay was aware of the tremendous publicity value that a free university would have in the capital, and willing to gamble on the fervor of the dissident students and Foss, and the considered endorsement of Wells. "I was somewhat surprised that Clay gave the project enthusiastic support," Wells related. Clay "waved aside the difficulties" and insisted that the new university be open for the fall semester, less than five months away. Gauging the magnitude and complexity of the task, Wells explained to Clay that the university "had to have a faculty, a library, laboratories, and so on" in addition to students. Wells had no doubts about getting enough students, but worried about the short timeframe. After listening to Wells's doubts, Clay remained firm in his decision and asked Wells "to put the machinery into motion."[60]

Wells, impressed by Foss's competency and passion for the issue, hired him as a special assistant to aid in the possible creation of a new university. Although nothing in Foss's background qualified him for the position, as Wells explained later, "[I]f you want to get something done, you get someone who is for it and has the ability."[61] Wells and his staff worked at breakneck speed and reported again to Clay in less than a week from the date of the student protests. Their report indicated that it would be feasible to start the operation of certain university activities by fall 1948, less than six months away, with strong aid from the U.S. Military Government – aid that would have to be rendered "discreetly as well as expeditiously," in the words of historian James Tent.[62]

Above all, Wells cautioned, "the new university should be a German university developed by German leadership" and "the enterprise would have to be carried out well if it was to be carried out at all." Cognizant of the superheated political environment and the merciless public scrutiny, the experienced IU president confided to Clay that this project, with all its difficulties, "would not be attempted in the States under ideal conditions in less than two years time."[63] Wells used his diplomatic skills to move back and forth between academic and military leaders, providing reassurance and hope in equal measure to all who came in his ambit. With the realization that his term of duty in Germany was ending soon, he paid less attention to the bureaucratic machinery than to the establishment of academic philosophy and principles of university governance. Historian Tent concluded, as Wells functioned as a catalyst for the creation of the Free University of Berlin, that he "was probably the most vital link in the American chain of officialdom" leading to its establishment.[64]

Wells completed his stint as cultural affairs advisor in late May 1948. The IU campus was beckoning: "So far as I am concerned, I prefer it to any place else in the world," he wrote the *Indiana Daily Student* editor.[65] With two successful overseas missions in two years, Wells was enhancing his national reputation and international network by leaps and bounds. It also provided him with new views and new ideas that he could bring back to Bloomington.

The expansion of foreign language and area studies during the war began paying rich dividends soon afterward. More and more international students were matriculating at IU, and increasing numbers of IU students were taking an expanded array of courses to learn about other languages and cultures. Foreign graduate students became instructors of courses in their native tongues. Linguistics became a separate program around 1948, and an autonomous department later.

Wells was an avid supporter of international education. His horizons were considerably broadened by travel and experience in other cultures, and he strove mightily to bring that broadened perspective to students at the Hoosier university. As Fraenkel later said, "All great universities are international in scope."[66]

Wells took advantage of every opening. In October 1948, when he learned that Thailand education minister H E Mom Luang Pin Malakul was stopping in Bloomington en route to a UNESCO conference in Beirut to visit two Thai graduate students who were studying at IU, he arranged an official reception in his honor. Wells said later of the Oxford-trained educator, "I enjoyed my visit with Mom Luang Pin from the moment of meeting. He was handsome, imaginative, and congenial." Wells spent much time with Malakul and his wife, showing them the university and discussing the educational situation in Thailand. The two men began a personal friendship that would lead to a close institutional relationship with IU and the development of higher education in Thailand.[67]

FOUNDATION GROWTH

After the war was over, IU Foundation head Lawrence Wheeler launched a new annual giving campaign. In 1946, the first annual giving to the "Greater Indiana Fund" was launched, and by June 1947 over 700 alumni gave a total of $14,215. In part, their gifts would be used to provide scholarships in honor of the 416 alumni who died in service to their country in World War II.

Wheeler and the Foundation board were active on other fronts as well. In summer 1947 the Foundation acquired title to the first land for future expansion of the campus. Gifts of real estate would become increasingly important for the Bloomington campus as well as other IU campuses and facilities, such as the Geology Field Camp in Montana. In February 1948, a gift of $38,000 from the Independent Clubs of America – known formerly as the Willkie Clubs of America – was received. Presidential hopeful Wendell Willkie was on the original board of the Foundation until his death in 1945; his brother, Frederick Willkie, replaced him.[68]

Wheeler produced a "Schedule of Investments" for the Foundation's assets at the end of June 1947. Over half of the total $80,000 was invested in U.S. Government bonds; the remainder was split between other bonds, stocks, and real estate.[69] The second annual giving campaign (1947–48) netted 623 donors who gave a total of $23,286.[70] In spring 1948, the Foundation sponsored a traveling exhibit of masterpieces from the Metropolitan Museum of Art. It was part of President Wells's master plan to put art and culture on the map at IU as well as foster good community relations. Nearly 70,000 attended the display in Alumni Hall in the Indiana Memorial Union. Its success demonstrated a hunger for such experiences, and the Foundation recouped a few hundred dollars after expenses.[71]

Near the end of 1948, Wheeler prepared a history of the work of the IU Foundation under the title "Outline of Projects Book: What the Foundation Has Done since June 1936." It provided a useful summary of how the Foundation contributed to the academic quality of the university. It cited various scholarship funds, including one of the first – the William Lowe Bryan Scholarship Fund, established in 1937, with thirty-four awardees to date. It highlighted the gift or purchase of several libraries (such as the Ernie Pyle Library) and rare manuscripts (such as Theodore Dreiser's original Dawn manuscript) over the years. The IU Foundation also held patents for the faculty, such as that for the "Harger Drunk-O-Meter" devised by physiology professor Rolla N. Harger.[72] It was clear that the pace picked up considerably after the war, when Wheeler was in full stride.

The consequences of the GI Bill were beginning to be felt at Indiana University. According to figures prepared by the U.S. Department of Education, in 1948 IU ranked ninth in enrollment nationally. One fifth of over 2.4 million students were found in only twenty universities, and Midwestern state universities were leading the way.[73] As a consequence, Indiana's alumni body grew rapidly.

The third annual giving fund was already receiving gifts, despite the fact the solicitation letter was in draft form. At the end of November 1948, Wheeler wrote the annual appeal letter to the alumni. He noted that the average gift was $10, the largest was $5,000, and contributions of $1 or $5 were common. He also pointed out that gifts to the university were tax-deductible.[74] But Wheeler's health was declining due to a series of heart problems, and the search for his successor was underway by early 1949. The third annual giving campaign attracted more than 1,200 donors and $23,000 dollars.[75] Although the annual giving campaign was steadily generating donations, IU was trailing behind such institutions as Northwestern, Ohio State, and Notre Dame, which had a comparable number of alumni but attracted ten times the amount of annual support. Closer to home, Purdue raised almost $70,000 from 1,800 donors.[76] Expanding the donor base became a perennial concern.

INDIANA UNIVERSITY PRESS

In the heady days of postwar expansion, Wells envisioned a scholarly press for the university.[77] Not only would it signal that IU deserved to be taken seriously in the scholarly world, but it also would provide another point of pride for Indiana citizens. Dean Payne, who along with faculty colleagues had been running a small nonprofit press – Principia Press – since 1931, shared Wells's enthusiasm. A parallel proposal to establish a semi-popular journal, along the lines of the *Yale Review* or the *Virginia Quarterly,* was also in the air. In 1946, history professor W. T. Morgan wrote to Wells, "The public is really interested [in] illuminating presentations of the problems of nuclear physics, hormones, Mid-Western history and Indiana literature – to mention only a few fields."[78] Although the journal idea was dropped eventually, Wells continued to believe in the twin goals of publishing scholarship and documenting the heritage of the region.

Wells and Payne agreed, as the frugal Hoosiers they were, that a press could be started on a shoestring budget, with just an editor and a secretary to start. The search for a suitable candidate led them to Bernard Berenson Perry in 1949, the son of Harvard philosophy professor Ralph Barton Perry, who had trade publishing experience as well as a good academic pedigree. Perry was skeptical about the proposed budget, but, after lobbying by new graduate dean Stith Thompson and consultation with other university press editors, he agreed to take the position in early 1950. Thompson suggested that his job title be "director" because "it would actually include the duties of editor but would be a more comprehensive position."[79]

Wells released an enthusiastic press release in March:

> The Press will be an ultimate expression of the influence of the University in scientific and intellectual publishing. . . . [It] will endeavor to extend the University's teaching and research beyond the library, laboratory, and classroom, thus performing a function of a university peculiarly important in a democracy. . . . While its interest will be wide, the Press is particularly concerned with the promotion of regional culture and literature in the Midwestern area.[80]

The catalog, containing six titles, appeared in spring 1951. Professor of French Edward D. Seeber's translation of *Travels in America, 1816–1817* by Edouard de Montulé, a nineteenth century French traveler, became the inaugural volume. About a year later, IU Press had published eleven books, and garnered one book club selection, a Pulitzer Prize in history, and nearly $25,000 in sales. In a report to the faculty, Perry boasted about the Press's superior marketing, confiding, "We feel that we are in position to solicit the best manuscripts on campus, not on the basis of institutional loyalty but on the basis of the self-interest of the faculty-author."[81]

Wells was pleased. Indiana University Press was another foundation stone to increase the stature of the university, serving both the scholarly needs of the faculty as well as getting the IU name in wider circulation.

He followed his usual practice in selecting its leader: find an ambitious person, give them unstinting support, and give them freedom to develop the enterprise as they saw fit. Perry fit the bill perfectly.

Many other academic initiatives were started at IU in the five years following the war. For instance, in 1948, Assistant Professor of Botany Barbara Shalucha, with the support of her colleagues Ralph Cleland and Marcus Rhoades, started a youth gardening program on undeveloped campus land on East Tenth Street. Wells was an enthusiastic booster of the one-acre Hilltop Garden, where nine- to twelve-year-olds learned the basics of gardening and nature study. In the late 1950s, Hilltop became nationally famous for its pioneering concept.[82] Another example was the 1950 co-creation of IU's FM radio station – WFIU – and the Department of Radio. With typical prescience, Wells supported the efforts of faculty and staff in the field of radio. WFIU grew directly out of IU's "School of the Sky," a fifteen-minute educational segment for K–12 students throughout the state that was broadcast every weekday beginning in 1947. These initiatives provided training for students interested in broadcasting and also served as another arm of the university reaching out to the state's citizens.[83]

World War II extended the boundaries of U.S. higher education, forever altering the landscape of the American university. Indiana, under the entrepreneurial leadership of Wells, responded to this new ecology of knowledge. The GI Bill, creating a new social contract between the university and the public, ushered the age of mass higher education in America. Wells managed the expansion and diversification of educational programs with foresight, and shaped the inevitable bureaucracy with the infusion of humane values. In the drive to internationalize the American university, Wells led the way for public institutions.

Be yourself, just be yourself;
Be yourself from day to day.
Be yourself, just be yourself;
That's the Herman B Wells way.
He avoids all ostentation,
No pretense or affectation;
He's a pleasant, humble, normal, friendly one.
He assumes no pose to please,
He has natural poise and ease,
Genuine, sincere, and honest, loving fun.
All these things endear the man;
Emulate him if you can.
Be yourself, just be yourself;
That's the Herman B Wells way.

Newell Long, 1938

ELEVEN

Music Appreciation

PERHAPS THE MOST UNUSUAL GIFT that Herman Wells received for his presidential inauguration in December 1938 was a song. It was composed by music faculty member Newell Long and his wife, Eleanor, and performed as part of a humorous show, *Inaugurating the Boy President,* put on by an ad hoc group of faculty and their wives. Long, a trombone player, had been a classmate of Wells's in the 1920s (they marched together in the University Band), and had been hired by IU in 1935. He was part of the good but not exceptional School of Music that Wells inherited.

Wells's predecessor, Bryan, had sound ideas for the administrative structure of the university. During his long term, he nurtured the development of various specialized professional schools, notably in the medical and allied health areas, education, business, and music. The School of Music was established in 1921, under the direction of Barzille Winfred Merrill. German-trained Merrill, "a thoroughly professional musician, a violinist, conductor, and composer," was hired two years before as professor of Music and head of the music department in the College of Liberal Arts. The new dean shared Bryan's ambitions to offer professional training for performance as well as music education as part of the liberal arts.[1] Despite the happy start of his tenure, within a couple of years Merrill made enemies among the faculty, numbering a half dozen, and Bryan had to implore him repeatedly to make peace with his colleagues. Most of the faculty agreed, however, about the direction of the school toward the conservatory model, in opposition to the reality that almost all of the students were in training to become public schoolteachers of music.[2]

Mitchell Hall, a frame building dating back to the 1880s, was the headquarters of the music school.[3] In 1921, a separate, very plain annex was constructed nearby to provide a classroom, two studios, and four practice rooms. The two buildings were painted the same color, at Merrill's insistence, to provide at least some visual continuity. Large concerts were held in Assembly Hall, a ramshackle barn-like structure that served as the largest performance space on the campus. It had a rudimentary stage and could be set up with 1,200 folding wooden chairs. Almost from the start of the school, the facilities were inadequate to meet the needs of the growing student body and faculty. Mitchell Hall's lack of sound-proofing was a continuing difficulty. Moreover, the buildings were insufferably hot during the summer months, and dogs and other animals even got underneath the structures. "One time there was so much barking they had to call off rehearsal," Long recalled. Dean Merrill longed for a "visible sign" in the form of a new building, to announce the shared aspiration for a true conservatory within the state university. "He recognized the great *symbolic* value of a good building," noted music school historian George Logan. Located in substandard facilities for its entire existence, in 1936 the school obtained a splendid new building, built with Public Works Administration funding, on East Third Street.[4]

Robert Frost Daggett designed the specialized structure, with irritating input from Dean Merrill, who had a high opinion of his own architectural skills. The exterior was clad in local limestone done in the collegiate Gothic style. It had touches of Art Deco ornamentation and fixtures, and the names of great composers were incised above the large casement windows. A relief figure of cloven-hoofed Pan playing his pipes was inscribed above the front entrance. Inside the three-story building, marble flooring and oak wainscoting added elegance and signaled refinement. The top floor was divided into forty-eight practice rooms, and the other floors and the full basement housed studios, classrooms, a large rehearsal room, a library, and a museum (which contained the first piano in Bloomington, owned by Baynard Hall, the university's first professor). Located at the heart of the building, Recital Hall, with seating for over four hundred, was the first performance space on campus that had excellent acoustics. Not only was sound subject to control throughout the structure, but temperature was as well, with the provision of central air conditioning, then a rarity. On January 15, 1937, Recital Hall was inaugurated with a concert, and a new era had begun.

A NEW ADMINISTRATION

Merrill was seventy-three when Wells was named acting president in June 1937. He was perhaps the only one among the longtime deans and department heads not urged to take his pension immediately.[5] But during Wells's first year, Merrill decided to relinquish his position, so the president began searching for his successor. Two candidates were eventually identified in early 1938, and Wells, trying to revive the dormant democratic spirit in the school, had each faculty member confer with him after the contenders' visits to campus. Wells ratified the clear faculty choice and invited Robert L. Sanders to become the dean.[6]

A composer on the faculty at the University of Chicago, Sanders had been trained at the Bush Conservatory in Chicago and had the bulk of his career in that city. He possessed virtually no administrative experience, but he had a charming manner and was liberal in outlook. Soon after he arrived, he took the measure of his domain, and found the school's "library inadequate, the talent of the students . . . often times mediocre, the faculty disunited, and . . . the scope of the School too narrow."[7] Despite its seventeen-year existence, the school had never attempted to obtain certification from the National Association of Schools of Music (NASM). Sanders became determined to achieve that benchmark, and invited the accreditation committee to examine the school a few months after his arrival. The school's broadened aims were expressed in the 1939–40 *Indiana University Bulletin*:

> The School of Music exists within the framework of Indiana University for three important services: It offers music courses of interest and value to all University students, that they may acquaint themselves with music as one aspect of liberal culture, either as appreciative listeners or as trained participants. It offers state-approved curricula for the preparation of music teachers and supervisors in all aspects of music teaching generally offered in public and private schools. It offers instruction designed to prepare students for careers in the field of professional music.[8]

In stark contrast to his predecessor, Sanders practiced democratic faculty governance and allowed his colleagues to have their say, resulting in frequent, almost interminable meetings.

The results of the NASM inspection revealed several inadequacies, specifically in the theory program and the public school music students' inability "to give a decent performance on any instrument." Rather than reject the School of Music's application for membership, NASM awarded the probationary status of associate membership, with a reinspection scheduled two years later. The problem of poorly prepared students was a perennial one, with IU admission open to any graduate of an Indiana high school. Another structural issue that precluded higher standards was that students could opt for a bachelor's degree in the School of Education, which required fewer courses in music.[9]

As the outside review called attention to problems in the music school, the IU internal self-study committee recommended an administrative reorganization into a Division of Music and Fine Arts, reversing the cherished autonomy of the separate school. Equally disturbing was their recommendation that all undergraduate programs be divided into Junior and Senior Divisions, each comprising two years of coursework. The Junior Division would be given over to general education, so students would not start specialized courses in a specific discipline until the third year. As the NASM review pointed out, students had difficulty reaching a professional level in four years. How could this task be accomplished in two?[10]

Luckily for the school, the Junior Division was cut down to a single year when the recommendation was eventually enacted. In fact, enrollment for music school courses increased when the College of Arts and Sciences and the Schools of Business and of Education started granting credit for applied music courses in their respective degree programs. In 1940, the accreditation examiner from the National Association of Music Schools found the music theory program much improved, but there were continuing problems with students' performing skills: "At almost any school where they might teach, the examiner's report said, 'students in the bands and orchestras will be able to outplay them.'" He noted that grades for seniors were unacceptably inflated. As a consequence, NASM decided against the acceptance of the IU School of Music as a full member, pending further progress. Sanders was allowed to plead the school's case at the annual meeting of the Association, however, and full membership was granted. In congratulating the dean, Wells said he "must have performed a miracle."[11] Sanders began an extensive set of curricular revisions. In September 1940, the Works Progress Administration gave the School of Music a grant of $200,000 to promote public school music instruction and subsidize public musical programs throughout the state.[12]

ROLE OF THE NEW AUDITORIUM

Meanwhile, Wells and Biddle had conceived the plan for the IU Auditorium in 1938 and were busy making it happen. A replacement for the aging Assembly Hall and the more modern but smaller Alumni Hall in the Indiana Memorial Union, opened in 1932, was sorely needed. As noted above, the new auditorium took shape in 1940, with the spectacular Thomas Hart Benton murals gracing the entrance lobby. Comptroller Biddle was a chief planner for the five-day dedicatory celebration, held in March 1941, and he succeeded in attracting Metropolitan Opera Company stars Lotte Lehmann and Lauritz Melchior and also actors Alfred Lunt and Lynn Fontanne in a production of Robert Sherwood's *There Shall Be No Night*. Historian George Logan summarized the influence of the new facility thus:

> The Auditorium provides an unsurpassed example of the benefits, both material and symbolic, the superior physical facilities can provide for the development of an educational institution. The perennially embarrassing Assembly Hall had epitomized the provinciality and relative poverty of the University and had strongly suggested that it was a place where the performing arts did not enjoy a high priority. By contrast, with the opening of the Auditorium the University suddenly had a cultural facility that rivaled or surpassed that of any other American university, and most commercial halls. This fact gave an enormous boost to the self-esteem and reputation of the University, and it enormously enriched the cultural life of students, faculty, and the surrounding community (indeed of the state as a whole), by making Bloomington an attractive venue for the full range of musical and theatrical performers.[13]

The auditorium series prospered under Biddle's ambitious guidance.

The IU Auditorium proved to be a boon for the embryonic program in theatre and drama. It played a special role in the evolution of the opera program of the IU School of Music. Not only did it provide space for student productions, it also attracted annual visits from the Metropolitan Opera Company starting in 1942. Previously, the company had made annual tours to Chicago, Boston, Cleveland, and Atlanta, but it had never appeared in a small university town. In a bold move, Biddle and speech and theatre faculty member Lee Norvelle successfully lobbied the Metropolitan Opera Company to visit Indiana University on their Midwestern tour. When Edward Johnson, the General Manager of the Met, "declared that no college facility in America could accommodate the Met," he was quieted by a look at the Auditorium's blueprints. Wells and Biddle had ensured that the stage was big enough for the production of grand opera. When Johnson claimed that the $13,500 cost would be prohibitive, the university came up with a plan meet the largest part through ticket sales of $9,000, and a university subvention of $4,500: "And so one of the most unlikely and charming events in the history of American music was contracted: the Metropolitan Opera Company, making its first appearance on a university campus, would perform in Bloomington, Indiana" in 1942.[14]

Biddle and Norvelle asked for Aïda, "an especially splashy opera," to mark the historic occasion. On April 13 – the new Auditorium just a year old – townspeople, faculty, and out-of-town visitors from as far away as Chicago and St. Louis flocked to the performance. Among the guests was Josiah K. Lilly, scion of the venerable family-run Lilly Company, a large pharmaceutical manufacturer in Indianapolis. The event was a great success, even netting a small surplus over budget. Met manager Johnson enthused, "the Metropolitan likes Indiana University and Bloomington. So we are not saying 'goodbye' but only 'au revoir.'" The advent of World War II a few months earlier would curtail the opera company's touring schedule, "but when we again leave New York, Indiana University need only beckon."[15] Wells, ever alert to the tremendous public relations value of this outstanding university facility, made sure to credit Biddle, his loyal right-hand man, for the accomplishment. Writing to Biddle to express the board of trustees' appreciation for the auditorium series, he added this "personal word" of gratitude:

> You have accomplished much in your years here, but no one thing more important than what you have done through the past semesters in the inauguration of

an outstanding Auditorium year. I realize that the amazing success in the use of the Auditorium this year has reflected credit upon this administration, and I want you to know that I feel that success is due almost entirely to your own vision, and your promotional and managerial skill.[16]

The war years passed, and the Met came to Bloomington again in April 1946, beginning a continuous string of annual I U performances that lasted until 1961. The Met performed two operas – *Tannhäuser* and *La Bohème* – during this visit. Wells noted in the programs:

> The visit of the world's greatest opera organization and your presence here are a part of a plan and of an objective of Indiana University. Both are steps in the program of the university to make the whole state of Indiana its campus, and to that ever-widening campus to bring the best in music and the finest in artistic expression. There are larger universities in America. There are older universities in America. There are none, however, more typical of the American ideal of educational opportunity for all youth and cultural leadership for all citizens.[17]

That confident declaration revealed that, in the ten years of his administration, the expansion and support of the arts, both fine and performing, was to be a continuing hallmark.

Unfortunately, Ward Biddle did not see the return engagement of the Metropolitan Opera Company. He was in an Indianapolis hospital in spring 1946, and died at the end of May of heart problems brought on by overwork and smoking. Wells was devastated by the loss of his close friend and colleague, confidant and mentor. The two worked together so closely it was sometimes difficult to distinguish whose fingerprints were on policies and procedures. Biddle was a true brother to Wells for nearly twenty-five years, and played an essential role in making Wells the man he was.

THE COMING OF WILFRED BAIN

From the outside, the School of Music appeared to be thriving. Student enrollment was growing, leading to increases in the faculty ranks, numbering twenty by the end of the war and thirty only a couple of years after. The Music Building and Recital Hall were functioning well, although, after only a decade of use, they were required to serve more personnel than they were originally designed for. But the Sanders administration was drifting. After war's end, the dean, never much interested in administration, wanted to return to composing. To be sure, his democratic leadership maintained good faculty relations, restored the school's balance between performance training and music education, and accomplished NASM accreditation. In order to accommodate Sanders's wishes, an assistant dean, Douglas Nye, was appointed to help shoulder some of the administrative burden in mid-1945. By March 1946, Sanders submitted his resignation, effective in September. Persuaded to stay on for an additional year and then go back to the teaching faculty, he changed his mind again and accepted an appointment at Brooklyn College as chairman of the music department.[18]

There were no overt clashes with Wells, and the two remained on good terms throughout Sanders's deanship. But Wells, maturing as an administrator, had refined his ideas about the composition of his leadership team of deans and other lieutenants. He believed that only second-rate men were expensive, and this ironclad conviction held true not only in faculty appointments but also more importantly hiring at the level of deans and other administrators. Sanders had been appointed in the early months of his presidency, even before the idea of a new auditorium was broached. Now he had another chance to help put music on the map at Indiana University. For Wells, music was more than another administrative puzzle – it was an essential nutrient of his soul.[19] He relished the immediacy and intimacy provided by musical performance of all types, and reveled in the deep human connection between performer and audience.

Contacting the Clark-Brewer Teaching Agency for available music teachers in early 1947, Wells was dismayed at the lack of turnover in available names since Sanders's hire. The agency consultant pushed Wilfred C. Bain, at North Texas State University in Denton, as "one of the five best music administrators in the nation." Just thirty-nine years old, he had brought the North Texas State's choral music program to national prominence with few resources other than the enthusiasm of young singers. Bain had served as vice president of the National Association of Schools of Music from 1941 to 1944, and was at that time secretary of the Music Teachers National Association.

Soon the university received Bain's impressive dossier from the employment agency. Bain, born in the province of Québec, Canada, had spent his twenties acquiring education in music, mainly piano and voice, culminating in a doctorate in music education from New York University in 1938. He wrote his dissertation on a cappella choirs in American colleges and universities. Then he spent the better part of a decade applying what he had studied at North Texas State.

In February, Wells interviewed Bain over dinner in St. Louis, where the Music Teachers National Association was meeting. Jotting notes to himself after the meeting, the president wrote,

> Nice appearance – looks fit; agreeable personality and undoubtedly has a flair for administration. Was a little nervous with me and didn't do himself justice. *Is a first rate prospect* although he smells a little of his long association with a teacher's college. He obviously is keenly interested in the job.[20]

Bain, for his part, was ambitious, and was eager to move to a better university. He recalled looking at a magazine picture of the IU School of Music building shortly after its construction in 1936, thinking Indiana *"looked* like a first-rate institution." The facility, as Merrill predicted, was serving its symbolic function well. In his memoir, Bain later expanded on the theme, and recalled "remarking to himself of the attractiveness of the building and wondering if at any time during his professional career he might be fortunate enough to be the administrative officer" in such an edifice.[21] The Indiana campus was exerting its spell, a silent ally in recruitment.

Wells went to Denton to see Bain in his home environment at North Texas State. The president attended student performances, including a dress rehearsal for Wagner's opera *Faust,* and came away with an appreciation of Bain's work in developing a solid music program that encompassed both academic work and performance training.[22] In conversations with Wells, Bain was eager to try something much more ambitious at Indiana: the development of a full-scale opera program. Opera, with its highbrow cultural cachet, was not an obvious choice for a university in the middle of the Middle West. But the shrewd Bain revealed his pragmatic rationale. Opera was an activity that incorporated most phases of musical expression (voice, orchestra, ballet, and drama) and auxiliary fields (music history, musicology, scene design, stage direction, lighting, and costuming). Only a school with a comprehensive program – and faculty to match – could meet the wide-ranging demands of opera.

The recruitment dance concluded with Bain's on-campus visit in May, when Bloomington was blooming. He had a room in the tower of the Indiana Memorial Union with a sweeping view. Looking out of his seventh-floor window, he reported that he was "much impressed with the solidity and elegance of the building and architecture of nearby build-ings." Touring the music facilities set Bain's entrepreneurial mind to thinking about the possibilities. At the end of the visit, Wells offered the deanship to Bain, promising to support his plan to start an opera program. In his letter to the IU Trustees asking for their formal endorse-ment, the president summarized, "[W]hile he has as high standards of musical performance as Dean Sanders, he is much more ready to popu-larize and participate in the general musical life of the University and State."[23]

Bain arrived in July 1947, intent on pursuing his strategic vision. Genteel and urbane, the new dean possessed a formidable, self-assured presence, aided by his cultured Canadian accent with its whiff of British formality. Impressed by Bain's energy and entrepreneurial drive, Wells backed the new dean unreservedly. In reference to his overweening am-bitions for opera, Wells dryly remarked, "he rode that pretty hard at the beginning."[24] A new era was beginning for the musical arts at Indiana University, and Bain's name became indelibly associated with the rise of the School of Music. "We put down musical roots," Long explained simply, "so when Bain came along, we were *ready*."[25]

GROWTH PAINS

During much of Bain's first year on campus, Wells was out of the coun-try, working on reconstructing the German educational system. An ad-ministrative committee, headed by trustee John Hastings and including Briscoe, Franklin, and Wright, was in charge of day-to-day operations. Before Wells left, Hastings asked, "What am I going to do with this guy Bain?" After giving it some thought, Wells replied, "Give him anything he wants."[26] Wells did everything in his power to support Bain's ambi-tious goals for the school, and Bain took advantage of this support.

Over time, Bain developed unparalleled access to the president's office, bypassing the dean of the faculties office and going "straight to

An aerial view of Indiana
University's campus
in 1922, with Dunn's
Woods and the crescent
of academic buildings.

Courtesy IU Archives.

Wells observing T. C. Steele
painting in Dunn Meadow,
near the Jordan River, 1923.

Courtesy IU Archives.

Drawing of the IU campus in 1923, showing the proposed fieldhouse next to the Men's Gymnasium.

Courtesy IU Archives.

Portrait of Wells as a college senior, in the 1924 *Arbutus* yearbook.

A 1924 advertisement for Indiana University, the "Spirit of IU" offering the cornucopia of the campus to all.

Courtesy IU Archives.

Riding Black Dynamite, probably on a trip to South Dakota, c. 1928.

Courtesy IU Archives.

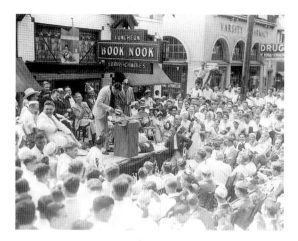

On stage, in a
white suit, at 1931
Book Nook mock
commencement.

Courtesy IU Archives.

With his maternal
grandmother, Ida
Belle Harting, in
Chicago to visit the
1933 World's Fair.

Courtesy IU Archives.

Front page of the *Indiana Daily Student* announcing
Wells's appointment as president, March 23, 1938.

Courtesy IU Archives.

Contemplating his promotion to the I U presidency, 1938.

Courtesy I U Archives.

The new president and his electors, the IU Board of Trustees, 1938.
From left, Albert Rabb, Nellie Showers Teter, Dwight Peterson,
Ora Wildermuth, Herman Wells, Ward Biddle (board secretary),
Paul Feltus, Val Nolan, and John Hastings. (William Kunkel
not pictured.)

Courtesy IU Archives.

At the 1941 dedication of the IU Auditorium,
with Thomas Hart Benton (third from left).

Courtesy IU Archives.

Discussing the shape of the postwar campus, with John
Neely, Francisco A. Delgado, and Zora Clevenger, 1945.

Courtesy IU Archives.

In conversation with President Emeritus William Lowe Bryan, 1946.

Courtesy IU Archives.

President Wells gets arrested by the Soviets in Berlin, in an editorial cartoon from the *Evansville Courier,* January 1948.

Courtesy IU Archives.

In 1949, signing every Indiana University diploma.

Courtesy IU Archives.

President Wells
congratulating IU
Nobel Laureate
Hermann J. Muller,
1949.

Courtesy IU Archives.

With Professor of Zoology Alfred C. Kinsey (left) and National
Research Council official George W. Corner, 1950.

Courtesy IU Archives.

Library director Robert Miller showing Wells a new acquisition, 1950.

Courtesy IU Archives.

With Notre Dame
University colleagues
Athletic Director
Edward "Moose" Krause
and Executive Vice
President Theodore
Hesburgh in 1950.

Courtesy IU Archives.

At dedication of the Lilly Library in 1960, with donor J. K. Lilly and
Frederick B. Adams, Jr., director of the Pierpont Morgan Library.

Courtesy IU Archives.

With Mother Wells and
Bill Armstrong, IU Foundation
president, at a Little 500 luncheon
in 1955.

Courtesy IU Archives.

Presidential portrait in front of open window displaying
the green foliage of campus, with personal icons of
school bell, globe, and Tibetan beggar's bowl, 1960.

Courtesy IU Archives.

With Howard University Board of Trustees, c. 1960.

*Courtesy Moorland-Spingarn Research
Center, Howard University Archives.*

Wells and Santa
Wells, 1961.

*Courtesy
IU Archives.*

Dedicating the Showalter Fountain in fall 1961, with donor
Grace Showalter, sculptor Robert Laurent, and Mimi Laurent.

Courtesy IU Archives.

At the dedication
of his bust outside
Kirkwood Hall in
1965, reminding the
audience that it was
to keep watch over
Dunn's Woods.

Courtesy IU Archives.

Wells as chairman of the Education and World Affairs organization,
meeting with President Lyndon B. Johnson, presidents of five
universities in South Vietnam, and other American educators, 1967.

Courtesy IU Archives.

With Dean Wilfred
Bain, administrative
maestro of the School
of Music, and donor
Elsie Irwin Sweeney
at the groundbreaking
of the Musical Arts
Center, 1968.

Courtesy IU Archives.

Talking with a
delegation of SDS
members, 1969.

Courtesy IU Archives.

An aerial view of the greatly expanded Bloomington campus, 1971.

Courtesy I U Archives.

Cruising the Nile River, near Aswan Dam, 1974.

Courtesy IU Archives.

Celebrating his seventy-sixth birthday with
friends and staff in his Owen Hall office.
From left: John Haste, Dorothy Collins,
Peter Fraenkel, John Davis, James Capshew,
Mary Jo Chandler, Matilda Hopkins,
Kate Mueller, and Darlene Heck.

Courtesy IU Archives.

Walking on campus with
cane and a pedometer,
summer 1977.

Courtesy IU Archives.

Holding a copy of the newly published *Being Lucky,* 1980.

Courtesy IU Archives.

Reprising his official
portrait after a quarter
century, 1983.

Courtesy IU Archives.

With Henry Hope, namesake
of the Hope School of Fine
Arts, at the dedication of the
IU Art Museum, 1982.

Courtesy IU Archives.

On his eighty-ninth birthday with his presidential successors,
Thomas Ehrlich, Elvis Stahr, and John Ryan.

Courtesy IU Archives.

Still working in his memento-
filled office in Owen Hall, 1994.

Courtesy IU Archives.

The iconic figure of IU,
painted by Alan Hirsh, 1992.

Courtesy IU Archives.

On the Bloomington
campus with President
Myles Brand, 1996.

*Courtesy Randy
Johnson.*

With the Dalai Lama on his visit to Bloomington, 1996.

Courtesy Garrett Ewald.

A drawing by Joe Lee entitled "We Are Bloomington,"
for the Bloomington postcard series, 2000.

*Courtesy City of Bloomington
Community Arts Commission.*

A layer of frost collects on the otherwise warm and jovial visage
of the Wells sculpture in the Old Crescent, January 2007.

Courtesy Chris Meyer and the IU Trustees.

Wells" with requests and problems.[27] Bain's ambitions for the School of Music accorded with Wells's basic administrative principles: to hire the best faculty and administrative leaders, and then leave them alone to do their work. Once he found a strong leader, such as Bain, Wells kept himself "primarily in a responsive rather than a directive mode."[28]

To build up the faculty, Bain kept his ears tuned to the world of performance. Concertizing artists would be approached just after the peak of their career, lured by the prospect of teaching, even if they had not had any pedagogical experience or training. Not infrequently, problems with performers arose because of their "artistic temperament" or limited experience in the academic world. Met star Dorothee Manski, on the faculty since 1941, was a prime example of this recruiting tactic, and provided a precedent for a continuing series of appointments of eminent performers.[29]

Bain adopted, with Wells's blessing, a simple form of the medical school geographical full-time model, in which doctors taught while continuing their professional practice outside the university, to the faculty performing artist in the music school. In this variation, music faculty would be allowed time to pursue their performance career away from campus as long as they could schedule time to fulfill their faculty teaching load.[30]

Bain was ruthless in building up the School of Music, and was not above cutting corners in his treatment of the faculty. There was at least one case of administrative misjudgment in the non-renewal of a faculty appointment, carried out with the complete support of the president's office.[31] Bain persevered, and five years after his appointment he reached, in his words, a "plateau of activity" in his quest to create a comprehensive music school with the ability to showcase opera.[32] Large enrollments were a necessary part of the dean's plan. In 1951–52, nearly five hundred students were enrolled, with about fifty faculty instructors. Bain achieved the goal of having an individual instructor for each orchestral instrument with the hiring of percussionist Richard Johnson that year. Johnson, who held a B.A. from Indiana and a diploma from the Paris Conservatory, became the first African American to join the Bloomington faculty. History was being made and Wells made additional progress on building a diverse community. But as Bain noted later, his appoint-

ment "caused little or no comment since there was not the general consciousness of the unequal representation of the races on the faculty."[33]

Among the dozen or so African American students enrolled in the
school during the late 1940s and early 1950s was David Baker, a graduate
of Crispus Attucks High School in Indianapolis. Coming to IU in 1949,
he found discrimination against blacks in Bloomington and some segregated facilities on campus, but the climate was different in the music
school. Blacks and whites played together, as did students and faculty;
he remembered intense camaraderie in the process of receiving an extensive musical education.[34]

An example of Bain's audacity and Wells's response to it occurred
in 1952 when the music dean wanted fifty grand pianos in the midst of
a minor recession. Wells decided to use the money derived from the
indirect costs that scientific research grants were bringing into the university. Characteristically, the president checked with the scientists to
okay this unusual (and possibly illegal) arrangement. Bain got his fifty
grand pianos, according to campus lore.[35] This story illustrates the flavor
of the cooperative spirit among faculty and administration in the 1950s.

On March 20, 1956, Marian Anderson returned for her third visit to
the IU Auditorium. Fresh from her belated debut at the Metropolitan
Opera Company the previous year, she proved a favorite once again with
the academic community. "Sweet and low, the golden voice of Marian
Anderson thrilled us with her melodies," the Arbutus enthused.[36] The
contrast from her two previous visits, both during wartime, was striking. Wells had been in charge for nearly twenty years, and the postwar
university was flourishing. Gone were the most visible signs of racial discrimination, on campus if not in Bloomington, and signs of growth – in
enrollment, in programs, and in quality – were manifest. As a young
president, Wells had reached out to Anderson as part of his anti-racism
initiative. Now a seasoned pro, Anderson's third visit was a homecoming
of sorts for Wells to show how the university had progressed.

As the number of students and faculty in the School of Music continually grew, facilities were an increasing problem. Less than ten years
into the Bain regime, plans were started in 1956 for a new structure to provide more classrooms, practice rooms, and faculty studios. Connected
to the existing music building on the north side, bids for the $2.5 mil-

lion Music Annex were let in April 1958, and ground was broken in June. Construction dragged on for over three years and costs crept up about 20 percent – to $3 million. It was dedicated during the last months of the Wells administration, in April 1962; Professor Bernhard C. Heiden composed "A Fanfare to the New Building" as part of the festivities. Wells and Bain were pleased that the new facility brought back together personnel and programs from widely scattered temporary structures into a unified physical plant, with one major exception – the cavernous performance space of East Hall, a former World War II airplane hangar.[37] A month after the annex's dedication, Wells was quoted in the *Indiana Daily Student,* and expressed great institutional pride in the growth and stature of the School of Music: "Once upon a time music was looked upon as something easy and 'precious' in the higher education curriculum of America. Today, however, no division requires more hard grueling work for a degree."[38] He had every reason to feel proud.

At the end of Wells's tenure as president in 1962, Bain publicly thanked him: "On behalf of the Faculty of the School of Music and its many students, I wish to thank the President of the University, the Board of Trustees, and the Administrative Committee for their continued efforts in creating and maintaining a climate in which the most advanced artist-teachers find satisfaction. The record of achievement of music at this University is a testament to the wise and vigorous leadership of one of America's great university presidents."[39]

Wells followed the fortunes of the School of Music after he traded his president's chair for the new post of chancellor after 1962. Serving as the chief ambassador and fundraising head for Indiana University, he was able to expand this role to become the institution's general factotum and emblematic leader.

In 1964, the music school instituted a year-round production of grand opera. The school was now sizable: 732 undergraduates and 440 graduate students gave 676 public performances, including 10 operas and operettas, in the academic year 1964–65. Responding to Governor Matthew Welsh's request, the school presented outdoor productions of *Turandot* on "Indiana Day" at the New York World's Fair on August 17 and 18, 1964: "It was said these attracted the largest audiences ever to see an operatic performance in New York." Wells, working in New York City for the Education and World Affairs organization at that time, was surely pleased with this public relations coup.[40]

RISING FROM THE ASHES

In January 1968, a major fire destroyed East Hall, the performance venue that had provided a home for the opera program since its beginnings. Historian Thomas Clark described it vividly:

> Standing gaunt and virtually stripped of any former glory the old World War II hangar might have enjoyed as the seat of campus opera performances, East Hall vanished in a roar of flame and smoke. The ashes of the crumpling old building seeded the ground with symbolic continuity. Here the new Musical Arts Center would rise in all its glory to give the university a permanent leasehold on both musical and operatic art.[41]

With the opening of the Musical Arts Center, Bain's administrative career as dean of the IU School of Music ended with a grand flourish in 1973. In the twenty-five years that he served as head, student enrollment increased from 225 in to 1,700 – an almost eightfold increase. Likewise, the number of faculty grew at a similar pace, from 25 to 150. Bain had achieved his dream of a full-scale opera program. With the essential support of Wells, the university rode high on the wave of the postwar growth of public universities, with the crest of the music school's reputation second to none in America. Reviewing *Parsifal*, the last of twenty-three IU productions of Wagner's great work, in 1976, *New Yorker* music critic Andrew Porter announced, "Indiana University Opera Theater is just about the most serious and consistently satisfying of all American opera companies."[42]

LOOKING BACK

In his autobiography, Wells wrote little about the rise of the School of Music during and after his presidential tenure, and was characteristically generous with praise for others and modest about his own contributions. Focusing on Dean Bain and his notable faculty recruits, Wells stated, "[H]e had developed within a relatively few years a school of international fame. He accomplished this through the rare spirit he was able to engender, not by an infusion of funds, for he was allocated much less money than he could have expected on the basis of the School of Music's rapidly rising enrollment." The last phrase was an acknowledgment of Bain's repeated budgetary entreaties; what was left unsaid was the truly extraordinary support, in moral and budgetary terms, that Wells had steadfastly provided.[43]

The University believes the human race has been able to make progress because individuals have been free to investigate all aspects of life. It further believes that only through scientific knowledge so gained can we find the cures for the emotional and social maladies of our society. In support of Dr. Kinsey's research the University is proud to have as co-sponsor the National Research Council. . . . With the chairman of that committee, I agree in saying that we have large faith in the values of knowledge, little faith in ignorance.

Herman B Wells

TWELVE

The Man behind Kinsey

WHEN HE PAUSED TO REFLECT ON THE POSTWAR SITUATION, Herman Wells took pleasure in the emerging shape of Indiana University – "his" IU. Not that IU belonged to him, or to any other person for that matter, but that *he* belonged to the university, and was happy and fulfilled in his public servant role.

Physically, Wells was also feeling good. Claiming he was too busy to stick to dietary regimens to control his weight, Wells continued to exercise his prodigious appetite for good food in the company of friends and to enjoy the occasional drink of Scotch whisky – preferably the Pinch brand. His rotund shape disguised a rude animal health. His apparently sedentary routine was actually a strenuous daily workout of meetings, consultations, correspondence and telephoning, and travel. Unlike most people, he rarely felt the need for retreat from human contact. There seemed to be a synergy between his level of social involvement and his personal vivacity.

Indiana was poised to move ahead. Certain areas, such as nuclear physics, mathematics, and biology, were already much further advanced than they had been during the Bryan administration. Other areas – such as fine arts, psychology, music, and folklore – had been newly revived with the addition of academic personnel and resources.

KINSEY'S RESEARCH

Biology professor Alfred Kinsey had dramatically expanded the scope of his sex research project with the help of a continuing series of grants from the National Research Council's Committee on the Problems of Sex. He was able to hire three colleagues to help gather sexual histories as well as additional staff to operate the library, translate foreign books and periodicals, and curate the growing collection of artifacts and artworks.

Wells watched the extension of Kinsey's territory with approval. Although Kinsey presented detailed reports to the president's office, and urged Wells repeatedly to come and visit the laboratory, the busy president begged off, time and again. But Wells was scrupulous in providing administrative support for the NRC grants and fending off continuing criticism of Kinsey's research.

Kinsey's periodic reports did not gather dust in the president's files, but were a valuable source of information to develop a comprehensive strategy to protect Kinsey's academic freedom. Although Indiana had but a short history of democratic faculty governance, now policies were in place to provide latitude to conduct controversial or unpopular research. In 1942, the board of trustees made IU a signatory of the 1940 Statement of Principles on Academic Freedom and Tenure, jointly issued by the American Association of University Professors and the Association of American Colleges and Universities. This brief statement outlined both the rights and responsibilities of faculty working in higher education institutions. Its purpose was

> to promote public understanding and support of academic freedom and tenure and agreement upon procedures to ensure them in colleges and universities. Institutions of higher education are conducted for the common good and not to further the interest of either the individual teacher or the institution as a whole. The common good depends upon the free search for truth and its free exposition.

In addition to offering a ringing endorsement of unfettered inquiry and the rationale for tenure, the statement also provided a general framework for the creation of institutional policies. Wells hewed closely both to the spirit and the formal dictates of the directive, which encapsulated his educational philosophy about the relation between the university and the commonwealth, and before long the university was in compliance.

With characteristic forethought, Wells looked ahead to the eventual publication of Kinsey's findings. The analysis of the several thousand male interviews approached completion in 1946, and Kinsey started writing in earnest in early 1947. In that period, Wells took several steps to protect the university and mitigate future controversy. In 1946, he suggested that Kinsey seek a well-established medical publisher. Kinsey agreed, explaining to one publisher that there would be "special problems in keeping the book identified as a very sober, scientific contribution . . . much needed in the medical field."[1] After several unsuccessful tries, following a lecture in Philadelphia Kinsey made serendipitous contact with Lawrence S. Saunders, president of the venerable medical publisher W. B. Saunders, who became enthusiastic about publishing what was soon called "the male volume" after its data source.

In that first postwar year, Wells attempted to sort out the complex administrative tangle surrounding Kinsey's growing project. Indiana University was still paying Kinsey's salary and providing space and utility services on campus. The National Research Council (NRC), a quasi-governmental scientific agency, funneled the grants to pay for the increased staff and the library and associated collections. The Rockefeller Foundation, which was the source of the NRC funds, also had a legitimate interest in the work and its products, but was less willing to be identified publicly as a supporter of sex research. To complicate matters further, Kinsey had started to bypass the NRC and dealt directly with the Rockefeller Foundation and its program officer Alan Gregg, much to the consternation of Robert Yerkes and his successor George Corner, chairs of the NRC's Committee on the Problems of Sex.

Playing always within the rules, Wells reasoned that the first line of defense should be legal in nature. The ingenious president suggested that Kinsey's research enterprise be incorporated as a private, nonprofit research entity. The legal status of a corporation would ensure the project's independence and provide a measure of jurisdictive distance from IU. The sex history interviews, as well as the books, art objects, and artifacts, would be the property of the organization and not subject to public inspection. Kinsey liked the idea because it offered protection for the project, particularly the confidentiality of the interviews, and reinforced his position as leader.

Both the NRC and the Rockefeller Foundation saw advantages in such a scheme. The NRC's Yerkes, who suggested that it be named the Institute for Sex Research (ISR), thought that the independent body would deflect fire from potential attacks on the NRC and its support. He was also anxious to "set the seal on the project he'd spent so much time supporting and defending" prior to his retirement in 1948.[2] For their part, Gregg and the Rockefeller Foundation, constantly worried about negative publicity, also believed that the establishment of the ISR would provide administrative clarity and open a prudent distance between the organizations.

After protracted negotiations, the Institute for Sex Research was incorporated in April 1947. The articles of incorporation listed the purposes of the ISR: "to continue research on human sexual behavior; to accept, hold, use, and administer research materials, a library, case histories, and other materials relating to the project; and finally, to acquire, own, hold, rent or lease such real estate and personal property as might be reasonably necessary to carry out the general purposes of the Institute."[3] To complete the organization of the new institute, Kinsey transferred his research materials, including its voluminous files of individual sexual histories, to the new corporation for the nominal amount of "$1.00 and other considerations."[4] An important clause was added to the transfer agreement. In the event of the corporation's disestablishment, its property would go either to the Rockefeller Foundation or to another educational institution where the research could be continued. That was to provide a safeguard in case IU withdrew its support or of Kinsey's death so the research would be continued regardless of its location. The original ISR board of directors was comprised of Kinsey and his core staff members – Clyde Martin, Wardell Pomeroy, and Paul Gebhard, who had arrived the previous year.[5]

With Kinsey's work now incorporated into the Institute for Sex Research, Wells had constructed another bulwark against criticism directed toward the university. He could honestly say that, although IU paid Kinsey's salary, his sex research was under the auspices of a separate, autonomous organization, which happened to be based at Indiana. Of course, this glossed over the extensive record of the university's support over the previous decade, but it had the advantage of literal accuracy.

Kinsey proposed, and Wells quickly agreed, that any earnings made from books or lectures by the institute's staff would be reinvested in the institute. That provision would prove useful in generating income as well as making Kinsey and his coworkers immune from the charge that they were personally profiting from the project.[6]

PUBLICATION OF THE *MALE* VOLUME

During the first few months of 1947, Kinsey worked tirelessly on the writing *of Sexual Behavior in the Human Male*. Although the prepositional term "in" was to confound many, the title reflected his conformance to technical biological usage by referring to behavior *within* the male of the human species and not *all* human males. Publication plans proceeded apace with W. B. Saunders, and Kinsey worked with their copyeditor and his coauthors to get the book in final form. Proofreading and indexing were accomplished by late October, and the publication date was set for early January 1948.

Wells, who had earlier suggested a medical publisher to maximize its chances for scientific impact and minimize potential sensational reactions, had also asked Kinsey to consider the Indiana General Assembly's legislative calendar when fixing a publication date. An astute observer of Indiana politics generally and legislators' fluctuating moods in particular, Wells knew that the Assembly was subject to "agitation" whenever it was in its annual sixty-one-day session, and cautioned Kinsey to avoid publication either shortly before or during the legislative session.

Wells remained active behind the scenes, regularly talking to individual trustees and the board as a whole to keep them apprised of Kinsey's controversial research. The trustees were well aware that one of their members, Nellie Showers Teter, had taken Kinsey's marriage course several years earlier, and her enthusiastic endorsement of the research was on the record. Wells urged the trustees to be united in their support of Kinsey's right to conduct his research if they were called on publicly. He reiterated that they could have any private opinions on the veracity and worth of the research, but that they needed to be unanimous in their backing of Kinsey's (or any other professor's) academic freedom.

Wells spread the same message throughout his administration. In September 1947, he circulated a memo to the University Executive Committee saying the book was bound to be controversial, and represented a crucial test of academic freedom:

> It seems to me it is essential that we stand firm in our support of the book and
> the research. We are not called upon to endorse the findings, but we are called
> upon to stand firm in support of the importance of the project and the right to
> publish it. Any less than that would be fatal. We would lose the respect and the
> services of our best faculty men and the respect of the scholarly world more
> generally.[7]

After all of this advance preparation, *Sexual Behavior in the Human Male* was published on January 5, 1948.

The Saunders publishing house, using market research, estimated the book would sell around ten thousand copies over time. Instead, the presses worked overtime to meet the overwhelming demand. Within two months, two hundred thousand copies had been sold. The first year's royalties generated $180,000 for the ISR coffers. Public reaction was swift and vociferous, as newspaper headlines screamed the report's findings and magazines debated its meaning. Among the topics receiving the most attention were the report's findings on "premarital sex, frequency of extramarital relations, homosexuality, and the commentary on out-of-date sex laws."[8]

Wells found himself fending off attacks to the university constantly. Irate alumni and ordinary citizens inundated his office with indignant comments and unsolicited advice to fire Kinsey. For example, one disgruntled alumnus wrote that Kinsey "has dragged the name of Indiana University low enough and it is time to get rid of him." Wells was calm and measured in replying to all but the worst of the crackpots, citing some or all of the following elements in his response: the value of Kinsey's comparative methods had long been established; the Vatican Library in Rome contained the largest collection of sexual, including pornographic, materials in the world; and that "Kinsey's materials were no more obscene than were the illustrations in the old medical standby, *Gray's Anatomy*."[9]

Although Wells and Kinsey stood side by side in defense of sex research, Wells's non-confrontational approach sometimes irritated the combative Kinsey. In 1951, Wells explored with Claude Rich, the director of the alumni association, the suggestion that a story about Kinsey and his research be featured in the *Indiana Alumni Magazine*. Such a story would be a departure for the staid magazine, but might give alumni useful information about the controversial project, Wells reasoned. When Kinsey heard about the idea, he exploded with annoyance. To soothe the professor's ruffled feathers, Wells wrote back mildly, taking responsibility for the suggestion of an article: "It occurred to me we owed it to our alumni to really give them the facts essential to their understanding of your project so they might defend you and the University when occasion arose. I may say that I was not prompted by any splurge of reaction but by the belief that in public relations the offensive and precautionary measures are the most effective."[10]

With two decades of experience in Indiana politics, Wells was a master player. Understanding his role as an agent of the state, he wielded his authority with restraint, using his intimate knowledge of the system and the forces at play within it to place the presidential office in an advantageous position. "The reason state universities can be the freest of all institutions is that you have all the forces bearing on them," Wells explained.

> You have labor and capital and manufacturers associations, and the farmers associations, the preachers, the Methodists, the Catholics, the poor, the rich, and they counteract each other. So, if they are handled right, correctly, they create a vacuum in the center, which gives you the freedom to operate. Now, this is frequently not true in a private institution, which is dominated by a certain group from the outside. You can't balance the forces. And this is part of the executive job to get a balance between these forces so that they counteract each other and leave you room for freedom in the middle.[11]

Wells performed this "balancing act" over and over in defending Kinsey and his work from outside interference.

THE PRESIDENT AND THE PROFESSOR

Both Kinsey and Wells maintained scrupulously dignified public profiles that contributed in no small way to their success in keeping the sex research going. Each was singularly devoted to their respective subjects at IU – biology and administration. Wells's increasing national stature, leavened by a winning personal charm, provided an effective screen against criticism. Careful to keep his scientific persona intact, Kinsey was the sober, serious researcher, and "his personality and private moral habits were tough shields against attacks upon him for frivolity or lasciviousness."[12] Each man could rely on the other to care for the project's public face.

Kinsey and Wells could not have been more different in personal style, academic career, and political affiliation, however. Although Kinsey was a scientific reductionist, counting orgasms and tallying sexual outlets, he treated his human subjects with compassion and respect. His staff and colleagues had varied descriptions of his managerial style along a spectrum from dominating to dictatorial, but all agreed he was the undisputed boss of the team. Beyond the "inner circle" of the project, he was forceful and controlling, and combative when under attack. A Republican, Kinsey was happily married with three children. In contrast, Wells, eight years younger than Kinsey, was a confirmed bachelor and a New Deal Democrat. Tolerant and genial, he was charmingly persuasive and tried to avoid direct confrontation. An administrative mastermind, he worked tirelessly to serve the interests of the university.

They never became personal friends, and there is only one photograph that pictures them both. The general outlines of their relationship are well known: the unconventional scientist pursued his increasingly controversial investigations, and the agile president steadfastly supported Kinsey's right to perform his research and publish his work. Two biographies of Kinsey published in the 1990s, plus recent film (both feature and documentary) and fiction treatment, have added new texture to enrich interpretations of Kinsey's life and career. Comparatively little has been added to the picture of Wells and his role, however, and the standard account verges on the hagiographic.

In their core beliefs they were remarkably alike. The two men shared a love of learning and academic life and had tremendous faith in the individual and collective benefit of knowledge. Kinsey, whatever his personal motivations to pursue sex research, was an avowed rationalist in his public pronouncements about the results of his research and implications of it. There is ample documentation in his published writings. A career scientist and educator, he burned with a desire to find out and let other people know. He had great faith in scientific knowledge and its power to liberate the mind, and by extension, society.

Wells, an economist by training, found it easy to navigate between theory and practice. He knew the value of empirical data, whether to use in a formula or to guide the creation of policy. He also was an avid collector – of financial data, antiques, friends, and travels – and fashioned them into an expansive worldview that placed learning and education as a superior good. Wells was convinced of the liberating influence of education on human potentiality and its contribution to individual and collective wellbeing.

Both had an Enlightenment vision about the unmitigated value of knowledge, although one might say that Kinsey devoted himself to depth whereas Wells preferred breadth. Each believed that academic freedom was paramount in the modern university. Ultimately, both men were social progressives, even radicals, in their faith that human liberation was made possible by knowledge and education. From this perspective, despite other differences, they shared a profound allegiance and interdependence.

Sex was the defining characteristic of Kinsey's life. Before his death in 1956, Kinsey was known throughout America as "Dr. Sex" for his controversial research. Forty years after his death, biographers revealed the spectacular sex life that fueled Kinsey's research. By that time, Wells was in his mid-nineties. Throughout these many years, he maintained an unshakable reticence about his private life.

Even Kinsey could not penetrate this reserve. Apparently, Kinsey never asked Wells to contribute a sexual history to the project – perhaps the exception that proved the rule that Kinsey asked anybody and everybody that he met – for the obvious reason that the absence of a personal interview would allow the president to maintain a clear distinction between any personal knowledge of the content of the research and the overarching principle of academic freedom. Wells could honestly say that he had no direct investment or personal stake in the results.

Wells's Sphinx-like silence on personal topics was a product of his upbringing in small-town Indiana, but it occasioned rumors and speculation about his psychosexual orientation and preferences throughout his adulthood. Yet, to my knowledge, he never told anyone about erotic or romantic longings.

Wells was a single child, and when he got to Indiana University as an undergraduate in 1921, he blossomed socially and intellectually. A proud member of the Sigma Nu fraternity, he greatly enjoyed the parties, the camaraderie, and living among his new brothers. In college, Wells continued his high school practice of having a wide circle of friends, both male and female, but apparently no romantic partners.[13]

During his year of doctoral study at the University of Wisconsin in the late 1920s, Wells lived at University Club, a male-only preserve. Afterwards, when he worked for the Indiana state government, he kept a room at the Claypool Hotel. In 1930, after a couple of years on the IU faculty, he rented the historic Bloomington Woodburn House with a high school chum. He still lived there when he became acting president and started to employ a series of student helpers, called "housemen" or "houseboys."[14] The first one was an African American student five years younger than Wells. He was succeeded by dozens of students over the years, of many colors – white, brown, and black.

Some of his advisors counseled him to find a wife to increase the chances of being appointed permanent president, but he made no moves to do so. In the world of higher education administration, he was often in the exclusive sphere of men, and was at ease in the gender-segregated facilities that men of his status and time benefited from, such as the posh University Club in New York, where he stayed periodically on business trips as president and chancellor. We might conclude that he was homosocial, but whether by natural inclination or social adaptation, one cannot be sure.

Over the years, various individuals have raised the question of Wells's sexual identity. Kinsey's recent biographers, James Jones and Jonathan Gathorne-Hardy, believe Wells was homosexual, as does former Kinsey Institute director Paul Gebhard. Several current and former IU faculty members have told the author that was a subject of speculation from time to time. In 2000, as this biography project was just getting underway, *Indianapolis Star* writer Bill Shaw stated the question baldly: "Was Herman Wells a homosexual?" Other people chimed in.[15] All of these opinions were based on inference from circumstances, not textual evidence or personal testimony.

Motivated by the cultural assumption of heteronormativity, there is a certain irony in these insistent questions about whether Wells had significant homoerotic inclinations. To a large extent, Kinsey brought homosexuality out of the closet, and contributed greatly to what some might call the hypersexualization of American culture. But Kinsey's preoccupation with the measurement of sexual expression left little room for qualitative insights into the erotic imagination or for the study of other forms of affiliative behavior. In short, Kinsey's system was poorly designed to capture Wells's psychosexual individuality.

It appears that Wells's life was lacking in traditional romance or sexual eroticism of any sort. A bout of childhood orchitis left him with persistent pain that lasted for at least twenty years. Psychologically, he faced the common presupposition that orchitis would impair his fertility, and, given cultural expectations that reproduction was the primary reason for matrimony, that prognosis closed off the marriage option. Whatever the impetus, he became a lifelong bachelor.

Wells, who had just moved to a larger town with a bigger high school, was a sensitive fifteen-year-old boy when this physiological trauma started. There were no road maps to guide him through recovery, and his parents, while supportive, did not have much to offer beside their example of Hoosier stoicism in the face of adversity. We know next to nothing of Wells's degree of consciousness about his situation and little about exactly how he managed to work through these challenges, but we do know that he did. From the time he was a sophomore to his high school graduation, he developed a remarkable capacity for friendship. Based on a discerning empathy, Wells made himself essential to any group that he found himself in, often by offering his communication skills and knowledge of business practices.

Starting as a coping strategy, the focus on filial love and friendship ripened into an unusually rich concern for others as Wells reached adulthood and extended his hand toward many, many people over the course of his long life. Not content with practicing the brotherly love that is called philia, he also was a student of agape, a transpersonal or spiritual love for humanity. Not having a single lover or partner, Wells could experience liberation: "Since I didn't belong to anyone, I belonged to everyone," in the words of his friend Theodore Hesburgh, Notre Dame president.[16] There is much evidence that Wells loved his fellows greatly, both individually and collectively, and pursued his life with remarkable vigor and éclat. But the riddle of his sexual orientation remains an open question, assuming it is relevant at all.

Taking the long view, Kinsey can be seen as the spirited outsider, clamoring to tear down the walls of ignorance and taboo in regard to sexual behavior, whereas Wells was the consummate insider, working a quiet transformation in public higher education. Each one exhibited a career verging on monomania, and, despite their surface differences, they were sons of the Enlightenment and belonged, in divergent ways, to the same iconoclastic brotherhood.

SEXUAL BEHAVIOR IN THE HUMAN FEMALE

After the explosive debut of the Kinsey report on men's sexual behavior in 1948, the staff of the Institute for Sex Research continued their work on a companion volume dealing with women. The interview team of Kinsey, Gebhard, Pomeroy, and Martin crisscrossed the country seeking sexual histories from a diverse array of women, including college students, prison inmates, sex workers, and housewives. Their labors were now in the public spotlight, which both helped and hindered the research.

For his part, Wells was in regular communication with Kinsey, and kept the IU trustees abreast of the research. To keep the critics in the Indiana General Assembly at bay, Wells invited members of the budget committee down to Bloomington to visit the ISR and see what was going on. Kinsey turned on his considerable charm as he led the group through the nondescript offices and explained the scientific importance of the research. Members returned to Indianapolis enthusiastic about the project.

About six months prior to the publication of the "female volume" in 1953, both Kinsey and Wells stepped up the public information campaign. Kinsey made up an elaborate set of rules for reporters covering the story. Privately, Wells again exhorted the IU Board of Trustees to show unanimous support of the controversial professor's right to conduct his research.

In the pages of the *Indiana Alumni Magazine,* Wells responded to a letter criticizing Kinsey sent by the Indiana chapter of the National Council of Catholic Women. His reply began, "Indiana University stands today, as it has for fifteen years, firmly in support of the scientific research project that has been undertaken and is being carried on by one of its eminent biological scientists, Dr. Alfred C. Kinsey." He reaffirmed the project's connection to the National Research Council and reiterated faith in the values of knowledge. "The University never approves or disapproves the research findings of its experimental scientists," Wells said, adding, "This is just as true of popular as of unpopular results." He reminded readers that the search for truth was a major function of all universities, the right to investigate was a foundational principle, jealously protected by the institution – but that the knowledge produced has to withstand examination and criticism by other scientists through the peer review system before it is accepted. "This final verdict frequently takes many years, perhaps decades," Wells wrote. Changing topics, Wells assured the Catholic women that Kinsey's research was "entirely divorced" from teaching. Touting IU graduates as second to none in regard to "morals, ideals, high-minded purpose, and integrity," he dared anybody to say otherwise. Turning conciliatory, Wells thanked them, as well as members of other denominations, for their efforts to provide facilities for worship and religious study close to campus.[17]

This was a classic Wellsian statement. It began with a moderate, even bland, rehearsal of a basic university tenet about the value of scientific research, coupled with a citation of the approval of an outside body, and ended with a common-sense truism. Any edge was tempered with his genuine expression of gratitude for the role of Catholic women in the education of students. Wells was inviting this audience, and a more general one, to disregard the media hype and focus on the real issue of academic freedom.

Owing to the overwhelming publicity about the female volume and strident criticism of its contents, the Rockefeller Foundation decided to stop channeling money to the Institute for Sex Research. Deeply hurt by this vote of no confidence, Kinsey and his coworkers faced the daunting problem of how to raise funds for the extensive program of research and publication. Characteristically, Kinsey redoubled his efforts to convince the public – and potential donors – of the need for and value of sex research. There was no interruption in the university's support of the ISR's institutional needs, and the cordial relationship with President Wells continued. But Wells was reluctant to solicit private gifts for the institute due to his longstanding principle that it was unseemly for the chief executive of a state-supported institution to participate actively in outside fundraising.

Kinsey drove himself frenetically as he expanded the project to encompass the filming of live sexual acts, occasionally participating as a subject. His private sexual experimentation became even more reckless, too. Kinsey's behavior was taking a toll physically. His heart problems, dating from a serious childhood bout with rheumatic fever, recurred, compounded by physical and mental exhaustion. In early summer 1956, Kinsey's wife, Clara (nicknamed Mac), had him admitted to the Bloomington Hospital despite his protests. Wells visited him there, sharing Mac's worries privately.

In August 1956, Kinsey was back in the hospital, suffering from exhaustion apparently compounded by an infection. Wells dutifully paid him another visit, and learned from the doctors that the famous sex researcher might not make it. Kinsey died after a few days, aged sixty-two. As Wells consoled the family, he was thinking about how to preserve the sex research institute that was created by Kinsey and remained synonymous with his name.[18]

As ideas are the fruit of the university and scholars the blood that give her life, so books are the university's sustenance.

Herman B Wells, 1960

THIRTEEN

A Metropolis of Books

TEXTS IN ALL THEIR FORMS ARE THE CENTRAL TOOL of scholarship and education. Institutions of higher education must have repositories to hold cumulated knowledge, ranging from the medieval monks illuminating sacred incunabula to specialized monographs and sleek modern textbooks. Libraries have evolved to fulfill this function. Detractors dismiss them as "warehouses for books," while aficionados celebrate them as the iconic records of the highest achievements of humankind. Whatever the attitude, libraries play a major role in the modern university and serve as fundamental symbols of the pursuit of knowledge.

When Herman Wells was an IU undergraduate in the early 1920s, the library building occupied a prominent location at the northeast corner of Kirkwood and Indiana Avenues. Not quite fifteen years old, the large but unpretentious collegiate Gothic structure was a stone's throw from the more boisterous Book Nook, where books were certainly not on the menu. The library was expanded in 1927 with an additional wing to the east, abutting the Student Building. In 1934, at the behest of President Bryan, workmen carved a favorite quotation from John Milton over the entrance: "A good book is the precious life-blood of a master spirit." Although Bryan gave up his active scholarship to become an administrator, he found the time to read seriously and thoughtfully. He promoted IU alumnus William A. Alexander to head librarian (and chief organizer of the Memorial Fund drive) in 1921, and followed the development of the book collection with satisfaction.[1]

When Alexander took over the library, collections were modest, numbering fewer than two hundred thousand volumes. These served the needs of the undergraduate population and also provided materials for the research activities of the faculty and the small number of graduate students who were involved in original work. A dozen or more departmental libraries containing specialized materials were also in operation. By February 1937, a month before Bryan retired, the library reached another milestone with its three hundred thousandth accession.

As an undergraduate student during the heyday of the Memorial Fund campaign, Wells had become aware of Alexander in his organizing role. When Wells served as acting president in 1937, he got to know Alexander personally as a member of the executive advisory committee. The following year, after his selection as permanent president, Wells saw no need to replace Alexander, then aged sixty-two, as head of the important academic support unit. He had other, more pressing university business at the time.

A NEW LIBRARY DIRECTOR

In 1942, after five years in office, Wells set his sights on improving the library and its services. It had garnered criticism in the self-study report and it needed fresh leadership. Following his usual practice, he talked to trusted faculty colleagues and outside advisors to get names of promising men. One name, Robert A. Miller, was on this short list, and he was hired. Miller, a human dynamo, was inspired by Wells's plan for the renaissance of the institution and believed that the library would play a key role.

Although the library dated from the earliest days of the institution, it had suffered two major fires in 1854 and 1883; each one destroyed the entire book collection. It had been under the direction of a succession of faculty and staff, all self-taught in librarianship, and grew gradually to serve mainly the needs of undergraduate education. Miller, with advanced training from Columbia's School of Library Service and a Ph.D. from the University of Chicago's Graduate Library School, broke the mold of previous IU librarians. Hired from outside the institution, he brought a fresh perspective that was in tune with modern trends in university librarianship. He had strong support from Wells to upgrade the collections and services of the library, but he would face an uphill battle to gain the resources to aid his efforts.[2]

Ever since he was a youngster, Wells loved reading. He was a serious student during his high school and undergraduate days, and he spent hours at the library – first the Lebanon Public Library and then the Indiana University Library. History and literature were two of his favorite subjects. His first jobs, in banking and academia, required long hours of reading and digesting data. As president, he was totally committed to raising IU's research profile, and relentless in his promotion of scientific investigation, humanistic scholarship, and artistic creativity by the faculty. He also had a great appreciation for the ideals that drove scholarly innovation and was genuinely pleased when a new book or article flowed from the pen of an IU faculty member. Although only specialists in the field could follow the details of esoteric studies, Wells used his broad-ranging intelligence to grasp the gist of the matter and relate it to something in his own experience. When faculty chanced upon Wells at a musical performance or at a meeting, they were often pleasantly surprised that he had read their latest book and, moreover, could ask interesting questions about it.

So it was natural that Wells supported the library system and understood the various roles in which it served in the university: undergraduate storehouse and meeting place, faculty workshop, and indispensable campus ornament. Early in his presidency, he supported the reallocation of the central library acquisition budget to provide a small amount of funds to separate departments in order to obtain specialized materials. Although the sums involved were trivial, they generated tremendous goodwill among the faculty.[3]

Wells was secure in his belief that the library was in good hands. Miller was au courant with the latest thinking about university libraries and had good connections with other librarians around the country. He also had building experience; under his direction the University of Nebraska was completing a $1 million library facility.[4] With Miller, Wells took what was fast becoming his standard administrative approach: find a dynamic academic leader (preferably in early mid-career), infect the person with the vision of a greater Indiana University, hire the person and give him (or her) unstinting support, and then "leave them alone" to do their work.[5] For the most part, Wells left the operation of the library entirely to Miller, routinely approving plans and budgets for the growing unit. In one area, however, he took special interest: rare books and special collections.

In December 1948 Wells addressed the Bloomington Faculty Council to provide ideas for future building projects. Plans were already underway for a $25 million expansion of campus facilities, and "Wells was looking to the future." In addition to several major projects, he "set university sights on a new library."[6] By 1950, with rising enrollments and continued modernization of the campus, the university tried to plan ahead for the next decade. Again, a new library was on the priority list.

GROWING INDIANA UNIVERSITY PRESS

Notwithstanding the first flush of growth at IU Press, money problems became a perennial refrain. By 1954, Director Bernard Perry was complaining to Wells that the Press's budget was not sufficient, given the realities of publishing books with a limited academic market. He wanted both moral and financial support, asking rhetorically, "[D]oes the university want a top press, which will earn respect and admiration around the country or shall we retreat and become a nice sleepy publishing organization?"[7] Wells soothed Perry's ruffled feathers by increasing support for the Press and giving him periodic raises to keep him at IU.

After a succession of temporary offices on campus, Perry and his staff landed in the historic Wylie House in April 1953. Built by Andrew Wylie, the first IU president, in 1835 to house his large family, it was acquired by the university in 1948 at Wells's urging. Interested in anything that displayed the university's "antiquity," Wells also knew that any structure with four walls and a roof could be a valuable commodity in alleviating the postwar shortage, and the mansion was pressed into service. By 1959, IU Press had a staff of nineteen and was publishing thirty titles a year.[8] The Press took over publishing the Graduate School monograph series – separate series in humanities, folklore, and social science – and gave them the same attention to details as books. The faculty committee, a successor to the original planning committee, was very active in editorial operations, and worked closely with Perry and his staff.[9]

In 1961, the Press published *The Addict and the Law,* the result of a joint commission sponsored by the American Bar Association and the American Medical Association and headed by IU sociologist Alfred R. Lindesmith. Controversially, the book approached drug addiction as an illness, not as a form of criminal behavior. Despite Lindesmith's eminence as a criminologist, the Federal Bureau of Narcotics made an attempt to suppress the report, even sending an agent to interview the Press's staff. One analyst opined, "the Federal Bureau of Narcotics' concern about the report suggests that the Press was pushing at the limits of academic freedom by publishing it."[10]

When Wells stepped down as president in 1962, the Press had been in existence for a dozen years and was firmly established. The choice of Perry as director was inspired. He made the operation of the Press his life's work, and headed it for twenty-six years. He shared with Wells the "idealism about the role of university presses in public life," and had the "perspective, nerves, and solid knowledge of publishing combined with a feeling for scholarship" to ensure success.[11]

RARE BOOKS AT INDIANA

Under the Bryan administration, the university would acquire rare volumes as gifts or bequests, but had neither the budget nor the expertise to have a special collections policy. By 1940, the library had a modest research collection housed in the library stacks. The few rare books were in a special room, and could be seen only by appointment. During the next few years, some significant collections came to the university, including the Ellison collection of western Americana and some items relating to the War of 1812. In 1942, a large mass of material relating to U.S. president Abraham Lincoln, called the Oakleaf Collection, was acquired by the Ball Brothers Foundation and others, and given to the university.[12]

Growing ever more comfortable with his presidential role as an agent of the state of Indiana, Wells took a special interest in the effort to acquire books of unusual scholarly or cultural value for the university. He thought that the state university should possess objects of great cultural and artistic value, along with the associated scholarly connoisseurship, to aid in the education of the state's citizens. Rare books fit the bill perfectly.

In his first year as librarian, Miller created a Department of Rare Books and Special Collections, and hired Cecil K. Byrd, who had recently earned his doctorate in the IU history department, to manage it. Housed in renovated rooms in the library, the new facility was opened in 1942 with a grand display of the recently acquired Oakleaf Collection. Wells was well aware of the power of exhibitions to foment interest among the public as well as contribute to the education of students, and he assiduously aided the efforts of the librarians to bring special collections into the university's orbit. By 1945, several notable collections had come to Indiana, including Defoe, Wordsworth, the War of 1812, Ellison's western Americana, and the archives of Jonathan Williams and Hugh McCulloch. That same year, the *Indiana Quarterly for Bookmen* was inaugurated; it contained information on new collections "for the bookmen of Indiana and friends of the University."

J. K. LILLY, JR.

One of the bookmen of Indiana was Josiah K. Lilly, Jr., the grandson of Colonel Eli Lilly, founder of the Indianapolis pharmaceutical firm. Known as Joe to family and friends, he had an older brother, born eight years before, named Eli Lilly, Jr. The two brothers, both shy and reserved, inherited the family business, working together well but with a deep undercurrent of sibling rivalry. Joe Lilly graduated from the University of Michigan School of Pharmacy in 1914 and joined his father and brother in the family business. This triumvirate oversaw the transition of Eli Lilly and Company into a large modern corporation during World War II and afterward.[13]

Hewing to the family tradition of providing support to civic and religious causes in Indiana without fanfare, the three men created a private philanthropic foundation, the Lilly Endowment, in 1937 to support worthy projects in religion, education, and community development. With capital from gifts of stock in Eli Lilly and Company, the foundation grew to be one of the largest in the nation. Remaining focused on their hometown, Indianapolis, and home state, Indiana, the Lilly Endowment has, from time to time, supported national or international projects, but the bulk of its money has remained expended towards improving the lives of Hoosiers.

The two brothers also cultivated intense avocational interests. Eli, Jr., was an amateur archeologist who became an expert on the Native American mound-builder culture along the Ohio River.[14] Joe Lilly was a collector of fine objects, amassing superb collections of rare books and manuscripts, as well as works of art, coins, stamps, military miniatures, firearms and edged weapons, and nautical models.[15] At first, Lilly kept his growing library in his Indianapolis home, but it was moved in 1936 to Eagle Crest Library, a specially constructed facility on family land northwest of Indianapolis.

Joe Lilly had the wherewithal to acquire the best of the best, and he pursued his passion with single-minded intensity: "He bought a book or manuscript only when he found pleasure in it, and rejected anything about which he could not muster 'enthusiasm.'"[16] Although he worked with rare book dealers, Lilly personally selected the books and manuscripts he bought. His collection was particularly strong in classic works in British and American literature, history of science and medicine, and Americana. As the Lilly collection grew in the 1940s and early 1950s, librarian Miller paid close attention to the development of library resources at Indiana University, making connections to book people around the country. He and Byrd were in sporadic communication with Lilly, occasionally visiting their fellow bibliophile at Eagle Crest Library.

Wells was kept apprised of these developments. He found out that Lilly was in the audience for the first visit by the Metropolitan Opera Company to the IU Auditorium, a performance of Aïda, and used the occasion to begin writing to Lilly about items of mutual interest. Both men had deep Hoosier roots and took their civic responsibilities seriously. Wells admired Lilly's business acumen and corporate successes, and Lilly could not help but notice how Wells was enhancing the stature of the state's flagship university.

In 1953, Joe Lilly retired as president of Eli Lilly and Company and became chairman of the board of directors. The following fall he confided to David Randall, his favorite bookseller at Scribner's, that he would like to divest his collection, and suggested setting up a joint business with his library as stock. But financial analysis deemed that the tax consequences would be too great.[17]

With no advance indication, on November 26, 1954, Lilly sent a letter to Wells signaling his wish that Indiana University would assemble "the most outstanding general collection of rare historical and literary material in the Middle West." He went on to say, "In what I hope to be a substantial beginning of this collection, I desire now to present to Indiana University all of the books in my general collection covering the period from 1469 to 1551, which embraces a total of sixty-nine titles." He requested no publicity, and trusted that delivery could be arranged soon, "not later than the first part of December."

Stunned at the university's good fortune, Wells wrote back with unbridled enthusiasm, saying "In the years of my presidency there has been no single event which has given me greater joy than the receipt of your letter of November 26th. We are profoundly grateful to you for your generous gift and accept the trusteeship of your books with full knowledge of the entailed responsibility." Wells then reviewed progress on storage and display areas for the growing rare book library and special collections, and told Lilly about future plans to build a new library in a more central location.[18]

So began a correspondence that was to include deeds of gift – three more in all – that comprised the entire book and manuscript collection assembled by Lilly over three decades of concentrated accumulation, totaling more than twenty thousand volumes, seventeen thousand manuscripts, fifty oil portraits, and three hundred prints. The bequest was truly breathtaking. Characteristically, Lilly wanted the bare minimum of publicity regarding his munificence, no involvement with the operation of the proposed library, and a name that reflected his family, not his person.

The IU News Bureau announced the gift in January 1956, over a year after events were set into motion. The release read, "It is regarded by rare book authorities as the largest and most valuable gift of its kind ever made to a American university." The *New York Times* estimated its worth at $5 million. The story was picked up both domestically and abroad, sometimes with fanciful elaboration. Wells, in his annual report on the state of the university, distilled the meaning of the contribution: "The character of the University Library was changed almost overnight with . . . the great gift of J. K. Lilly, Jr., of rare books, first editions and manuscripts. Our former concept of the Library as an agency of local service must be modified to include its new responsibility to national scholarship . . . and to lay the foundation for a wider scholarly use of its rare books and special collections."[19]

THE LILLY LIBRARY

Perhaps not surprisingly, the first curator of the Lilly collection was David A. Randall, manager of Scribner's Rare Book Department in New York since 1934 and a major source of books purchased by Lilly. For over two decades Randall and Lilly shared their mutual interest in book collecting, with their acquisitive acumen reinforcing each other. Randall knew the Lilly collection better than anyone besides its owner. He was appointed rare book librarian and professor of bibliography in July 1956.

Because books were his passion, Randall made the transition from the book trade to academic life easily. He recalled in his autobiography,

> I had gone into my profession because I liked to be around books which, individually, I could never have aspired to. But the trouble was (or so I rationalized), someone was always buying them and taking them away just when we were becoming friends. Here I could get them and keep them – and what a lot of old friends I had to begin with.[20]

The Lilly gift underscored the woefully inadequate library facility. Squeezed into a corner of the main library, the Department of Rare Books and Special Collections had hardly enough space for its modest collection, much less for the Lilly gift. Miller, Byrd, and Wells immediately started to think about how to protect, preserve, and make accessible this literary treasure trove. Waiting for a new main library was rejected on the grounds that getting such a large appropriation approved would be a lengthy process, in addition to a long period of construction. Wells also worried that a facility for rare books might be considered a frivolous expense by state legislators because it would not directly serve undergraduates.

Revisiting the master plan for a "cultural quadrangle" on Seventh Street, Wells reasoned that a special library dedicated to the literary arts might fit well. The IU Auditorium, opened in 1941, was the cornerstone of that ambitious dream. That dream turned into a vision for a group of fine arts facilities as Wells successfully persuaded others of the desirability of the idea. But cultivating enthusiasm was only part of the slow and arduous process of laying the groundwork. The plan included a circle of buildings surrounding a monumental fountain. Sketches for a fountain had been completed a few years before, but private funding for construction proved elusive. In addition to the auditorium, a fine arts building that included studios and exhibit space and a large outdoor amphitheatre, inspired by the Hearst Greek Theatre on the Berkeley campus of the University of California, would complete the ensemble.

Although the gently sloping ground on the south side of the emerging plaza was ideal for an amphitheatre, the Indiana climate was not. But a library would fit nicely. By 1958, architects Eggers and Higgins had designed a dignified collegiate Gothic building, built of local limestone, for the site. With touches of Art Deco styling and no windows in its façade, it resembled a museum, which was one of its functions.[21] It was privately funded by Joe Lilly, who again insisted that it not carry his name, but only the family's surname.

The Lilly Library was dedicated in 1960, nearly twenty years after the anchor building for the fine arts plaza, the IU Auditorium, was opened. In his remarks at the ceremony, Wells declared "these treasures of the written word [have] fourfold significance" to the campus, by simultaneously serving the mature scholar, the student, the state's citizens, and, indeed, the nation. "Their presence here is proof again of our determination in America to bring to *all* of our people, wherever they may live, the inspiration and sense of creative excitement which derive from personal acquaintanceship with the original evidence of man's highest intellectual achievement," Wells explained. "In America we have never sought to construct a capital of culture," he continued. "[I]nstead, we have attempted to distribute across our land the rich fruits of man's mental effort" much like sharing "the wealth of our farms and factories."[22]

TOWARD A NEW GENERAL LIBRARY

Although the Lilly gift instantly put IU in the select company of other rare books libraries, nearly all of which were located either on the East or West Coasts, director Miller and his staff were making important improvements to other areas of the library system.

During the McCarthy era, patriotic zealots singled out the I U library for attacks. In June 1952, Hal Denman, a Kokomo citizen and editor of *Counter Action Magazine,* spoke to a meeting of the Veterans of Foreign Wars. Waving around foreign periodicals with a library stamp, he charged that the I U library had become a "transmission belt for Communist propaganda." How he got such non-circulating materials, if indeed they were what he claimed them to be, was never explained.

Wells, always taking such assaults against the university seriously, worked with the library administration to craft a reasonable response: "Indiana University would have a very inadequate library if it did not provide students with all types of literature. How else could scholars and students analyze and develop defenses against Communistic ideas and goals if documents and reports of Communistic materials were not available?" The statement went on to say that faculty and students study propaganda just as they would any other fields.[23] This measured but firm rejoinder successfully countered any sustained attack against the library housing "un-American materials."

In the meantime, the library had run out of room to house its bulging collection or to seat its patrons. Books were moldering in storage or simply piled on floors. In 1956, Wells successfully lobbied the Budget Committee of the Indiana General Assembly for an addition to the stack area, assuring the legislators that it would be adequate for fifteen to twenty years.[24] The new stacks looked out over Dunn Meadow. Now the library was an agglomeration of three buildings – the 1908 original plus two additions completed in 1927 and 1956 – all with different interior elevations.

Ironically, the construction of the Lilly Library – a "rare book temple" – exerted a downward pull on the longstanding priority of a new library.[25] Meant primarily to house Lilly's magnificent gift, it had little effect on the overcrowding of the general stacks. During the final years of the Wells administration, Miller was joined by other voices in lamenting the deteriorating physical condition of the main library. Although the building was only about fifty years old, the growth of the university after World War II made its insufficiency apparent to nearly all. Collections had increased almost geometrically, from 382,453 in 1938 to 2,300,000 in 1957.[26] Emphasis on research meant that specialized monographs and periodicals continued to be acquired to serve the needs of mounting numbers of faculty and graduate students. The only bright spot was the construction of the Lilly Library.

Now that provisions were made to store and show the treasures of rare books and other special collections, Wells was gratified. Although he was concerned about the state of the library's main facility, he had long been accustomed to under-built university facilities with their inevitable crowding and jostling for space. He also knew that he could use that as a compelling argument for increased facility budgets during presentations to the Indiana legislature. Although he could be audacious in his requests, he also understood the limits to the state's largess.

In 1961, IU political scientist (and future IU president) Joseph Sutton and historian Robert F. Byrnes emphasized to the faculty council and the administration that a new library should have priority in the next ten-year plan. Byrnes said that he "could not conceive of a project that should supersede the library as the no. 1 item in our building program. The only major dissatisfaction with the University among faculty and, even so, among students [is] the library. . . . We are now behind and shall lose valuable faculty members if we don't get going right now."[27]

Although Wells did not agree, his difference of opinion was clad in conciliatory language. He was not opposed to the building of a new library per se; he argued that the $15 million price tag "would place too serious a drain on faculty facilities and other buildings that had even greater priorities." In a time of rising enrollment, meeting the needs for classroom and office space would be a continuing problem. Warning that faculty might have to double up in offices and that "many departments that might have expected new buildings would have to be content with rehabilitated older buildings," he even floated the suggestion that the course of the school day might have to be extended to the evening hours or perhaps Saturday.[28]

Despite Wells's cautionary remarks, the library director was already taking steps toward the construction of the building. With the support of the administrative committee, Miller asked the architectural firm of Eggers and Higgins to put together a preliminary design plan for a modern library.

When Elvis Stahr succeeded Wells as president in 1962, plans were revived yet again for the construction of a new general library. Miller had been on the job for twenty years at this point. Under his administration, Indiana had emerged as "a major purchaser in both the rare and current book markets" and library's collection had "grown phenomenally" to support the university's greatly ramified programs.[29] In 1964, the university's budget request to the state included $11,900,000 for a new library. At last, in 1966, final planning got underway. The chosen site, at the corner of Tenth Street and Jordan Avenue, just beyond the old Memorial Stadium on Tenth, would mark the transition between the academic precinct and the student residential area. The imposing building, set on a slight hill, provided a visual anchor to the newer parts of the campus. Constructed of irregular limestone blocks, prefabricated on large panels, the structure contained more cubic feet than any other academic library in the nation. Opened in 1970, the new structure towered over the deteriorating Tenth Street stadium, used just once a year to hold the Little 500 cycling race.

By the time library director Robert Miller retired in 1972, the libraries at Indiana University boasted the fourteenth largest collection in the United States, in addition to the literary treasures contained in the Lilly Library. That was truly a staggering achievement, from a provincial storehouse to a cosmopolitan metropolis in less than thirty years.

After his retirement from the president's office, Wells replied to a reporter's question about whether he would have done anything differently in his administration. He pondered long and hard before answering, "Well, I suppose if I were to do it over again, I would put more money into the library collections." Perhaps he was remembering his occasional foot dragging when it came to the library's needs. His assistant, Dorothy Collins, mentioned the remark to Carl Jackson, Miller's successor, who was astonished: "When I was at Iowa, we thought of Dr. Wells as the model university president for a university librarian to have because he paid so much attention to the needs of the library."[30]

During the 1950s American institutions of higher education began to shed their parochialism and slowly embrace the concept that the world is education's parish.

Herman B Wells, 1980

FOURTEEN

Expanding the University's Universe

BY THE EARLY 1950S, no longer was higher education for the lucky few, but now a birthright for all Americans as the age of mass post-secondary education dawned. The GI Bill opened the floodgates of access and Cold War policies continued to keep them open. Quantitative changes in the student body led to qualitative changes in student expectations and culture, at Indiana and elsewhere. For the expanded middle classes, going to college became a rite of passage to adulthood. Students spent four years of relative freedom in varied ways, ranging from passionate study and deep scholarly immersion to an equally fervent pursuit of intoxication through romance, relationships, and chemical compounds. With bigger classes, an expanding university bureaucracy, and a loosening of social mores, students were presented with a paradox. On the one hand, they had more autonomy and freedom to choose their courses and college lifestyle. On the other hand, more and more of their lives were caught up within an increasingly complex and differentiated institution. "Student services" replaced in loco parentis and "residence halls" supplanted dormitories. Student personnel work professionalized and became a recognized adjunct to traditional concern with pedagogy and curriculum in schools of education, including that of Indiana University.

President Wells enjoyed a sustained popularity among members of the student body. He requested his office staff to remind him when classes were in the process of changing, and he timed his strolls through campus in order to meet as many students as possible.

STARTING A STUDENT FOUNDATION

In July 1949, Laurence Wheeler stepped down from his post as executive director of the IU Foundation to become professor of journalism and director of communications. Howard ("Howdy") S. Wilcox, an Indianapolis advertising executive, succeeded him. A 1942 IU journalism alumnus, he served in World War II, reaching the rank of lieutenant colonel before discharge from active duty.

Wilcox had several interesting ideas to increase the scope of the IU Foundation. One of the first things he did in 1950 was to organize a student foundation committee, with thirty-six student leaders from the residence halls, Greek houses, and off-campus communities. If student ambassadors were to tell the story of the IU Foundation, Wilcox realized, "undergraduate interest [could] project itself into future alumni support."[1] The fourth annual giving, concluding in May 1950, netted $32,597, an increase of a third over the previous year.

The pace picked up for the academic year 1950–51. The IU Foundation Board of Directors named a national chairman, Byron K. Elliott, to coordinate the fifth annual giving, created a faculty foundation committee to improve communications with this important constituency, and appointed an internal wills and bequests committee to oversee fund raising efforts in that area. Wells also noted that the IU Foundation should set up a research division to handle several large federal research contracts that were in process.[2]

Wilcox put the student committee to work on an idea that was inspired by an informal bicycle race that he witnessed taking place around a residence hall on campus. Steeped in automobile racing traditions, Wilcox had served as the press agent for the Indianapolis Motor Speedway, where his father won the 1919 Indianapolis 500 race shortly before his birth. The first Little 500 bicycle race took place on May 12, 1951. Patterned after its namesake, thirty-three teams of four students raced for fifty miles along an oval track in Memorial Stadium on Tenth Street. Through his contacts, Wilcox attracted many famous Indianapolis Speedway personalities to the first race, including Wilbur Shaw and Tony Hulman, who rode in the pace car with him and President Wells.[3]

The effort was designed to raise money for student scholarships to aid working students. Under the theme "To Help Those Who Are Helping Themselves," sixty scholarships of $100 each were distributed to needy students not supported by academic or athletic scholarships. The success of the first race garnered much publicity for the I U Foundation and plans were made to make the Little 500 an annual event.

Meanwhile, the returns were in for the fifth annual giving: 1,400 donors contributed over $46,000.[4] At an I U Foundation board meeting, Wilcox suggested renaming the effort the Alumni Fund campaign and setting a goal of $75,000. He also recommended that more letters be sent to the alumni and that a test mailing program be established to assess various categories of donor groups. Wells reported that the Foundation's Research Division got contracts amounting to more than one million dollars, but the university was still lagging behind other institutions.[5]

In February 1952 Wilcox sent a letter to the faculty stating that the I U Foundation would be glad to receive requests for aid, and in turn would appreciate gifts and other forms of support from the faculty. The question of faculty relations was raised formally at a board meeting later that spring. The minutes noted, "It has been suggested that an energetic campaign to solicit annual gifts from members of the faculty. Also as a part of working with the faculty, that they be constantly exposed to the objects, aims, plans and materials of the Foundation that they, in turn, can become salesmen of the Foundation."[6]

The second running of the Little 500 was held in May 1952. It was even more lavish than the first, with assorted celebrities and business executives. Tony Hulman, owner of the Indianapolis Speedway, promised to host the winning team as guests at the "big" 500. In addition to planning the Little 500, Wilcox was drumming up support for the I U Foundation, speaking to service clubs around the state. Dixie Heighway, who was serving as secretary, wrote the board of directors: "It would seem that the Student Foundation Committee idea is beginning to pay off . . . 25% of all contributions to annual giving this year have been from those who have been graduated in the last three years."[7] But Wilcox informed Wells that he intended to resign in the summer, to become director of personnel and public relations for the *Indianapolis Star* and *News*. After the 1952 race, Wells wrote, "The Little 500 has caught on; it is here to stay.

I, for one, am certain that we have succeeded in establishing a new and colorful tradition at Indiana University, thanks to you."[8]

The annual giving campaign reached a record $65,000, a 40 percent increase over the previous year. In his resignation letter of August 1952, Wilcox reiterated his belief that good student relations will lead to good alumni relations. He suggested "that Indiana University reconsider the possibility of building a University Chapel – either as a University proj- ect or, still better, as a Foundation project where all alumni can be asked to join in building something that they all recognize as needed. If we had a beautiful chapel on this campus, we would have couples return- ing for years to come to see the place where they were married, attended services, etc. It would represent one strong connecting link between I.U. and the boys and girls whom we turn out each year."[9]

MARKETING THE UNIVERSITY

Wilcox's replacement was William S. Armstrong, known as "Bill" or "Army" to his many friends. Armstrong, who joined Sigma Nu before finishing at IU in 1942, was working as a salesman for an Owensboro, Kentucky, dairy when he was recruited by Wells. An outgoing and gre- garious man, he put his stamp on the IU Foundation during his thirty- one-year tenure. First and foremost, Armstrong was a superb salesman for his dearly loved alma mater. He had an infectious wit and an ability to make connections with alumni and friends of the university. Always smiling, he liked golf, gaudy sports jackets, and porkpie hats.

One of the first things that Armstrong did was to create the "Varsity Club," to funnel private support to the athletic department, in 1953. It became the first in a long line of "gift clubs" that were used for fund rais- ing for particular areas or programs of the university. In the mid-1960s, it was joined by the Friends of Music and Friends of Art gift clubs, which provided scholarships and outreach programs. For a time, gift clubs pro- liferated at the IU Foundation, supplying a way to organize the pool of donors in a rational manner.[10]

In the 1950s an Indiana University scientific research team con- ducted clinical research on stannous fluoride as a tooth-decay preven- tive. Professors William Nebergall and Harry Day from the chemistry department and Joseph C. Muhler at the IU School of Dentistry in Indianapolis entered a patent agreement with the IU Foundation in 1952. Procter and Gamble agreed to fund and patent the research, and it eventually led to the creation of Crest, first commercial fluoride toothpaste. The IU Foundation received half of the patent royalties, and the research team the other half. By 1976, the IU Foundation had received over $500,000 in royalties from sales of Crest.[11]

THE PRESIDENT'S HOUSE

When President Emeritus William Lowe Bryan died on November 21, 1955, a few days after his ninety-fifth birthday, Wells took the lead to memorialize his mentor at the funeral service. His remarks were collected in the *Indiana Alumni Magazine,* which featured a lavish spread on Bryan's career and legacy. Earlier, Wells penned a tribute to Bryan for the Newcomen Society of America. Published under the title *A Man, An Institution, and An Era,* Wells evoked the history of IU in Bryan's long administration and lovingly paid respect to Bryan's character and personal friendship.[12] There was a kaleidoscope of memories of Bryan that Wells could choose from. For instance, in 1952, the Monroe County Fall Festival organizers planned to honor Bryan, who was ninety-one. A few days prior to the event, however, organizers found out that Bryan was in the hospital. Wells assured them that he would be happy to represent Bryan in his place. After visiting with Bryan in the hospital and telling him of this plan, the former president told Wells, "I am capable of receiving my own certificate. If you want to do something to help, you can come and take me over there." A worried Wells consulted with Bryan's physician, Neal Baxter, who advised him to comply with the frail man's wishes. Still concerned, Wells blurted, "In his condition, what if he dies?" Baxter responded, "He needs to be where he'll be happy!" The day came, turning out to be extremely hot, and Wells and Bryan made their way to the festival and back with no further incident.[13]

Now both of his fathers – biological and academic – were dead. Granville Wells had taken his own life seven years before at the age of seventy-three. Will Bryan, his academic mentor, died of natural causes as an old man. In his last years, Bryan still could be seen walking around the

woodland campus he nurtured, living year after year as the sole occupant of the President's House under the shelter of a grove of big trees.[14]
Ambling by construction sites that were literally transforming the university, Bryan was amazed and pleased by Wells's success. But he kept the
President's House as a shrine to the times when he shared life with his
beloved wife, Charlotte, who died in 1948. In a marriage that lasted fifty-
nine years, they shared nearly a quarter century in that house, which she
planned and furnished. Bryan remembered, "The inside, where her mind
touched everything, is judged to be exquisite. The house will remain for
her a monument."[15]

As Bryan attempted to preserve the ambiance of his home, he was
touchy about workmen disturbing the peace and quiet of his residential
sanctuary. He postponed regular maintenance of the utility systems,
politely turning away physical plant staff. When the house was inspected
after his death, several years of benign neglect made major renovations
necessary. Although Wells and his mother were living comfortably in
the Woodburn House downtown, he thought it best to move into the
now-empty President's House. But painting the walls, sanding the floors,
and upgrading the appliances came first, followed by a complete redeco-
ration using Wells's extensive collections of antique furniture and fine
artworks. It was over a year before the house was ready for occupancy.

President Wells, Mother Wells, and the entire household moved
into the refurbished President's House in early 1957. The busy social life
of the president and his mother did not skip a beat with the change in
location, but the venue was more convenient, particularly for receptions.
Wells continued to look on the Woodburn House with affection. It had
served him well as a home since 1932, a constant place of refuge and re-
generation in the evolving panorama of his life. It saw him through his
meteoric rise to the IU presidency in his public life and also witnessed
his private struggles and personal triumphs. Living there for twenty-
five years – longer than anywhere else in his life – he created an elective
family, starting with his childhood buddy Sam Gabriel as a roommate,
and then incorporating generations of houseboys, and his own mother
in 1948.

Thanks to James Woodburn's gift of the house to IU in 1940, Wells
knew that his former home would find another use in the life of the uni-

versity. Treasurer Joseph A. Franklin and his wife, Beatrice, lived there after Wells. In 1976, the Alumni Association was put in charge of the management, and Tom and Barbara Cosgrove lived there full time as hosts and caretakers. It has since been refurbished to give a sense of the time it served as the Wells residence, complete with period photographs on the walls. It continues to be a popular place for IU-related receptions and parties.

In 1924, when the President's House (since renamed the Bryan House) was new, it stood by itself on the margins of campus. As the campus footprint expanded over time, the house was now closer to the heart of campus rather than the periphery. Through the trees a small chapel could be seen in the shadow of the massive Indiana Memorial Union. Constructed in 1957 and named in honor of Frank Beck, the University chaplain, the ecumenical chapel was built adjacent to the old Dunn family graveyard on the banks of the Jordan River. Wells was pleased with the symbolism of its placement, suggesting that spirit was the true heart of a university.[16]

TOASTING CARNEGIE

By the 1950s, Wells was a regular visitor to New York. Since being selected as a board member of the Carnegie Foundation for the Advancement of Teaching in 1941, he faithfully attended their meetings in Manhattan. Black-tie dinner parties were held the night before, and Wells socialized with the intellectual and social elite. Wells delighted in the scintillating conversation, excellent food and drink, and the presence of "men of eminence and global perspective," as he put it later. The following day was devoted to foundation business, until the board members adjourned for a private luncheon in the rich ambiance of the Century Association, another private men's club. By custom, the chairman of the board offered a toast to the memory of Andrew Carnegie at the conclusion of the luncheon.[17]

In 1953–54 Wells served a chairman of the Carnegie Foundation, and made a speech toasting the founder in November 1954. Determined to make a good show, he made careful preparations. On a trip to Europe in spring 1954, Wells visited Scotland, the ancestral home of Carnegie, visiting both Carnegie's modest birthplace and the palatial Skibo Castle, where he lived after he became a magnate.[18] Reflecting on Carnegie's great wealth and equally great benefactions, Wells called on his own background as a fifth-generation Hoosier to craft a speech about the "cultural transformation in the American hinterland" in progress for fifty years.[19]

At the turn of the century, Wells said, small towns in the Midwest and West "were still close to the frontier," and men "who could conquer raw nature" were greatly admired, whereas "the professor and the fiddler were equally suspect, if not in fact the subjects of derision." Into such communities, Andrew Carnegie, a preeminent self-made businessman, donated libraries and organs, "thus proclaiming the importance of the things of the mind and things of the spirit." In Indiana, 139 libraries were established for every city and county seat as well as many smaller towns.[20] He reminded his listeners of the ripple effects:

> It is generally recognized that Mr. Carnegie through the creation of his founda-
> tions stimulated other men of great wealth to follow his example. Less well un-
> derstood, however, is his influence upon men of modest means. The small-town
> banker, farmer, and merchant have received their stimulation to contribute to
> public causes from Mr. Carnegie's local gifts, and, if they falter in their idealism
> or attempt to revert to selfishness, Mr. Carnegie's omnipresent library at the
> corner of the courthouse square reminds them of their duty.[21]

Wells went on to recount how many colleges, playhouses, and other cul-
tural venues were built upon the donations of the leadership of small communities. "Nowhere else in the world is there such emphasis upon civic beneficence in contrast to family inheritance," he stated.

The gift of organs and Carnegie's example of attending concerts broke down "the contempt of the practical man for music and the arts," Wells explained. "Local leadership could ignore the endorsement of the arts inherent in his construction of Carnegie Hall, but they could not do so in the local church organ."[22]

Wells concluded his speech by talking about the roots of Carnegie's motivation to philanthropy. He cited the "bleakness, drabness, and nar-
rowness of the small town" in which Carnegie grew up and how he re-
belled and "sought escape through books and dreamed of a day when life would be richer in his village" of Dunfermline. When he created a

community trust, Carnegie talked about bringing "sweetness and light" into Dunfermline workers' lives, specifying the provision of classes in music, arts and crafts, and the building of parks, playgrounds, a community theater, concert hall, and library. "What he did for Dunfermline directly," Wells declared, "he has helped to do indirectly for thousands of American communities." Remembering his long hours reading in the Lebanon Public Library, Wells could have been referring to himself when he concluded that Carnegie found a way "to open windows which allowed 'sweetness and light' to enter the minds and the hearts of the people of the American heartland."[23]

COMMITTEE ON INSTITUTIONAL COOPERATION

The Council of Ten, composed of the presidents of the "Big Ten" universities, occupied a special place in Wells's aspirations for the educational commonwealth. The Big Ten – comprising the state universities of Illinois, Indiana, Iowa, Ohio, Michigan, Minnesota, and Wisconsin, plus the private Northwestern University – was an academic and athletic powerhouse. (Its formal name was the Western Collegiate Athletic Association.) Automatically becoming a member upon his selection as IU president in 1938, Wells became chairman a decade later, and served until 1962.[24] Meeting semiannually, the Council was a place for frank and confidential discussion of issues and problems of Midwestern research universities. Athletics was only part of the agenda, but it got the lion's share of public attention because of media attention to intercollegiate sports.

In 1956 Wells chatted with James Perkins, the vice president of the Carnegie Corporation of New York, whom he had known through his membership on the Board of Trustees of the Carnegie Foundation for the Advancement of Teaching. Perkins remarked that all of the publicity associated with the annual Council of Ten meetings had to do with athletic matters, asking Wells, "Don't you ever discuss education?" In reply, Wells responded that, on the contrary, the council spent most of its time conferring about common educational problems. Athletic decisions, he explained, were arrived at efficiently with the aid of a council secretariat that prepared background materials and released them to the waiting press. Perkins pressed on and inquired why there was no publicity surrounding the educational discussion, noting that "your institutions carry a lot of weight, and any pronouncements of the presidents as a body on educational issues would not only be interesting but useful and important in promoting consideration of academic policies regionally and nationally."[25]

Wells pointed out that an additional secretariat would be needed to keep track of the exchange of educational ideas. Perkins then inquired how much that would cost. Wells guessed $50,000 per year. Perkins expressed interest in the project, but wanted Wells to get the endorsement of his fellow presidents. When Wells brought the proposal to the table at the next meeting, in December 1956, the presidents were enthusiastic. Two subjects were identified for cooperative study: "the changing nature of student migration, and the philosophy of student fees."[26] The Council of Ten organized the Committee on Institutional Cooperation (CIC) at their next meeting, in April 1957, and made a formal proposal to the Carnegie Corporation. The CIC's membership included the Big Ten plus the University of Chicago, a former member of the Big Ten.[27]

The following year the Carnegie philanthropy appropriated $40,000 to cover expenses for the CIC, the initiative for an academic counterpart to the Big Ten's athletic focus. Wells argued that individual institutions, particularly in the public sector, did not possess all of the resources in faculty and facilities to meet the demands of the present world. Preaching the virtues of cooperation, he stated "academic isolation has long been impractical; in today's world, it is impossible." The idea behind the creation of this regional consortium was to encourage each member institution to develop in depth and exploit its own areas of strength, and then to make the combined strength available to all. Wells referred to the CIC as "perhaps the world's greatest common market in education," borrowing the phrase "common market" from recent attempts in Europe to enhance economic cooperation.[28]

Each university would send a top administrator (a president, chancellor, or provost) to thrice-yearly meetings. The CIC possessed a simple, laissez-faire structure: programmatic decisions were not binding on the entire membership, and member universities were free to select the programs offered according to their needs and interests. Oriented toward specialized graduate education, the CIC's signature program was a traveling scholar program that enabled graduate students at any of the eleven member institutions to study for a semester at any other member university without paying special fees or meeting residential requirements. Student needs for specialized courses, faculty, library, or research facilities would be met by this sharing of resources.[29]

"This voluntary cooperation, within the framework of flexible agreements, has been the strength of CIC," Wells summarized.[30] Not only did Wells provide the original impulse to its creation, but in many ways it also was an institutional embodiment of his personal style of generosity and concern for the larger community.

ANTIRACISM, ON CAMPUS AND BEYOND

Back at the Indiana University campus, race relations had improved in the 1950s, but black students still had to deal with a campus oriented to cater to the white majority. Although the "reserved" signs in the IMU Commons had long disappeared, students were self-segregating and there were still "subtle signs of racism."[31] True to their tradition, the Bethel AME congregation and the Second Baptist Church on the Near West Side provided a home away from home for generations of African American students.

Wells kept his fingers on the student pulse, using his wide network to obtain information about particular individuals, particularly emerging student leaders. Contact with those at the heart of the university's educational mission put things into perspective for the busy executive, and these exchanges never failed to energize him.

One such student, Orlando Taylor, an African American studying for a master's degree in speech and hearing science, came to Wells's attention in 1953. Taylor, a member of the local chapter of the NAACP, admitted that he was surprised when the IU President greeted him by name the first time they met. The two struck up a friendship as Wells invited him into his large elective family. Taylor never forgot that initial encounter which revealed Wells's deep concern for minorities, and returned to campus in the late 1960s as a faculty member.[32] Taylor moved to Howard University in 1973, eventually becoming dean of the Graduate School.

In the midst of his work on behalf of the nation's educational commonwealth, Wells received an invitation from Howard University to become a member of their board of trustees in 1956. Founded in 1867 and located in the District of Columbia, Howard was a federally chartered institution focused on the higher education of African Americans. It was known as the flagship of black higher education in the U.S., and its longtime president, Mordecai Johnson, was a widely respected leader. Wells and Johnson probably first crossed paths during the war years, when Wells spent a significant amount of time in Washington.

Wells had received countless invitations to joint corporate, foundation, and university boards since he was named president nearly twenty years before, but he had rejected all of them on the principle that there was an inherent conflict of interest by his service as president of Indiana University. He represented the institution with all of its varied constituencies, including alumni, and he could not be sure that service on a board would not give someone an unfair advantage. But this invitation was different. It might allow him to put into practice, in a different context, his egalitarian ideals of access to higher education. Wells considered the invitation seriously and eventually accepted, making an exception to his own policies of self-regulation because of the importance of the task. Joining the largely African American board, Wells quickly became a valued trustee of Howard, sharing his immense experience and wide contacts to further its mission.

In 1957, the U.S. Congress passed the first civil rights bill since the decade following the Civil War. Both Wells and Johnson celebrated this achievement, but knew that more needed to be done to insure access and fair treatment of minority students. Two years later, Wells served on the screening committee for Howard's new president, in anticipation of Johnson's planned retirement in 1960, after thirty-four years in office.

In addition to his work as a Howard trustee, Wells paid attention to academic community building at the historically black university. During the institution's centennial in 1967, Wells and his mother gave the university an ornate "chain of office," finished in silver, for the use of the president in ceremonial occasions such as commencement.[33] Wells was aware of the power of such symbols in dignifying ancient academic rituals. Indiana University had a chain of office used by the president since its gift in 1958 by the local chapter of Sigma Chi. Attached to the chain was the jewel of office, presented in 1946 by the campus chapter of Beta Theta Pi. Emblematic of Indiana University's historic mission and emblazoned with synthetic jewels and diamonds, the jewel and chain were around the president's neck at public ceremonies.[34]

During Wells's presidential tenure, another color barrier was broken in 1959, when Nancy Streets became the first African American "Miss IU." In 1960, another historic first was achieved when IU students elected Thomas I. Atkins the first African American student body president. He was also the first in the Big Ten. Atkins, a senior, hailed from Elkhart, Indiana, where he was a trailblazer upon his election to president of his high school senior class. Graduating with Phi Beta Kappa honors in 1961, he went to Harvard University, earned both M.A. and J.D. degrees, and went on to become a nationally prominent civil rights lawyer in Boston.[35]

FOREIGN STUDENTS ON CAMPUS

Wells was committed to increasing the number of foreign students on campus. He encouraged faculty and staff to recruit them, and intervened personally in the case of Bolivian student Peter Fraenkel, whom he met on his 1941 South American trip. In 1943, when international enrollment was about fifty students, he appointed business instructor Leo R. Dowling to the new position of counselor to foreign students. In 1948 Dowling was an organizer of the National Association of Foreign Student Advisers, which provided assistance to the growing flood of foreign students attending U.S. institutions of higher education.[36]

Volume 1 of *Education for One World* appeared in 1948–49 and listed U.S. universities with the largest international enrollments, including six of the Big Ten schools. Indiana, with fewer than two hundred international students, was not among them. In spring 1951, president Wells invited Dowling to a brainstorming session about ways to increase foreign student enrollment. Dowling thought that a permanent meeting space on campus would help promote social intercourse between U.S. and foreign students. Although since 1916 IU had an active Cosmopolitan Club (its motto: "Above All Nations Is Humanity"), which sponsored an annual International Night with food and music, they did not have a permanent facility. Dowling outlined his proposal in a memo:

> Having a central place of social and educational activity for foreign students would give a definite stimulus to our overall program, it was felt. We had in mind a place that offered, (1) facilities so that the foreign students could entertain their teachers and friends with teas or dinners which they themselves would prepare, (2) office space for the foreign-American social clubs, (3) a small library with international appeal, (4) a foreign record library, etc. In short, our thinking was in the direction of facilities for an international relations workshop on the student level.[37]

Wells agreed with the plans, and a house at 111 South Jordan Avenue was secured.

In December 1951, the Cosmopolitan Club held its first party there. The International House was an immediate success, and, when the Jordan Avenue house was torn down for the construction of Read Residence Center, it moved in the early 1950s to the Thomas House on East Third Street. By the mid-1950s, the International House was bursting at the seams.[38] International enrollment was growing, standing at 359 in 1955 and at 531 in 1960. In 1958, the facility changed its address again, moving back to Jordan Avenue into a former sorority chapter house and sporting a new name – International Center – and an address – 111 South Jordan – inherited from the original International House. Members of the Cosmopolitan Club were pleased with this expansive new facility. Its president, A. Kumar Parikh, wrote to Wells in appreciation: "I am sure that the foreign students on the campus are proud of their new American home," recognizing the president's "exalted desire to lay roots of international understanding in their youthful hearts." Wells responded, "Of course all of us hope that our students from abroad will find this Center a happy and convenient place, and that it may serve the purpose of bringing together our foreign students and American students in a relaxed and home-like atmosphere."[39]

THAI CONNECTION

Wells took advantage of every opening to strengthen IU's international connections. He had met the education minister of Thailand, Mom Luang Pin Malakul, when the minister visited the Bloomington campus in

1948. Five years later, Thailand turned its attention to modernizing its system of teacher training. With the assistance of the U.S. International Cooperation Administration (a precursor to the Agency for International Development), a report, authored by Willis Porter, a professor at New York's State Teachers College at Oneonta, was issued that called for a national school of teacher training. It came to the attention of the IU administration, which was asked to consider undertaking the ambitious project. Two vice presidents – Graduate School dean John Ashton and School of Education dean Wendell Wright – made separate trips to Bangkok to negotiate the deal. The program would require an ongoing personnel commitment of IU faculty to advise on administration, develop curriculum, and plan for specialized facilities, such as a library.

In 1954 an agreement was signed by the School of Education, the Prasan Mitr College of Education in Bangkok, and the Thai Ministry of Education, with funding from the U.S. Foreign Operations Administration, to develop a four-year program leading to a bachelor's degree. At that time, the recently founded Prasan Mitr College was small and undistinguished, and the contract "envisioned its complete rehabilitation and major expansion."[40] Assigning expert faculty to the contract, Wendell Wright himself spent several weeks in Thailand collaborating with officials there to work out detailed plans. The IU administration, convinced that Porter would make an ideal director, gave Wright permission to offer him a tenured position on the faculty.

An average of four senior faculty members, graduate students, and staff were on the ground in Thailand at any one time, advising and assisting with the College of Education at Prasan Mitr. That same year, in a related effort, IU's School of Education started a graduate program in the Department of Education at Chulalongkorn University, Thailand's oldest and most important university. That program metamorphosed over time to a full-blown Faculty of Education.[41]

SCHOOL OF PUBLIC ADMINISTRATION, THAMMASAT UNIVERSITY

Strengthening governmental infrastructure through public administration training and assistance was also an important concern among developing countries. The U.S. Foreign Operations Administration helped fund institutes of public administration in various parts of the world, including Thailand, in the 1950s. Growing out of previous contacts between Indiana University and the College of Education at Prasan Mitr College, and an early visit in 1953 by future IU political scientist Walter Laves,[42] the university negotiated a contract in 1955 to create a new Institute of Public Administration at Thammasat University in Bangkok. The cooperative agreement stipulated "IU was to provide personnel to advise and train staff for a new institute of public administration and to give guidance on its organization, teaching methods, library development, research and consultative services, publications program, and conference and training programs." A special aspect of the program was to train Thai graduate students to the master's in public administration level in the United States, mostly at Indiana University.[43]

The $1.5 million contract – the biggest ever for IU – was for a period of three years. Pomp accompanied the signing on May 3, 1955. The ceremony occurred in Washington, D.C., with President Wells representing IU and Prime Minister P. Pibulsonggram, who was also Rector of Thammasat University, representing Thailand.[44] "Manifold benefits will accrue to both the participating universities and the governments involved," Walter Laves told the Indiana Daily Student, adding "IU will have an added role in the current struggle of the free nations of Southeast Asia to erect a bastion of freedom and stability in that part of the world."[45] Democratic education was a key nonmilitary tactic during the Cold War.

The Institute of Public Administration was staffed by a handful of IU faculty members, usually accompanied by their families. A two-year assignment was the norm. The chief of party in Thailand was Joseph L. Sutton, professor of political science, and Lynton K. Caldwell, a public policy expert, served as coordinator of the program on the Bloomington campus.[46] Many Thai students pursued graduate work in the United States, mostly at IU. Student exchanges also went the other way, as a few advanced graduate students from IU went to assist the IPA and to conduct research for their doctoral degrees. For example, John W. Ryan, a doctoral candidate in political science, went between 1955 and 1957 to finish his dissertation on "Bangkok Government and Administration:

Appearance and Reality."[47] Wells took an active interest from the beginning of IU's technical assistance efforts in Thailand, and visited on a number of occasions.

In print, Wells reviewed the surge in overseas contract programs occurring at U.S. universities. By 1957, fifty-three American colleges and universities had signed eighty-three contracts with foreign universities in thirty-eight countries for exchange programs and technical assistance in academic administration and curriculum development. He observed benefits accruing to both university partners and urged the expansion of federal support while preserving institutional autonomy. Taking IU's contracts with Thailand as an example, Wells boasted, "tens of thousands of Hoosier citizens now have an increased awareness of the Orient and its economic and diplomatic significance." Watching "horizons widen" from the "depths of the Hoosier hinterland," Wells avowed that these "university contracts offer Americans new perspectives and enlarged vistas of understanding, and political maturity so vitally needed in the solution of the problems of today's chaotic world."[48]

NATIONAL EDUCATIONAL AFFAIRS

During the 1950s Wells was a fixture on the IU campus. The university continued to make its meteoric rise in reputation under his care. Some viewed him and his small group of lieutenants as a benevolent cabal; to most he was beloved figure, always in the thick of things, leading by serving the needs of the academic community.[49] Wells's stature as an educator continued to grow as he stepped up his already heavy involvement with national education affairs in the 1950s. After early seasoning in the war years and afterward in the National Association of State Universities and the American Council on Education, he was known throughout the community of educational administrators and had a reputation as a smart and cooperative group member. Wells, who found it difficult to turn down invitations to serve on committees, was a member of a host of national committees, commissions, and boards.

Wells continued his service to ACE and NEA throughout the 1950s. Postwar growth in higher education, fueled by federal involvement in paying for veterans' college costs and in national defense research and development, spawned a range of problems that the large national associations tackled. Wells represented ACE on the U.S. National Commission for UNESCO from 1951–1955, serving as vice chairman of the group in 1953–54 under chair Walter Laves.[50]

Wells renewed his involvement with the National Education Association in 1954 by becoming a member of its Educational Policies Commission. The next year he became chair, and served until 1958. Wells had wide experience, good sense, and "staying power" in the presidency that made him sought after for such jobs. He also had a powerful work ethic and was able to instill high morale among his committee peers and staff members.

One growing problem in education was a lack of trained personnel, particularly teachers. The commission investigated the national predicament, probed its range, and surveyed the human resources that could be mobilized to alleviate the crisis. Their findings and recommendation were published in a report, *Manpower and Education,* in 1956.[51] One review stated, "The great strength of the report is its sanity and its moderation."[52]

Under Wells's chairmanship, the Educational Policies Commission moved on to one of the biggest issues facing universities: faculty salaries. The commission "began to look toward the future and discuss the question of how much of the gross national product (GNP) could be devoted to education – particularly higher education – without doing damage to other social needs."

Concerned that the commission was not being bold enough in its projections, Wells commissioned two IU Business School colleagues, John Lewis and George Pinnell, to perform an economic study of potential scenarios. Lewis and Pinnell did the work, and Wells "furnished the enthusiasm and the excuse for its preparation," as he later recounted. The paper, "Needs, Resources and Priorities in Higher Education," was privately circulated in 1956 to interested parties at the NEA and the ACE. The IU team "called for a doubling of higher-education salaries in constant dollars by 1970 and through careful analysis argued that a substantial percentage increase in the amount of GNP devoted to higher education was feasible and socially desirable."[53]

The paper had its intended effect and expanded the parameters of the conversation. It "was something of a blockbuster" for the commission, Wells dryly noted, and in the commission's 1957 final report, *Higher Education in a Decade of Decision,* they called for a sizable increase in faculty salaries over the next few years.[54] As it happened, the goal of doubling faculty salaries by 1970 was met, and Wells was justifiably proud in prodding the conversation along. His autobiography offered an ironic note, "Actually our projections, instead of being daring, turned out to be rather conservative."[55]

Higher Education in a Decade of Decision was shaped by Wells's belief that "the academic way of life must itself be safeguarded" and "the condition of living as a professor must be attractive to people of ability and integrity." The report decried loyalty oaths and manifestations of anti-intellectualism in American life, and argued for the responsibility of the general public to increase the reputation and standing of the professoriate. The report maintained, "Academic freedom to search for truth and to propound the truth is essential."[56]

Also evident were Wells's concerns about university leadership and administration. Because he mediates various interests, "the presidency thus calls for statesmanship and 'wrap-around vision' of the highest order." Such statements, if not actually written by Wells, went out under his imprimatur. "The American college president has become a responsible pivot on which with system of higher education turns," the report continued.

> He is the chief executive of the board of trustees; he is the motivating agent for internal institutional examination and appraisal; he is the chief solicitor of funds for the institution; he should also be chief educational leader of the faculty and students, and the prime interpreter of the institution to the public. Because his role has become so sensitive and complex he is able, in a degree unapproached elsewhere, to translate a "grand design" into reality. In the same degree, shortsightedness of his vision may leave lasting defects and disharmonies in the institution. The presidency is both a source of strength and a sharp target for criticism. It is the center for communication within the total organization, capable of becoming either a "bottleneck" or an expediting force.[57]

Philosophically, this view of the president's role resonated with Emerson's nineteenth-century dictum that an institution is the lengthened shadow of a man, but with one important proviso: "that the lengthened shadow is of the corporate personality symbolized by the individual."[58]

UNITED NATIONS SERVICE

In June 1957, soon after his fifty-fifth birthday, Wells received a call from John Foster Dulles, the U.S. secretary of state. Dulles asked if he might be interested in serving as a delegate to the upcoming twelfth General Assembly of the United Nations. The cabinet official cautioned that this was a preliminary inquiry, and that the actual nomination, should it materialize, would be proffered by President Eisenhower. For Wells, the prospect was tantalizing–yet another opportunity to put into practice his deeply held egalitarian and humanitarian ideals. It would also represent a high-water mark in his government service career. Wells talked confidentially to board of trustees president John Hastings, and they both agreed that the chance would be too good to pass up. Even though IU was in the midst of a sustained period of growth and Wells could ill afford to be away from campus during the Indiana General Assembly's three-month session, it would burnish the institutional reputation of the university tremendously.[59]

In August, Wells read in the newspaper that both Indiana senators, Homer Capehart and William Jenner, had given their recommendation. In typical Wells fashion, he wrote lovely notes of thanks. On August 8, the president's office called with the news that Eisenhower had signed his nomination letter.[60] Wells was the first Hoosier to be a delegate to the UN, although Robert Brokenburr, a Republican state senator, had been selected as an alternate in 1955.[61]

The U.S. delegation was made up of five persons. Henry Cabot Lodge, former senator from Massachusetts and UN ambassador since 1953, was chief; two members of the House of Representatives–A. S. J. Carnahan (D-Missouri) and Walter H. Judd (R-Minnesota); the president of the AFL-CIO George Meany; and Wells. Alternates included popular actress Irene Dunne. The UN's membership had a total of eighty-two nations. The twelfth General Assembly began on Sept 17, 1957, and lasted until December 14, 1957. Although the UN had evolved differently than its founders expected, it served as "the most important agency for mobilizing and reflecting world opinion." It had an official, formal agenda, but the work of the organization was accomplished mainly through informal contact and conversation among the assembled delegates. A major agenda item was disarmament, a perennial issue made even more salient with the advent of nuclear weapons. The question of seating Communist China was on the table, and Greece and Turkey were still fighting over the island of Cyprus.[62]

Wells made plans to spend the workweek in New York and fly back to Bloomington on the weekends to take care of IU business. He was back on the shuttle schedule, doing two full-time jobs, as he had been during World War II. In New York, he resided at the Vanderbilt Hotel. The U.S. delegation's chief, Lodge, had a suite of rooms on the top floor of the Waldorf Towers.

Wells had a very active social life in connection with his UN service. Being single, he was more available than other members of the delegation, and Lodge came to rely on him to attend the myriad of official social gatherings. Wells recalled that Ambassador Lodge would look over and say, "Herman, you're a university president and accustomed to standing in line. You go." Thus, at the end of a long and exhausting day, he found himself attending up to three evening receptions, making sure to stay long enough so that the host and others registered the presence of a U.S. official. Picking up useful information for the delegation, he was often too busy shaking hands and conversing to eat much. After the parties were over, sometimes he had his driver stop at the Oyster Bar at Grand Central Station, where he fortified himself with a bowl of oyster stew.[63]

The General Assembly had been in session for less than three weeks when the Soviet Union launched the world's first artificial satellite, *Sputnik 1,* which effectively derailed work on the UN's official agenda. Although it was ostensibly part of the global scientific effort of the International Geophysical Year, it was seen as a severe defense threat to the U.S. and marked the beginning of the Cold War–inspired Space Race. After a spectacular failure to launch its first satellite, the United States countered with the launch of *Explorer 1,* a navy scientific satellite, in January 1958. It returned data that led to physicist James Van Allen's discovery of the natural radiation belts surrounding the Earth.[64]

THE RUSSIAN AND EAST EUROPEAN INSTITUTE

Wells had long been interested in the Communist Bloc countries in the orbit of the Union Soviet Socialist Republics. He encountered individual Russians at meetings connected to the United Nations, supported the formation of area studies at IU dealing with Russia and Slavic-speaking regions, hired émigré scholars, and defended the IU Library's importation of Communist materials against critics. In 1949, the university established a Department of Slavic Languages, with Russian émigré scholar Michael Ginsberg as chair. Two year later, an interdisciplinary East European Institute was established. Despite its impressive faculty, student enrollment was not enough to sustain a focus solely on Eastern Europe.[65]

The chair of the history department, Russian specialist Robert F. Byrnes, was hired in 1956. Wells was impressed by Byrnes's dynamism and drive, and assured him that six additional faculty lines would be supplied in the Russian and Eastern European field. In 1958, Byrnes circulated a memo arguing for a new Russian and East European Institute:

> Indiana is already the leading Mid-Western institution specializing upon Russia and Eastern Europe. Our goal now should be the establishment of an institution and program with the national and international reputation now held by Harvard and Columbia. The foundations have been created; we should complete the structure and collect upon the investments made.[66]

The Wells administration approved the formation of the Russian and East European Institute in 1958.

International events played a significant role. The Cold War had been heightened with the successful orbit of *Sputnik 1*. The U.S. Congress responded with the National Defense Education Act, of which Title VI provided appropriations for National Resource Centers to study foreign areas considered to be critical to security.

The new REEI successfully applied for Title VI funds during its first year, and also received a major Ford Foundation grant for new faculty and fellowships. Its mission was "the development of a broad interdisciplinary curriculum offering the best possible language and area training relating to the Soviet Union and the countries of Eastern Europe."[67]

The Russian and East European Institute was the first full-scale language and area studies center at IU, and provided a model for the development of others. Primarily a grant-seeking and coordinating office, it did
not have control of its own faculty lines and had to depend on specialists hired by regular departments of the university. With help from the
faculty, Wells set the basic "obligation to international studies: that any
university must place a high priority on the international dimension of
higher education, that it must define its focus in global terms and that
it must infuse its programs and studies with the universalist outlook
suggested by its name."[68] The pattern was simple: encourage faculty interest, provide incentives, develop faculty strength within academic departments, and support auxiliary enterprises that facilitate international
engagement. But the process of building a coherent curriculum and program could be contentious.[69]

JOURNEY TO THE SOVIET UNION

Wells was eager to see the Soviet Union for himself, but was frustrated
by the U.S. ban on travel to Communist countries. His closest encounter
with Soviet soil was during his brief arrest by the Russian police in East
Berlin in 1948. After the death of Josef Stalin in 1953, the Soviet Union
was increasingly open to exchanges with non-Communist countries.
Likewise, the United States was "eager to pierce the Iron Curtain and
to establish direct contacts with the Soviet people."[70] In 1958, the Soviet Union and the United States signed a two-year bilateral cultural
exchange agreement that would bring agricultural, industrial, scientific,
and artistic delegations from each country to the other.

Nine months after the launch of *Sputnik 1,* Wells got his chance to
make his first visit to the USSR through his old friend, Edward Litchfield, chancellor of the University of Pittsburgh, who had served, like
Wells, under General Clay a decade before. Litchfield chaired an official U.S. delegation to observe Soviet higher education. The trip was
organized under the auspices of the Governmental Affairs Institute – a
nonprofit research, survey, and operations organization begun in 1950, of
which Litchfield served as chairman of the board. Wells joined the small

group, which included seven university presidents, staff members, and a few wives, for a strenuous fifteen-day journey covering eight thousand miles of the vast country in July 1958. It was the first group of university presidents to have a firsthand look at Soviet higher education since World War II.

Although it had official status as a U.S. delegation, the trip was financed privately by the Scaife Foundation, whose officers (and principal donors) Alan Scaife and his wife, Sarah, accompanied the group.[71] The independent financing was, as Wells remembered it, "unprecedented in the experience of the Russians," and it seemed to allow more flexibility and freedom from bureaucratic monitoring. The itinerary took them to the usual cities of Moscow and Leningrad, but also off the beaten track to Tbilisi, Samarkand, Tashkent, and Alma-Ata.

Members of the group were seasoned pros, and they divided up the work of talking to university faculty, administration, and students as they were shown around a wide array of educational facilities. Within six months of their return, a *Report on Higher Education in the Soviet Union* was published.[72] The concise report detailed the general structure of Soviet higher education, paying particular attention to its place within a socialist government. Despite the limitations of the Soviet academic program, their faculties enjoyed the highest prestige of any professional group, gained plentiful support from the government, and were highly regarded by students. Noting, "the Soviets attach a greater value to higher education and have adopted a more pragmatic approach to it than we have in this country," the authors went on to say. "If we must live in competition with the Soviet Union, every educator, legislator, alumnus, taxpayer, student, and parent must develop a deeper appreciation of the values of higher education and be prepared to accept a greater commitment of his financial resources to higher education."[73]

The group found much to criticize in the Soviet system, however, ranging from its instrumentalist ethos to overspecialization, prescribed curricula, and limitations on enrollment. The research enterprise was channeled to fulfill utilitarian goals, in contrast to the U.S. system that the group believed emphasized "unordered creativity." The multiplicity of Soviet research facilities outside of the university structure curtailed robust communication between disciplines and led to a fracturing of the community of scholars. The report's findings were short and to the point, and couched in dispassionate language. Widely reviewed, it led to some serious reexamination of American educational methods.

We cannot hold a torch to light another's path without brightening our own.

Ben Sweetland

FIFTEEN

Passing the Presidential Torch

AS THE 1960S DAWNED, WELLS WAS HAVING THE TIME OF HIS LIFE. He had overseen a tremendous increase of academic quality at Indiana University that was based upon judicious investments in faculty, programs, and facilities over the past two decades. Indiana was on the move in the national rankings, and Wells had reached the status of a respected national spokesman for American higher education. Just fifty-eight years old in 1960, his roly-poly physique disguised his great physical endurance. He had fashioned a method of working at capacity for over thirty years, and there was no question of slackening his vigorous pace now.

With rare ability for interpersonal engagement, Wells helped to create a robust academic community with a vibrant culture on the Bloomington campus. Sure of the commodious boundaries of his executive position, he was secure enough to share power with the faculty and his administrative subordinates. He presided at meetings of the Bloomington Faculty Council, knowing that the faculty often came up with effective policies even if their deliberations were slow.

There was a downside to this comity between the leader and the led, however. The university community placed unmitigated trust in Wells's vision and decision-making abilities. This simple, unquestioning faith was personally disturbing to Wells. He enjoyed the scope of action that being a chief executive gave him, but he worried that, in their responses to his judgments and opinions, the faculty and administration had let their critical faculties atrophy. His private discomfort about what he jokingly referred to as his "deification" was a major reason to step down.[1] That process was on his mind when he told the trustees in advance about his desire to retire from the presidency in 1962, two years hence. The *Indiana Daily Student* picked up the story on April 7, 1960.[2]

As word of Wells's impending retirement spread, construction of new facilities continued. A new Memorial Stadium was under construction on the site of the old Faris Farm property on Seventeenth Street. Purchased by the university in 1955, the property, mostly woods and fields, was slated for athletic facilities. Wells was out of town when the site was bulldozed to bare ground in preparation for building. When he returned to Bloomington, he displayed a rare burst of anger at the wholesale destruction of trees.[3] Wells had cultivated his famously calm, imperturbable demeanor. One longtime secretary remembered that he never lost his temper, "although there were occasions when we on the staff lost our patience with him" due to the heavy workload that he imposed. Realizing that he had pushed too hard, Wells sent a dozen red roses as a form of apology. Red roses were his trademark, and he sent them "when he had annoyed someone, when someone was ill, as a condolence, or as a token of congratulations or appreciation."[4]

A couple of weeks after Wells announced his plans to retire, the National Collegiate Athletic Association (NCAA) suspended IU, barring postseason play in any intercollegiate sport for four years. The football program under new coach Phil Dickens had been on probation since 1958, when recruiting violations that apparently originated in the actions of alumni and boosters were discovered. When the NCAA discovered continuing irregularities, they threw the book at the university and levied unprecedented sanctions. Wells, as chief executive officer, was deeply upset at this breach in ethical behavior on the part of football program, but he thought the penalties were too severe. Although the Big Ten commissioner, K. L. "Tug" Wilson, was supportive of the investigation's findings, he thought that only the football program should be penalized, because there was no evidence of any other sports involved. The university appealed the NCAA decision, and Wells and Wilson appeared personally in front of the NCAA Infraction Committee, but the decision stood. The news was especially devastating to the basketball and swimming programs. IU basketball was a perennial contender, and the swimming and diving program, under new coaches James "Doc" Counsilman and Hobie Billingsley, was poised on the brink of national dominance.[5] In 1961, business faculty member John Mee, IU's faculty representative to the Big Ten, wrote to the newly installed IU athletic director, Bill Orwig, "[T]hrough the years Indiana has been a champion contender in virtually every sport except football. The king of sports, football, seems to be our nemesis."[6] Although the athletic program persisted, redoubling its efforts to scrupulously conform to the rules, a cloud hung over IU sports teams for several years. For Wells, the dedication of the new Memorial Stadium and the new fieldhouse in fall 1960 was bittersweet.[7]

Wells also faced challenging issues concerning faculty personnel. On January 16, 1961, Associate Professor of Spanish Glenn Willbern was one of fifty-two individuals indicted by a federal grand jury in a nationwide crackdown against distributing male pornography through the mail. The teacher, winner of the Brown Derby Award for the most popular professor in 1953 and said to be a quiet, kind person, had taught at IU since 1929. The next day, concealing himself behind an overpass abutment on North College Avenue, he ran directly in front of a car in a suicide attempt. He survived, but with a shattered right leg and pelvis and a dislocated shoulder. The crackdown, led by Postmaster General Arthur E. Summerfield, was part of a larger homophobic campaign by the federal government. The indictments targeted members of the Adonis Club and the International Body Culture Association and readers of the physique magazines *Vim* and *Gym* who exchanged addresses and corresponded with each other, and allegedly swapped obscene materials.[8]

Placing Willbern on sick leave, the university promised to conduct an internal investigation, and a local Methodist minister, Benjamin Garrison, wrote to the Bloomington newspaper, saying, "I shoved that professor under the car – and so did you. . . . We are co-guilty." Wells, keeping abreast of the developing situation, wrote to Garrison to thank him: "I am glad you wrote it." In the meantime, history and philosophy of science professor Roger Buck, who had just been hired a few months before, was "steamed up" about the case and cautioned Wells not to rush to judgment. He explained, "Willbern was unlucky – he should have lived in classical Athens" or patronized the local brothel, "thereby eliciting nothing worse that some sly chuckles and cocktail-party remarks about 'gay old Glen [*sic*].' Under your guidance Indiana University has come to occupy a position of moral leadership in this State. It would be splendid to see that position used for the defense of this unfortunate man."[9]

Wells agreed as a matter of course, and led university officials to rally around the indicted professor. Dean of the Faculties Ralph Collins wrote to his probation officer, Wells gave a deposition and agreed to serve as a character witness at the trial, and the university extended Willbern's leave. Wells was optimistic about winning the case and implied that Willbern could continue his IU employment. The jury trial, held in Chicago, occupied most of the month of January 1962. The fifty-eight-year-old Willbern, now using a cane to walk, admitted to writing some letters, but denied other involvement and stated that he was not a homosexual. At the trial's end, he was found guilty of "conspiring to mail obscene matter." He appealed the conviction but was soon turned down. The judge ruled his punishment to be one year of probation, commenting, "This man deserves another chance." By summer Willbern had another position lined up, at the Modern Language Association, and he officially resigned in September 1962.[10]

REMEMBERING ANDREW WYLIE

As Wells neared the end of his presidential term, he began to consider the shape of his institutional legacy. Looking back over the ten presidents that had preceded him, he had known only one personally (Bryan), and he frequently invoked the name of Jordan, who represented the start of the modern institutional enterprise. Although he was familiar with the first president's house and had engineered its purchase by the university, Andrew Wylie the man and his influence on IU was something of a mystery. As the IU Press vacated the premises of Wylie House in 1959, Wells renewed his attention to this ambiguous landmark that was associated with the original campus at Second Street and College Avenue. In support of the idea that the house should be restored to its original appearance, he publicized the legacy of Andrew Wylie.

In November 1960, six months after the NCAA sanctions were announced, Wells gave a speech at Louisville's Filson Club, a venerable history society dedicated to Kentucky and the Ohio River Valley. Relying on research by IU librarians and archivists, Wells sketched "The Early History of Indiana University as Reflected in the Administration of Andrew Wylie, 1829–1851."[11] He claimed that Wylie, almost forgotten outside of IU circles, was a "notably important figure in the early development of western state universities." Justifying the biographical approach, Wells said,

> Educational institutions no less than business, religious, or political institutions are deeply indebted to men of the past. The state of Indiana is deeply obligated to this man who guided the pioneer institution on the western frontier. With a single-minded devotion to higher education, he laid the cornerstone of which his successors could build the present educational structure.[12]

The more he knew about Wylie, the more determined he became to bring his legacy to light.

Wells pieced together his narrative account from the few surviving sources, including contemporary reminiscences from peers and students, to portray Wylie's personality and career as an educator. He summed up his contributions under four categories: establishing the curriculum, promoting good student-faculty relations, serving as chief spokesman for higher education, and mounting successful defenses of the university against outside forces.[13] As an example of the last category, he dissected one legislative investigation of Wylie that occurred in 1839, at the end of which Wylie was absolved of all of the charges against him. Ever the pedagogue, Wells explained that at that time, "investigations were a quick and democratic method of gathering information and ascertaining the truth or falsity of rumor," and that "the management aspects of the University were in their infancy and areas of responsibility of the citizens, the Legislature, the trustees, and the president were not clearly defined by custom, statue, and usage."[14]

Wells concluded with a salute to his predecessor:

> If the Indiana University of today is an institution of immeasurable value and service to the state and nation, and I firmly believe that it is, we must revere the memory of the first president who offered the intellectual and moral leadership so vital and necessary to the University in its infant days. He gave it stability in a period characterized by instability. A university is a durable institution, built on the accumulated experience of the past. How fortunate that our past included Andrew Wylie![15]

By the time Wells's article appeared in print in 1962, the Wylie House restoration was well underway. In the 1960s, on every Founders Day following the campus ceremonies to recognize outstanding students, Wells initiated a pilgrimage to the gravesite of Andrew Wylie in Rose Hill Cemetery, a few blocks northeast of the original campus.

Wells no doubt measured himself against his predecessor. Alive to the importance of individuals in social progress, he empathically narrated Wylie's actions in dealing with the perennial issues of higher education. Even the choice of categories to characterize Wylie's accomplishments could be read, with some adjustment for context, as a list of the Wells administration's most notable contributions.

Wylie became a touchstone for the university's past, and his house was an important part of that legacy. It became a visible sign of the university's rich cultural heritage. Wells, with his self-confessed interest "in anything that was a living reminder of the antiquity of the University," maintained his concern about the Wylie House for decades. Currently, it is open to the public as the Wylie House Museum, operated by the IU Libraries.[16]

INDIANA MEMORIAL UNION

Wells continued his efforts to promote the physical campus and its associations as a form of cultural glue, binding together the diverse academic community, both past and present. In 1961, a year before he stepped down as president, he rededicated the Memorial Room at the heart of the Union Building. A great book, containing the names of students and alumni who served in the nation's armed forces, and a polished bronze seal are focal points of the room, which also contains medieval stained-glass church windows, a portrait of William Lowe Bryan, the standing desk of Indiana novelist Ring Lardner, and ornamental wrought-iron bank gates at the entrance. Amidst this collection of relics commemorating the past, Wells revealed a glimpse of his interior life. In a remarkably poetic turn of phrase, he remarked, "What man in his inner self does not have a small room of memory, where, if he stops to look, are stored reminders of the things in his life which have made it full of wonder in the having of them, and of sorrow at their loss?" In his six decades, Wells had fashioned a life of service to others, relying on a remarkable ability to integrate the bad with the good.

In 1961, looking ahead to President Wells's retirement date the following year, the Indiana Memorial Union Board of Directors created an award to honor his many accomplishments and celebrate his signal place in the university's history. The Herman B Wells Senior Recognition Award has been given annually to a senior who has an outstanding academic record as well as a strong commitment to leadership and service on the Bloomington campus. The award also reaffirmed the connection between Wells, who served as Union Board treasurer in 1923–24, and succeeding boards.

Publicly, Wells graciously received the honor. After all, the honor was student initiated. Union Board was a student organization of long standing – one that he participated in nearly forty years earlier – dedicated to the very same ideals that he had championed for so long. It might have given him some secret satisfaction that the IU organization that was part of his developmental matrix as a servant-leader earlier now was using him as an exemplar of the highest and best qualities of an IU undergraduate. The award has been presented at an annual dinner where Wells was a regular guest while he lived. The recipient's name is inscribed on a plaque on permanent display in the IMU near the South Lounge.[17]

Another organization, the local chapter of the NAACP, gave Wells their annual "Brotherhood Award" for 1961–62. The citation recounted the "partnership" that the group had with Wells over the preceding quarter century to "lessen prejudice and unreason" and to promote healthy race relations. It expressed appreciation for his support, "usually quiet and unobtrusive," for their programs and also praised him for efforts to "purge official University policy of all discrimination."[18] As he looked back, Wells could take some satisfaction about steps he had taken, but the road ahead was still filled with obstacles.

COMMENCEMENT 1962

Wells took special care preparing his commencement speech for 1962, his last year as president. Just a few days shy of his sixtieth birthday, Wells was feeling bittersweet about giving up the position that had become synonymous with his person. He had dedicated his whole being to the welfare of IU and in turn had received untold benefits, which redounded to everybody's gain, thus starting the cycle of beneficence over again. Characteristically, Wells did not dwell on the past, however, but used it to provide a useful contrast to the present and the future.

The ceremony, held in the capacious old Memorial Stadium, took place Monday, June 4. The stage was set up on the field, with the four thousand graduates assembled in chairs in front, and the audience filling the horseshoe-shaped bleachers on the eastern side. The platform party included two giants of education, Wells and Notre Dame President Theodore Hesburgh; various administrators, including Graduate School dean John W. Ashton; and some members of the IU Board of Trustees, among them Willis Hickam, their president. Hesburgh, slated to receive an honorary doctorate, was a good friend and close colleague of Wells. His decade of leadership, with an assist from a fabled football program, had guided Notre Dame to the front ranks of private liberal arts colleges.[19]

Wells's black cap and academic gown hid his bulky frame but not his animated face. He noted in his speech that, in his 25 years as president, he had presided over thirty-six commencement ceremonies, due to the multiple ceremonies during and after the war. He cited a statistic that revealed the educational growth during his administration: in the last 25 years, the university had granted two and one third times as many degrees as it had during the entire previous 118 years of the university's history. And, he said with pride, today's university gives more advanced degrees each year than all degrees awarded 25 years ago, illustrating "not only the scholarly growth of our university but also the increasing need of our society for men and women with the highest degree of competence."[20] Continuing to weave a story using numbers, Wells told the graduates that he had personally signed 62,621 diplomas in the last 25 years. He explained,

> This has given me a sense of direct identification with each graduate. Many of the names I have recognized, recalling pleasant contacts and mutual experiences during college days. In other cases the names have brought to mind fathers, mothers, or other relatives of my undergraduate era or earlier. But whether I recognized the name or not, in the act of signing I felt some individual participation in the joy and satisfaction of each graduate who had won his degree with conscientious work and application.

> Moreover, I wished to sign individually because in André Gide's words, "*Man is more interesting than men.* God made *him* and not *them* in his image. Each *one* is more precious than *all.*"
>
> And this is the attitude of our Alma Mater – each man, each student scholar, is precious in her eye. Each stands for a unique individuality and each represents a divine opportunity. These precious individuals carry with them the responsibility of the University's future distinction, for it is by their performance the University is measured and by their dedication and devotion the University is nurtured.[21]

Wells resisted the current pessimism about the state of the world, and harkened back to the age of discovery in the fifteenth and sixteenth centuries, predicting that the space age will bring new vistas to humankind. He counseled, "Make no small plans. They are too difficult to achieve and unworthy of your ability and your opportunity."[22]

At that point, Notre Dame President Hesburgh was presented an honorary Doctor of Laws degree from Indiana University by his friend and colleague IU President Wells. After graciously accepting the honor, the smiling priest turned to go to his seat. Wells, in the process of returning to the speaker's stand, was surprised as Dean Ashton and trustee president Hickam stepped forward quickly. Ashton wrested control over the microphone and announced, "There may be a bit of confusion at this point." He directed Wells, with mock seriousness, to return to his seat and await further instructions. The portly president complied, wondering – as the audience did – just what was in store.

In the months before commencement, the IU Honorary Degree Committee had hatched a plan to award Wells an honorary doctorate for his service to the university, to be presented at the 1962 commencement ceremony, the last one Wells was to preside over. But there was one problem: if Wells were to hear of this plan, he would surely quash it. So the plan was kept secret from all but a few of the principals, including Ashton, Hickam, and Hesburgh. The assembled spectators murmured expectantly, and Wells wondered what was up.[23]

Ashton, speaking on behalf of the faculty, recommended that Wells receive an honorary Doctor of Laws. He then read a beautiful tribute to Wells, starting with a quotation from his inaugural speech in 1938: "Universities must be maintained as watch towers of human progress, from which men may gain a view of life in its entirety, and in which there will be maintained the calm and quiet necessary for objectivity and comprehension." In the ensuing twenty-five years, Ashton declared, Wells's "leader-ship never wavered in its insistence on the necessity for the *whole* view, the far-ranging quest for ever fuller knowledge of man and the world – the universe – he lives in." The dean admitted that the ideal of "calm and quiet" was replaced by "energy and excitement" as Wells "swept along those associated with him in the building of a great university."

Ashton marveled at Wells's close association and familiarity with "Hoosier life" from birth onward, so "that his judgment has been sought in many phases of the educational, the economic, and the social prob-lems of the state." Wells was "one of those rare people who manage to maintain their identity with their home community, and yet at the same time become citizens of the world." Ashton illustrated this quality by juxtaposing his ability to "identify a succulent bit of ham from a Boone County hog" with gourmet accuracy and to offer sage advice to the U.S. State Department on developing a cultural exchange program between Germany and the United States.

Although Ashton took note of the immense physical growth of the campus – the campus had grown from 140 acres to over 1,800 – he em-phasized the profound changes in educational opportunity and resources that the Wells administration brought, "carefully enlisting at every step the support of faculty and staff." He lauded the president's staunch de-fense of academic freedom, protecting the faculty from threats without or within. Ashton closed his encomium by addressing Hickam, board president, and conveying the faculty's recommendation, "enthusiasti-cally and affectionately (albeit without consulting him)," that Wells be presented with an honorary Doctor of Laws degree, *summa cum laude*. The audience erupted with cheers and applause.[24]

Hickam took the microphone to read the citation, which began,

> To you, Herman B Wells, educator, statesman, leader of men, devoted Hoosier, but also wise citizen of the world, who have been associated with this University for forty years and have engineered its growth and development as its President for the last twenty-five years, and who have distinguished yourself not only by your administrative wisdom, but also by your warm humanity, by your tolerance of all except evil and dullness and stupidity.

Hickam conferred the degree – "with great affection" – and assisted Wells as he donned the ceremonial hood.[25]

Wells was literally speechless. He understood the profound honor that the degree represented. The unprecedented signifier *summa cum laude* further embellished the honor. He had worked to the utmost of his abilities, and now his alma mater was expressing its formal appreciation. The audience waited patiently for Wells to conclude the ceremony. In a voice choking with emotion, he thanked the faculty and trustees. Recovering his wit, he shrugged, made a gesture of helplessness, and remarked, "This shows how quickly a lame-duck loses control of things!"[26]

PART THREE

At Large in the World, 1962–2000

Cultural activities are not instruments capable of affecting the immediate maintenance of peace. This depends on the intelligent use of other dimensions in the conduct of international relations. The cultural dimension, however, is indispensable as a longer-range means of creating the genuine world community of values and experience that our ever-growing interdependence requires. The imaginative, purposeful development of this dynamic new dimension therefore presents a challenge of major significance to both the government and the people of the United States.

Walter H. C. Laves, 1963

SIXTEEN

Education and World Affairs

WELLS HAD IDENTIFIED TWO MAJOR POSSIBILITIES for his post-presidential career. The first was to release himself from a self-imposed restraint regarding fundraising on behalf of the university. Although he had been serving as president of the IU Foundation since the start of his university presidency, he followed a personal rule against initiating contact with potential donors. Because he viewed the IU president's office as an extension of state government, and the state then provided the bulk of the university budget, it would be unseemly to seek outside funds. For its part, the IU Foundation was eager to unleash Wells, with his unparalleled network and tremendous charm, on its growing donor pool.

The other possibility took him away from campus to focus on organizing international education. International education was a yeasty brew of technical development assistance to foreign universities, student and faculty exchanges, area studies at American universities, and UNESCO initiatives. Wells had been a part of this changing environment since the Second World War, and developments in the early 1960s held great promise of cooperative endeavors between the federal government, the academic community, and private foundations to make real progress.

Upon stepping down from the presidency, Wells accepted the title suggested by the IU Board of Trustees. He would become the first-ever "University Chancellor." The honorific title was devised to keep him within the high administrative ranks while allowing him latitude in developing his portfolio.

THE UNIVERSITY AND WORLD AFFAIRS

In December 1960, Wells received a letter from the president of the Ford Foundation, Henry Heald, asking him for comments on a recently released report, *The University and World Affairs*. It was the product of a top-level committee formed in 1959 at the request of U.S. Secretary of State Christian Herter. Chaired by former University of Minnesota president J. L. Morrill, it included leading educators, businessmen, foundation officials, and government representatives. Although Wells was not a member of the committee, he knew most if not all of its members from his service on the national educational scene.

The concise report surveyed the history and current status of American higher education and its operations across national borders. In order to reap the benefits of internationalizing American universities, it called for a new organization to coordinate the manifold activities performed by universities, state and federal government, foundations, and private enterprise:

> It would provide a mechanism through which universities and colleges can consider together educational planning, the development and employment of educational competence in world affairs, and the systematic accumulation and appraisal of growing educational experience in world affairs. It would facilitate communication for these same ends with agencies of government, business and foundations in the United States, and with the institutions of other nations.[1]

In his letter, Heald asked Wells and a select group of other university presidents specifically about the recommendation to form a new organization and wondered about participation. "Should it be an independent enterprise," Heald continued, "or perhaps be organized under the aegis of some existing agency of educational association, such as the American Council on Education, the Association of American Universities, the Institute of International Education, or some other?"[2] As a group, the university presidents generally endorsed the idea of a new, autonomous organization.

Further discussion led by the Ford Foundation in early 1961 detailed the functions of the proposed organization. A staff memo outlined a "top level planning and programming group . . . to provide long-range guidance for university and college activities in world affairs." Such a group or organization would coordinate and mobilize resources on behalf of international education, and "deal with specific problems such as exchange management, sister-university relations, the philosophy of area centers, etc." But the memo cautioned against becoming "involved in operations or take over the functions of existing agencies. It should not finance institutional developments or be a means of certifying individual programs to foundations or government."[3]

As news filtered out to existing educational associations, the American Council on Education (ACE) and the Institute of International Education (IIE) lodged concerns that the new organization might provide unwanted competition. Things were fluid in the first few months of 1961, with the Carnegie Corporation and the Ford and Rockefeller Foundations still studying whether a new organization would be feasible and desirable.[4] The Ford Foundation appointed a task force that would consult with a wide variety of stakeholders in international education, including government agencies and ACE and IIE, and study "the possible establishment of a new organization, its role, function, budget, geographical location, and autonomy." Heading the task force was Franklin D. Murphy, chancellor of UCLA and a member of the original Morrill committee. Four university presidents – Robert F. Goheen (Princeton), John A. Hannah (Michigan State), Douglas M. Knight (Lawrence College), and Herman Wells (Indiana) – rounded out the small committee. All except Hannah had been involved in prior discussion with Heald.[5]

The Murphy task force completed its work by September and reported back to the sponsoring foundations. Not surprisingly, they strongly advised creation of a new, autonomous organization that would direct studies in the realm of policy, planning, research, and evaluation studies, but not operate programs. Mindful of other players in the field, they stressed the formation of cooperative relationships with existing government agencies and educational associations. Suggesting the name of the Center for Education in World Affairs, the task force thought that foundation support for the fledgling organization should extend for at least ten years, and provide $3 million for the first five years.[6] Despite some serious reservations about the function and scope of the proposed organization, both Carnegie and Ford approved; Rockefeller declined support. Agreeing in principle with the task force's recommendation about the initial term of ten years, Carnegie gave $500,000 and Ford gave $2 million for the first five years.

With this generous showing of support, expectations were high. But a substantial string was attached to the money. As the grant from Ford specified,

> If the new agency can help to improve our educational leadership in world af-
> fairs, break the bottleneck of American competence and enlarge the educational
> resource base, stimulate the initiation of better practices and institutional
> arrangements and thereby lift international cooperation in education to a
> higher level of performance – if it helps to do these things, the new agency will
> have made an invaluable contribution in the national interest. If it does not, the
> agency can be terminated.[7]

The new organization had its budget and mandate.

Members of the Murphy task force were invited to become founding members of the new organization, and they met several times in 1962 to hammer out details, with foundation staff contributing to the discussion. After deliberation, the board decided on the simple name, Education and World Affairs (EWA). Excellent leadership was a concern, because the "reputation and prestige of American higher education were very much at stake" in overseas activities. Cold War concerns were in evidence as members of the board agreed "that the basic national interest of the United States is affected by the way we perform and the wisdom we show in our international educational relations." The board was expanded with men from business and government, and the Ford Foundation declared, "The trustees of EWA are of top quality, keenly interested in the agency, and aware of the need to clarify program priorities."[8]

EWA CHAIRMEN

After assembling a top-flight board of trustees, EWA asked Wells to become chairman in June 1962. The offer was made by John Gardner, president of the Carnegie Corporation. Wells, convinced of the worth of the initiative and yet unsure of his post-presidential plans, accepted the position on a quarter-time basis. That would allow him to continue to reside in Indiana and to keep working for the IU Foundation. Despite some opposition to appointing a foundation official rather than a university president, William Marvel, executive associate of the Carnegie Corporation and EWA trustees' board executive secretary, was appointed EWA president.[9]

EWA's trustees interpreted the mission of the new agency broadly. It was to

> promote the investigation and consideration of means by which United States educational institution and resources can contribute to international cooperation in education and to the advancement of education in other nations; [and] to encourage and facilitate communication and contact on the part of the educational community of this country with all relevant institutions and groups in this and other countries and thus to foster a widening network of educational interchange, of both persons and ideas.[10]

To accomplish its objectives, the organization would sponsor research and conferences, and publish and distribute materials dealing with international educational activities.[11]

Wells was in his element in getting EWA off the ground. Mobilizing his extensive network, he relished being involved in promoting international education. He fervently believed that education was the key to individual self-improvement and social progress. The early 1960s was a heady time, with unprecedented American prosperity and great hopes for the export of democratic values around the world. The inherent contradictions in modernization and third-world development had not yet been generally perceived. It was a boom time for higher education, and there seemed to be no reason not to extend the purposes and methods of American higher education beyond the borders of the United States.

In 1963, Education and World Affairs moved into their permanent offices at 522 Fifth Avenue. Its quarters were described as "opulent" and even "posh." Wells used his EWA office as his New York headquarters, finding it a convenient base of operations. The first order of business was to publicize EWA's work and make linkages with other institutions. In the first full year of operation, the organization sponsored six regional conferences to bring in faculty and administrators to discuss opportunities and challenges of international educational activities. The conference locations – Santa Fe, New Mexico; East Lansing, Michigan; Hanover, New Hampshire; Pebble Beach, California; White Sulphur Springs, West Virginia; and Princeton, New Jersey – revealed a sensitive concern with pleasant surroundings for the proceedings. As Wells described it, "EWA had an active program of conferences, seminar studies and reports, consultation with colleges and universities, consultation on international educational policy making, and an active, functioning program of committees and councils dealing with specialized problems."[12]

One early publication was *The University Looks Abroad*. Its purpose was stated in its subtitle: *Approaches to World Affairs at Six American Universities*. A series of case studies, it examined international programs at Stanford, Michigan State, Tulane, Wisconsin, Cornell, and Indiana in hopes of providing useful examples for other universities. The imprint of Wells was evident in the description of the wide-ranging efforts at IU. Using the trope of the small Hoosier village of Birdseye, Wells explained the rationale for involvement with international education:

> Through the years Indiana University has tried to preach the gospel that to be a university of the first rank in this day and age, it must keep its eye on Birdseye *and* on Bangkok, and, of course, on Bloomington.... Birdseye is our constituency, but there is more than one Birdseye. The steel workers of Gary are Birdseye; the Indiana Federation of Women's Clubs are Birdseye; the State Chamber of Commerce is also Birdseye. And the colleges and high schools of Indiana are among the most important of our Birdseyes. Birdseye can thus be reached in many ways.[13]

Once again the cosmopolitan University Chancellor was reaching out to his listeners, trying to build bridges between the local and the potential global constituency of Indiana.

Although the main functions of EWA were communication and policy making, two operational services centers were created. The first, the Overseas Educational Service (OES), provided logistical support to the U.S. higher education community for technical assistance work abroad, and facilitated recruitment of U.S. staffs by foreign institutions. Located in EWA headquarters, the OES had numerous cosponsors, including the American Council on Education, the National Academy of Sciences, the American Council of Learned Societies, the Social Science Research Council, and the Institute of International Education. The second, the Universities Service Center, located in Hong Kong, was to facilitate access to Chinese scholarly materials by Americans and other Westerners in the wake of the 1949 ban on travel to mainland China. The EWA created a special advisory board composed of "leading figures in the fields of Chinese studies, higher education, and public affairs in Canada, Great Britain, and the U.S." to oversee the work of the Universities Service Center.[14]

FREELANCE EDUCATIONAL CONSULTANT

Wells was also in demand for his professional services. In the summer of 1963, he was appointed a consultant on higher education by the New York legislature to review the operation of the entire state university system. The mammoth State University of New York (SUNY) had been created as an amalgamation of many public institutions of varying size and quality all over this large and populous eastern seaboard state, and the state had launched a huge multi-campus building program. Aided by associates John A. Perkins, president of the University of Delaware, and G. Russell Clark, board chairman of the Commercial Bank of North America, Wells spearheaded the study. Working closely with Wells was study director Sidney G. Tickton, a Ford Foundation staff member, who drafted the final report.[15]

The "Wellsian approach" was deceptively low key. In his soothing Hoosier cadence, he said calmly, "I don't know how this will work out. We'll figure it out as we go along." But he displayed his usual sense of organization as he spoke to key legislators and leading educators in the state, and had his staff assistants research the history and policy of state aid to education in New York. Study director Tickton noticed: "He has the sort of mind that can absorb a great deal of information quickly and reduce it to fundamentals. When he sits down to talk to a legislator, he knows what he wants. More important, he knows why he wants it."[16]

Their sixty-five-page report was released to the press at the end of 1964.[17] It called for more autonomy and freedom from "governmental procedures now hampering its operations." Avoiding direct blame on the New York Assembly, it cited "jurisdictional and policy conflicts with the board of regents, the state executive departments, and the Governor's office" that only the legislature could remove. Several administrative and business reforms to halt duplication and to streamline procedures were outlined. Taking a cue from state or regional cooperative agreements elsewhere in the nation, the report urged that SUNY devise a management plan to share faculty and facilities with private institutions in the state. Asserting that future college enrollment estimates were too low, the study presented revised figures, saying that private colleges in the state would increase from 290,000 to 500,000 by 1985, and public universities from the current 260,000 to 1,000,000 in the same period – altering the private-public balance.[18]

TROUBLE AT EWA

As chairman of the board of Education and World Affairs, Wells remained committed to the organization, and was careful not to micromanage the work of EWA president Marvel. But by 1965 he found himself in the hot seat. Foundation officials from Carnegie and Ford were dissatisfied with the EWA, and one complained that the influential board of trustees had not been well utilized, becoming a "bomb that has been defused."[19] Wells, as board chairman, explained that the trustees "have deliberately stayed in the background." He also noted that the presence of representatives from ACE and IIE prevented frank discussion when areas of possible competition arose.[20]

Taking the criticisms to heart, Wells led a revamping of the organization structure, making the trustees even more involved, and rethinking the EWA mission statement. In May 1966 the Ford Foundation continued their financial commitment with a grant of $3 million for the next six years, and in March 1967, the Carnegie Corporation renewed its $500,000 pledge for the next five years.[21] EWA boosted its publishing program, and several individuals connected with the organization were involved in lobbying Congress for the International Education Act, which President Johnson signed into law in October 1966. No appropriations were ever made, however, as the escalation of the Vietnam War strained federal coffers.

By January 1968, five years after his resignation as university president, Wells had started thinking about stepping down as chairman of the EWA. The IU Foundation was ramping up to a major fundraising campaign to coincide with the university's sesquicentennial in 1970. He wrote to his friend John Gardner – who had recently announced his departure from the president's cabinet as secretary of the Department of Housing, Education, and Welfare – about taking over the chairmanship of EWA. Gardner, who was president of the Carnegie Corporation when EWA was founded, decided to pursue other options.[22] By spring 1968, IU president Elvis Stahr, feeling embattled by student activism, stated his wish to resign, and the trustees called on Wells to step in as interim president while they conducted a search for Stahr's successor. Inexorably, Wells found himself drawn into the day-to-day administration of the university as he served as executive officer from July through November. Although he retained his position in EWA, Wells's energies were drawn back to Bloomington.

The EWA faced a changed environment, and the foundations that had supported it over the years had new leadership and new priorities. In 1970, various plans were broached to reorganize or merge the organization. On June 22, Wells resigned as chairman of the board. Later in the fall, EWA went out of existence, merging with the Center for Educational Enquiry to form the International Council for Educational Development.[23]

Looking back, Wells regretted the demise of EWA and the waning interest in international education on the part of American universities following the Vietnam "catastrophe." The 1970s' focus on the internal problems of the American university was lamentable, Wells maintained: "Once more we academics learn that we cannot retreat within our own quarters, but must continually interest ourselves in what is occurring beyond our borders."[24]

FRIEND-RAISING TO FUNDRAISING

Although Wells retained his title as president of the IU Foundation after 1962, his behavior was subtly transformed. For the past thirty years he had steadily enlarged his networks of associates, and his remarkable social intelligence made him a superb friend-raiser for the university. Knowledgeable about university needs and possessed of an evolving vision of what IU could become, Wells infected nearly every one he met with a positive enthusiasm for the future. He had learned long ago, as a paperboy, that wholehearted belief was necessary to be a successful salesman. People responded to his genuine concern for the university as a human institution as he brought them into the IU orbit. Fundraising for Indiana University and international educational policy served as the twin axes of his work during most of the 1960s, until he was drawn back to service as a full-time administrator in 1968.

As the IU Foundation grew in wealth and influence, it became the target of periodic criticism. A few critics saw it as a "private conclave that controlled the institution itself." Some objected to its tax-exempt status; others argued that it provided unfair competition with local businesses and government. In October 1962, Indiana Governor Matthew Welsh declared that the state had no wish to audit the books of the IU Foundation. Criticism continued, and matters came to a head in 1964 when the Monroe County prosecutor, Thomas Hoadley, filed suit against the IU Foundation, the Hoosier Realty Corporation (the real estate arm of the Foundation), and the IU Board of Trustees in order to force them to open their books to the Indiana Board of Public Accounts. Wells responded in his characteristic manner, explaining that a board of "respectable Indiana citizens" set policies and that the books received an annual audit by certified public accountants. The land gifts and purchases were made in mind of future university expansion. The IU Foundation and the Hoosier Realty Corporation paid taxes on the property until the university acquired them. The suit generated publicity, but the charges were not sustained by a court decision.[25]

Nevertheless, the IU Foundation volunteered a public report on its holdings in 1967, the first ever. In his prefatory remarks, Wells stressed that the IU Foundation played an increasingly important role in achieving quality in a public university. The report listed assets of $8,600,000, earnings of $2,600,000, and expenses of $2,400,000. The IU Foundation had received $1,149,000 in annual gifts earmarked for faculty, student, and departmental support in 1967.[26] Critical voices were muted but not silenced.

FOREIGN UNIVERSITY MISSIONS

Under the Wells presidential administration, Indiana University had technical assistant programs ranging from teacher education to public administration in Brazil, Cyprus, Indonesia, Korea, Nigeria, Pakistan, Si-

erra Leone, and Thailand. As chief executive, Wells encouraged these developments and often went to the field to consult with IU colleagues and
make ceremonial calls on foreign officials. After he became chancellor in
1962, Wells continued his foreign travels on behalf of international education, with IU projects in Indonesia, Pakistan, Peru, Philippines, Saudi
Arabia, Thailand, Uruguay, Venezuela, Yugoslavia, and Afghanistan.[27]

In 1966, Wells was invited to visit Kabul University by President
Tooryalay Etemadi, who obtained his M.A. at Indiana in 1954. Kabul
University wanted to modernize its curricula and programs, and con-
tracted with several U.S. universities to provide onsite assistance. To
effectively oversee the modernization process, the university administration needed training and guidance, and they turned to Indiana University. Indiana and Kabul agreed on a three-phase program that included
a group of KU administrators visiting IU and observing various administrative offices and functions for one semester, and then sending selected
administrative staff to IU to pursue graduate education – leading to master's or doctoral degrees – in relevant programs. The exchange program
was initiated in January 1967 when nineteen Kabul University administrative staff came to the Indiana campus, lived in Wright Quadrangle,
and learned firsthand about U.S.-style university administration.[28]

Among the Afghani staff was Hussain Farzad, who was director of
programs and chief of protocol for the university. Meeting Wells during
his first visit to Kabul, Farzad provided essential links to the developing
exchange relationship, hosting IU education professors Willis Porter,
Chris Jung, and Thomas Schreck on subsequent visits. In 1970, Farzad
received a scholarship for graduate study at IU, and completed two master's degree programs (in student personnel administration and student
college union administration) two years later. He was back working at
Kabul University as director of dormitories when a military coup took
over the government in 1973, making things uncomfortable for those
who had studied in American universities. The next year Farzad emigrated to the United States and returned to Bloomington to study for a
doctorate in education and to work at IU in residential life.[29]

I believe that any community of scholars would agree that *no* special interest group, internal or external, should be allowed to impose its particular point of view upon the university. This does not imply any restrictions on questioning, making suggestions, seeking information or peaceful and orderly advocacy – although usually there are more direct sources of information than the President of the University. It does mean that the policy of an open campus in which freedom of inquiry is protected is of highest importance to the university community. Indiana University has an unblemished tradition of preserving an open campus.

Herman B Wells, 1968

The support of great universities is the most lasting of all investments, for universities have a life of their own that maintains the validity and character of the gift.

Herman B Wells

SEVENTEEN

Back to Basics:
Management and Marketing

WELLS, A NEW DEAL DEMOCRAT, CARED DEEPLY ABOUT POLITICS, whether at the local, state, or national level. After eight years of the Eisenhower administration in the 1950s, he was happy about the election of John F. Kennedy in 1960. The note of hopeful idealism evaporated as Kennedy was assassinated and the United States became mired in war in Vietnam. A host of other problems surfaced – the lack of civil rights for minorities, the degradation of the natural environment, the oppression of women – leading to antiestablishment sentiment and reform legislation. Youth culture became an unmistakable social force, nowhere more evident than on the nation's burgeoning college and university campuses.

The university was approaching its 1970 sesquicentennial, and planning began to launch a major fundraising campaign. Wells, a key player in the IU Foundation, provided important input for shaping the appeal and fundraising strategy. Planning started about five years before the launch, to give plenty of lead time.

Another reason was more urgent. When Elvis Stahr officially resigned as president in early July 1968, the indefatigable Wells was at the helm again, appointed as interim president, thirty-one years after his first taste of that office.[1] Stahr had resigned after a strenuous six years of continued growth in campus enrollments, academic programs, and the physical plant. In spring 1968 he was caught in the middle of a racially charged civil rights controversy. Black students activists had demanded that historically white fraternities remove discriminatory clauses in their charters that barred students of color from membership. That demand was reinforced by a sit-down strike, involving about fifty African American students, on the Little 500 track in the old stadium. Although twenty of the twenty-four fraternities had already complied, the matter was still not resolved when race day dawned, overcast and rainy, on May 11. The race was postponed for a week as negotiations continued with the four remaining houses. In short order, all of the fraternities, except for Phi Delta Theta, removed these restrictions, bringing their policies into closer conformity to the university's nondiscriminatory policies. Acting upon a request from the mediators, Phi Delta Theta withdrew its team, "for the good of the University," and Stahr assumed "personal responsibility for the decision."[2] In a show of concern for the demonstrators, Wells, Professor Orlando Taylor, and other university administrators and faculty paid visits to the stadium.[3]

The Little 500 action was the proximate cause of Stahr's citation of "presidential fatigue" in his letter of resignation, but only the latest in a series of confrontations with increased student activism across a broad front. Earlier in spring 1968, black students founded the Afro–Afro-American Students Association (AAASA) "'to cooperate with individuals and organizations dedicated to the eradication of those impediments to human progress,' such as racism and segregation."[4] They put pressure on Stahr to increase the numbers of black faculty and students and to start a black studies program, but found his response too cautious and measured when he delivered his remarks at the National Conference on Negroes in Higher Education. Registering their displeasure, on April 1 several AAASA members marched to Stahr's campus residence, the President's House, and milled about on the grounds. Stahr was still out of town, but Mrs. Stahr and their three young children were at home. Although the students were nonviolent, they stayed for six hours outside the house, terrifying Stahr's family. They finally left after Stahr acceded to their demand to abolish the university's committee on discrimination because the students had no input on the composition of its membership. Three days later, Martin Luther King, Jr., was assassinated, which raised fears about the escalation of violence as the nation dealt with the consequences of the blow.[5]

INTERIM PRESIDENT WELLS

From the beginning of July 1968, "most of the problems of the presidency landed on my desk," Wells recalled. The Board of Trustees had turned to the former president once again to nurse the university through another administrative crisis. They urged Wells to accept a two- or three-year appointment, but he refused, thinking that it would not be in the best interests of the university. Wells suggested that the title interim president be used. It would help emphasize the brevity of his tenure as well as signal his disinclination "of being only a caretaker president for even a short period of time."[6] His love for the institution was stronger than ever, and he felt secure in his ability to take another turn at the helm to guide it through the coming days.

In the nearly five decades since Wells's own undergraduate days, the proportion of all youth attending college went from 10 percent to almost 50 percent, and IU Bloomington had grown to be the eleventh largest university in the nation. With rising enrollments and more students on campus, students found their voice. Idealistic students got involved in the issues of the day in unprecedented numbers.

A keen student of politics, Wells was well aware of the rise of student activism, both in the United States and around the world, in the 1960s. As president of IU, he had firsthand experience as far back as the 1954 "green feathers incident," in which progressive students protested the McCarthy hearings by scattering green chicken feathers around campus. He was careful to draw a sharp distinction between the university's obligation to protect academic freedom and its official apolitical stance. "The University should not take a position pro or con on controversial issues," he maintained.[7] Historian Mary Ann Wynkoop explained that Wells "felt he could and should protect those members of the university community whose activities provoked attacks that brought into question the principle of academic freedom. He did not see his role as defender of those who criticized political adversaries from within the walls of the university itself."[8] In his 1961 Founders Day address Wells offered a mild rebuke to the methods of some student activists:

> In our institution, therefore, it is a little surprising that students would elect to
> substitute demonstration for discussion and debate. The articulate intellectual
> frequently criticizes the noisy demonstrations of a political campaign as an
> appeal to mass emotions. Perhaps this is necessary in an era of mass communica-
> tion. Nevertheless, it hardly seems compatible with the campus atmosphere.[9]

But Wells had been insulated from the day-to-day demands of university
administration for six years when he stepped back into the president's
office in 1968.

Characteristically, one of the first things he did was to invite student activists to meet with him to share their concerns. That open door
policy had worked in the past, most notably in rectifying cases of racial
discrimination. He was confident in his ability to find common ground
with the young idealists. But after a couple of futile meetings with the
students, Wells was bewildered and a bit crestfallen. He was mystified
that he was not able to establish a productive dialogue with them.

After the academic year started, Wells delivered the president's annual report on the state of the university. Ostensibly addressed to the
faculty, the report highlighted the achievements of the Stahr administration. This retrospect, Wells stated, would be followed by part 2 of the
annual report, dealing with budgetary issues, "about December 1, if we
don't have a new president by then."[10]

Drawing parallels to the great IU president David Starr Jordan, Wells
noted that the Stahr administration lasted six years, just like Jordan's,
and that both presided over a period of "revolutionary change in knowledge, thought, and patterns of social behavior." Noting that faculty
salaries had lost ground competitively, he explained that the state's appropriation had fallen short "in the last three biennia through no one's
fault" because of unpredicted rises in enrollment and inflation. Several
changes in the university's structure occurred under Stahr, including
the establishment of the School of Nursing as an independent entity;
the incorporation of the Herron School of Art; creation of the Division
of Allied Health Sciences, the Graduate Library School, and the Honors
Division; and the conversion of the School of Law's Indianapolis Division into a freestanding Indianapolis Law School. The centerpiece was
a plan, begun July 1968, to reorganize the university into three areas:
the Bloomington campus, the Indianapolis divisions, and the regional

campuses, each with a chancellor responsible for academic programs.[11] Wells noted that the regional campuses came into their own during the past six years, with strong increases in enrollment (and the part-time instructional staff) and a shift from two-year to four-year institutions.

Wells mentioned the rise of student activism, pointing out "the difficulty of decisions that rest on the thin lines between request and demand, between consensus and represented opinion, between felt needs and desired goals. One of the easiest things in the world is to say 'no' to change; one of the hardest, to provide for its reasoned and orderly occurrence." The Stahr administration, he thought, managed those challenges well, with a huge increase in student representation on all-university committees, and the creation of a student affairs committee in the Bloomington Faculty Council. A pass-fail option was added to the grading system, and "regulations concerning student life were liberalized."

Sponsorship of research activity flourished, rising from $31 million in 1962 to $89 million in 1968, and Stahr continued the presidential tradition of heavy involvement in regional and national educational affairs that was started by Wells. The physical plant continued to expand, with new residence halls, the Optometry Building, a new library, and the Musical Arts Center completed or under construction in Bloomington, as well as new facilities on the Indianapolis campus and many of the regional campuses.[12]

Wells concluded with an encomium to Stahr and his administration:

> I wish this [address] to be a tribute to the remarkable period of accomplishment which was guided by Indiana University's twelfth president. The University's forward movement during his administration has made her, near the eve of her Sesquicentennial, a much greater and finer institution than has been true in all of her long and eminent history. It was a period of reasonable and thoughtful response to student activism. It was a period of vigorous response to aspirations of faculty members for scholarly development. It was a period of resourceful response to the many demands for public service. It was a period of sensitive response to the social issues of the time. In all, it was a period of courageous, imaginative response to growth and change.[13]

Publicly, Wells accentuated the positives in this time of transition, but his private fears about finding adequate leadership in this turbulent era were lurking.

RESPONSE TO THE SDS

For taking the trouble to try to meet with student activists soon after he took over from Stahr, Wells was rewarded with a list of points formulated by the Students for a Democratic Society (SDS). They accused the university of being "a subservient, uncritical flunky of the military establishment and of the agencies formulating American policy" and demanded that Wells remove all traces of the military from campus and end secret research for the Vietnam War effort. His first impulse was to accept their invitation to a public forum, putting his faith in rational discourse. But other administrators convinced him that radical students might attempt to disrupt the occasion, so he reconsidered. A plan was made for a point-by-point refutation of these charges to be published in the *Indiana Daily Student*.

On November 1, the interim president's statement came out.[14] With close attention to detail, Wells and his staff prepared a lawyerly brief, "comprehensive but unyielding."[15] He emphasized that the SDS demands did not raise questions about student life, such as university regulations or extracurricular activities, but "invade the area of academic programs and the scholar's freedom to pursue his research interests."[16] Wells had faced down threats to the university's autonomy before, in the 1940s and 1950s, from outside groups on the right, such as the American Legion. Now the attacks were coming from the opposite end of the political spectrum and mounted from within the university by members of the student body.

"The impropriety of 'demands' as a form of questioning policy and practice in an academic community should be evident to every member of the community," Wells averred, explaining the university should be above interest group politics. Of course, there were no restrictions on questioning or advocacy by members of the academic community, only that the university should not (and would not) take an official position on political questions despite strong partisan pressure to do so. "The policy of an open campus in which freedom of inquiry is protected is of highest importance to the university community," Wells affirmed, adding, "Indiana University has an unblemished tradition of preserving an open campus.[17] After enunciating this basic philosophy and remarking how the war in Vietnam was causing "national stress," Wells launched into his defense of the university administration.

In response to the first SDS demand, calling for the elimination of ROTC programs, Wells responded with a lengthy history of military training on campus, pointing out that ROTC was started in 1917, at the urging of students, and had been optional for male undergraduates since 1965. He argued that, due to the presence of ROTC units on civilian campuses, "the large majority of the men in the officer ranks are R.O.T.C.-trained college men and partly because of this, the United States fortunately has not developed a narrow professional group with a stake in militarism." Wells resisted demands to bow to political pressure, whether to cancel ROTC programs now or, in earlier instances, to "cease teaching anything about Karl Marx, Russian history, and Slavic languages and literature." Finally, he appealed to the students' concern for their peers in this era of a mandatory draft: "Opposing R.O.T.C. may satisfy your hunger for actions but its crucial effect will be to remove the option of valued training for many of your classmates."[18]

SDS objected to military recruitment on campus, vociferously claiming that the university was "actively channeling" students into employment in the Defense Department, the Central Intelligence Agency, and the armed services, among others. Wells countered that "the University is not engaged in 'actively channeling' students into anything other than its instructional programs," and gave a brief historical review of placement services, citing both the Bloomington Faculty Council's and Union Board's policies as supporting the "open campus" principle. "Pressure to use the University for promotion of any group's particular position on an issue constitutes an assault upon the integrity of the University," Wells argued, adding, "Yielding to that pressure would make the University vulnerable to any and every special plea."[19]

The next SDS demand called for the elimination of military-funded research at the university. President Wells pointed out that no research on weapons was taking place, and disclosed that the Department of Defense provided $1.2 million in the previous year to support various basic research projects. In all cases, the faculty member had initiated such projects, and in no cases were the results classified. Wells concluded,

Let me reaffirm in the strongest terms our intention to defend the right of every
faculty member to carry on without fear of censure or disruption the research
in which he is interested. We will seek support for him from any and all legal
sources. I need only mention the Kinsey research to illustrate that the University
has braved heavy criticism to prevent the subjects of research and of classroom
instruction from proscription by external or internal pressure groups.[20]

The next set of demands concerned police and student political activity. Wells feigned bafflement when he encountered the first – "all special
training programs for police forces, foreign and domestic, be ended" – responding dryly that he thought there was general agreement "on the
desirability of the best possible training for police forces everywhere."
No response was possible to the allegation that the university had special training programs for military and intelligence because it had none.
The SDS wanted the university to "cease intimidation of student political activity" by "removing plainclothes and secret police from campus."
Denying that there were secret police on campus, the president stated
that the university's policy was one of cooperation with law enforcement.
In a matter-of-fact tone, Wells admitted, "We do have three investigators
on the Safety Department staff at Bloomington in addition to Director
Spannuth who customarily do not wear uniforms. There is nothing ei-
ther secret or sinister about their presence. They are here to protect the
University community, its property and the University's property."[21]

Concerned about unfriendly witnesses at student political events,
the SDS stipulated that "only clearly labeled administrative observers"
be sent. With tongue in cheek, Wells mused, "I do not know what useful
purpose labeling of individuals would serve, but if that is generally desired, I suggest that everyone be labeled – students and faculty members
as well as administrators." In a serious vein, he defended the right of
anyone to obtain firsthand information by attendance, and reminded the
group that accurate observation (including cameras and other recording
devices) was in the best interest of the students by protecting them from
wrongful complaints. A further demand was removal of "all implements
of political repression such as tear gas, chemical mace and riot clubs,
whose only use could be against students." Wells, resisting the SDS's
belligerent assumptions, reviewed the Safety Division's report for September 1968, during which time they were called upon to investigate 134
incidents ranging from larcenies and vandalism to suicide and attempted

rape. "It is patently absurd to charge that provisions for protection are disguises for intimidation of student political activity. Campus elections, Dunn Meadow political gatherings, marches around Showalter Fountain, discussions in the area south of Woodburn Hall have always been carried on without Safety Department interference with legitimate activity."[22] He went on to state that the presence of law enforcement to control crowds had prevented accidents from occurring and allowed the resolution of partisan differences among groups.

After giving a point-by-point rebuttal to the demands put forward by the SDS, Wells had a word to say about the university's foreign contracts, which had been criticized for supporting reactionary governments abroad. He pointed out that all of the contracts were with universities, not governments; that they were concerned with advising universities on training programs for educational leadership; and that six were funded by the Ford Foundation and two by the federal Agency for International Development. Wells concluded his response with a restatement of his views: "I strongly oppose the exclusion of recruiters and the banning of R.O.T.C., just as I have successfully opposed efforts to have the University oust individuals active in anti-military and other controversial causes. I fully support the discussion and study of issues involved in the Vietnam War, in war itself, and in the presence of the military on campus." He made an appeal to the disaffected students to rededicate themselves to the larger objectives of higher education: "Each of us has a crucial stake in seeing to it that Indiana University enters the post-war period, which will come, still invulnerable to the pressures that would erode its strength and violate its cherished principles: freedom to teach, to learn, to seek new knowledge and to serve society."[23]

Wells, with the benefit of time to hone his responses to the SDS demands, made a tight, even legalistic, defense of the actions of the university administration. In certain ways, however, the president and SDS leaders were talking past one another. Students wanted change, and sometimes expressed their concerns in naïve and uninformed ways. Wells, a master academic politician, knew the university inside and out, and was able to point out inaccuracies and misinformation in the protesters' demands. Students were rightfully concerned about "secret police," as there were FBI undercover informants who were infiltrating campus groups. Wells might not have had direct knowledge, "but it was unlikely that he was unaware of the FBI's interest in Bloomington's New Left leaders."[24]

A NEW PRESIDENT

The presidential search committee made their selection in November 1968, and recommended Vice President and Dean of the Faculties Joseph Sutton for the post. At IU since 1953, he was a political scientist specializing in the Far East, and served as chief of party to set up an Institute of Public Administration at Thammasat University in Bangkok in 1955. Sutton took office on December 1, and Wells returned to the chancellor's office in Owen Hall. The new president struggled with alcohol-related problems during much of his first year, and Wells stood in for him on various formal occasions, such as Founders Day and commencement ceremonies. "In fact, with the help of the other administrative officers of the university, I carried on many of the presidential functions," Wells blandly revealed.[25]

In spring 1969, shortly after Wells gave up the title of interim president, student activism reached a high tide in Bloomington. In response to state budget cuts, the IU Trustees, seeing no alternative, raised tuition a breathtaking 67 percent, from $195 a semester to $325 a semester for in-state students. Galvanizing even apathetic students, in late April more than eight thousand students trekked to the new fieldhouse and met with administrators to talk about the budget. On May Day, three thousand students rallied in the Old Crescent and called for a two-day boycott of classes. Shortly after, an unexplained fire occurred in the library building next to the Kirkwood campus entrance at Indiana Avenue (the library's collections would be moved within the year to the massive new edifice being constructed at the corner of Tenth Street and Jordan Avenue). Working in his office, Wells rushed to the scene, where smoke poured out of the library's window and a growing crowd watched firemen attempt to control damage to a campus landmark. Not only did it cut him deeply to see this institutional symbol of learning injured, he also had warm personal memories of spending time in its welcoming confines ever since his student days. Business School professor William Scott observed Wells "standing there all by himself in stunned disbelief." As they talked about the unfolding tragedy, Wells said, with tears in his eyes, "Who would do such a thing?"[26] Nearly everyone suspected student protesters at the time, although later investigations pointed to arson by a disgruntled library employee.[27]

During the same period, Founders Day was celebrated to showcase the efforts of high-achieving students. In the midst of the ceremony, nearly 500 of the student honorees got up and left. In the newspaper, Wells backed students' demands for increased state support and praised them for their peaceful exit.[28] Students continued the boycott of classes for a week. A group of about fifty students, administrators, and faculty met in the faculty lounge of Ballantine Hall to attempt to resolve the boycott. A group of 150 African American students joined the meeting and proceeded with a lock-in, demanding that the university trustees meet with them. President Sutton called the campus police and obtained an injunction ordering the black students to release everyone and leave the building. State and local police mobilized with full riot gear and were ready to storm Ballantine Hall. The locked-in administrators convinced the students that their voices would be heard, and the brewing crisis was peacefully averted. Although no threats or actual physical violence, either to persons or property, took place, and the administrators and faculty members involved refused to press any legal charges, the Monroe County sheriff sought a grand jury investigation. Several indictments of "riotous conspiracy" were forthcoming, and several student leaders and one faculty member, Orlando Taylor, received the charge. Taylor's pending nomination for vice chancellor was withdrawn, and the opening of a new Black Studies Institute, of which he would have been the inaugural director, was delayed for a year as a consequence. (Taylor was eventually acquitted, but he had already left the university for a faculty position elsewhere.)[29]

Never backing down from the principle of academic freedom, Wells urged the students to honor the university and respect the academic community as they sought political change. Stories abounded about the venerable leader who loved students as the biggest wave of student activism sweep over Indiana. A faculty member reported that, in the late 1960s, Wells was speaking to a crowd of students when a young protester cried out, "Be quiet, you old f– –!" Finishing his sentence, Wells turned in her direction and said disarmingly, "Now, my dear, you had a comment – could you repeat that? I didn't quite hear." The young woman – with all eyes upon her – was not bold enough to repeat the insult. Of course, it was clear that Wells had heard it perfectly.[30] Another time, around 1970, some concerned students living at Foster Residence Hall sought an informal dialogue with senior IU administrators. All of the invitations were turned down, with one exception. Chancellor Wells met with about one hundred students gathered in a lounge at the residence hall. A participant recalled,

> There were no guards or assistants, just himself, a glowing, enthusiastic spirit that seemed to fill the room with calmness, integrity and respect. He really had no answers to all the present issues that were burning in our young souls. What he had to offer was his sense of where the university had been and a sincere vision of what he believed it should be and could be. He impressed me with his faith in young people. . . . It was puzzling because here was the symbolic anchor of the university establishment who in his thoughts, convictions and actions was far beyond and above what I thought the "establishment" stood for. Basically he said all this would pass and humanity and the university would do just fine. It was a wise but frustrating message for those who wanted change and wanted it now.[31]

In contrast to the SDS activists, Wells connected with these students and communicated his vision of Indiana to yet another generation, in trademark style.

But some student activists remained critical of Wells. The IU chapter of the New University Conference, a "national organization of radicals who work in, around, and in spite of institutions of higher education," published a booklet, *Disorientation: Like It Is at IU*.[32] The last chapter in the section "The Power Structure" was entitled "The Grand Old Bastard," consisting of a three-page profile of Wells. Admitting that he had a generous and benevolent image, the anonymous author cautioned, "behind that façade stands a greedy ambitious man who works for his own political and economic aggrandizement, using students, and prostituting education to business, government, and military interests to make himself richer and more secure." Making fun of his holiday persona, the article promised muckraking and exposure: "Santa Claus is a lie. Herman Wells at 67 is the most successful manipulator of them all.

Want to hear about the 'elf'? There's a lot to tell." What followed was a paranoid interpretation of his *Who's Who* entry, using Marxist-flavored innuendo to question his activities, associations, and affiliations; and painting him as a power-hungry bureaucrat. The piece accused him of lying to students, citing his published response to the SDS in the IDS in November 1968. The author could not resist insulting Wells's appearance, characterizing him as "rich, fat, old and busy" – the "bulbous and over-stuffed granddaddy of all the bureaucrats."[33]

In January 1971, following the death of his wife, President Sutton suddenly resigned.[34] His two-year tenure had been a stormy one, and the university was once more plunged into a crisis of leadership. This time the board of trustees decided that the interests of the university would be best served by an immediate appointment. There was no formal search committee, and the trustees consulted few of the faculty before appointing one of Sutton's former faculty colleagues, John W. Ryan, who was serving as vice president and chancellor of the regional campuses. Ryan had obtained a Ph.D. in political science from IU in 1959, and spent time as a graduate student working for the IU mission in Thailand. Although he took office in late January 1971, Ryan's formal inauguration took place on January 20, 1972, the 152nd anniversary of the university's creation. The circumstances of his appointment without a formal search would create difficulties from time to time – especially with the faculty – during his nearly two decades in office.

NOBEL NOMINATION

In the mid-1960s, British astrophysicist Robert d'Escourt Atkinson served as a visiting professor in the IU Astronomy Department. Becoming en-amored of the university community, he subsequently retired and stayed in Bloomington. Impressed with chancellor Wells and cognizant of his role in international education, Atkinson hatched a plan to nominate Wells for the Nobel Peace Prize. President Stahr counseled patience. Atkinson complied; then after two years he launched a campaign to get Wells considered for the international honor. In 1969, the nomination letter to the Nobel Committee went out with the signature of twenty distinguished faculty and administrators at IU, including President Sutton.

The nomination cited Wells's many accomplishments at Indiana, including the support of foreign languages and area studies, and his continuing service to the nation on behalf of international cultural diplomacy. The letter stated,

> Convinced that education is the key to human relationships, he became persuaded that only as young people, lawmakers and citizens generally developed an intelligent interest in and appreciation for the diverse peoples and cultures of the world could there be any hope of creating a climate and dialogue for permanent peace.[35]

Atkinson wrote to many notable figures who had worked with Wells and asked them to support the nomination by writing recommendations. Among the letter's recipients were former vice president Hubert Humphrey, UN Undersecretary General Ralph Bunche, Columbia University President Andrew Cordier, Indiana Representative John Brademas, former Harvard president James Conant, and Ford Foundation President McGeorge Bundy.

Wells's multifaceted efforts to foster international study, promote scholarship on foreign areas, and augment understanding of diverse people during the Cold War were esteemed among IU faculty as well as national dignitaries from politics, diplomacy, and education. His nomination for the Nobel Peace Prize went forward in 1969, but it proved unsuccessful.[36]

150TH BIRTHDAY FUND

As the IU Foundation reorganized in 1969, Wells was made chairman of the board and Armstrong received the title of president. Wells continued to provide valuable counsel and a sedate counterpoint to Armstrong's breezy style. He was adept at identifying prospects, making personal connections, and informing them about opportunities and needs of the university. Blessed with a vision for the enduring health and vitality of IU, Wells knew that friend-raising and fundraising were long-term propositions, and he cultivated accordingly, patiently waiting for the fruits of his labor.

A few years earlier, various senior administrators, including Wells, realized that IU would be marking its sesquicentennial in 1970, and started planning for what became known as the 150th Birthday Fund. As plans progressed, individual objectives were made and shared with faculty, alumni, and potential donors.

The official kickoff of the Indiana University 150th Birthday Fund campaign occurred in December 1968, at the end of Wells's temporary presidential service. Its stated goal was $25 million. The 150th Birthday Fund campaign changed the organization of the IU Foundation from a small, entrepreneurial operation with well-oiled annual giving program to "a multidimensional foundation managing, in addition to the annual giving program, corp[o]rate and foundation relations, and planned or deferred giving programs."[37] Four building projects were identified as priorities: the Musical Arts Center, Hoosier Heritage Hall (of which the Glenn A. Black Laboratory and Mathers Museum are now a part), the Fine Arts Pavilion (now called the IU Art Museum) and Assembly Hall. Old friends of Wells's were put in charge. Claude Rich resigned as the Alumni Association secretary to become the director of the Sesquicentennial Program, and Major General Joseph O. Butcher, former dean of students, resigned from the Marine Corps to direct the 150th Birthday Fund. A variety of initiatives were conducted on the local, state, and national levels, with the cooperation of an army of volunteers coordinated by the Foundation's increasing specialized staff. Wells was in the thick of things, with friendships cultivated from near and far for decades, as he persuasively told the University's story and made clear the unmet needs to donors who had the wherewithal to contribute.

At the large victory party, attended by five hundred people, in February 1971, the total was announced: $27 million, more than $2 million beyond the original goal. But the IU Foundation was on a roll. Campaign director Butcher declared, "I am convinced that the final chapter will be written in much larger figures," and a new goal was set, at $35 million. When the books were closed a year and a half later, in July 1972, the IU Foundation had raised more than $51 million – double its starting goal.[38] Wells found deep satisfaction in this collective accomplishment, and later declared, "A quantum leap forward in the affairs of the Foundation came with the success of the 150th Birthday Fund drive in 1970."

Wells practiced what he preached. In the mid-1970s, he asked for a confidential report on the total amounts given by top donors since the

Foundation's beginning in 1936. The donor list was headed by James Adams, a New York corporation executive. He was one of the student captains of the Memorial Fund drive in the 1920s, and had continued his philanthropy to his alma mater, most notably by providing funds for art objects purchased by the IU Art Museum, beginning in the 1950s at Wells's urging. The second person on the list was Wells himself. Characteristically, Wells did not share this information with anybody.[39]

ANOTHER RETIREMENT

Reaching his seventieth birthday in 1972, Wells was hale and hearty, still moving from one activity to another in a busy schedule. Despite a few medical setbacks, he was remarkably healthy given his minimal physical exertion and rich diet. He officially retired from his professorship in the School of Business after forty-two years on the faculty. Soon afterward, the school created "The Herman B Wells Seminar on Leadership," an undergraduate capstone course, to honor and extend his legacy.[40]

Less than a year passed before the death of his beloved mother, in April 1973, at the age of ninety-one. After a fall that broke her hip, Bernice Wells was taken to Bloomington Hospital. As the medical personnel transported her from her second floor room at 1321 East Tenth Street, she clutched the banister desperately, fearing that she would never return to the house that she had shared with her son for the past ten years.

Wells was emotionally devastated and remained disconsolate for a time. Their relationship supplied both the pattern and the impetus for his preternatural talent for human affiliation. In his seventy-one years, he had spent well over half of his life living under the same roof with her. She was his constant companion since 1948, going through nearly everything with him for the past twenty-five years. She had blossomed from a small-town housewife into the figure of "Mother Wells," carving out a role as the first lady of the campus during her son's presidency.

Although his mother could be irritating at times, Wells missed her presence in the chancellor's residence. Her large suite on the second floor was quiet. Without a word said, the housekeeper kept everything as it was. Except for the occasional overnight visits from the Heady cousins, Helen and Esther, the room's place in the home's fabric was undisturbed.

Nearly every morning before coming down for breakfast, Wells shuffled along in his slippers to the open doorway of his mother's room and spent a few minutes in silent contemplation. Finished with his daily visit to the household shrine, Wells padded to the elevator in his robe, went down the first floor, and commenced breakfast.

The aroma of coffee filled the spacious kitchen. The housekeeper had started her day several hours earlier, the houseboy would be off to class, and the chauffeur would soon arrive. Wells greeted each person cordially, and then gave his breakfast order to the housekeeper as she poured him coffee. There were only two constants: coffee and cooked fruit (homemade applesauce in the fall and winter, and homemade rhubarb in the spring and summer). Depending on the strength of his appetite, the rest of the menu ranged widely, from bran cereal with skim milk to bacon, eggs, and toast. Wells read newspapers – the local *Herald-Telephone* and the *New York Times* – while he ate. Thus fortified, he started his business day at the breakfast table by checking in with his office and by phoning associates.

In May 1973, just weeks after his mother's death, Wells injured his back. The injury was severe enough to keep him at home, curtailing his appointments at his office and elsewhere. Within the month he was a patient at Bloomington Hospital. The original estimate of three weeks of reduced activity stretched into three months of convalescence.[41]

A bright spot occurred a week after his seventy-first birthday, on June 7, when Professor Frank Edmondson and President Ryan visited him in the hospital. Edmondson, an astronomer in charge of the asteroid program at IU's Goethe Link Observatory, had the privilege of naming many newly discovered minor planets. Confirmed by the International Astronomical Union on June 15, minor planet 1721, located in the constellation of Leo, was officially designated "Wells." The chancellor asked, "How big is it?" Edmondson replied, "About 100 miles in diameter." Wells deadpanned, "Gosh. There's something with my name on it that's bigger than I am."[42] When Eli Lilly heard about the asteroid, he contributed a bit of doggerel to his friend:

"How appropriate it befalls / That the planet is named Herman Wells / Against all odds / He now orbits with the gods / So let's turn out & ring all the bells."[43]

By September Wells felt well enough to travel. Still grieving for his mother, he wrote a tribute to her when he was traveling at sea off the coast of Spain, in commemoration of her October birthday. He recounted her outgoing personality, her dramatic change of life when she came to live with him, and her role as campus host and traveling companion. Away from Bloomington, Wells found himself in a reflective state of mind, recalling her presence and missing her profoundly.[44]

REDEDICATION OF THE BROWN COUNTY PLAYHOUSE

As he moved into his mid-seventies, Wells maintained his residential headquarters on Tenth Street and his office in Owen Hall. Houseboy David Eibling, studying medicine, had just started working at the Wells residence when Mother Wells died. He continued until 1977 when I, as an undergraduate psychology major, succeeded him.

I learned quickly about the responsibilities and privileges that demarcated the life of the houseboy. I paid attention to the chores and duties, such as serving food and drink, mopping the kitchen floor nightly, and the occasional chauffeuring. Some privileges were obvious, like having the run of a beautiful furnished house or the excellent food in copious quantities or tickets to almost any campus event. Others were more subtle and incremental pleasures, such as having conversations with Wells himself.

In the first summer of my employment as the chancellor's houseman, I drove Wells to Nashville, Indiana, to see a theatrical performance at the Brown County Playhouse. On the way, Wells regaled me with tales of living in Nashville in the 1930s and the history of the playhouse. The summer stock theater, begun in 1949, owed its existence largely to the efforts of Professor Lee Norvelle and Nashville businessman Andy Rogers. Located on the main street of the village, Van Buren Street, it consisted of a barn with a proscenium opening in one wall and dressing rooms in the basement, and a large tent sheltering the audience who were seated on backless benches. Eventually, a tin roof replaced the tent. The playhouse served an important pedagogical function by providing an outlet for student performers in the summer season. Nashville had the distinction of being the only county seat in the state with live theater and no movie house.

The previous winter, the playhouse had been completely reconstructed to serve as a modern indoor venue. To initiate the new structure, Tennessee Williams's *A Streetcar Named Desire* was chosen. Perhaps the most important amenity was the addition of air conditioning, which was appreciated by both the actors and the audience. It was the opening night of the first show of the summer season, and the occasion of a rededication ceremony. Wells stopped and talked with nearly everyone he encountered before taking his seat.

I recall that midway through the dedicatory remarks, Chancellor Wells was recognized and the entire crowd rose to its feet clapping. Wells slowly drew himself upright, hanging onto the chair in front of him, nodding and smiling, his eyes looking from one face to the next. The applause continued. Wells kept smiling. The applause kept coming. Wells kept smiling, although a note of embarrassment crept into his smile. Finally, after what seemed like a long while, but what was actually about five minutes, the clapping died down and ceased. Wells and the audience took their seats again, and the crowd burbled softly, energized by the spontaneous outburst of affection. The impromptu exchange of tender feelings left a glow throughout the audience as the lights were dimmed and the curtain rose.

Pretentiousness Hoosiers will not accept. It's what you are as a private person that counts (a frontier tradition), not your offices, titles, degrees, honors, or fortune. Whatever you have accomplished or acquired is attributed to luck, and you're no different fundamentally from your poor, uneducated, or unrecognized neighbors. This is a fiction, of course, but it is preserved by the graciousness of those who have moved ahead. Perhaps it makes an easier society.

Howard Peckham, 1978

EIGHTEEN

Being Plucky: Covering the Distance

INDIANA UNIVERSITY CELEBRATED A MAJOR MILESTONE – its sesquicentennial – in 1970. Wells's association with the institution had endured for nearly a third of that period – and his leadership as a senior administrator had lasted for a third of a century. A few years earlier, President Stahr launched a major fundraising campaign, the 150th Birthday Fund, and recruited Thomas D. Clark, a historian from the University of Kentucky (and a former professor of his), to write a history of Indiana University. Clark took on the immense job of synthesizing voluminous archival sources and published records, which he augmented by conducting many oral history interviews. The history project, covering the entire span of the university's existence from its founding in 1820 to the end of the Stahr administration in 1968, eventually yielded three substantial narrative volumes and one book of reprinted historical documents.[1] Indiana University Press provided editorial supervision.

At the Press, Editorial Director John Gallman had succeeded Bernard Perry as director in 1976. With a pedigree that included growing up in several countries as the son of a diplomat and education at Yale University, Gallman renewed the Press's focus on the academic strengths of IU – including area studies, folklore, and music. He was also interested in publishing books of regional interest. The scholarly history of the university was a hybrid form. As the Clark history was being researched, Gallman broached the idea of having Wells produce an autobiography. At first, Wells scoffed at the notion, begging off even considering the idea because he was too busy. But he believed in the value of institutional history and was a great supporter of Clark's project, providing moral support as well as several oral history interviews.[2]

Clark himself urged Wells to "record [his] own perceptions" of his administration, reminding him that he was writing about the university's history and not that of Wells, even though Wells's fingerprints were all over it.[3] Wells was deeply ambivalent about setting down his own version of events, knowing that it would focus more attention on him as an individual rather than the institution he loved. The very act of writing an autobiography verged on immodest behavior. Besides the potential violence done to his personal standards, this form of taking stock of his life would force him to come to grips with the reality that he had already reached whatever high point in his career – and that the coda, however long it lasted, would be only that.

However, Wells realized that his iconic status and the cult of personality that had grown up unbidden could be harnessed for the greater good of the university. Universities, like other human institutions, need heroes, exemplars, and model citizens. But if he could provide a true accounting of his legendary career, readers could see that he was an ordinary mortal, however fortunate. A deeper problem remained: How could a man who had devoted his whole persona to representing other people and other causes depict himself?[4] His reluctance was exacerbated by the self-knowledge that he did not like to write, especially in a formal genre such as biography. The communicative arts he had used so successfully in his career were face-to-face and telephone conversations, letters, speeches, and memoranda. Although comfortable compiling bureaucratic reports, his literary output in the form of published material was small for an academic, amounting to several book reviews, a few professional journal articles, and the occasional book introduction or chapter.

Wells finally gave in to pressure to write his personal history. Gallman was pleased that his unremitting campaign to convince the university chancellor had finally paid off. Although Wells had kept busy with multiple activities, he had no major project on the horizon. The Foundation's sesquicentennial fund drive had been completed a few years before, and the books had been finally closed. His trusted lieutenant, Dorothy Collins, had proved herself a superb researcher and writer since joining the chancellor's staff in 1969, and she joined the chorus urging him to start.

Once Wells decided to do the autobiography, the entire chancellor's office's staff added one more item to their already full agenda. There was no question about how the form of the rough draft was generated – it was dictated, not written out. Wells had a rough scrawl, used only for taking notes or correcting drafts of letters and memos. Since he always had secretaries available during his career, there was no incentive to improve his handwriting. So he began to dictate chapters, starting at the beginning, and after the secretaries typed them up, Collins would read and comment on them. But it was slow going. Wells would get distracted and go off on a tangent. Dates and names would be incomplete or missing, necessitating research in the voluminous files in the office or at the presidential archives in Bryan Hall. Or Wells simply could not find the time to record his memories and thoughts verbally. Collins was not only the chief editor, but also the head cheerleader, trying to get her boss to get back on a task he did not care for. The current houseboy, John Haste, was recruited to serve as a research assistant – checking facts, hunting down names, and a myriad of other detail work. In addition to the chancellor's office staff, David Warriner, a Ph.D. student in history, served as another research assistant. His own dissertation dealt with the impact of veterans on Indiana University after World War II – an eventful time during the Wells presidential administration.[5]

As the autobiography project was getting started, the third volume of Clark's new IU history was prepared for publication. Wells not only gave an extensive oral history interview, he also read and commented on Clark's book in draft form. The author thanked him in the book's acknowledgments, and added that Wells did not "suggest 'editorial' changes in the treatment of his administration."[6]

Even with all the help, the book draft proceeded slowly. Wells's heart was simply not fully engaged in the project. Not only did he misremember things, much to his chagrin, he was also inhibited by his personal injunction to always be nice. Averse to expressing verbal criticism, he was loath to commit even mild disapproval to paper. He bent over backwards to give other people the benefit of the doubt in an effort to provide fair and balanced treatment. The resulting skew meant that astute readers would have to add their own intensifiers. Trying to provide a model, Gallman gave him a copy of Machiavelli's *The Prince,* a classic early modern treatise on gaining and using political power, and suggested, "Pretend you are Machiavelli telling the University world how you did it." The suggestion had the opposite effect, and Wells stopped working on the book for a while. Finally managing to get his advice cancelled, Gallman later had a meeting with Wells in his Owen Hall office. "I read that book you gave me," Wells said. "You're right. I was like that. But I can't write that kind of book." Reflecting on this afterward, Gallman mused, "What could he have told us if he were not a Victorian gentleman?"[7]

WRITING AUTOBIOGRAPHICALLY

Although Wells had an intuitive grasp of history and its potential uses, he was naturally disposed to think ahead, planning and strategizing to see how potential could be turned into actuality. Once he completed a task, whether big or small, his forward-looking constitution impelled him to move on to the next thing. This memoir-writing project could be a challenge to his normal way of operating in the world. But he set off, thinking that the autobiography might set the record straight and perhaps demystify his career.

Wells had growing awareness of the distance he had covered in his life, from humble beginnings in Jamestown to a respected leader of an international university. The twentieth century had revolutionized transportation and communication several times, and Wells eagerly embraced new technology in his quest to build community and cultivate the cultural landscape. From the cart and pony of his childhood to modern jet travel, his horizons had expanded remarkably – from Boone County to the entire globe. His trajectory was different only in the details from Andrew Carnegie's story that Wells recounted in 1954. Symbolically, Carnegie's transit from his birth in a drab weaver's cottage in Dunfermline to the lofty turrets of Skibo Castle possessed the same elemental meaning as Wells's journey from obscurity to fame in the Hoosier State had.

When recalling his childhood and youth, Wells tapped into a deep vein of pride and nostalgia for the vanished time before World War I.

"Hoosiers were most distinctively their own people in the period from 1900 to 1920," regional historian Howard Peckham asserted.

> They were rural in background and outlook, without being rustic or uncouth. By then they were pleasantly mature but not sophisticated or urbane. They read their own authors (so did everyone else) and patronized their own paint-ers. Since hard work, perseverance, thrift, and honesty seemed always to be rewarded, they clung to the old virtues. . . . No one was ashamed to be known as a Hoosier; in fact, it was a badge of honor. They knew who they were and what they were, and thus they were stable.[8]

In resonance with this framework, Wells presented a stable picture of his formation in Boone County. Local schools, the Methodist church, the Jamestown Boys' Band, and the circuit Chautauqua were the institutions that instructed and entertained him.[9]

"As I look back, it seems to me that I was born in the best of all times and under the best of all possible circumstances," Wells wrote, reflecting in his words what Gallman identified as his Victorian optimism.[10] The atmosphere depicted had much in common with Meredith Nicholson's 1912 fictional work, A Hoosier Chronicle, whose narrator concluded, "It's all pretty comfortable and cheerful and busy in Indiana, with lots of old-fashioned human kindness flowing round; and it's getting better all the time. And I guess it's always got to be that way, out here in God's country."[11] Wells, a fifth-generation Hoosier, took genuine pride and satisfaction in his roots in the Indiana countryside.

At the heart of Wells's narrative were his parents: "My best fortune of all was to have as parents an ambitious young couple who were wise, encouraging, and loving."[12] His father, schoolmaster and banker Gran-ville Wells, was described in a reverent, even sacramental, tone: "A man of nearly sacrificial industry," serious and virtuous, and able to relate well to people. Wells wrote of his father, "I have never known a better man, a man of more unswerving integrity, morality, and decency."[13] Granville died in 1948, when Wells was forty-five. The unblemished idealization of his father was followed by a tribute to his mother, Bernice Harting Wells, with whom he had a longer, day-to-day relationship until her death in 1973, when Wells was seventy. Describing her as outgoing and optimistic, he said she "made a great contribution to our physical and psychologi-cal well-being."[14] What follows is an admiring account of her life after her husband's death when she came to live with Wells and fulfilled the social role of IU's "First Lady." He credits her with drawing him further into campus social life and increasing his "personal popularity." Mother Wells accompanied her son nearly everywhere, including his extensive foreign travels. Wells wrote of her kind graciousness, "extraordinary memory," and "deep personal interest in each friend," concluding "her contribution to my professional career was incalculable."[15]

A careful reader might pick up the few hints that Wells left indicating his family life presented some obstacles. In one paragraph on his father, Wells stated his father was introspective and a perfectionist, liable to depression if he did not achieve the high standards he set for himself. "He had to take the hard blows of the Great Depression and his mother's suicide," Wells wrote.[16] Not committed to paper was the reality that Granville's wife and son had to accommodate his black moods all through his life, until his own death by suicide. In the tribute to his mother, Wells disclosed his own emotional struggles in a single sentence as he described her social involvement as first lady, saying it "helped to cure me of the periods of acute loneliness I had suffered periodically before, almost to the point of depression."[17]

In describing his own youthful activities, Wells presented a laundry list of high school activities, both academic and extracurricular, and working with his father at the bank after school and during school vacations. The image portrayed was that of a driven boy, always doing something, endlessly busy. His packed schedule left "little time for dating, dances, or social functions other than those held at school."[18] One could ask, Why didn't this bright and personable lad ever date? And why did he turn into a lifelong bachelor? One small clue is offered in Wells's description of the family move in 1917 from the village of Jamestown to the county seat of Lebanon, in which he briefly mentioned his and his mother's coming down with mumps.

Entering Lebanon High School as a sophomore well after the start of the school year was a social adjustment. But it probably was not as severe as the changes in his body. Wells suffered from orchitis, a complication of mumps common among adolescent boys. At the time, folk knowledge held that orchitis caused a reduction of fertility, even sterilization. We don't know whether his parents ever discussed his condition with him, or what he thought about this physiological problem. What we do know is that Wells, at the age of thirty-four, had a complete workup to discover the source of his chronic groin pain, apparently suffered since his bout with orchitis at fifteen.[19]

No one can know Wells's interior life but it is a reasonable surmise that his psychological environment and physiological conditions during his formative years affected his adult way of being in the world. Work was his most reliable anodyne, and serving others before himself was deeply ingrained. He made friends easily, and was adept at keeping them close but not intimate. Reading his accounts of his family and high school years, he selected events and stories that prefigure his career as a public servant, told in a friendly yet dignified manner, with a positive twist always. Just in case the reader were to miss his idealistic portrait of his parents, Wells reiterated, "As a look back on my life, I am sure that they were more responsible for the kind of career I have had than was any other influence."[20] Determined to keep on the sunny side in retrospection, he relegated any shadows to the margins or eliminated entirely in this relentlessly upbeat personal narrative.

Another problem Wells faced in composing his autobiography was how to treat his wide-ranging career without appearing to boast. One good way was to use humor. Wells loved nothing better than a good joke, and his sense of humor was as wide as the Wabash. He hit upon recycling a speech, given as a valedictory to the National Association of State University in 1962 two months before his retirement as IU president, entitled "Maxims for a Young College President, or How to Succeed without Really Trying." This ironic reference to a recent pop culture phenomenon, *How to Succeed in Business Without Really Trying,* was probably not lost on his audience.[21]

The tone was set by the first maxim – "Be lucky." The speech recapitulated the philosophy and the practices that Wells followed in his administrative career. The advice blended earnestness – "save time for student contacts of all types" – and unsubtle wit – "the first rule of public relations is never to get into a contest with a skunk!" On the personal role of the president, Wells quipped, "Be born with the physical charm of a Greek athlete, the cunning of Machiavelli, the wisdom of Solomon, the courage of a lion, if possible; but in any case be born with the stomach of a goat." The telegraphic style was perfect for an after-dinner speech, and suited Wells's aversion to pomp and preening. But the pages do convey the gist of his personal style. The last maxim was the same as the first – "Be lucky!"

The speech also provided the title of the book. Subtitled *Reminiscences and Reflections, Being Lucky* was, in equal parts, an engaging autobiography, a manual of higher education management, and an artful spoof of his stellar career. In it, he repeated old stories that had become encrusted with myth, such as the serendipitous way he came to be acting president in 1937. He was fond of saying "Don't ever let the facts get in the way of a good story." There was a kernel of truth in his stories – always – but later embellishments added juice and a moral point.

The title *Being Lucky*, on its face, valorized chance and the interplay of circumstance at the expense of individual agency and personal will. Although it would be hard to doubt Wells's genuine gratefulness for his life's chances, the book's narrative minimizes his own role in shaping his destiny. Modesty and unpretentiousness were bred to the bone in this Hoosier, and even listing the accolades that he earned from others was simply not done in his book. Reading between the lines, "being lucky" could mean responding in a creative way to life's fortune.

Wells practiced a radical form of unselfconsciousness in his life that was displayed in the life story he presented. Secure in his own being, he was able to meet others on common ground. With highly developed interpersonal skills and an intuitive grasp of John Donne's dictum that "no man is an island, entire of itself," he understood that humans were social creatures first and foremost. With that stance, it was natural for Wells to emphasize the contributions of others in shaping events and to downplay his role, however central it was. There are countless examples in *Being Lucky*.

A master practitioner of the Hoosier penchant for understatement, Wells told his story in a neutral, diffident, "aw, shucks" style. One prime example: "My college fraternity afforded me many opportunities. I suppose I had a natural affinity for fraternity life, and my experience in Sigma Nu was a very happy one."[22] The reader gets little sense of the profound influence on Wells that communal living and the development of lasting friendships entailed.

Perhaps the easiest chapters to draft were accounts of his travels and memorable hotels, meals, and chance encounters with other people. Wells built his entire career around extensive travel, and he made little distinction between traveling for business and traveling for pleasure, because they were deeply intertwined in his experience. This peripatetic lifestyle, with constant movement through changing environments, suited Wells like a favorite pair of shoes. In January 1978, in the midst of writing, he embarked on a five-week, around-the-world air cruise to exotic destinations in the company of old friends Hansi Mendel and Kate Mueller. Wells wanted to join the Travelers' Century Club, which had the requirement of documented travel to at least one hundred countries. The club, which was started in the 1950s as an informal social club connected to the Hemphill Travel Company, adopted as its slogan "World Travel . . . the passport to peace through understanding" in 1960. Despite his intense travel schedule over the years, Wells remained a few countries shy of the century mark before the air cruise.[23] After the trip, Wells qualified for membership in the Century Club, joining about three hundred other enthusiasts. But he was not as successful in getting all of the accounts of travel and meeting colorful personalities included in the autobiography; IU Press director Gallman had them cut.[24]

The draft was finished in 1979, and the book entered production. Once the book was finally done, Wells was generous in the acknowledgments. He cheerfully admitted Collins's central role as "stern taskmistress and a constant source of inspiration," keeping him at the assignment "when the temptation to chuck the whole thing was great."[25] Collins, with her English studies background and long experience as an administrative aide, appreciated the delicacy of the task and provided the appropriate editorial direction. "The difficult part about collecting and producing the book, Dorothy Collins once confided, was in getting Wells to stay in one place long enough," one reporter noted.[26]

As publicity plans for the book were devised during the first few months of 1980, they got added steam by the announcement that Wells would deliver the baccalaureate address at the May commencement ceremonies. In the buildup to the book's launch, scheduled for fall 1980, Wells talked about its contents to local audiences during the spring and summer. To the IU Men's Faculty Club, Wells joked that writing a book "is really a very traumatic experience." When asked about the title, *Being Lucky,* he said it referred to his good luck in being born in Jamestown, Indiana.[27]

Coincidentally, one of Wells's fellow presidents, Frederick L. Hovde, who led Purdue University between 1946 and 1971, was the subject of a biography that appeared in July 1980. The two friends occupied the trenches of Hoosier higher education for many years, and cooperated faithfully. In side-by-side reviews of *The Hovde Years* and *Being Lucky* in the *Indianapolis Star,* one can glean the public image conveyed by the titles of the respective stories: "Purdue's 'Beer-Drinking' Educator" and "Folklore Shrouds Ex-I.U. President."[28]

Pre-publication copies of the book were made available to the press. *Indianapolis News* reporter Bill Pittman made the perceptive comment, "And beneath the sheath of joviality there ever was a reservoir of energy and diamond hard determination yet to be fully plumbed." Speaking of his deepest attachment, "From 1933 to about 1935, I didn't even have time for a date," he once said in an interview. "I guess I married a university." Pittman concluded, "From his memoirs comes the understanding that I.U. is his monument."[29]

The IU News Bureau sent out a press release inviting the media to the book party on October 16, 1980, in the IMU's University Club. The original print run for *Being Lucky* was two thousand copies. At the reception, Gallman introduced the book and its author to the nearly thirty people in attendance. After making a few humorous comments, Wells autographed copies of *Being Lucky.*[30] What would turn out to be his most robust literary brainchild was taking its first steps into the world.[31]

THE CRITICAL RECEPTION

The first serious review of the book was done by a student, appropriately, in the *Indiana Daily Student.* Puzzling over the maxim "Be Lucky," which gave the book its title, staff writer Jonathan Evans thought it was a curious choice, both grammatically and logically. "Good luck is not contingent upon adequate performance," he wrote. But he went beyond these considerations and saw the main theme of Wells's life and work as "unsuppressable [*sic*] optimism":

One may not be able to control the fates and demand their good graces, but one *is* able to make the best of what one has, to work hard, to refuse to compromise one's ideals and values and thus to come as close to fulfilling the terms of the paradoxical imperative as is humanly possible. In "Being Lucky," the reader sees that Wells followed such a plan. In these terms, he *was* lucky.

Wistfully, Evans contrasted the optimistic tone of the book with contemporary skepticism about institutional leaders. Not only did it tell the story of one of the university's "greatest personalities," but could also serve as a textbook of conduct for similarly successful lives.[32]

A review appearing in the *Indiana Magazine of History* called Wells "a president's president."[33] David D. Henry, president of the University of Illinois from 1955 to 1971, opined, "*Being Lucky* is a readable account of an unusual, interesting, and noteworthy career" in higher education, although the book's "tedious recitation of names of colleagues" became irksome.[34] James Perkins, former president of Cornell University and the head of the successor organization to Education and World Affairs, took note of Wells's efforts to desegregate the campus and of his defense of Kinsey, shrewdly observing, "The more volatile and emotional the issue, the lower the Wellsian key and the less hurried the pace of decision making, but the more direct his quiet personal involvement." In American higher education circles, Perkins argued, "Wells is Father Hesburgh's only serious competitor for the prize for durability, institution building, and automatic chairman of the meeting." He also appreciated the book's wide focus: "Not the least of the pleasant discoveries was that of Herman the gourmet, Herman the aesthete, and Herman the compleat voyager."[35]

Amidst the general approbation of *Being Lucky,* one reviewer dared to raise serious questions about Wells's role in shaping national and international polices and the extent to which Indiana University "served American interests as defined by the State Department" in its own programs or by the president's official federal appointments. Reviewer Harvey Neufeldt, from Tennessee Tech, noted the development of IU from provincial to distinguished, and saw parallels with Wells, who "grew with the institution." The Kinsey chapter merited special attention, with its vigorous defense of unconventional research and controversial publication. The review highlighted Wells's declaration that if a university "bows to the wishes of a person, group, or segment of society," it cannot

be free, and the university, as a corporate body, must preserve its neutrality on contentious public and political issues. Neufeldt saw inconsis-
tencies in this stance, and questioned whether Wells's involvement in
national and international service affected "the presumed neutrality of
the university at its highest administrative levels."

Although Neufeldt criticized *Being Lucky*'s optimistic, even boosterish, tone, he saw value in the book as a window into the Cold War world:

> Its importance for the student of higher education lies less in the narrative that
> unfolds than in the mindset it portrays of university administrators, like Wells,
> who exercised power during the years of rapid growth after World War II, and
> who consciously or subconsciously worked to have higher education serve
> national governmental policies abroad.[36]

There is no evidence that Wells looked at this review or any others, or
that he cared about the critical reaction. After all, it was another project
done, there were many more in progress, and he was not going to get
distracted now by indulging in the habit of looking back.

Four months after its publication, *Being Lucky* was in its third print-
ing, and Wells was still in the news, talking about his life and career. In
yet another profile of the book in the local paper, civic affairs editor of
the *Herald-Telephone,* John Fancher, used Shakespeare's lines about the
world being a stage and "one man in his time plays many parts" as a hook:
"Among those many parts Wells has played is his recent role as author."
The full-page spread was lavishly illustrated by photographs of Wells
playing different parts at various points in his life. Much of the text was
quotations from *Being Lucky,* with some comments by Wells about how
things have changed since his term as president. Speaking to the success
of IU's legislative program, Wells noted that due to conservative state
fiscal policy, the university does not suffer from "peaks and valleys" in
financial support. Making a virtue out of Hoosier frugality, he said, "I
have an abiding faith in the people of Indiana who have confidence in
their university."[37]

IU RETIREMENT COMMUNITY

As Wells was researching and writing his autobiography, he was also
lending his support to the idea for a university-affiliated retirement com-

munity. Growing out of the Annuitants' Association, the Indiana University Retirement Community (IURC) was organized in March 1977, with a twelve-member board of directors. Wells gave an initial contribution to its treasury, and soon $48,000 was raised to formulate a plan of action. After an extensive search, a thirty-acre parcel of land, north of the football stadium, known as the Kerr Farm, was located. The old farm was a beautiful tract, with wooded hills, old pastures covered with tall grass, and a small pond. Located close to Griffy Lake, its northern boundary abutted protected municipal land. Kerr Farm had been acquired by the IU Foundation, and they rented the ground to the Annuitants' Association on a thirty-year renewable lease.[38]

After discussion of architectural design, the IURC decided that 184 living units (apartments and garden condominiums) would be arrayed around a central common building that would include facilities for dining, nursing care, and social interaction. Marketing efforts were ramped up, the name "Meadowood" was agreed upon, and membership requirements were loosened to include surviving spouses of retired employees, IU alumni or trustees, and "other persons determined by the board of directors to be significantly associated with the University." The projected cost of the development was estimated at $13 million. Financing the construction costs would be accomplished through a hefty residency fee (a contract for lifetime occupancy, not ownership) and by the sale of tax-exempt bonds.[39]

In summer 1979, the City of Bloomington Common Council authorized economic development bonds, contingent upon selling at least 50 percent of the proposed units. Despite the requisite number of contracts not being sold, the IURC remained sanguine, and held a formal groundbreaking ceremony in July 1980; shovel-wielders were John Ryan (IU president), Frank McCloskey (mayor of Bloomington), Frank B. Jones (IU Alumni Association president) and Wells. In short order, 114 residency contracts were in hand, paving the way for the marketing of the bonds and the beginning of construction.[40]

In April 1981 construction was started. Site preparation revealed a large sinkhole where the mid-rise apartment buildings were to be located, so work shifted to the completion of the garden units. Near the end of the year, Meadowood's first residents moved in, and lived in a construction site without paved streets or common dining facilities.[41] IURC President Harry Day, an IU chemist who was part of the team to develop fluoridated toothpaste, wrote Wells in October 1982 and disclosed deep worries about the slow pace and high costs of construction and the inadequacy of income from residency fees. Day suggested that a "substantial low-interest loan or a good line of credit" be obtained from the IU Foundation to finish construction and place the community on firm financial ground. Wells replied, "I think it is unrealistic to think of the Foundation supplying funds directly to Meadowood. In fact I would not recommend it." That amounted to a firm "no," but he ended on a soft note, saying things would work out eventually.[42] Wells, ever the fiduciary watchdog, wanted to avoid IU Foundation entanglements.

By July 1983, the health pavilion and the community building were completed, street paving and landscaping were substantially done, and the Meadowood population was more than one hundred residents. But as more employees and more services to residents were added, expenses were greatly exceeding revenue. Estimates of construction cost overruns ran as high as $2 million, and the IURC was forced to sue the general contractor and architect.[43] Reversing its stance, the IU Foundation agreed to bail the retirement community out with a loan of $1 million, with Wells personally guaranteeing the sum.[44]

Not surprisingly, Wells invested in a Meadowood condo himself. Snuggled up to Griffy Woods at the northeast corner of the Meadowood property at 1025 E. Sassafras Circle, it was decorated in Wells's eclectic, tasteful style. Antiques, artworks, and oriental rugs combined to make a comfortable home environment. But Wells rarely, if ever, stayed overnight, preferring the comforts of his Tenth Street home. The condo was used as a hideaway and guesthouse, and Wells joked that it functioned as his own "Camp David" retreat. Ever the optimist, the aging chancellor retained his public enthusiasm for Meadowood: "We would build the kind of community where you just don't go and vegetate!"[45]

Wells began his octogenarian decade still vigorous in body, mind, and spirit. One of his cherished projects, the Indiana University Art Museum, was completed that year, and marked the architectural finale to the Fine Arts Plaza. Over the preceding forty years, Wells patiently assembled funds and mobilized the university's will for this magnificent complex of facilities surrounding the Showalter Fountain, including the ɪᴜ Auditorium, the Fine Arts Building, the Lilly Library, and the Art Museum, dedicated to artistic expression and humanistic understanding. In a profound sense, it deepened the university's core identity to preserve and transform the fruits of human aspiration, and can serve as a fitting monument to Wells's vision.

Another major fundraising drive, the Campaign for Indiana, came to its successful conclusion in 1989, and Wells and his cochairman, Danny Danielson, each received the university's highest honor, the University Medal, in a surprise ceremony. Other honors, from national, state, and fraternal bodies, continued to rain upon the genial chancellor, who noted, "Each and every one of these I appreciate and treasure for the regard of fellow laborers in the vineyard."[46] Harvest time, indeed.

As his eighties wore on, however, Wells started having difficulty with his hearing and mobility. It was a frustrating decline. He obtained hearing aids, which helped some, but his trips to the theater became increasing rare. His arthritis made him stiff and creaky, and no longer able to readily withstand the rigors of flight. After a full lifetime of free movement around the state, the nation, and the globe, he discovered limits to easy mobility, and found his orbit increasingly circumscribed.

Father Time is not always a hard parent, and, though he tarries for none of his children, often lays his hand lightly upon those who have used him well; making them old men and women inexorably enough, but leaving their hearts and spirits young and in full vigour. With such people the grey head is but the impression of the old fellow's hand in giving them his blessing, and every wrinkle but a notch in the quiet calendar of a well-spent life.

Charles Dickens, 1841

NINETEEN

An Icon Aging in Place

WELLS STAYED REMARKABLY ACTIVE DURING HIS EIGHTH DECADE. With a lifetime of achievement behind him, he was still looking for new challenges and for opportunities to help care for his vast network of friends and his beloved Indiana University. His good health continued, although there were some medical issues. Ever the optimist, Wells had an indoor swimming pool installed at his house on Tenth Street in 1983 so he could enjoy his favorite recreation at home. The following year marked the twentieth anniversary of his residence across from the Main Library, and he continued to host intimate dinner gatherings regularly and large cocktail parties on occasion. Still in possession of the "stomach of a goat," he relished good food wherever he was – at his home, in Bloomington restaurants, or on the road.

Wells did not flag in his attendance at administrative meetings, although he occasionally had his eyes shut, leading other committee members to the assumption that he was asleep. But if the conversation hit a rough patch, Wells would rouse and summarize the discussion, often contributing a unique insight that would move the dialogue further or suggest a solution to the problem on the table.[1] Likewise, he was a constant at social events – receptions, operas, ballets, plays, and athletic events. He made sure never to miss commencement or Founders Day.

This demonstration of a lifetime of allegiance to the mission of IU and its people and the radiance he exhibited in putting his educational ideals in practice while he aged in place was a source of inspiration and comfort to many members of the academic community. Not only were people used to his constant presence, he added a certain magic to the proceedings. As one longtime faculty member said, "If he was there, a sense of rightness and completeness possessed the crowd."[2]

Fundraising continued to occupy a large part of Wells's time and energy during this period. He cultivated relationships with donors, worked with IU Foundation officers on complex financial transactions involving trusts and estates, and strategized with presidents John W. Ryan (1971–87) and Tom Ehrlich (1987–94).

When Kenneth R. R. Gros Louis became the chancellor of the Bloomington campus in 1980, Wells was pleased at the selection of a robust believer in faculty governance. Gros Louis, a literary scholar, joined the English department in 1964 and rose to become chair of that distinguished department and then dean of the College of Arts and Sciences. Gros Louis had been an admirer of Wells ever since they meet in 1956 at a national conference of Sigma Nu. At that time, President Wells was serving as national chairman of the fraternity and Gros Louis was an undergraduate delegate from Columbia University.

One of the first things that Gros Louis did as the new Bloomington chancellor was to institute an open telephone line to his office one day each week; he fielded calls from students, faculty, or citizens about university concerns and issues. Forty years before, Wells, as president, instituted public office hours for the same purpose. Both men realized that keeping a pulse on the university played a vital role in ensuring that communication channels remained open and accessible.

In 1982, the old Tenth Street stadium – unused except for the yearly running of the Little 500 – was torn down, opening up several acres of prime space for redevelopment on Tenth Street. President Ryan faced strong pressure from members of the board of trustees and some faculty to pave it over to serve the growing parking needs of this burgeoning sector of campus, or to reserve it for future buildings. The night before the June commencement, Ryan consulted with Gros Louis about how best to deal with competing demands for use of the space. The two administrators agreed that the best long-term use would be to relandscape the site as a greenspace, which would provide several benefits to this vital campus area: visual relief from the streetscape, a striking backdrop to the massive bulk of the Main Library, and a pleasant place to walk or wander. The idea was to symbolically "give" the embryonic arboretum as a gift from the president to the graduating class, thus short-circuiting lobbying efforts from interested parties. Gros Louis, a fine wordsmith, hit upon an apt phrase, "a stadium of green." The two men rewrote Ryan's commencement speech, weaving descriptions of the trees, flowers, colors, and scents that would grace the emerging "stadium of green." The address took nearly everyone by surprise, and Wells was delighted by this ingenious compromise to tastefully extend the woodland character of the campus.[3]

FOUNDATION REALIGNMENT

With the success of the 150th Birthday Campaign behind it, the IU Foundation continued to grow and diversify its operations throughout the 1970s. President Bill Armstrong had added two able vice presidents, James Elliott and Jerry Tardy, to his staff. Elliott, who had legal and accounting experience, proved to be Wells's right-hand man in counseling major donors. A new building, christened Showalter House, was constructed in 1974, and brought together staff members – previously scattered through eight locations in Bloomington – under one roof. By 1975 annual gifts exceeded $10 million.

Armstrong, under occasional fire for his free-spending ways, retired in March 1983 and was succeeded by W. George Pinnell, IU's executive vice president since 1974 and former dean of the School of Business. Pinnell, who had obtained his doctoral degree in 1954 from IU, and Wells had been colleagues for decades. Pinnell had a sterling record of fiduciary management, and it was thought that he would be able to put an end to any sloppy bookkeeping or financial irregularities.

Pinnell re-emphasized fundraising for academic programming, and reorganized the IU Foundation staff. Instead of a handful of officers directing the fundraising efforts of all the campuses and schools from a central location, now there were forty or more development specialists, working out of their respective academic units, throughout the IU system. Those staff had ready access to "the resources of the Foundation's research, legal, corporate relations, data processing, and other departments" in Bloomington. New management systems were established, and business operations were overhauled, including a central registry of all donations, administered jointly by the university and the IU Foundation. Among the new initiatives were telemarketing (soon to be known as the IU Telefund) to alumni and parents of current students and the planning for a major capital campaign.[4]

In June 1985, Wells wrote of the upcoming Campaign for Indiana, a five-year fundraising plan to enlarge endowment income. Looking ahead to the next century, he provided a rationale:

> As I see the American scene at the moment, of the thousands of post-baccalaureate institutions, only about 100 are true universities. Out of that group, after all of the reshapings of the next century, a couple of dozen will remain truly distinguished in the world sense. Indiana University has been one of that group, and I know that you wish to keep it in those ranks.[5]

Wells, now serving as vice chairman of the foundation board, had been selected to chair the new campaign. Fundraising practice had changed significantly since the time of the 150th Birthday Fund and the campaign had a "silent" launch prior to the public unveiling in mid-October. That allowed IU Foundation staff time to contact major donors and to conduct a campus campaign for faculty and staff.

The Campaign for Indiana goal was $203 million, divided into the major categories of endowments ($80 million), programs and equipment ($20 million), facilities ($53 million), and annual support ($50 million). The public launch was elaborate. On Homecoming Eve, October 18, 1985, five hundred guests observed a two-hour program in Assembly Hall. Over television, cable, and satellite networks, many more alumni and friends of the university across the country saw the kickoff festivities. The scripted program, "Distinction in the Heartland," was designed to showcase "the solid traditions, the academic strengths, the wealth of basic intellectual capital, and the necessary people-oriented philosophies" that characterized the University. Notable alumni and friends, including Richard Lugar, Chris Schenkel, Josef Gingold, Harvey Feigenbaum, Desmond Wong, Harold A. Poling, Jane Pauley, Dick Enberg, and, of course, Herman Wells, appeared, as well as a host of students, faculty, and staff. President Ryan announced that the silent phase of the campaign had raised $102 million, a little over half of the goal.[6] The following year was a banner year for the foundation, with over $50 million in gift contributions in 1986, raising the total for the Campaign for Indiana to $178 million.

In 1987, Thomas Ehrlich succeeded John Ryan as IU president, and automatically became chairman of the board of the foundation. Wells continued his service as vice chairman. In summer 1988, Pinnell retired and Curtis R. Simic was hired as president of the IU Foundation. Simic, who had graduated from IU in 1962, held a variety of fundraising posts in other universities, mostly recently the University of California at Berkeley, before coming back to Bloomington. As an undergraduate, he was active in the student foundation, and he was a rider in a Little 500 cycling team. A gifted communicator and administrator, he was faced with a public relations disaster soon after he arrived when former foundation president Bill Armstrong, Vice President of Finance James Elliott, and Director of Real Estate Richard Beard were indicted for felony conversion by a federal grand jury in late September. Aware of his very public fiduciary responsibility, Simic had to maneuver delicately, keeping lines of communication open with stakeholders, including alumni and donors, foundation staff members, and University faculty and administrators. As the legal challenge came down, Simic emphasized the bottom line. "The Foundation is not a party in any of it," he said. "There's no money missing from the Foundation."[7] After protracted legal wrangling, all of the charges against foundation executives were dismissed by June 1989, but the affair left a cloud that lingered.[8]

WELLS SCHOLARS PROGRAM

In the mid-1980s, Gros Louis floated another idea past the administration. A new scholarship program designed to attract the best high school students in Indiana would help staunch the college "brain drain" to other states. Scholarship funding, whether need-based or merit-based, for public universities was always lagging behind student requirements. The program, Gros Louis reasoned, would not directly address this problem, but it might have a leavening effect on the intellectual quality of the student body. In the historic polarity between access and excellence, this represented a move toward the latter.

There was no question that the new scholarship program would have to be funded through private sources, which the IU Foundation was quite willing to take on. A suitable name was sought, and Gros Louis hit on a splendid idea. It should be named after Wells, since he did so much to nurture the environment for student learning and empowerment. But Gros Louis knew of Wells's modesty and his dislike of special attention, and carefully prepared the case surrounding the new program and the added interest it would generate if Wells consented to have his name associated with it. At first, Wells demurred, but as he gradually became convinced of the soundness of the naming proposal, he gave his consent.[9]

Cast as a living memorial to the chancellor, then in his mid-eighties, the program would be known officially as the Herman B Wells Scholars Program. In 1986, fundraising officially began at a dinner of potential donors and notable friends of the university, including Governor Otis Bowen and Father Theodore Hesburgh. A souvenir publication was prepared for the event. Consisting of material that had been cut from Wells's autobiography, some recollections, and a speech or two, it was fashioned as a *Being Lucky Postscript*.[10] Not only did Wells provide the text for the publication, he also spoke at the project inauguration. He first made a deprecating joke about his "legend," and, turning more serious, said how pleased he was that his name would be associated with such a distinguished program that would bring, year after year, the best students in the state to Indiana University.[11] In 1990, the first class of Wells Scholars was welcomed to campus. Numbering 20, the successful students had been picked from 379 nominations from Indiana high schools on the basis of their academic performance and promise. Their reward was four years of full support (tuition, fees, living expenses), special seminars, and an optional year of overseas study. When he met this first class, the shining eyes of the program's eighty-eight-year-old namesake told the depths of his joy.

During his ninetieth birthday festivities, Wells was formally presented with the program named after him, although it had begun a couple of years before. Funded by a host of friends and admirers, it was a tribute to his unparalleled contribution to the university. Answering the question, "Why does only this Program carry Chancellor Wells' name?" an IU Foundation brochure stated, "The creation of an entire academic scholarship program in the name of a living member of the University Community is unique. But, then, we believe the contribution Chancellor Wells has made to Indiana University is likewise unique."[12]

To finance the Wells Scholars Program, the IU Foundation announced a $16 million endowment goal, to fully fund one hundred stu-
dents (up to twenty-five students per class), and another $6 million goal
to endow the Wells Enrichment Fund (to support colloquia, lectures,
seminars, retreats, and extracurricular activities), the Study Abroad Stipend Fund (to make possible an optional year abroad for all Scholars),
and the Wells Program professorships (to provide opportunities for University faculty to create special learning experiences for the Scholars).
The funding of the Wells Scholars Program offered some options for
donors. They might choose to support the program's general fund or
designate funds for a named scholarship. For a contribution of $100,000,
donors were entitled to name an individual scholarship.

By the end of 1990, $10 million had been raised. As the Foundation
cast its net widely for potential donors, someone suggested contacting
the former houseboys of Wells. The unflagging Dottie Collins, still working in the chancellor's office in her late seventies, was a key organizer who
had a wealth of personal knowledge of workers for Wells household for
the past twenty years and access to Owen Hall records. The IU Foundation chose Marita Sherer, a talented development director based in the
Indianapolis office, as a member of the organizing group. By January 1991
Ray Maesaka, a professor at the IU School of Dentistry and an avid IU
supporter, had been recruited by the foundation to provide leadership to
the group. The energetic Maesaka was a personable Hawai'ian who, as a
beginning dental student, served as Wells's houseboy in 1956–57. He had
finished his D.D.S. degree at the IU Dental School in Indianapolis, won a
position on faculty there after graduation, and later served as Chancellor
Wells's personal dentist.[13]

Maesaka sent a letter to more than thirty of the housemen whose
addresses could be located, inviting them to a "houseboy reunion" in
June to coincide with Wells's eighty-ninth birthday. The letter contained
information about the Wells Scholars Program and its fundraising campaign.[14] Many of the former houseboys responded enthusiastically that
they would attend, even though in some cases that meant traveling great
distances. As plans evolved, the date was set on Alumni Weekend, June
15–16, for a reception at the Chancellor's Tenth Street residence before
a special dinner with Wells at the Showalter House on Saturday; and,

on Sunday, a brunch at the Woodburn House featuring some special Hawai'ian dishes. Reminiscences and anecdotes of working for Wells were solicited from the houseboys, and I edited them.[15] After the reunion, the houseboys were urged to contribute towards a "Herman B Wells Houseboys Scholarship" and $75,000 (out of a goal of $100,000) was raised by spring 1992. New houseboy James Stevens received the first Houseboys Scholarship as an internal Wells Scholar in 1996, followed by another Wells houseboy, Adam Spaetti.

MEADOWOOD FORECLOSURE

Wells had a large moral stake in Meadowood, as well as a financial investment in his personal condominium. After the main building was completed in 1983, "[T]he next few years became very shaky ones for Meadowood and its owners," retired business professor and chair of the Annuitants' Association Harry Sauvain noted. "In addition to dealing with cost overruns, the corporation struggled with lawsuits and countersuits over construction quality, inclement weather which halted construction for extended periods of time, labor strikes, delays in occupancy, an as a result, lower-than-expected revenue."[16] The mortgage had briefly defaulted around 1985 and bond interest payments were often late, causing the Indiana Securities Commissioner to issue a "cease and desist" order to prevent Meadowood from selling more residency contracts.[17] A debt of unpaid interest to bondholders kept accruing, reaching $1.3 million in 1986, and in May, bond issuer American Fletcher National Bank filed a suit to force foreclosure.[18]

The problems came to a head in early 1989 when foreclosure proceedings were initiated, sending shock waves among the two hundred residents. On February 10, Wells attended the foreclosure hearing, conducted by a Boone County Superior Court judge. The judge ordered that Meadowood "be sold to the highest bidder at a sheriff's sale in Bloomington in March."[19]

As it happened, the sheriff's sale took place in April, with four bidders putting in offers. The highest bid, $13.4 million, was proffered by the OFC Corporation, a group of three individuals consisting of two bond traders from New Jersey, brothers Don and Bob Wheeler, and IU law alumnus Tom Mathers (son of former chemistry professor Frank Mathers). "The three had formed the corporation, OFC ("Our Favorite Community") specifically for the purpose of purchasing Meadowood."[20] Several conditions were attached to the sale, including maintaining the standards and philosophy of the community.

Despite some bumps and a substantial increase in rental rates, most residents were pleased with life under the new owners. As the management listened to the residents' concerns, longstanding problems were addressed systematically. The occupancy rate increased to 100 percent and a waiting list was begun. The old IU Retirement Community Board of Directors relinquished administrative and operational control to the new owners under the terms of the sale, and a new "Resident Council" was formed. This elected body served to communicate residents' concerns to management and to oversee programming.[21]

Wells was pleased with these changes, particularly the strengthening of the financial picture. When the Resident Council was contemplating how to honor Meadowood's greatest supporter, Wells's longtime associate Dottie Collins – a Meadowood stalwart – suggested that a gazebo be constructed on the grounds. She recalled Wells's admiration of a garden gazebo at the estate of J. K. Lilly.[22]

On October 1, 1995, an anniversary celebration was held, marking the fifteenth anniversary of Meadowood. The invitation quoted Wells: "Dreams Do Come True in Bloomington." The centerpiece of the event was the dedication of the "Herman B Wells Sanctuary," a gift from his fellow Meadowood residents. Wells graciously accepted the honor as a simple sign was unveiled on the path leading to a handsome new gazebo on the shore of the Meadowood pond.[23] A few days later, Wells sent Bob Wheeler, the president of OFC, warm thanks:

> I continue to marvel that you and your brother have carried on so admirably in the operation and development of this retirement center. We did the best we could during the years we had it and were happy to have you take it over. I've been especially pleased with the way in which you have added facilities. You're meeting all of our dreams for development.[24]

The future of Wells's "Camp David" seemed assured.

A GALA NINETIETH BIRTHDAY PARTY

As Wells approached his ninetieth birthday, various groups of friends and associates conspired to mark the occasion with a special tribute. IU Press director Gallman – along with Rosann Greene, former director of Faculty Records; Jim Weigand, dean of continuing studies and professor of education; and Doug Wilson, IU Vice President for University Relations and External Affairs – collected stories about Wells from IU administrators and staff, alumni, and friends of the beloved university chancellor. The group became aware of the Wells houseboys' similar effort the year before, and included some of those stories as well.[25] After judicious editing, they were arranged in a slim book, descriptively titled *Herman Wells Stories: As Told by His Friends on his 90th Birthday,* and published by IU Press in both hardcover and paperback.[26]

Most of the stories told of an event that revealed some aspect of Wells's character, especially his steadfast devotion to the university and his immense love for other people. But a few stories started to take the measure of the man beyond the local legend. For instance, Dottie Collins mentioned that former president of the University of California Clark Kerr, in his 1969 Patten Lecture, told of his search to understand IU's "rapid rise in academic respectability" that led him directly to Herman Wells, its "secret weapon."[27] Tom Ehrlich, then IU president, spoke about his recruitment to the position and how thrilled he was to meet Wells for the first time after decades of reading about "this great man of higher education, one of the two or three most important American educators in our century." Ehrlich revealed later that he considered Wells to be in "that magic troika" with James Conant of Harvard and Clark Kerr of Berkeley.[28]

The book was released during an all-university party in the IU Auditorium on June 7, 1992. The venue was packed with well-dressed men and women of all ages. When Wells entered, slumped in a wheelchair being pushed by houseboy Christopher Raver, the crowd erupted in cheers and clapping as people got to their feet. Wells raised his head as far as his neck would allow and beamed at the gathering, extending one of his arms in collective greeting. The current was strong between the servant-leader and his admirers. With Wells there, the circle was complete.

Keith Michael, chair of the Department of Theatre and Drama, served as the emcee as successive acts of music and ballet were performed. Soprano Angela Brown, a music graduate who had recently debuted successfully at the Metropolitan Opera Company, sang "Were You There?" an African American spiritual, to great emotional effect. Janos Starker, the world-renowned cellist on music school faculty, performed his own arrangement of Franz Schubert's Sonatina in D Major, D. 384, one of the greats of the classical repertoire. *Herman Wells Stories* was presented to Wells, and Michael and a faculty colleague – Marion Michael, his wife – read aloud from the book. A giant birthday cake, ablaze with ninety candles, was ceremoniously wheeled on stage, and three thousand voices were lifted in a hearty rendition of "Happy Birthday" to the chancellor, providing a fitting climax to the party.

Afterwards, as people spilled out into the warm air, they were greeted with red and white balloons, festive lights, and the sound of splashing water flowing from the Showalter Fountain. Wells held court at the top of the auditorium steps. Dozens upon dozens greeted the aging icon and verbalized their personal good wishes. For his part, Wells flashed his radiant smile, and, even if he could not catch every word, he reciprocated fully as each individual shared good wishes on this spirited occasion. Wells's heart was full. Forgetting about his physical infirmities, he could reflect with great pride, almost parental, about how hard work – his and others – and a sure touch had transformed his alma mater. The seeds he had planted had yielded a bountiful harvest, to be sure, and would keep on producing.

DOCUMENTING A LIFE

The hoopla surrounding the celebration of Wells's ninetieth birthday had barely died down when Gros Louis and other senior administrators came to grips with the aging chancellor's mortality: What would the university do if Wells died on their watch? Of course, it was not a question of "if" but "when." His immense contributions to the university needed to be documented and included in any obituary, although everybody involved was reluctant to call it an obit piece. The chancellor was generally in good health, but he *was* ninety, after all. The news media would be clamoring for video and audio, trying to describe the impact of his giant influence on education.

One of Gros Louis's aides, Perry Metz, took the lead in devising a solution to this quandary. He talked with Don Agostino, the head of IU's Radio and Television Services, about the possibilities. Soon it was decided that a video documentary of Wells's career, suitable for broadcast on WTIU and other Public Broadcasting Service stations, would be produced, and a veteran director, Eugene "Gino" Brancolini, was assigned to the project.

Although Brancolini was aware of Wells's stature on campus, he was not conversant with the scope and scale of the IU leader's accomplishments. He read *Being Lucky* and other materials relating to Wells, and talked with Metz, who had been employed in IU administration since his graduation from Indiana a decade before. Brancolini spent a lot of time in the IU Archives poring over its collection of photos, documents, and film, and persistently searched for other moving images in every corner of the university. He started to identify persons who knew Wells best and to notice themes in his career. The veteran director was pleasantly amazed by the way doors were opened upon hearing that he was working on a documentary on Wells. The typical response was this: "Is there any way I can help you?"[29]

For example, Wells's conviction "that Indiana University needed to be a center of beauty and culture for the entire state, and that students performed best when were in beautiful surrounding and had access to wonderful examples of culture" was one of several leitmotifs.[30] Topics such as educational access, academic freedom, racial integration, and internationalism were identified and became the basis for building sequences. After considering the pros and cons of reinterviewing Wells for the documentary, Brancolini decided against it, owing to the existence of earlier interviews. The director quipped, "Anything that he was going to say now, he had said better in one of those previous interviews."[31] Several individuals were interviewed for the project, and answered carefully worded questions posed by Brancolini.

After the content areas were framed, the real creative work began. Using a combination of taped interviews (both new and archived), still pictures, and audio and film clips, Brancolini started building sequences.

He likened it to assembling a jigsaw puzzle, but without an existing picture to guide him. In addition to the "talking heads" of newly interviewed
persons, Wells appeared repeatedly through various sequences. Father
Theodore Hesburgh, interviewed at Notre Dame University, called his
good friend Wells "the very model of the good university president."
Faculty stalwarts, such as Henry Remak, emeritus professor of Germanic
studies, recalled the skepticism that greeted Wells as he was pulled from
the ranks of the business school into the presidency, which quickly disappeared once his views on the centrality of academic excellence were
known. The section on racial integration of the campus was particularly compelling, relying on the powerful, eyewitness testimony of two
alumni, LaVerta Terry and George Taliaferro.

In fall 1993, Brancolini had a rough cut of the documentary, appropriately entitled *The Vision of Herman B Wells*.[32] Wells was offered the
courtesy of a preview, but he declined, placing his faith in the professionalism of the people involved. Before its broadcast on WTIU, the
campus affiliate of PBS, it was shown for the first time in Whittenberger
Auditorium on December 1, fifty-five years to the day after Wells's presidential inauguration. The audience, including Wells and a number of
his longtime associates, filled about half of the seats in the small lecture
theater. When the hour-long program ended, the audience clapped and
clapped. All eyes were on Wells, who acknowledged the crowd with a
slight nod. Later, Wells revealed that he enjoyed the documentary, and
wrote a thank-you note to director Brancolini.

Reaching a modest public audience through PBS, *The Vision of Herman B Wells* was considered an artistic success in the realm of documentary film. The erstwhile "obit piece" turned into an absorbing historical
drama in Brancolini's hands, as he showed how Wells's vision became
reality.

ÉMINENCE ÉNORME

Aging gracefully into his nineties, Wells became an iconic figure on
campus and well beyond. He came to personify the Hoosier university
because of his great accomplishments on its behalf. A frequent attendee
at concerts, receptions, and basketball games, he was a comforting, lu-

minous presence. He stoically weathered the bodily storms of old age as his legs, his hearing, and his eyesight faded. Afflicted by macular degeneration, his once-excellent eyes became useless for reading, much to his consternation, and his household staff added reading aloud to him to their duties.

Wells still had the energy to lend his support to various initiatives during this period. One was WFHB, the community radio station in Bloomington – a long-held dream of a band of enthusiasts. Brian Kearney, one of the chancellor's aides, emerged as a leader of this group. When Wells first heard of the concept, he was reluctant to give his support, given his understandable loyalty to WFIU, the university station. Kearney was persistent and persuasive as he made his case for the noncommercial enterprise, pointing out the benefits to town and gown relations, and in 1987 Wells wrote a letter of support. He also allowed his name to be used when the radio project approached Cecil Waldron for financial support. That personal connection led to a gift of $225,000, which allowed the nascent station to be located in the old Bloomington firehouse and the necessary permits obtained. The station, first of its kind in the state, was named WFHB (for Fire House Broadcasting) and went on air January 4, 1993 (broadcasting from a temporary location for about a year until the firehouse was renovated). In February 1994, Wells gave the keynote address at the "Firehouse Warming" to celebrate the completion of the studio renovation, and said, "the goal of establishing a radio station that will entertain us and inform us by giving the community an opportunity to be an integral part of the day-to-day operations of the station demonstrates a belief in grass-roots education." Kearney had found the station's "single greatest ally," who also became a generous financial backer.[33]

After a lifetime putting all of his being into advancing the university, Wells's investments had generated enormous returns. Like King Midas, his golden touch had marked nearly every part of the institution. The university community cherished this *éminence énorme* that had unselfishly poured his soul into the education of others. Harvest time was sweet for Wells. His actions had done so much for the university, so long and so well; now he could simply be a part of the beloved community and humbly enjoy his exalted status.

When he celebrated his ninety-fifth birthday in June 1997, Governor Frank O'Bannon honored him with an Indiana Statehouse reception where he received a Sagamore of the Wabash award. The governor's award, created during the administration of Ralph F. Gates (1945–49), referred to the American Indian term for "tribal chief," and was given for extraordinary service to the state. Wells had received it five or six times previously. O'Bannon explained, "When you think of the person who has had the biggest influence on the state – there is no question in my mind the person you would call Mr. Indiana is Herman B Wells."[34]

Wells's public appearances were marked by spontaneous outpourings of affection. When in 1996 the Dalai Lama came to speak in the biggest indoor venue in Bloomington, IU's Assembly Hall, the all-ages crowd broke into voluntary applause when Wells was wheeled on the stage. As the Dalai Lama appeared shortly after, the crowd broke into another wave of applause. The two men beamed at each other on the stage, and the emotional contagion spread throughout the hall. This event, like so many others at Indiana University, was the fruit of Wells's patient cultivation of the community of learning on the Hoosier campus and of the intentional reach well beyond it.

Do not seek death. Death will find you. But seek
the road which makes death a fulfillment.

Dag Hammarskjöld, 1976

To have a sense of place is to sense limits, to sense our own
deaths. . . . By accepting limits a place imposes, we gain the ability
to leave a mark. By being a part of a place, we become it.

Michael Martone, 2006

TWENTY

A Peaceful Passing

IN 2000, INDIANA UNIVERSITY STUDENTS – at least those who attended class – began their spring break peregrinations at the close of classes on Friday, March 10. Soon the campus would be empty. Few cars would disturb the peace on East Tenth Street, where the University Chancellor was housebound. Herman Wells, three months shy of his ninety-eighth birthday, had been struggling to maintain some semblance of normal activity.

Confined to a wheelchair for the better part of a decade, he had relied on houseboys to move him around. One of his favorite assistants, Randy Norris, who was thin as a rail, had perfected the art of transferring the chancellor's odd bulk back and forth to the wheelchair. Norris's touch was sure and steady, and Wells enjoyed his assistant's outsize sense of humor.

The power of Wells's eyes and ears had gradually left him, forcing him to adjust to the growing dim silence. His office and house staff had to adjust, too, by reading the newspapers to him, encouraging him to wear his hearing aids, or by shouting to get through to him. Wells had not gone to his cherished office in Owen Hall since before Christmas, so his secretary Linda Bucklin came to the Tenth Street house nearly every day. She and Wells went through correspondence, replied to invitations, and consulted about other university business as well as the management of his residence.

Two days before the start of spring break, the Indiana University–Bloomington website erroneously posted a tribute to Wells, referring to him in the past tense. That sent a shiver down the collective spine of the

IU community. Web managers quickly caught the mistake and removed the announcement. Trying to minimize the fallout, communications spokesman George Vlahakis said the offending message was an "upbeat" salute to Wells's many accomplishments, and Wells was "alive and well." Public affairs and government relations vice president Christopher Simpson said the incident was the result of "human error," and relayed a message from Wells's office that "the chancellor's health is fine."[1]

But people close to Wells knew otherwise. He was not acting like his normal self. The previous weekend he had missed Founders Day ceremonies. When friends noticed his absence on the podium, they were alarmed. His attendance at concerts and other public events declined. But Wells had gone through similar health crises before and had always pulled out of them.

President Myles Brand paid him a visit a few days after Founders Day and noticed the chancellor was unusually agitated. After some chitchat, Wells bluntly asked the president, "Is there anything else you want me to do?" Momentarily puzzled, Brand replied, "No, Chancellor, you've done enough." Wells persisted, "Are you sure?" Brand repeated his assurances. Wells relaxed and appeared relieved. After a slight pause, he said, "Then I want to say goodbye." The conversation ended shortly thereafter, and Brand walked away from the house on Tenth Street feeling sure that Wells knew his time was coming.[2]

When Wells showed no sign of emerging from this depressed state, the house staff started bracing for the worst. Wells's prodigious appetites – whether for food, entertainment, conversation, or diversion – were waning. The most public of men was now withdrawing into himself. Spring break was particularly trying. Ominously, the houseboys could not cajole him into the van to drive around and visit new buildings on campus and look at construction sites. Previously, that had never failed to buoy his spirits.

THE LAST DAY

The chancellor's residence on East Tenth Street was a beehive of activity amidst the quiet of campus. Houseboys, nurses, cooks, housekeepers, and office staff visited regularly. Wells's physician, Jean Creek, was called to consult on more than one occasion. If the end was indeed coming, Wells's wishes were clear – no heroic medical interventions. "Do Not Resuscitate" orders were posted in his medical chart. He was determined to leave this world as he happened to come into it – in the home of his family.

Five days passed without any IU classes. Saturday came, March 18, and students still were scattered to the four winds. Fifty-two years ago on this day, a sorrowful Wells had witnessed his father Granville's funeral and burial in Jamestown. After dinner, Wells followed custom and went up to bed. The houseboys and the nurses – current members of his elective family – found themselves taking turns standing watch as he lay on his antique bed in his small bedroom. Occasionally Wells roused himself to consciousness, and took note of his surroundings and his human companions, murmuring a comment or request. His lucid periods grew more infrequent until he was simply sleeping comfortably.

A random trio from his staff was in the room when he finally stopped breathing at 8:45 in the evening. Liz Egan, a nursing assistant, Andy Halsey, a houseboy, and Susan El-Sayyad, a registered nurse, were with him as he "slipped into forever," in the words of houseboy Nathan Zapf.[3] Silently, each member of the group looked into the eyes of each of the others in the sacred stillness. After a few moments they calmly left the bedroom. Going downstairs, the trio shared the news with other individuals in the house. People spread out to the phones and started calling.

Soon Dr. Creek was notified, and a hearse was dispatched to carry the body to the Day Funeral Home. The media got word, and the TV stations carried the news on the late daily broadcast. Before long, members of his elective family began arriving at the house for an impromptu wake to heal the rupture of their collective reality. Although his body had been taken away, Wells's presence was everywhere in the house. Munching on chocolate ("soul food," according to office manager Terri Crouch), they exchanged stories about their beloved boss and university icon.[4] The tone was lighthearted and respectful, touched with equal measures of relief and disbelief.

There were some teary moments as people struggled to grasp the finality, but the overall mood was one of tranquil acceptance after the initial shock wore off. The staff knew that Wells had given his all, up to very end, until his corporal frame had reached its limit. Now their responsibility for the care and feeding of the great man had ceased and other persons would join in the work of grieving. They recognized that the entire university family had entered a liminal state with the passing of its great leader and paterfamilias.

Word spread quickly, and the machinery of public communication was activated as IU officials were notified. It was the end of spring break, and not everyone was back on campus. Not surprisingly, the IU Office of Communications and Marketing was poised to respond quickly with a news release reporting Wells's death early on Sunday, March 19. The lead paragraph noted that Wells was the only person to lead IU three times during its 179-year history. This obituary was cobbled together from various sources – and quoted several IU leaders. President Brand called him "quite simply, a great man," adding that without his leadership "IU would not be the university that it is today." Board of trustees president John D. Walda quoted "John F. Kennedy who said: 'Things do not happen; things are made to happen.' Chancellor Wells made wonderful things happen not only at Indiana University, but in the lives of everyone with whom he came in contact." Walda was grateful to be included in that company. Wells's lifetime achievement awards – "Man of the Century," "Hoosier Living Legend," "Hoosier Millennium Treasure," and "B'nai B'rith Great American Traditions Award" – were interwoven with some of his well-worn yarns from *Being Lucky*. Perhaps the most thoughtful comment was made by Bloomington Chancellor Gros Louis: "He always said that the spirit of a place was its most important attribute, and he always worked tirelessly to enhance it at Indiana University. For me, the warmth of his being is his greatest legacy." A two-page chronology of his life followed, as well as an editor's note announcing that photographs and digital images of Wells were available.[5]

MEDIA NOTICES

The office of the *Indiana Daily Student* was closed during spring break. As the reporters started drifting back on Sunday, editor-in-chief Olivia Clarke was anticipating a "tanned, relaxed and eager staff" as the newspaper prepared for Monday's resumption of publication. Instead the newsroom was hit by the largest campus story in decades. Slated to graduate in May, Clarke had worked at the IDS for four years, and knew many editors "who lived in fear of the day Wells would die," wondering whether the paper could rise to the challenge.[6]

Luckily – and inadvertently – Clarke had done her homework before the break. She had commissioned several administrators and faculty members to write about Wells in preparation for a special tribute, to be published at the end of the semester, about a month before his ninety-eighth birthday. Final versions of those stories were already in hand. IDS reporters and designers worked through the night to produce a comprehensive look at Wells's character and career. Monday morning's headline blared, "Losing a Legend: Herman B Wells, 97, Dies at Home Saturday." The entire front page, with a huge photograph of a smiling Wells, was devoted to the story.

The lead story, by veteran reporter Joseph Pete, said that the cause of death was pneumonia and heart failure. Liz Egan, one of the three people that were with Wells as he died, told the reporter about his last moments. "He was aware at the time," she said. "And he slipped away quietly and comfortably." The story included details of visitation at Day Mortuary the next evening, the funeral service scheduled for Wednesday, and family wishes that donations be made to the IU Library in lieu of flowers.[7]

An extra eight-page section – "A Tribute Issue" – was folded into Monday's newspaper, announced by a graphic that included his name, birth and death dates, and a cameo photo of Wells with two fingers touching his temple. The special section contained in-depth analysis of the influence of Wells on nearly every facet of Indiana University, enlivened with interviews from university notables. A double-page spread presented a chronology of his long career. Sidebars included quotations culled from Being Lucky, Herman Wells Stories, and personal interviews.[8]

On Tuesday, the New York Times published an obituary, illustrating it with a 1996 photograph of a white-headed Wells with reading glasses. Noting that Wells "was quietly devoted to progressive causes," it cited his efforts to desegregate IU and his defense of Alfred Kinsey. The life sketch mentioned his determination "to make the university a cultural center for the Midwest," exemplified by the 1942 Metropolitan Opera Company performance of Aïda in the IU Auditorium, which marked the first visit by the Met to a college campus. Wells's service to the federal government and educational consulting were highlighted. The obituary concluded its impersonal, dispassionate sketch with one sentence on his private life: "Mr. Wells, who did not marry, left no immediate survivors."[9]

Many Indiana and regional papers took note of the death of one of the greatest Hoosier educators of all time. The *Louisville Courier-Journal* stated, "If one person can be said to have given Indiana what Kentucky never has had – a truly distinguished public university – it was Wells. No Hoosier did more for his state."[10] The *Indianapolis Star* reflected on his career: "Wells' simple, two-point creed – 'education for all' and 'all knowledge is useful' – was applied both to his university work and his service in 1957 as a delegate to the United Nations."[11] Providing a personal angle, nursing assistant Egan suggested, "He was the best grandfather anybody ever had. Everybody who ever worked for him, just loved him. Maybe that's why he lived so long. He just had so much love."[12]

Outside the Sigma Nu house on North Jordan Avenue stood a large limestone boulder painted white to symbolize consistency and strength. One of their brothers, full of years and honors, had died, and for the first time in the chapter's history, the rock was painted black. A black sash was hung diagonally over the fraternity sign. Inside the chapter house, a portrait of the departed brother, hanging in the foyer, was also draped in black. Two days after Wells's death, the brothers joined together in the evening "for a candlelight service to remember their most prestigious brother, the man they simply referred to as Herman B."

Wells had remained engaged with the chapter for nearly eighty years – ever since he pledged Sigma Nu as a sophomore in 1921. That fraternal relationship formed a foundation stone for his extraordinary life. Even during his declining years, Wells visited and dined at the chapter house a couple of times a semester. "Every time he was over here he was just glowing," said one current member. Although his deteriorating hearing made it increasingly difficult to interact with him, the Sigma Nus remembered, "just being around him was enough."

A hundred brothers – nearly the entire membership of the chapter – were there for the private service, dressed in coats and neckties. Lighting candles near the black rock, they started walking with solemn steps down Jordan Avenue, passing by the chancellor's residence and through the Arboretum to the Fine Arts Plaza and into the woods to end at Beck Chapel (Frank Beck was a founding member of the Sigma Nu chapter in 1892). Extinguishing their candles, the silent brothers entered the chapel and conducted a memorial ritual honoring their brother Wells.

A further sign of the depth of the Wells–Sigma Nu connection was his request that chapter members supply the pallbearers for the funeral. Scheduled two days after the private Sigma Nu rite, the fraternity called upon six of its brothers to serve. One was Andy Choate, a sophomore, who was also serving as one of Wells's houseboys. With a double connection to the elective family surrounding Wells, Choate was impressed by Wells's authentic modesty. "A lot less important people try to act imposing," Choate said. "He was the most important man I ever met yet he was also the most humble."[13]

A SIMPLE, METHODIST FUNERAL

As he planned ahead for his demise, Wells insisted on a simple Methodist funeral. He left strict instructions with his office staff and church pastor that there would not be a eulogy or other special considerations. Everybody associated with planning the funeral strove to fulfill these final instructions, at least in spirit, because the event presented a formidable logistical challenge.

The venue was the easy part – the First United Methodist Church. Wells had first started coming to the church on the corner of Fourth and Washington Streets as an undergraduate in the early 1920s, and probably formalized his membership as a young professor.[14] A large, prosperous church, the facility was undergoing renovations in the spring, but luckily the sanctuary had just been reopened for public use. Deciding who was to preside was equally automatic – Wells had no particular individual in mind, but just specified the pastor on active duty to serve as the officiant. Knowing that Methodists practice local control over their churches, Wells was content to follow his congregation. As it happened, the current pastor was the Reverend Philip Amerson, a good friend and church colleague of Wells.

Amerson had been pastor at the First Methodist Church since 1992. He and Wells had worked together on the church's administrative council, known as the Pastor-Parish Committee, and Wells had chaired a major fundraising campaign in 1996–97, as he had done for a previous drive sixty years earlier, in 1936–37. Amerson remembered that when he first came to Bloomington, Wells had suggested cultivating church-university connections, and urged him to get to know IU administrators and faculty.[15]

As Amerson composed his funeral sermon, in the conventional form of "Words of Christian Hope," an elaborate ushering plan was made to accommodate the large crowd anticipated. The church sanctuary held about seven hundred people, with overflow directed toward the adjacent Great Hall, with a capacity of nearly five hundred. Television monitors were set up in the Great Hall so that attendees could view the proceedings. Reserved seating in front of the sanctuary was saved for family and personal staff of Wells and federal, state, local, and IU officials. Members of the press were assigned to the balcony; no cameras were allowed on the main floors. A total of seventeen ushers were required to seat the overflowing audience.[16]

On Wednesday morning, people started streaming into the church well before the 11:00 AM starting time. The casket bearing Wells's body, draped with the white IU flag and a white khata (a gift from the Dalai Lama), lay on a bier at the front of the church. As expected, several dignitaries, including Senator Richard Lugar, Father Theodore Hesburgh, and various state, local, and university officials, were there, as well as cousins Esther Heady and Helen Heady and a host of former staff and houseboys. The Sanctuary and the Great Hall were full. Church organist Charles Webb, former dean of the School of Music, played a somber prelude while people settled into their seats. Reverend Amerson opened the service with a cordial greeting. The hymn "For All the Saints," was sung, and Psalm 23 was intoned in unison. After a reading of Romans 8:35–39, the chancel choir resounded with a stirring interpretation of "How Lovely Are Thy Dwellings" from Brahms's *German Requiem*. John 14:1–7, 15–17, and 27 were read as the Gospel lesson, and Amerson offered his "Words of Christian Hope."[17]

"And so, we find ourselves on our own; suddenly left to our own devices," he began. "We did not think it possible but the standard bearer has left the scene. The constant, the template, the archetype, the exemplar, a measure and personification of our highest aspirations has finished his earthly life." Amerson noted the exquisite timing of Wells: the funeral took place sixty-two years to the day after he was selected as president, and the sanctuary was again open for use after a period of renovation. Wells's request for a simple, religious service, Amerson explained, was in keeping with his "humble yet proper" character: "It *is* his faith in something beyond himself and not his biography that marks his greatness. It *was* his faith and not his countless citations which caused his eyes to dance and his countenance to shine. It is faith in the good people of Indiana, faith in human intellect, but more, faith in his Creator."

Referring to Alexis de Tocqueville's observation about American civic virtue, Amerson argued, "Herman was great because he was good." He went on to suggest that this ethical virtue was rooted in a profound spirituality, a conviction that he was a beloved child of God. Wells learned of this "belovedness" from his parents, the concept was reinforced by Methodist Sunday school classes and other experiences, and he applied it to everyone else. Amerson enumerated some marks of Wells's greatness:

> his incessant curiosity, his genuine humility, his steadfast generosity, his practiced sense of humor and his sure hospitality. But more, here was a man who saw the world comprehensively, who entertained paradox naturally and who would never be too full of his own self-importance to recognize his family connection with every other human being. For Herman the secular never negated the spiritual. . . . [He] saw each one of us as a Child of God.

To illustrate Wells's comprehensive vision in action, Amerson pointed to the location of Beck Chapel near the center of campus. In a departure from the colonial colleges, which placed the house of worship at the focal point, Thomas Jefferson's plan for the University of Virginia placed the library at the center. In contrast, Wells's syncretic idea "allowed for the paradox that made room for intellect, imagination and spirit to each be honored as central to discovering the best of who we are. And so at the center of Indiana University there is a place for libraries and laboratories, the performing and visual arts and, yes, a chapel."

Amerson went on to mention briefly Wells's efforts to encourage freedom of inquiry, racial justice and civil rights, respect for nature, and international institutions for peace. He had a vision "of who we can be," the pastor continued. "His dreams were so large they shaped us and in turn shaped the culture around us. We all need somebody who believes in us – somebody who sees us as we are and also as we are yet to be. This was his genius."

Amerson told a story about attending a panel discussion where he encountered Wells. When he asked Wells if he was a participant, the elderly leader joked, "No, I'm just adding a little weight to the occasion." Later, Amerson reflected the weight did not mean gravitas or self-importance, but rather weight in the Biblical Hebrew sense of *kabod,* which he glossed as "the glory of God's presence.... the weightiness of being beloved." Returning to the theme that he started with, Amerson assured the audience that, even though the materiality of Wells is gone, we still have access to his glorious legacy through stories and shared experiences:

> Some people spend their years and leave behind memories – wonderful times with friends and families. Others are blessed enough to leave behind legacies – institutions or compositions or new systems of knowledge. But only a few of us come and walk this human path and leave behind a culture which has been reshaped by our presence. Only a few marvel in the glory of who they are and who we all can become. Only a few encourage us to become our best because they know we are all beloved.

Thus Amerson concluded his stirring "Words of Christian Hope" for the soul of Herman Wells.[18]

After receiving the pastor's oration, the assembly repeated the Lord's Prayer, speaking as one voice. Standing for the final hymn, "God of Grace and God of Glory," people sang. Amerson bestowed his final blessing and the choir responded while the Sigma Nu pallbearers shouldered the weight of the casket and slowly carried it out of the sanctuary to the hearse waiting curbside. Once the casket cleared the church door, the gathering reluctantly dispersed, never to be called together again. The soaring strains of the organ filled the sanctuary with a mournful requiem for Wells's last visit to his home church.[19]

A CELEBRATION OF LIFE

Within a few days of Wells's death plans were laid for a public memorial service. University Ceremonies, operating out of the board of trustees' office and closely aligned with the president's office, was the lead unit to coordinate the myriad of details. The IU Auditorium was picked as a suitable venue. The Auditorium was one of the most beautiful and functional performing spaces on campus, and, to the history minded, it also was an emblem of an early fruit of the Wells vision. Care was taken to observe university customs and protocol. Remarks were made by representatives of the IU administration, faculty, and students, as well as by local community notables. Music was also an essential part.

A Celebration of a Life: Remembering Herman B Wells took place the evening of Wednesday, April 5, almost three weeks after the chancellor's demise. The program opened with a medley of Hoagy Carmichael songs performed by the Singing Hoosiers. President Brand welcomed the assembly and Reverend Amerson gave the invocation. A special video, *Herman Wells: The Man Who Was Indiana University,* was shown on the giant screen at the front of the auditorium. The film, produced quickly by cutting and pasting other images, many from the documentary *The Vision of Herman B Wells,* was narrated by James Mumford, director of the Afro-American Choral Ensemble; his resonant voice lent an air of majesty to the production.

Not surprisingly, administrators were the first to speak of their memories of Wells. Brand took the lead, followed by presidents emeriti John Ryan and Thomas Ehrlich and trustees president John Walda. A stirring rendition of "Climb Ev'ry Mountain" was performed by soprano Angela Brown, a notable new talent with the Metropolitan Opera Company and a graduate of the IU School of Music; former dean Charles Webb accompanied her on the piano. Current students Emily Chui, a Wells Scholar, and Michael Gosman, president of the Union Board, read from letters received from Wells's friends and admirers.

Next the audience heard from John Fernandez, mayor of Bloomington, and Viola Taliaferro, Monroe County judge. Janos Starker, distinguished IU cellist, performed his interpretation of Schubert's Sonatina in D Major. Longtime faculty member and good friend of Wells's, Henry Remak, spoke movingly about Wells's radiance, charm, and intellect. More letters were read by the students and some lighthearted moments – "Being Himself" – in Wells's life were recalled. Another faculty member, writer and director of the Wells Scholars Program, Scott Sanders, told of his remembrances, followed by longtime Bloomington Chancellor Gros Louis, who had a fund of insightful stories to tell.

Angela Brown closed out the program by singing "Were You There?" followed by everyone singing "Hail to Old I.U." A benediction was offered by Amerson. People clutched their handsome programs, which contained a selection of stories about Wells, as they left the Auditorium.[20]

Not only was Wells an IU alumnus, he started his career as a professional educator when he became a member of its faculty in 1930. Although he spent only five years in the teaching ranks (two of these on leave) before moving into administration, he cherished being a member of the professoriate, and, for the last twenty-eight years, professor emeritus. In keeping with custom, the Bloomington Faculty Council sought authors to write a fitting memorial resolution – in which the deceased faculty member's biography, concentrating on their contribution to IU, was sketched. I was selected for the task, and shared the draft with senior colleagues Don Gray and Henry Remak, who advised on stylistic matters and suggested some minor rewording.

On April 18, near the start of a regular Tuesday meeting of the council, I read the memorial resolution aloud. Because of Wells's long career as a university leader, the text was much longer than usual. The resolution noted various biographical milestones, from his experience as an IU undergraduate in the early 1920s to his dynamic presidency to his years as university chancellor, when he served as chief fundraiser and beloved icon.[21] Soon thereafter the academic year would be over, and the official *Indiana University Register* would omit Wells's name for the first time in seventy years.

"Hermie's Army," so named by Wells's secretary Bucklin, would have its regular meeting on June 7, but the birthday boy would not be in attendance. Around fifty people – office and house staff members and their families – met at Karst Farm Park for a cookout and potluck. The day was sunny and pleasant, and the usual banter and conversation was leavened with laughter and the occasional pathos. It was exactly like an extended family reunion after the death of its aged patriarch – healthy enough to go forward, with the human life force rebounding after a confrontation with death. In different ways, Wells had touched each one of Herman's Army and his spirit inhabited everyone.

Magazine coverage of the passing of Wells lost the advantage of immediacy but gained perspective. Judy Schroeder, the editor-in-chief of the *Indiana Alumni Magazine,* had an historian's appreciation of the facts coupled with devotion to her audience. Like many other campus stalwarts, she had occasionally received notes of appreciation and encouragement from Wells, the last one within six months of his death.

The May/June issue of the magazine featured a color photograph of Wells – wearing a black pinstriped suit with vest, smiling and placing his right hand on an antique globe symbolizing the global reach of the IU – in his Owen Hall office. Anne Kibbler, former managing editor, began her feature story with a dramatic scene, recounted by Wells in *Being Lucky,* about his selection as acting president in 1937, and then went on to describe some highlights of his life in lively prose punctuated by quotations. President Brand got the last word, about the plan to rename the library – "the heart and soul of the university" – for Wells, "a champion of knowledge and discovery."[22]

Wells died, as the saying goes, full of age and honor. Few educators of his generation had a higher reputation or greater distinction. Yet Wells possessed something even more rare: moral stature. Profound ethical insight allowed Wells to operate from his own moral center, unselfishly serving others as the highest good. He saw his vocation as enabling education and learning, and so releasing the human potential in each person. He was not above or outside this process, but always sought the heart of human relations, fully present to the other, and shared in the ongoing struggle to actualize individual potential and to contribute to the commonwealth of humanity.

Those who knew Wells grieved, of course, at his death. They lamented the end of chances to connect with this radiant human being, they were saddened by the finitude of human existence, and they cried about the loneliness of the human heart. Yet one might heed the wise words of Thornton Wilder:

> All that we can know about those we have loved and lost is they would like us to remember them with a more intensified realization of their reality. What is essential does not die but clarifies. The highest tribute to the dead is not grief but gratitude.[23]

Only connect! That was the whole of her sermon. Only connect the prose and the passion, and both will be exalted, and human love will be seen at its height. Live in fragments no longer. Only connect, and the beast and the monk, robbed of the isolation that is life to either, will die.

E. M. Forster, 1910

TWENTY-ONE

Keeping the Memory Green

THE PASSING OF WELLS BEGAN A NEW ERA at Indiana University. No longer would its popular former president and revered chancellor be seen walking around his beloved campus or driving to his haunts in Brown County. No longer would he be sitting in his Owen Hall office, ready to take a call from a donor, to cope with an administrative problem, or to simply meet with interested students. But his gift to the university continued. Everywhere one looked his presence was indelibly, lovingly imprinted on his alma mater. From its tended verdancy and beautiful buildings to superior programs ranging across the academic and professional spectrum to its global stature as a leader in international education, all were the shared products of Wells and his colleagues.

The Wells family circle was diminished by several deaths in the next year and a half. The death of cousin Esther Heady, aged ninety-three, followed Herman's. She had spent her career as a nurse in Jamestown. Single and living with her unmarried sister Helen, Esther was a fun-loving raconteur who relished visiting her cousin. Next to pass was Loretta Nixon, who had served as the housekeeper at the chancellor's residence for nearly two decades. Her children and grandchildren enjoyed visiting Wells at his house. Personal assistant Randy Norris died in January 2002. He had worked for the chancellor in a variety of capacities since the mid-1970s, most recently propelling Wells from his house on Tenth Street to the nearby arboretum for his morning constitutional.

WELLS PLAZA

The university lost little time in commemorating Wells. A bronze statue, underway at his death, was finished and installed in the Old Crescent in a ceremony in October. The artistic creation was the centerpiece of the Herman B Wells Plaza, located on a piece of ground midway between Owen Hall and the Rose Well House and consisting of three bronze park benches and a low, curving limestone wall surrounding a brick patio. Depending on the season, one might find pink rosebushes in bloom behind the wall, or petunias or mums in the front flowerbed.

The idea for a statue of Wells came to Bob LeBien, IU alumnus and friend of the IU Foundation, in the late 1990s. Soon it was the talk of foundation staff, and president Curt Simic easily persuaded donors to underwrite the cost. A talented sculptor was commissioned, Tuck Langland, professor of art at IU South Bend, and work began in summer 1999. The artist realized the special attributes of the commission: "He's a real part of Indiana University – he's kind of THE man," adding, "I feel extraordinarily honored to be working on this statue."[1]

Although Wells was apprised of the sculpture plans and met with Langland, he was too frail to sit for the artist for long periods. Instead, photographs were used to provide two-dimensional views of the subject. After considering various ages, Langland settled on depicting Wells at around seventy years of age. Wanting to convey his physical appearance but also his character and spirit, the artist had several conversations with Wells as the design was being refined.

Wells was not to be elevated on a pedestal, but sitting down on a bench extending his right arm, palm downward, in his distinctive greeting. He was dressed in a business suit, with necktie blowing in the wind, and a Homburg hat with the brim snapped down lay on the bench beside him. The sculpture slowly took shape over the winter as Langland and his student assistants worked in his South Bend studio. "As I worked, somebody began to appear in the studio and look back at me each day," the artist reported.[2] The clay form was nearly done when Wells passed away in March 2000. Langland was disappointed that Wells would not live to see the unveiling of the statue. "But it's a timely passing," the sculptor noted. "[H]e will be very fondly remembered."[3]

Within weeks the clay sculpture was cast in bronze at the Tallix Art Foundry in Beacon, New York. During the casting process, a curious thing happened. As the piece was nearing completion, foundry workers paused to look and smile at the unnamed figure. Langland asked the employees about their unusual reaction, and one explained: "He makes me feel happy."

The finished sculpture was transported to Bloomington and the plaza readied for its Homecoming Day dedication, on October 21, nearly seven months after Wells's death. The day was brilliantly clear, with a brisk snap in the air. The fall colors were at their peak. Several dozen people had gathered to witness the statue's unveiling. Langland and President Brand lifted the crimson velvet cover and the audience gave an appreciative gasp. The beaming sculptor recounted the story about the foundry workers and the appeal of the mystery figure, adding "that was also the secret of Herman Wells' success," making "the people around him feel good about themselves." Bloomington Chancellor Gros Louis spoke of Wells's self-deprecating modesty. "Despite our desires," Gros Louis said, "we knew we would not have Herman Wells with us much longer when this sculpture was commissioned. He would have been embarrassed at this ceremony. 'Too much tribute, over the top,' he would be muttering. But here in bronze we have him with us again – and forever – always approachable." To conclude the ceremony, Brand said simply, "Welcome home, Herman Wells."[4]

Always vigilant, the Wells statue is a welcoming sentinel to passersby at all hours. The bronze figure symbolizes the man who embodied Indiana University and made Bloomington an academic center known the world over. The Wells Plaza is within the hallowed Old Crescent where the campus took root in the 1880s. After forty years of slow expansion, the crescent of buildings surrounding the original plot of Dunn's Woods extended from the intersection of Indiana and Kirkwood Avenues on the west to the southern border of campus on Third Street. The view from the plaza is much the same as it was in the 1920s, when young Wells fell in love with the campus and the university as an undergraduate student.

THE WELLS ARCHIVE SYMPOSIUM

In September, a month before the dedication of the Wells statue, the IU Library sponsored an academic symposium in honor of Wells. Titled "The Wells Archive: Exploring the World of Higher Education," its purpose was to showcase the massive archival collection that Wells produced during his long association with IU and to reflect on his contributions to education at the state, national, and international levels. The symposium was originally scheduled for late March, with the expectation that Wells would be in attendance. The unavoidable postponement turned what was meant to be a happy celebration of a life in academe into a more somber commemoration.

Notwithstanding the focus on his person, perhaps Wells would have been pleased by the academic tone of the symposium. Dean of University Libraries Suzanne E. Thorin opened the session with remarks on the opening of Wells's papers and records to the public. Such noted historians of higher education as Roger Geiger, Hugh Hawkins, Helen Horowitz, and John Thelin addressed some of the events that shaped his career and put his efforts into context. Two distinguished administrators, Robert O'Neil and Kenneth Gros Louis, both of whom had worked with Wells, provided insights into his characteristic style and academic judgment.[5]

An illustrated booklet on the Wells Archive accompanied the symposium. Edited by Philip Bantin, director of the IU Archives, and myself, it contained a useful introduction to the life and career of Wells, a description of the archival collections, a chronology, and three tributes by friends and colleagues. The biographical sketch was brief, entitled "*Alma Pater:* Herman B Wells and the Rise of Indiana University" and outlined major facets of his career. Care was taken to include Wells's voice (in the form of quotations) whenever possible. Assistant archivist Thomas Malefatto co-authored the "Note on the Records and Papers of Herman B Wells," which described the major divisions of the 1,100 linear feet of material. The chronology detailed his extensive service to the university, to the state of Indiana, and to national and international affairs. Tributes were authored by Henry Remak, a longtime IU professor; Otis Bowen, former Governor of Indiana; and Theodore Hesburgh, former president of Notre Dame University.[6] The handsome front cover reproduced the striking portrait of Wells in his ninetieth year, painted by Allen M. Hirsch, and the back cover reproduced his characteristic signature.[7] The booklet was heavily illustrated with photographs, documents, and quotations from *Being Lucky* in its margins.[8]

MATTERS OF ESTATE

Wells's estate was valued at nearly $3 million. Years before, he left it all to Indiana University, save a trust fund to support his Jamestown cousins. After his death, his attorney, Tom McGlasson, saw that his will was probated. Wells's secretary Linda Bucklin took responsibility for the dispersal of his belongings from the Tenth Street house and his Meadowood condominium. Working for over a year, she laboriously inventoried his material possessions and tagged them for various organizations on campus, including the IU Art Museum, IU Foundation, Indiana Memorial Union, Bryan House, Wylie House, and Woodburn House. His last wishes allowed friends and associates to select souvenir items or mementos from his personal effects.[9]

After a lifetime of owning automobiles, Wells's last car was a purple 1999 Chrysler minivan, which was specially equipped to accommodate a wheelchair. In excellent repair, it was donated to the Bloomington Hospital Ambulance Service. Repainted in ambulance fleet colors of white, red, and yellow, it found use as a transport vehicle for non-emergency runs. On its back window, stenciled in white letters, was the phrase "In memory of Herman B Wells."

"LIVING WITH ART" EXHIBITION

After the estate was settled, the household furniture, furnishings, and artwork were dispersed. The site of one of his proudest accomplishments, the IU Art Museum, was favored in death as well as life, and received numerous bequests. Fine paintings, sculptures, and other decorative pieces from his eclectic personal collections made their way to the IU repository.

In fall 2001, the IU Art Museum mounted an exhibition, "Living With Art: The Legacy of Herman B Wells." Designed by Kathleen Foster, curator of twentieth century art, the show recreated the ambiance of his campus home, with its antique furniture and artwork. The intent was to honor the great patron of the arts at IU with a didactic flair: "Wells brought art into his own life and into the educational experience of the university."[10]

The opening reception, held on October 5 in the atrium lobby of the IU Art Museum, gathered together a cross-section of the community. Artists, donors, professors, students, and townspeople all were caught up in the excitement of seeing a glimpse of how Wells surrounded himself with fine objects, both at home and in the public space of the campus. The first section of the gallery served as a devotional space, with pictures of Wells on the walls and a video loop highlighting his biography. Then visitors flowed into a room containing the Empire sofa that stood in his living room, a portrait of his mother painted by noted Brown County artist Marie Goth, and other two- and three-dimensional objects. For viewers who had seen the inside of his house while he lived, seeing his possessions in the museum context was perhaps initially jarring, then energizing with its new juxtapositions, but ultimately soothing with its familiar objects and associations.

Wells collected fine objects for the better part of sixty years and displayed them in a series of homes – the Woodburn House, the President's (now Bryan) House, and 1321 East Tenth Street, his residence as university chancellor. His first finds were antiques, collected in Southern Indiana and Kentucky. As a young bachelor in his thirties, he favored the British clubroom style and bought nineteenth century English watercolor landscapes and hunting prints. As he got older, his aesthetic tastes expanded into a wide-ranging eclecticism: "He collected works by Brown County artists, by lesser-known Renaissance artists, and by Japanese, Chinese, and Turkish artists from various time periods."[11] A self-taught amateur, Wells's artistic discrimination was gradually refined through study and exposure to artwork, but he remained an open-minded collector. As Foster explained, "he bought things that appealed to him or that he thought the university would benefit from, not because they were done by famous artists."[12]

Included in the exhibit were sounding pieces. One was a large brass temple gong from eighteenth-century Japan that summoned guests to dinner. Another was a metal kinetic sculpture by Harry Bertoia that consisted of about two dozen small cylinders atop four-foot rods set into a sturdy base. When the rods were pushed, the cylinders struck together, producing a pleasantly loud, harmonious chime. In his Tenth Street home, Wells encouraged the houseboys, by word and by deed, to strike the sculpture whenever they passed it (When he used a cane, he would whack it with that).

Wells believed that fine things were to be enjoyed in daily life, not stashed away in vaults. He filled his houses with art and antiques, and "considered the Union Building an annex of his living room," Foster cracked. The overflow of his antique collecting passion accounts for the plethora of chests of drawers scattered around the building. As the Indiana Memorial Union evolved into a gathering place for the IU community, Wells lent his strong support to furnishing and decorating with fine objects to enhance the cultural environment.

Efforts by Wells to make the Bloomington campus a work of art by championing notable architecture, landscape design, and beautiful decoration were also represented. His first, and perhaps most remarkable, trophy was the acquisition of the Benton murals for the lobby of the IU Auditorium. The exhibit mounted a photograph of the murals as well as one of Benton's preliminary drawings. A small scale-model of Robert Laurent's sculpture the *Birth of Venus*, the centerpiece of the Showalter Fountain, reminded the viewer of his forty-year campaign for the Fine Arts Plaza and its constituent structures.[13] A sketch of the bold red stabile by Alexander Calder stood for the massive sculpture located on the front lawn of the Musical Arts Center, one of Wells's favorite edifices.

Studying his collecting patterns led Foster to observations on his character. "He treated people as though they, too, were works of art, to be treasured and treated with kindness, courtesy and respect," she noted. "He also lived with art; beautiful art because he loved it and it enriched his life on a daily basis, adding to the civility, grace and poetry of his life."[14]

THE WELLS CENTENNIAL

Several months before June 7, 2002, a small group of infantry of Hermie's Army started planning a gala celebration to mark Wells's hundredth birthday. With the knowledge that the university was not planning an official observance of the anniversary, a small committee of IU faculty and staff met regularly to organize what came to be called the Wells Centennial.[15]

Keeping in mind Wells's personal modesty on the one hand and his love of a good party on the other, the celebration sought to intermingle a simple and dignified academic ceremony with music and refreshments. Choosing a location was easy; the Wells Plaza was the obvious choice. (In case of inclement weather, the South Lounge of the Union was only a few yards away.) Care was taken to recruit a diverse set of speakers representing students, faculty, staff, and administrators – many with a personal connection to Wells. The potential problem of selecting the music, given Wells's eclectic tastes, had a brilliant solution: the jazz of friend and fellow alumnus Hoagy Carmichael. The Café Jazz Society – featuring Jack Ost (cornet), Michael Lucas (piano), Gary Potter (bass), and Karl Schuessler (clarinet) – was hired. Finally, publicity was arranged and orders were put in at the IMU for gallons of lemonade and several vanilla sheet cakes with bananas, Wells's favorite birthday cake. Along the way, the Wells Centennial celebration received official university endorsement.

Friday, June 7 dawned bright and sunny. The air was unusually clear and dry when people started gathering for the 2:00 PM ceremony. Perhaps 250 spectators, sitting on temporary chairs, were present when the jazz band played the dedicatory song, "Ole Buttermilk Sky," a favorite of Wells's. Brian Kearney, development director for the IU Art Museum, welcomed the crowd with remarks about the playful yet respectful intention behind the celebration. I followed with a brief reminiscence, quoting Wells on memory. President Brand spoke of Chancellor Wells's last days, when they met for the last time and Wells was wondering what more he could do for the university. Paul Musgrave, an undergraduate Wells Scholar, argued that Wells was highly ambitious, not for himself but for society, and we need to remember that forgotten virtue. Bloomington Chancellor Sharon Brehm, who had never met Wells, nevertheless saw many signs of him at the university.

Additional jazz numbers provided a welcome musical interlude. After the break, Arnell Hammond, a graduate student in education, told of

Wells's efforts to eliminate barriers to students of color. IU Foundation President Curt Simic gave colorful anecdotes about the amazing extent of Wells's human network and intergenerational friendships. The last speaker was Ken Beckley, president of the IU Alumni Association, who addressed the audience with uplifting stories about Wells, alumni, and the progress of the university. After making his remarks, Beckley led everyone in an enthusiastic rendition of "Happy Birthday," and the formal program was concluded.

DEDICATION OF THE WELLS LIBRARY

Shortly after the death of Wells in March 2000, Dean of University Libraries Suzanne Thorin floated the idea of naming the Main Library building in his honor. The IU Bloomington Library was in sore need of renovation and rehabilitation. A large fundraising campaign was in the works, and a strong association with the venerable leader would give it a welcome boost.

President Brand went along with the plan until the All University Committee on Names pointed out that to name it after Wells immediately would violate the custom of waiting at least five years until after the named person's death. There were all sorts of good reasons for the tradition of waiting, not the least of which was to avoid being swept away by current fashion. Ironically, Wells himself was the longtime chair of the naming committee.

But the plan was not scuttled, only postponed to a date five years down the road. During the ensuing years, the library's fundraising program toiled away, making incremental gains as it inched slowly upward on the university's priority list. As 2005 approached, plans solidified. June 17, 2005, was picked as the date of the dedication, speakers were recruited, and carving of inscriptions in the limestone over both entrances to the library lobby began. Stone carvers erected high scaffolding to gain access and draped it in opaque plastic to protect the workplace. It also obscured exactly what they were doing up there as people passed in and out of the library.

The ceremony took place in the afternoon, outside of the south entrance on the sward where the 1979 class tree was planted. Luckily, the weather was nearly perfect: low humidity, abundant sunshine, and clear blue skies. Thorin opened the event, welcoming the audience of nearly two hundred, who were sitting on folding chairs or standing on the grass. President Adam Herbert, appointed nearly two years before, gave an up-beat speech linking the current accomplishments of the university to the foundation laid by Wells. Referring to the 1970 dedication of the library, Gros Louis, senior interim chancellor, noted that Wells said, "the library is the most precious of jewels, not to be compared with other University possessions." Khalil AbuGharbieh, a senior business student and Wells Scholar, gave a student's-eye view of the event, lamenting that he was among the first of the Wells Scholars who had not gotten to meet Wells in person. IU Foundation President Simic gave an impressive recount-ing of the names of many donors and friends and the consequences of their gifts.

Steve Ferguson, president of the IU Board of Trustees, officially ac-cepted the renaming on behalf of the university. At that point, a white sheet covering up the inscription was raised and the audience could see the handsome carving that read simply Herman B Wells Library. It was a fitting monument, although some wondered whether the designation too tightly circumscribed his impact on the entire university. Now genera-tions of students will proceed to the library, walk under the inscription, and perhaps wonder who Herman B Wells was.[16]

Several months later, in fall 2005, as President Herbert faced criti-cism about his leadership, former Bloomington Faculty Council presi-dent Robert Eno suggested, "I think what's happening is Indiana is fac-ing a long-delayed and long-overdue realization that we can't remain the same university we were under (former President) Herman Wells forever."[17]

DEDICATION OF WELLS LIBRARY BUST

In the afternoon of October 19, 2007, the lobby of the Main Library was crowded with people waiting for the dedication of a bust of Herman Wells. The crowd stopped milling when newly installed President Mi-chael A. McRobbie swept inside the south doors with his retinue of as-sociates and staff members a few minutes late. The new president was the seventh since Wells stepped down forty-five years before. McRobbie welcomed the diverse group, ranging in age from retired faculty members who worked with Wells decades ago to curious freshman who wondered what all of the fuss was about.

Patricia Steele, acting dean of the libraries, spoke next. She reminisced about the beginning of her undergraduate days at Indiana in 1961. Her first assignment was to watch President Wells on TV speaking to the freshman class and to write a composition about it. What she had written had long been forgotten, but she vividly recalled "Wells' large spirit and the great affection the campus had for him." The dean continued,

> Everyone has a story, it seems. And that was his greatest legacy, perhaps – to build relationships through the generous force of his personality and to infuse this institution with a great spirit. He championed academic purpose and community. He encouraged discovery. He propelled us forward.[18]

Steele concluded her remarks with a verbal salute to the new president, prophesying that his administration would provide a marker for student life just as President Wells did during his day.

The climax of the dedication occurred when sculptor Marc Mellon, a nationally recognized artist, unveiled his bronze interpretation of Wells's head, more than twice life size. The artist captured Wells's smiling face, with its thick, unruly eyebrows and distinctive mustache. Oriented toward the south entrance, the bust was mounted on a handsome pedestal with an attractive wooden kiosk behind it. After the ceremony was over, people walked up to the bust like an old friend, and students posed next to Wells for pictures taken with their cell phones.

All rising to great place is by a winding stair.

Francis Bacon, 1625

No revolution changes the essentials so long as it only changes the institutions and ignores the men who live by them. If humanity is a function of institutions, so are institutions a function of humanity. For a transformation of the world to be radical it must grasp things by the root. The root is man. Education changes man. This is the path that is given to us.

Otto Fenichel, 1919

Reflections on a Hoosier Antæus

A MONTH AFTER WELLS'S DEATH IN 2000, I wrote a memorial resolution for the Bloomington Faculty Council. Trying to encompass his unsurpassed contributions, I declared, "Herman B Wells built an institution, and in the process, became one himself. Like a Hoosier Antaeus (the giant son of Gaia and Poseidon from Greek mythology), Wells drew his prodigious strength from his connection to the Indiana soil. He planted so many seeds of compassion and kindness and learning that his memory will be everlastingly green as long as there remains an Indiana University."[1]

The story of Antæus symbolizes the spiritual power that accrues when one rests one's faith on the immediate fact of things. Wells was grounded, geographically as well as psychically. This native Hoosier knew where he came from and was secure in his own self. Coming to college at Indiana fostered an epiphany of a lifetime. This realization did not announce itself all at once, but Indiana's genius loci worked its magic on this sensitive student. As a leader, Wells never stopped learning from Indiana University. He lived in intimate contact with the university, harmonized with its development, and cultivated the place and its people.

Like every human being, Wells was a creature of his cultural landscape. Like few, however, he was able to utilize his native endowments to learn to mold and shape one of its essential pillars – the institution of higher education. Indiana's genius loci became Wells's guiding star, associated with past experience as well as future promise. The campus was "expressively potent" and served "as a trigger to memory, imagination, and mythic presence."[2] And the campus drew him back, over and over again, throughout his life.

His contributions grew organically out of his life experiences and his gift for paying attention to the natural and social environments in which he was a participant. In college, he discovered a love for learning that went beyond the urge to excel and the usual avidity for good grades to please others. He caught a glimpse of the transformative power of education as a moral relationship between the individual and the community, a microcosm of culture in the making, and a way to invest in common wealth.

Making Bloomington his home for the last seventy years of his life, he poured his heart and soul into enhancing the university that was his nourishing mother. Never forgetting his own introduction to academic community in the 1920s and his conversion to its ideals, he sought to maintain Indiana's liberal spirit while improving nearly every aspect of its educational program and cultural milieu. Over the years, he infused his campus presence with a cosmopolitan prescience that enriched the culture of the local community and rippled out beyond it.

A MORAL EXEMPLAR

Wells experienced Indiana University – the physical campus and the human community, its material manifestations and its spiritual elements – as a theater of energies, both actual and potential. He was deeply fascinated and embarked on a lifetime affair of the heart. Wells idealized his beloved university, felt its animating energy, and was exquisitely attuned to its moral directives and ethos. But he also was aware of its lacks and imperfections. In fact, helping and healing those negative aspects never failed to inspire and invigorate him.

An aspiring servant-leader, he was able to exercise benevolent authority because of his complete identification with the interests of the institution. His relationship with the university could be characterized as an "I–Thou" exchange, as he related to its landscape and people as consecrated subjects, not as separated objects to be experienced or used.

With this empathic attitude, Wells had a simple modesty about his work. Although he took his leadership role quite seriously, his basic orientation was non-exploitive and humble. He belonged to the university, and not the other way around. A striking illustration of this occurred at a 1970 university dinner at which Wells's accomplishments were feted. As he accepted the accolades, he was overcome with emotion. "The university doesn't owe *me* any thanks, as much as I appreciate your," he paused and gulped a couple of times to maintain control before continuing in a clear voice, "your beautiful tribute. Quite the contrary. The obligation goes the other way, because it's given me a chance to have wonderful work with wonderful people for a whole lifetime."[3]

As Wells became ever more involved with the university, he came to embody its moral core and highest purposes. Selflessly engaged with his mission – to enhance the quality of Indiana University – he won the hearts and minds of nearly everyone he came into contact with, from students, faculty, and staff at IU to alumni, donors, Hoosier citizens and legislators, and others as he journeyed on behalf of the institution. He did this by being mindful of the multiplicity of the university and being present as he dealt with its embodiment in members of the academic community as he strove to serve the larger whole. Wells's personal charm and wholeheartedness about his mission was crucial in leading the university to expanding its academic territory and increasing its stature. Bridging the old establishment of the 1920s and 1930s with the new regime of the postwar period was a stunning accomplishment made all the more striking by Wells's ability to keep everybody moving forward under the banner of university improvement.

His brilliant leadership and charisma were widely noted. People of all statuses and stations in life felt comfortable in his presence. He was also a comforting presence when emotions were heightened. He could savor joy in the achievements of others and buoy people up when they felt discouraged by difficulties. Above all, he silently transmitted his belief in the inherent worth of each and every individual he came into contact with, and inspired many to achieve a fuller measure of their potential – a potential that they might have not been entirely aware of. Simply put, people felt affirmed in his company.

A PERSONAL ENVOY

This book is my attempt to convey my understanding of the life of Herman Wells and his relationship with Indiana University. Although I have relied on my professional skills as a trained historian, my perspective has been seasoned with three decades of reflection on Wells and his impact – on the university, on other people, and on me. As I pondered the roots of his eventful life, I kept returning to his deep connection to the Indiana landscape and Hoosier culture. Doubtless there are other worthwhile perspectives, and I hope that my work will stimulate the production of different ways to analyze Wells's life and career.

Someday, most likely before the end of the present century, a moment will come when Herman B Wells slips silently from living memory. But undoubtedly he will live on in books such as this and endless stories told about him, his home, and his time. His bronze presence will continue to grace the campus he steadfastly loved and courageously protected, and his ghost will inhabit those with empathetic discernment. And future historians will find new ways to compose songs of his life, in honor of the dead who are all among us and give us life.

MEMENTO MORI

The prospect of death
is reason enough
to embrace life.

Memorial Resolution

CHANCELLOR HERMAN B WELLS
(JUNE 7, 1902–MARCH 18, 2000)

Herman B Wells was born on June 7, 1902, in the village of Jamestown, Indiana. He was the only son of Joseph Granville and Anna Bernice (Harting) Wells. Growing up amidst the farms and small towns of central Indiana, Wells developed a radiant personality and a talent for serving others. First enrolled at Indiana University in 1921 as a sophomore transfer student from the University of Illinois, he fell in love with the historic woodland campus with its stately limestone halls. Active in social affairs on campus, including his fraternity, Sigma Nu, Wells was an average student, garnering respectable B's and C's in courses such as journalism and psychology. He completed his undergraduate degree in commerce in 1924. Among his classmates were Hoagy Carmichael, Nelson Poynter, and Ernie Pyle.

After graduation, Wells returned to his native county and worked in the National Bank of Lebanon for a couple of years. He came back to Bloomington for the academic year of 1926–27, obtaining a master's degree in economics. At the urging of his professors, he became a doctoral student at the University of Wisconsin, a noted center for the study of social science and political life. His degree requirements were not yet completed when he became the field secretary of the Indiana Bankers Association in 1928. Charged with performing applied research on the sorry state of Indiana banks, suffering since the 1921 agricultural recession, Wells was able to put his academic training to good use. He visited banks and bankers all over the state, traveling to each one of Indiana's 92 counties, and laid the foundation for his later work as an educator.

Wells got his first taste of college teaching in 1930 through his appointment as a lecturer at Indiana University. He was a natural, able to convey the latest in business concepts and techniques with enthusiasm and wit. Eschewing marriage, the next five years would be crucial to his career. Wells juggled several full-time jobs for state government during this period and his work culminated in plans for the overhaul of Indiana's banking laws. Governor Paul McNutt, a former dean of the IU law school, shepherded the reform bill through the state legislature in 1933 and it soon became a national model.

William Lowe Bryan, IU president since 1902, recognized Wells's tremendous passion for public service and appointed him dean of the School of Business Administration in 1935. At that time, the school was growing significantly and Wells used his organizational skills to attract new faculty and reform the curriculum. He possessed other gifts as well, including an elephantine memory that allowed him to connect faces with names and other personal details.

DYNAMIC PRESIDENT

In 1937, Wells was named Acting President as the IU trustees searched for Bryan's replacement. Nine months later they found the ideal candidate and appointed Wells as the eleventh IU president. He was the first president drawn from the social science/public policy arena. He had already traveled over 33,000 miles in search of new faculty for the university, persuading new as well as established scholars to share his vision for the renaissance of Indiana University.

At the head of a small but extremely capable administrative staff, Wells modernized the institution in almost every conceivable way while dealing with unprecedented growth. Over his twenty-five-year tenure, the student body expanded to 29,000 statewide; the Bloomington campus mushroomed with new academic buildings and residence halls; and programs proliferated at an amazing rate. With deep historical awareness, Wells was able to build on IU's institutional strengths in scientific research and professional education that were a legacy of his predecessors, David Starr Jordan and William Lowe Bryan. But he kept his keen eye on the future as well, and launched an ambitious plan to develop the visual and performing arts, especially music.

Wells and the institution he led reached a turning point with World War II. Before the war, Wells became sensitized to the global context in a journey to South America, and his work during the war with national agencies, such as the U.S. State Department and the American Council on Education, made him a true internationalist. After the war, Wells managed to deal with burgeoning IU enrollments due to the G.I. Bill while he took on additional duties as an educational diplomat in Germany and other countries. In 1947, for instance, he played an essential role in establishing the Free University of Berlin.

Had he chosen, at this juncture in his career Wells could have joined the select company of high counselors who moved all around the world performing important tasks for foundations, national associations, international commissions, and government agencies. Instead he stayed in Indiana, maintaining his vow to reside in Bloomington, his adopted city. His interest in the world scene was reinforced by frequent travel to get new ideas and to enlarge his wide acquaintance with political and educational leaders. Wells translated his global understanding into strong support for a wide array of international programs at IU, particularly the study of exotic languages in their cultural contexts.

Wells vigorously promoted the growth of IU in Indianapolis and nurtured regional campus development to ensure that higher education was in reach of every interested and qualified citizen of the state. He also developed excellent relations with other Hoosier colleges and universities. Leading by example, Wells laid a strong foundation of cooperation and goodwill, resulting in a peaceful commonwealth of higher education institutions in Indiana.

One of Wells's bedrock principles was intellectual freedom. He provided faculty and students with physical space and material resources to conduct teaching and research, but he was equally concerned that they have the liberty to venture into uncharted academic territory. In what became perhaps the most celebrated instance of the protection of

academic freedom in the middle years of the 20th century, Wells doggedly took on biology professor Alfred Kinsey's detractors, giving the
university an enviable reputation as a bastion of free inquiry.

Wells practiced environmental stewardship at IU, balancing tremendous growth in the physical plant with deference to the natural woodland setting. Over the term of his presidency, he acquired more than
1,700 acres of land for the Bloomington campus, providing ample space
for future expansion. Like his forerunners, Wells was intent on maintaining the forested character of the campus, and he was fiercely protective of
trees and green space. He said, "To cut a tree unnecessarily has long been
an act of treason against our heritage and the loyalty, love, and effort of
our predecessors who have preserved it for us."

BELOVED CHANCELLOR

At his retirement from the presidency in 1962, Wells received an honorary LL.D. *summa cum laude* from Indiana University. It occupied a
unique place in his growing list of honorary degrees, which eventually
totaled 26. Only sixty years of age, Wells received a lifetime appointment to the new post of University Chancellor. He was free to create
his own job description. Eventually that came to include raising enormous sums for the university, serving as interim president, and just being there. He enveloped generations of students, faculty, staff, alumni,
and friends in his warm, ecumenical embrace. He served as the wise
patriarch of the great IU clan. Substance was his style, and he became
a ubiquitous presence and a precious resource to all in his long tenure
as chancellor.

In his 98th year, his body weary and his mind intact, Wells died quietly at his campus home at 1321 E. Tenth Street on the evening of March
18, 2000. A few members of his loyal staff – a nurse, an aide, and a houseman – were at his bedside. The funeral was held on March 22, exactly 62
years to the day after his selection as president of Indiana University.
The eager sophomore of 1921, the dynamic president of 1938, the beloved
chancellor of 1962, had come full circle to rest, earning the eternal gratitude of his *alma mater*. Herman B Wells built an institution, and in the
process, became one himself. Like a Hoosier Antaeus (the giant son of

Gaia and Poseidon from Greek mythology), Wells drew his prodigious strength from his connection to the Indiana soil. He planted so many seeds of compassion and kindness and learning that his memory will be everlastingly green as long as there remains an Indiana University.

James H. Capshew, with the assistance of
Donald J. Gray and Henry H. H. Remak

Read at the Bloomington Faculty Council,
April 18, 2000; Circular B32-2000.

Notes

The sources of the book's epigraphs are: Pope, *Epistle to Burlington*, line 57; Durrell, *Justine*, 41; Jaspers, *Existential Elucidation*, 242; Williams, "Kenneth Burke," 6; Sanders, *Staying Put*, 114.

PREFACE

The source of the epigraph is Stanton, "Biography," 60.

1. Westfall, "Newton and His Biographer."

2. See Geiger, *To Advance Knowledge.*

3. See Graham and Diamond, *The Rise of American Research Universities;* and Geiger, *Research and Relevant Knowledge.*

4. Stephen Graubard, personal communication, September 25, 2006. See also his "Notes toward a New History."

5. Gardner and Laskin, *Leading Minds,* 129.

6. Nevins, *The State Universities and Democracy,* 104.

7. Thelin, *A History of American Higher Education,* 246.

8. Curti, review of *Indiana University,* by Thomas D. Clark, 1101.

PROLOGUE

The source of the epigraph is Ernie Pyle, "It's In the Air."

1. Chamness, "Mother of College Presidents." See also Capshew, "Indiana University as the 'Mother of College Presidents.'"

2. In 1817 Michigan Territory established a "University of Michigania" in Detroit before Michigan achieved statehood in 1837 and the university moved to Ann Arbor. See Peckham, *The Making of the University of Michigan.*

3. In 1867 Indiana University became the first state university in the United States to admit women on the same basis as men.

4. James A. Woodburn, *A History of Indiana University;* Clark, *Indiana University,* vol. 1.

5. Jordan, *Days of a Man,* 1:295.

6. Jordan made this statement in his 1888 report as a trustee of Cornell University; quoted in Hewett, *Cornell University,* 286.

7. Jordan, *Days of a Man,* 1:295.

8. Ibid., 295–96.

9. Ibid., 300.

10. Minuscule gains were made in racial diversity by 1920, with African Americans accounting for about 1 percent of the of the student body. Although Marcellus Neal became IU's first African American graduate in 1895, it was not until 1919 that Frances Marshall became the first black female to obtain an IU degree.

11. Jordan, *Days of a Man,* 1:385.

12. Bryan's older brother, Enoch Albert Bryan, class of 1878, was president of Vincennes University and the State College of Washington.

13. Chamness, "Mother of College Presidents."

14. Terman's only child, Frederick Terman, became Stanford's famous dean of engineering after World War II.

15. Chamness, "Mother of College Presidents," 49.

16. Swain, "Forty Years of Indiana," 394.

17. Rothblatt, "A Note on the 'Integrity' of the University," 280.

18. For an instructive discussion on the importance of milieu, see Rothblatt, "Consult the Genius of the Place."

1. IN THE LAND OF JORDAN
The source of the epigraph is Shively, *Initiation*, 122.

1. HBW to IU Registrar, April 8, 1921; Registrar to HBW, April 8, 1921. IUA/ C286/279/Well–Welz 1917–1923.

2. Capshew, "Boone County Days."

3. BL, 29.

4. Herman B. Wells's official transcript, University of Illinois at Urbana-Champaign; WBP files.

5. BL, 31.

6. Ibid., 16.

7. Ibid., 29.

8. Jane Wells, Granville's mother and Herman's grandmother, committed suicide in 1914, when the elder Wells was forty and the younger, twelve. See Capshew, "Boone County Days."

9. BL, 18.

10. Wells had mumps at age fifteen, right before he started high school, and his case was complicated by orchitis, which left him with chronic pain in his private parts. See Capshew, "Boone County Days," 9–10.

11. See Capshew, "Encounters with *Genius Loci*."

12. Hall, "Monroe County Leads All Parts of State," 48.

13. Davis, *The Adventures of an Ultra-Crepidarian*, 240.

14. When he left for Stanford, Jordan recruited a number of the members of the

IU faculty to accompany him. Such faculty "raiding" from one institution to another was not uncommon at the time; perhaps the most famous example was University of Chicago's rise at the expense of Clark University. See Koelsch, *Clark University*.

15. Davis, *The Adventures of an Ultra-Crepidarian*, 240.

16. BL, 457.

17. Ibid., appendix B.

18. "As an only child I found the fellowship of the fraternity family an especially pleasing and satisfying experience" (ibid., 35).

19. The former fraternity residence is still standing, now the home of small stores, a restaurant, and a coffeehouse.

20. Owen and Owen, *Greek-Lettered Hoosiers*, 23.

21. Moore, *Citizen Klansmen*, 48–50.

22. "Public Gazes at Klansman Parade and Ceremonies."

23. Thomas D. Clark, HBW oral history, January 1968.

24. BL, 22–23.

25. Ibid., 29.

26. Waldman with Klemkosky, *The First One Hundred Years of Education for Business*, 33–37.

27. Ibid., 36. Rawles, who grew up in Bloomington and lived next door to the Woodburn's house on North College, had been hired in the Department of History in 1894, and then served as an assistant professor in the Department of Economics and Social Science in 1899. That department developed a number of business courses, and in 1902 announced a two-year program of "commercial courses" leading to the baccalaureate degree. By 1916, Rawles, who had been put in charge of the commercial courses, recommended that a School of Commerce be established. The School of Commerce and Finance was opened in 1920, with Rawles as dean.

28. Wells cites his college teachers in BL: J. E. Moffat and Lionel D. Edie in

economics; U. G. Weatherly in sociology; William A. Rawles in corporation finance; William E. Jenkins in English; John L. (Jack) Geiger in music appreciation; and "many others who stimulated me" (33–34).

29. Sousa visited Bloomington in November 1925. See "History of the Indiana University Marching Hundred," Indiana University Marching Hundred website, 2010, www.indiana.edu/~bands/history.php.

30. BL, 34.

31. Ibid.

32. Ibid.

33. Clark, *Indiana University*, 2:275.

34. Peter Costas, oral history interview by Bobbie Taylor, July 17, 1974; Monroe County Public Library Indiana Room.

35. See Sudhalter, *Stardust Melody*, 54–68 for a vivid account of Moenkhaus.

36. Names of bands mentioned in Clark, *Indiana University*, 2:276.

37. Carmichael with Longstreet, *Sometimes I Wonder*, 54–55.

38. Sudhalter, *Stardust Melody*. As a college students, Wells and Carmichael were not close friends, but later they became close. In the late 1970s, for instance, Carmichael telephoned Wells at his residence every month or so.

39. Thelin, *A History of American Higher Education*, 211.

40. Carmichael, *The Stardust Road*, 7–8.

41. Quoted in Sherratt, "The Long Journey," 143.

42. James Elliott, oral history interview by James Capshew, June 2, 2005; WBP files.

43. Currently, Indiana Avenue between Third and Kirkwood is the site of Bryan Hall (1936) and the Law School (1957).

44. The site is close to the present-day location of the Law School. H. W. Hammond et al. to Board of Trustees, January 17, 1922; IUA/C286/237/Sigma Nu, undated.

45. Bryan to H. W. Hammond et al., January 25, 1922, ibid. Only two fraterni-

ties – Phi Gamma Delta and Phi Kappa Psi – had constructed specially built houses for their membership.

46. "The architectural legacy of the expanded student body in the early 1900s was the student union. This building provided an alternative to eating clubs and secret societies. It acknowledged that the campus was not a cohesive residential entity but rather was characterized by diverse living arrangements, including the arrangements of commuter students. It also represented an attempt by college administrators to exert some influence, perhaps control, over the patterns of student life. The student union movement was a truly nationwide phenomenon" (Thelin, *A History of American Higher Education*, 192–93).

47. Clark, *Indiana University*, 2:152.

48. Myers, *History of Indiana University*, 38ff.

49. Ibid., 191.

50. James Whitcomb Riley, the famed Hoosier poet, author of "Little Orphant Annie" and "Happy Little Cripple," died in 1916. Friends and associates decided that a suitable memorial would be a hospital for children. See Myers, *History of Indiana University*, 309–10.

51. Clark, *Indiana University*, 2:156.

52. Ibid., 159.

53. He was criticized, however, for his "heavy expenditures," although the university administration was generally pleased with his efforts. Blake, *Paul V. McNutt*, 15–16, cites letters from Alexander and Bryan.

54. Clark, *Indiana University*, 2:159.

55. Wells made a pledge to the Memorial Fund drive, amount unknown, based on a letter enclosing a payment for September 1. HBW to Paul Thompson, August 16, 1924; IUA/C286/279/Wells, Herman B. 1921–34.

56. Steele, Steele, and Peat, *House of the Singing Winds*, 161.

57. Senour, *Art for Your Sake,* 2.

58. Steele, Steele, and Peat, *House of the Singing Winds,* 162.

59. Ibid., 199.

60. Senour, *Art for Your Sake,* 1–2.

61. Ibid., 28–29.

62. Ibid., 31–32.

63. "He liked to watch Steele paint, and to listen to the artist talk about art. These sessions, Dr. Wells said, left him with a lifelong interest in the visual arts, and a deep appreciation for Steele's achievement and his intellect" (Finkelstein, "Remembering Herman B Wells").

64. See Myers, *History of Indiana University,* 424–35.

65. BL, 35.

66. Ibid.

67. There has been controversy about the date – 1824 or 1825 – the university first opened its doors. Recent research has established April 4, 1825, as the date classes began. Hackerd, "The Complex History of the Date Classes Began at the State Seminary of Indiana."

68. Similar scenes were enacted for the 1916 Indiana statehood centennial and the 1920 IU centennial.

69. "Centennial Celebration of the Opening of Indiana University," 380 [punctuation added].

70. Woodburn, "Since the Beginning," 317–18.

71. William Lowe Bryan, "Alma Mater and the Dark Ages," reprinted in Bryan, *Farewells,* 21–22, quotation 22.

72. "Commencement 1924." Currently the painting is located on the balcony of the IU Bookstore.

73. BL, 42.

2. BETWIXT BANKING AND SOCIAL SCIENCE

The source of the epigraph is Turner, "Pioneer Ideals and the State University," his 1910 Indiana University commencement address. See also Ridge, "Frederick Jackson Turner at Indiana University."

1. Austin and Austin, "The Indiana Bankers Association," 12.

2. Hazelwood, "Better Banks and Bankers."

3. HBW, audio recording by Brian Kearney, 1995, WBP files.

4. See Myers, *History of Indiana University,* 270–90.

5. Brennan, "From Tree to the Trade"; JoAnn Campbell et al., *The Greater Bloomington Chamber of Commerce.*

6. Kuykendall, "The Negro at Indiana."

7. Herman B. Wells, Indiana University transcript; *Indiana University Bulletin,* 1926. Wells dropped the period after his middle initial in the late 1930s.

8. Austin and Austin, "The Indiana Bankers Association," 6–7, 16.

9. HBW to Forba McDaniel, March 25, 1926 [1927]; McDaniel to HBW, March 26, April 18, and April 27, 1927; IUA/C75/3/McDaniel.

10. Wells, "Service Charges for Small or So-called Country Banks" (M.A. thesis), 117.

11. Ibid., 87, 88.

12. Wells, "Service Charges for Small or So-called Country Banks" (article).

13. McCarthy, *The Wisconsin Idea,* quoted in Frederick Rudolph, *The American College and University,* 363.

14. McDaniel to HBW, telegrams (2), July 21, 1927; HBW notes to McDaniel, July 21, 1927; IUA/C75/3/McDaniel.

15. McDaniel to HBW, July 22, 1927; HBW to McDaniel, n.d.; McDaniel to HBW, July 27, 1927; IUA/C75/3/McDaniel.

16. The manager of the University Club wrote to Wells with room rates ($24–$29 a month) and board expenses ($10 a week), and said, "We sincerely believe you would enjoy residence in the Club" (D. Bush to HBW, August 24, 1927; IUA/C75/4/U, general); Cronon and Jenkins, *The University of Wisconsin,* 11, 333, 527–31.

17. BL, 38.

18. Lampman, *Economists at Wisconsin,* 35. It was estimated that around 70,000 students took Kiekhofer's classes.

19. Ibid.

20. BL, 39–40.

21. Herman B. Wells's official transcript, University of Wisconsin, 1928; WBP files.

22. McDaniel to HBW, October 5 and November 12, 1927; McDaniel to HBW, telegram, November 16, 1927; IUA/C75/3/McDaniel.

23. HBW to Charles Zigler, January 7, 1928; HBW to McDaniel, January 7, 1928; IUA/C75/3/McDaniel.

24. HBW to J. Dwight Peterson; IUA/C75/3/Pa–Ph, general.

25. Williams's Bloomington, Indiana City Directory, 1927–28, listed Gabriel's address as 423 E. 5th St.; Carson's Bloomington City Directory, 1929–30, listed Gabriel's at 106 S. Indiana Ave. When he was pursuing his master's degree, Wells arranged to have Gabriel visit the Sigma Nu chapter at Wabash College in Crawfordville with a selection of clothes. He also corresponded with a part owner of the business, Pat Lynch, about the sale of his shares in the firm in 1928 (HBW to Sigma Nu Fraternity, Crawfordsville, March 7, 1927; Pat Lynch to HBW, January 17, February 1, and March 7, 1928; IUA/C75/22/Investments Gabriel's). William E. Sullivan was the majority shareholder, and he eventually bought the other partners out, including Gabriel, and continued the business under his own name.

26. HBW to McDaniel, telegram draft, n.d.; IUA/C75/3/McDaniel.

27. IUA/C75/9/The Country Bank (thesis) – outline, n.d.

28. *Hoosier Banker* 13, no. 5 (February 1928): 18.

29. See Musgrave, "A Primitive Method of Enforcing the Law."

30. HBW to C. O. Holmes, January 27, 1928; IUA/C75/2/Holmes.

31. HBW to McDaniel, March 5, 1928; IUA/C75/2/Holmes.

32. Announcement and picture of HBW in "The Watch Tower," 13.

33. "The History of Banking in Indiana," 118.

34. Ibid., 116.

35. HBW to Kiekhofer, March 13, 1929, reprinted in BL, 45; "First Banking Exhibit," 5.

36. Biddle to HBW, March 2 and April 19, 1928, May 1, 1929; IUA/C75/1/Biddle.

37. HBW to Biddle, April 2 1929; IUA/C75/1/Biddle.

38. McDaniel, "Annual Report of the Secretary," 18, 54.

39. "Hoosier Highways," February 1930, 30.

40. Ibid.

41. "Hoosier Highways," March 1930, 30.

42. "Hoosier Highways," April 1930, 30.

43. Ibid.

44. "Hoosier Highways," May 1930, 30.

45. Cleveland to HBW, April 9, 1930; IUA/C75/1/Cleveland.

46. Biddle to HBW, February 24, 1930; IUA/C75/1/Biddle.

47. Ibid.

48. Biddle to HBW, March 26, 1930; ibid.

49. Wells presents a drastically foreshortened and dramatically simplified account of the recruitment process, and omits mention of his ambivalence. In February 1930, Professor Weatherly, head of the IU Department of Economics and Sociology, invited Wells to Sunday dinner. In addition to Professor and Mrs. Weatherly, the other senior professor, James Moffat, and his wife were in attendance. After a fine meal, the men retired to the study, where Professor Weatherly, after fiddling with his pipe and clearing

his throat, said that there might be an opening for an instructor in the department in the fall, and, if so, would Wells be interested in the position? Wells accepted on the spot. He noted that his work with the IBA was not only interesting but also relevant to his teaching duties, and the senior professors agreed that he could maintain his links to the association. There was no discussion of salary, as befitted conversation among gentlemen. After visiting with his mother and father the next day, he wrote to Weatherly: "They were enthusiastic over the idea. Consequently I now confirm the favorable decision I gave you Sunday." Looking back fifty years later, Wells reconstructed his rationale: "I would be receiving a salary less than half of my current rate, but, so long as I had enough money to live on, that salary reduction seemed a small matter compared to the prospect of being a member of the faculty.... The very thought of being on the faculty was exhilarating to me." No doubt Wells remembered accurately his joyful emotion, but the timeline was severely compressed. Instead of two or three days to reach a mutual agreement with the department, hiring negotiations were protracted – and salary considerations played a key role (BL, 46–47).

3. THE POLITICS OF BANK REFORM

The source of the epigraph is IUA/C75/50/ "Economic Security" outline, c. June 1933.

1. HBW to U. G. Weatherly, 15 Oct 1930; quoted in BL, 47.
2. BL, 50.
3. IUA/C75/2/Greenough, Walter S. The article is missing from the bound volume of the 1930 Hoosier Banker in the Indiana University Libraries.
4. His employees were Paul DeVault, a law student completing A.B. and J.D. degrees; Lyman D. Eaton, a master's candidate specializing in accounting and

statistics; Charles M. Cooley, a master's candidate in economics; Elizabeth Chapman (Parrish), an undergraduate student; and Evelyn McFadden (Cummins), a recent A.B. recipient (BL, 52).
5. Ibid.
6. Ibid.
7. Musgrave, "Fractional Reform," 42.
8. Study Commission for Indiana Financial Institutions, Report, 81; quoted in Musgrave, "Fractional Reform," 46–47.
9. Musgrave, "Fractional Reform," 47–48.
10. Ibid., 49–60. Wells came to regret some of the proffered policies, such as shareholder's double liability, which did not perform its intended service but prevented investment in banks. Other policies, such as the ban on state deposit insurance, were overtaken by events, as shortly after the report was issued a federal deposit insurance scheme was implemented.
11. Peter Costas, interview by Bobbie Taylor, July 17, 1974, Monroe County Public Library Indiana Room.
12. Clark, Indiana University, 2:278.
13. Carmichael, Stardust Road, 143.
14. See The Presidents' Homes.
15. Myers, History of Indiana University, 434–35.
16. Kotlowski, "Launching a Political Career."
17. Musgrave, "Fractional Reform," 68–69.
18. Ibid., 70.
19. Ibid., 78.
20. For the 1932–33 academic year, IU salaries were reduced by 8 percent. For Wells, that meant $2,208 (reduced from $2,400) (WLB to HBW, September 5, 1932; IUA/C286/279/Wells, Herman B, 1921–1934).
21. Harold Stonier to HBW, February 3, 1933; HBW to Stonier, February 8, 1933; quoted in Musgrave, "Fractional Reform," 84–85.

22. Musgrave, "Fractional Reform," 79–80.

23. Ibid., 80.

24. HBW to Granville and Bernice Wells, February 25, 1933; reprinted in BL, 58.

25. BL, 59.

26. Ibid.

27. Ibid., 60.

28. Foster, Brewer, and Contompasis, *Thomas Hart Benton and the Indiana Murals;* Doss, *Benton, Pollock, and the Politics of Modernism.*

29. HBW, interview by Kathy Foster and Nan Brewer, October 13, 1989; IU Art Museum.

4. FIRST TASTE OF ACADEMIC STEWARDSHIP

The source of the epigraph is BL, 79.

1. HBW to Mother, May 2, 1934; IUA/C75/4/Wells, Mr. & Mrs. Granville.

2. Myers, *History of Indiana University,* 453–57, partially quoting Rawles, "Historical Sketch." See also Waldman with Klemkosky, *The First One Hundred Years of Education for Business.*

3. Retirement for former dean William Rawles was short: he died on May 17, 1936, less than a year after he stepped down.

4. Hugh McK. Landon, Fletcher Trust Co. to WLB, March 26, 1935; IUA/C286/279/Wells, Herman B, Jan–Sep 1935.

5. Walter Greenough to William G. Irwin, January 8, 1935; IUA/C286/279/Wells, Herman B, Jan–Sep 1935.

6. Clare W. Barker to WLB, April 1, 1935; Greenough to WLB, April 16, 1935; IUA/C286/279/Wells, Herman B, Jan–Sep 1935.

7. To cite but three examples: Vance L. Sailor, Supervising Examiner, Sixth Federal Deposit Insurance District, who worked closely with Wells, said, "Mr. Wells showed a very comprehensive grasp of the entire banking situation in Indiana

and was most versatile in dealing with difficult cases" (Sailor to WLB, April 16, 1935). George Weymouth, Indiana Farmers Guide, who worked with Wells as a member of the Study Commission, said, "It was during our prolonged work on the Commission that I learned to know Mr. Wells and to appreciate his ability and his great industry, and I think it is not too much to say that whatever success we may have had in drafting the state's banking law was due in considerable degree to the work of Mr. Wells. We were more fortunate than we realized at the time in having him for our secretary" (Weymouth to WLB, April 18, 1935). R. L. Hopkins, Supervising Examiner, Federal Deposit Insurance Corporation, lauded Wells: "I have known Mr. Wells intimately in his work and have always found him to be a man of high moral courage, estimable character and great ability" (Hopkins to WLB, April 19, 1935). All IUA/C286/279/Wells, Herman B, Jan–Sep 1935.

8. F. B. Bernard to William Rawles, April 20, 1935; IUA/C286/279/Wells, Herman B, Jan–Sep 1935.

9. HBW to Weatherly, April 29, 1935; IUA/C286/279/Wells, Herman B, Jan–Sep 1935.

10. In IUA/C286/279/Wells, Herman B, Jan–Sep 1935.

11. Wells, "Top Heavy Bank Supervision," 13–15, 81.

12. For example, Bryan appointed Paul McNutt, now the Indiana governor, as IU law dean in 1925 at the age of thirty-four, and Bryan himself was the beneficiary of liberal policies for advancement, having been named IU vice president in 1891 at thirty-one and president eleven years later.

13. WLB telegram to HBW, May 18, 1935; IUA/C286/279/Wells, Herman B, Jan–Sep 1935.

14. W. H. Kiekhofer to HBW, May 1, 1935; IUA/C286/279/Wells, Herman B, Jan–Sep 1935.

15. BL, 70.

16. Ibid.

17. Edward E. Edwards points out, "The reason why I think it was very important that Herman be away from the campus in [1933–34 and 1934–35] was that if he had stayed on the campus he would have continued to develop a reputation as a good teacher. . . . To jump from Assistant Professor to Dean and particularly from Assistant Professor of Economics to Dean of the School of Business, I just don't think it would have happened . . . I don't believe there would have been anything here that would have demonstrated his ability as an administrator, as a leader and motivator. But to go to Indianapolis and jump into what was a horrible mess, and to get it straightened out, to have wide acceptance, this, it seems to me, was very, very important" (Edward E. Edwards and HBW, oral history interview by Thomas Clark and Dorothy Collins, August 5, 1974; IUA/74-011).

18. Biddle's 1930 dream that Wells "might some time become the Dean" of the School of Commerce came true five years later. Biddle to HBW, February 24, 1930; IUA/C75/1/Biddle.

19. BL, 75.

20. BL, 75.

21. HBW to Walter Greenough, September 16, 1935; IUA/C75/2/Greenough, Walter S.

22. Wells taught throughout his deanship. He was listed as an instructor in 1936–37 for these business school classes: 100 Introduction to Business; 230 Business Research (senior level; with others); 270 Supervision of Financial Institutions (alternate years); 271 Business Policy (senior level; omitted 1936–37); 331 Graduate Research (with others). For 1937–38: 100 (with Silverstein), 230, 270, 274 Bank Portfolios and Management; 508 Graduate Seminar (with others). Indiana University Catalog, School of Business, 1936 and 1937.

23. BL, 87.

24. Ibid.

25. HBW to Bernice Wells, September 28, 1935; IUA/C75/4/Wells, Mr. and Mrs. Granville.

26. See Crump, *The Story of Kappa Alpha Psi.*

27. Stewart, *Yesterday Was Tomorrow,* 230–34.

28. Stewart, *Yesterday Was Tomorrow;* BL, 91. The baroque term "polemarch" was a reference to an ancient Greek term for leader or president.

29. Beck Chapel, constructed in 1957, was named after Frank Beck.

30. Beck, *Some Aspects of Race Relations at Indiana University,* 16.

31. Ibid., 34–35.

32. *Bloomington Evening World,* March 16, 1937. IU officials probably came up with this figure by summing the student body count each year, combining new students with continuing students. Wells continued his praise of Bryan, noting his leadership of IU's physical growth as well as to the "spiritual life of the institution": "I shall miss President Bryan's guidance. Ever since I assumed my present position, I have felt free to take my problems to him, certain that l would receive wise and sympathetic counsel. I shall always be grateful that I had an opportunity, for even this short time, to serve under him as a member of his administrative staff" (4).

33. The correct quotation is "There is a tide in the affairs of men, / Which, taken at the flood, leads on to fortune" (*Julius Caesar,* 4.3.218–19). Greenough gave a nonsensical reference to the quotation: II Psalms 32:4. Walter Greenough to HBW, no date; IUA/C75/1/Greenough, Walter S.

5. ACTING LIKE A PRESIDENT
The source of the epigraph is BL, 90.

1. Alexander, "The Indiana University Library," 611.

NOTES TO PAGES 90–96

2. Chamness, "Mother of College Presidents."

3. Clark, *Indiana University*, 2:375–76.

4. Ibid., 376–77.

5. See Norvelle, *The Road Taken.*

6. Alfred C. Kinsey to Edgar Anderson, February 7, 1935; KI Archives/Kinsey Correspondence/Anderson, Edgar.

7. McNutt was a brilliant student, excelling in the classroom and dramatic productions. After earning an LL.B. from Indiana in 1913, he entered Harvard Law School, graduating in 1916. While attending school in Boston, he was reporter for United Press, covering the World Series of 1914, 1915, and 1916, when the Boston Braves and the Boston Red Sox vied for the championship. After serving as a major in World War I, he returned to IU as an assistant professor of law, advancing to the deanship in 1925. McNutt continued his service in the Army Reserves Corps, achieving the rank of colonel in 1923. He was also very active in the American Legion, serving as national commander in 1928.

8. The IU Board of Trustees did not accept McNutt's resignation on January 4, 1933, but granted him a leave of absence. Clark, *Indiana University*, 2:321.

9. Ibid., 251.

10. Norvelle, *The Road Taken*, 249–50.

11. An explanation for the resignation was given by Fesler's brother, Bert. "Paper Read by Bert Fesler"; a rejoinder by Trustee Benjamin Franklin Long follows on 434–35.

12. *Bloomington Telephone,* March 20, 1936. The report also noted that Mrs. McNutt, whose father was a Bloomington industrialist, favored a return to the campus.

13. Quoted in Blake, *Paul V. McNutt,* 170.

14. *Bloomington Evening World,* December 23, 1937.

15. Clark, *Indiana University,* 2:397.

16. Blake, *Paul V. McNutt,* 174.

17. Ibid., 175.

18. *Bloomington Evening World,* February 18, 1937, 1.

19. *Bloomington Evening World,* February 20, 1937.

20. "Dr. Bryan to Remain at I.U. Helm Until New President Selected," *Bloomington Evening World,* March 16, 1937.

21. Kinsey to George A. Ball, March 16, 1937. IUA/C286/212/Presidential candidates' letter of reference/Hill–Trunk, 1936–37.

22. Wildermuth wrote to Ball a week after the announcement, "[W]e can not expect Dr. Bryan to look up and dish out to us as he does in most of the problems that arise" (OLW to George A. Ball, March 23, 1937; IUA/C286/212/Presidential selection).

23. OLW to Walter A. Jessup, March 29, 1937; IUA/C286/212/Presidential selection.

24. Presidents Jordan (1885–91), Swain (1893–1902), and Bryan (1902–37) had been faculty members before their appointments; President Coulter (1891–93), a botany professor at Wabash College, had been recommended by Jordan as his successor. Coffman quotation in OLW handwritten notes, April 10, 1937; IUA/C286/212/Presidential selection.

25. OLW to Board of Trustees, April 12, 1937; IUA/C286/212/Presidential selection .

26. OLW to WLB, April 12, 1937; IUA/C286/212/Presidential selection.

27. WLB to OLW, April 14, 1937; IUA/C286/212/Presidential selection.

28. OLW to W. L. McAtee, May 4, 1937; IUA/C286/212/Presidential selection. In addition to his key role conducting IU's business affairs, Biddle was a committed Democrat. He served in the Indiana House of Representatives in 1931–32 before being elected to the Indiana Senate from 1933 to 1937. A fierce partisan

for the interests of the university, he used his political connections and business acumen to advance I U.

29. OLW to George A. Ball, May 19, 1937; I U A/C286/212/Presidential selection.

30. Arthur M. Banta to OLW, May 19, 1937; I U A/C286/212/Presidential selection.

31. OLW to Johns S. Hastings, May 22, 1937; IUA/C286/212/Presidential selection.

32. WLB to OLW, May 18, 1937; WLB to OLW, May 21, 1937; I U A/C286/212/Presidential selection.

33. "Report Trustees Cable McNutt Offer to Take University Presidency," *Bloomington Evening World,* May 19, 1937.

34. OLW to WLB, May 24, 1937; I U A/C286/212/Presidential selection.

35. OLW to George A. Ball, May 24, 1937; I U A/C286/212/Presidential selection.

36. Banta wrote: "the politically-minded is the worst for a university president!" Arthur Banta to OLW, May 22, 1937, John S. Hastings to OLW, May 24, 1937; I U A/C286/212/Presidential selection.

37. OLW to Albert Rabb, cc to Val Nolan, John Hastings, May 26, 1937; I U A/C286/212/Presidential selection.

38. Arthur Banta to OLW, May 26, 1937; IUA/C286/212/Presidential selection.

39. Val Nolan to John Hastings, May 28, 1937; I U A/C286/212/Presidential selection.

40. Rabb to OLW, May 28, 1937; I U A/C286/212/Presidential selection.

41. *Bloomington Evening World,* May 20, 1937, June 4, 1937. Before they reached retirement age, faculty members were to contribute 5 percent of their annual salary, which would be matched by the university.

42. This is how Wells expressed the exchange, forty years later, in B L, 90. Meant for public consumption, this account was sanitized of politics and embellished for effect. Clark cites an interview from 1970 with John Hastings. Hastings said, "unequivocally that President Bryan recommended Dean Herman B Wells of the Business School to be his successor. For some reason which remains unexplained, the trustees waited from March 15 to June 10, 1937, to select a temporary successor to President Bryan" (*Indiana University,* 2:398–99). The account goes on to note the telephone call placed by Wildermuth to Wells in Brown County that *Being Lucky* repeats. The present account complicates the story, based on documents from the presidential selection archive, which might not have been available to Clark, and raises some doubts about the accuracy of Hastings's recollection of events of thirty years before.

43. *Bloomington Evening World,* June 11, 1937.

44. *Bloomington Evening World,* June 12, 1937.

45. Thomas A. Cookson to H. L. Smith, June 21, 1937; I U A/C286/242/ Smith, H. L. May–Sept 1937.

46. *Bloomington Telephone,* June 30, 1937.

47. James B. Conant to Albert L. Rabb, June 9, 1937; Rabb to HBW, June 12, 1937; HBW to Rabb, June 16, 1937; I U A/ C213/139/Conant, James B. Committee suggested to recommend men . . . 1937–38. In 1934, the American Council on Education issued a report on leading graduate programs. I U was listed in botany, chemistry, education, English, geology, German, mathematics, psychology, sociology, and zoology (Hughes, "Report of the Committee on Graduate Instruction"). A decade earlier, the Association of American Colleges performed a similar survey; Indiana was listed in education, German, history, and zoology (Hughes, *A Study of the Graduate Schools of America*).

48. B L, 103.

49. Ibid., 99.

50. OLW to M. Clifford Townsend, July 14, 1937; IUA/C286/212/Presidential search.

51. IUMP, 6.

52. Clark, *Indiana University*, 2:367.

53. IUMP, 6.

54. HBW to OLW, August 13, 1937; list of candidates prepared by search committee [late August 1937]; IUA/C286/212/Presidential selection.

55. OLW to Lewis M. Terman, September 3, 1937; IUA/C286/212/Presidential selection.

56. OLW to Walter A. Jessup, September 3, 1937; IUA/C286/212/Presidential selection.

57. OLW to George A. Ball, September 3, 1937; IUA/C286/212/Presidential selection.

58. OLW to Walter A. Jessup, September 16, 1937; IUA/C286/212/Presidential selection.

59. Frank O. Adyelotte to George A. Ball, September 29, 1937; OLW to Board of Trustees, October 25, 1937; handwritten notes, OLW, n.d.; IUA/C286/212/Presidential selection.

60. O. W. Douglas to OLW, September 3, 1937; W. L. Benson to OLW, September 21, 1937; IUA/C286/212/Presidential selection.

61. *Chicago Daily News* article clipping, September 23, 1937; IUA/C286/212/Presidential search.

62. Walter A. Jessup to OLW, November 3, 1937; IUA/C286/212/Presidential selection.

63. OLW to Ward Biddle, December 13, 1937; OLW to M. Clifford Townsend, December 13, 1937; IUA/C286/212/Presidential selection.

64. OLW to Walter A. Jessup, November 6, 1937; IUA/C286/212/Presidential selection.

65. OLW to HBW, December 6, 1937; IUA/C286/212/Presidential selection.

66. Ibid.

67. Wildermuth/Bryan presidency search files: Memo from OLW, December 7, 1937; IUA/C286/212/Presidential selection.

68. "McNutt Is 'Not in I.U. Picture,' Trustee Friend Says." Trustee Hastings rejoiced privately to Wildermuth over the newspaper article, believing "it has done more to instill a feeling of public confidence in our job than anything I have heard mentioned" (John S. Hastings to OLW, December 14, 1937; IUA/C286/212/Presidential selection). It got the information of the trustees' dissatisfaction with the McNutt possibility on the table without a public confrontation.

69. Hastings to OLW, December 21, 1937; IUA/C286/212/Presidential selection.

70. OLW to Henry M. Wriston, December 24, 1937; IUA/C286/212/Presidential selection.

71. OLW to Walter A. Jessup, n.d.; IUA/C286/212/Presidential selection.

72. Hastings to OLW, January 8, 1938; IUA/C286/212/Presidential selection.

73. Ibid.

74. Claude Rich to OLW, January 6, 1938; IUA/C286/212/Presidential selection. Rich was a distant cousin of Wells, although that connection was probably not well known at that time.

75. OLW to Walter A. Jessup, January 13, 1938; IUA/C286/212/Presidential selection.

76. HBW, Bloomington Chamber of Commerce speech, January 31, 1938; IUA/HBW presidential speech files.

77. The vote did not split along party lines. Rabb was a Republican, and Wildermuth a Democrat.

78. OLW to Val Nolan, March 2, 1938; OLW to Albert Rabb, March 3, 1938; IUA/C286/212/Presidential selection.

79. One such paper was the *Gary Post Tribune*.

80. OLW to Hastings, March 14, 1938; IUA/C286/212/Presidential selection.

81. OLW to [illegible], March 17, 1938; OLW to Johns Hastings, March 18, 1938; IUA/C286/212/Presidential selection.

82. Reprinted in BL, 103–04.

83. Ibid.

84. "This was in fact the groom, after a year of trial marriage, explaining his ambitions on this his wedding day to the university" (Clark, *Indiana University,* 2:404.)

85. Reprinted in BL, 105.

86. WLB to OLW, March 23, 1938; IUA/C286/212/Presidential selection.

87. OLW to WLB, March 25, 1938. Wildermuth wrote to Wells, conveying the gist of Bryan's advice; OLW to HBW, March 25, 1938; IUA/C286/212/Presidential selection.

6. A VISION FOR INDIANA UNIVERSITY

The source of the epigraph is HBW's inaugural speech, 1938; reprinted in Clark, *Indiana University* 4:378.

1. Renamed Bryan Hall in 1957.

2. BL, 107–108.

3. Payne, *Memories and Reflections,* 73–74.

4. BL, 100–102.

5. IUA/C213/Self-Survey Comm. 1937–39.

6. Although both Wells, as an undergraduate student, and Kinsey, as an assistant professor, were on campus in the early 1920s, there is no evidence that they interacted. Wells was likely aware of Kinsey's existence as a member of the professoriate, however.

7. Cattell, *American Men of Science.*

8. HBW, "Foundation Day Broadcast," May 4, 1938; IUA/HBW presidential speech files.

9. Kinsey to Wells, quoted in Christenson, *Kinsey,* 101.

10. See Capshew, "The Legacy of the Laboratory."

11. Gathorne-Hardy, *Alfred C. Kinsey,* 147–48.

12. Quoted in Jones, *Alfred C. Kinsey,* 412.

13. Thompson, *A Folklorist's Progress,* 113.

14. Ibid., 152.

15. Ibid., 160.

16. Sachar, "Ten Years at Indiana," 5; IUA/Ref Files: Hillel Foundation.

17. Ibid., 5–6.

18. "The Hillel Foundation," 516.

19. HBW to A. L. Sachar, May 9, 1938; IUA/C75/4/Sa–Sd, general.

20. "The Hillel Foundation," 516.

21. IUA/Hillel Foundation reference file. By his efforts to hire Jewish faculty members as well as his support of Jewish students, Wells was a key agent in the emergence of a vibrant Jewish community in Bloomington. See Spechler, in "Remembering Herman B Wells"; Himm and Eisenberg, *There are Jews in Southern Indiana.*

22. Daugherty, "Six-Ton, $20,000 Mural History of State Decaying at Fair Grounds Awaiting Home Big Enough to Hold It," 1.

23. Daugherty, "Suggestions for Preservation Of Murals Given by Lieber," 3.

24. Ralph Thompson to HBW, April 16, 1938; IUA/C213/67/Benton, Thomas Hart – Murals.

25. Thomas Hart Benton to Harry Engel, August 4, 1938; IUA/C213/67/Benton, Thomas Hart – Murals.

26. IUMP, 143–44.

27. BL, 106.

28. Ibid., 196.

29. Ibid., 197–98.

30. Dick Heller to HBW, September 27, 1938; IUA/C213/67/Benton, Thomas Hart – Murals.

31. Karl Detzer to Walter Greenough, September 24, 1938; IUA/C213/163/Detzer, Karl 1939–40.

32. HBW to Detzer, October 5, 1938; IUA/C213/163/Detzer, Karl 1939–40.

33. In early November, Detzer wrote an effusive thank-you letter: "I want you to

know how deeply I appreciate all you did for me, and to cuss you out for not letting me pay my own bill at the Union. You were swell all round, and I do hope the story goes over properly, and that even Walt Greenough will agree that I've done you justice. Knowing Walt, it will be difficult, for he'll expect me to set down enough virtues for make God look like a piker" (Detzer to HBW, November 6, 1938; IUA/C213/163/Detzer, Karl 1939–40).

34. Karl Detzer, "Culture to the Crossroads," *Kiwanis Magazine* 24, no. 3 (March 1939): 136ff. Condensed as "This College Campus is the Whole State," *Reader's Digest,* March 1939; reprinted in BL, 459–62.

35. BL, 462.

36. HBW to Clifford Townsend, March 23, 1939; IUA/C213/67/Benton, Thomas Hart – Murals.

37. BL, 200. Wells's initiatives for the arts became a common refrain in the media. For example, the *Louisville Courier-Journal,* in a profile on Wells celebrating his thirty-seventh birthday, noted that he was moving away from the concept of "a cloistered temple of learning" and toward the idea of "a cultural spa for all Indiana, where middle-aged business men and club women as well as wide-eyed youth, can soak in the waters of science and arts." Louisville *Courier-Journal,* June 7, 1939.

38. For a picture of Wells, Bradford, and others, see "History," Bradford Woods website, 2008, www.bradwoods.org/about/history.htm.

39. Ryan Lee, personal communication, January 18, 2007.

40. Perley, *Without My Gloves,* 256.

41. Ibid.

42. Of the $2,500 appropriated by the trustees for the installation ceremony, $2,000 went to the graduate school research fund and $500 to the professional school research fund.

43. Newspaper estimate quoted in Stewart, *Yesterday Was Tomorrow,* 314.

44. Perley, *Without My Gloves,* 255.

45. "Bryan Lauds Ideals and Principles of Successor."

46. Clark, *Indiana University,* 4:376–84, quotations 382.

47. *Time,* April 4, 1938; reprinted in BL, 438; "Newsboy to College Head"; Bostwick, "Wells Takes Oath as Head of Indiana U.," 3.

48. HBW notes; IUA/C213/268/Union Board.

49. Matthews, *Kirtland Cutter,* 249.

50. Perhaps the inscription was inspired by a passage in "Old Christmas" by Washington Irving, first published in *The Sketchbook* (1820): "It is, indeed, the season of regenerated feeling – the season for kindling, not merely the fire of hospitality in the hall, but the genial flame of charity in the heart" ("Old Christmas," 15, Open Library website, August 12, 2010, openlibrary.org/books/OL14032074M/Old_Christmas).

7. CHARTING A NEW COURSE

The source of the epigraph is IUMP, 6–7.

1. The National Normal College of the American Gymnastics Union, headquartered in Indianapolis since 1907, merged with IU in 1941, under the name of the American Gymnastic Union of Indiana University, with students coming to Bloomington to complete their fourth year of coursework and to receive a Bachelor of Physical Education from the School of Education. In 1945, an expanded new School of Health, Physical Education, and Recreation was established. It was the only new school established under the Wells administration. IUMP, 48–49; HBW to Governor Clifford Townsend, November 14, 1940; IUA/C213/540/Townsend, Gov. M. Clifford, 1940–41.

2. Warriner, "The Veterans of World War II at Indiana University," 72.

3. IUMP, 4.

4. Davis, *The Adventures of an Ultra-Crepidarian,* 350–51.

5. "From 1940 to 1962 the self-study report served as a detailed blueprint by which the Wells administration operated, and it was the basis on which most of the fundamental changes in the operation of the institution were made during this quarter of a century" (IUMP, 6).

6. In a 1962 speech to his fellow state university presidents, Wells made light of his impulse in suggesting the self-study; reprinted in BL, 142. Contrast with James M. Elliott's story about asking Wells about the differences between acting president, president, and interim president. Wells looked straight at Elliott and said "rather pointedly, 'You should understand that I was never Acting President, I was always the President'" (HWS, 21).

7. "Minority Groups and the Expression of Student Thought," 152–61.

8. Yokley, "The Negro Community in Bloomington." She thanked faculty member John Mueller for his help; Mueller was the husband of Dean of Women Kate H. Mueller.

9. Pyle, "Ernie Eats a Big Dinner with a College President."

10. Pyle, "President Hermie Wells and 'This Job' He's Got."

11. Ibid.

12. Ibid.

13. Beğdeş became a prominent businessman in Turkey and was a founding member of IU's International Council. Maintaining a lifelong friendship with Wells, he received the Distinguished Alumni Service Award in 1999. "In Memoriam [Kutsi Beğdeş]," *International News* (November 2002): 41; Patrick O'Meara, personal communication, April 29, 2011.

14. Clark, *Indiana University,* 2:308.

15. IUMP, 7, 12. Payne withstood some criticism from physics faculty member Rolla Roy Ramsay about the cyclotron plan.

16. See Heilbron and Seidel, *Lawrence and His Laboratory.*

17. Berger, "The IU Cyclotron as a Scientific Instrument," 12–15.

18. IUMP, 173.

19. Berger, "The IU Cyclotron as a Scientific Instrument," 15. For later developments, see Catt, "From Opportunities to Obsolescence."

20. The same date, three years before, Wells was selected as president. Coincidentally, March 22 was also the day of Wells's funeral, in 2000.

21. IUMP, 470.

22. Quoted in IUMP, 469; emphasis added.

23. Later, DeVault became the medical director of the Foreign Service in the U.S. State Department, and then the international secretary general of the International College of Surgeons. BL, 270–71.

24. Ibid., 271.

25. Ibid., 275–76. Eventually, Fraenkel attended IU on a scholarship and later became an assistant to Wells.

26. Ibid., 267.

27. Ibid., 279–80.

28. Ibid., 363.

8. WAR STORIES

The source of the epigraph is HBW, remarks to War Convocation, December 16, 1941; IUA/HBW presidential speech file.

1. Forba McDaniel to Oliver Field, July 1, 1943; IUA/C68/Correspondence, 1939–1948, undated.

2. IDS [extra, published on December 7], December 6, 1941, 1.

3. The meeting included administrative staff Biddle, Bartley, and Cookson; and deans Stout, Wiemer, Sanders, Smith, Gavit, and Payne. Ross Bartley to Oliver Field, May 27, 1943; IUA/C68/Correspondence, 1939–1948, undated.

4. HBW, remarks to War Convocation, December 16, 1941, 1–2.

5. Ibid., 10.

6. IDS, December 17, 1941, 1, 3.

7. IUMP, 121. The plan was published in the IDS, January 17, 1942.

8. The formation of the Junior Division was a part of the self-study report that had been rejected earlier.

9. IUMP, 122.

10. Ibid., 40–41.

11. Zirker, "The Way It Was," 8.

12. Kibbey, "Original IU Cyclotron Contributed to the American War Effort."

13. IUMP, 87.

14. Sumner Welles to HBW, March 12, 1943; NAII/DoS archives/851r.01/858a.

15. There is no record of his reply to the offer.

16. Secretary of State Hull established the Office of Foreign Economic Cooperation by Order #1166 on June 24, 1943. Dean Acheson to HBW, July 12, 1943; NAII/DoS archives/111.56.27A.

17. IUMP, 87. Official appointment, DoS Order #1183, August 9, 1943; NA II/DoS archives/111.56/33, also 111.017/676; Press release about the appointment, August 12 1943; NAII/DoS archives/111.56/31.

18. HBW to Acheson, memo to outline the functions of the Office of Advisor on LA, October 27, 1943; HBW appointed Special Advisor on Liberated Areas, November 6, 1943, Order #1210 from State Dept., E. R. Stettinius, Jr., Acting SoS; NAII/DoS archives/111.653.

19. Acheson, Present at the Creation, 78.

20. BL, 321.

21. Ibid., 322.

22. Ibid., 323.

23. Ibid., 325–26.

24. Acheson to HBW, December 10 1943; NAII/DoS archives/111.653/2a.

25. HBW to Dean Acheson, January 5, 1944; NAII/DoS archives/111.682/1.

26. DoS Order #1218, January 15, 1944, 13–14; NAII/DoS archives/111.017/711.

27. Acheson to HBW, February 8, 1944; Cordell Hull, SoS to HBW, February 8, 1944; NAII/DoS archives/111.682/1.

28. Hawkins, Banding Together, 198.

29. The process by which HBW was elected is not clear.

30. Presidential address, National Association of State Universities, Annual Meeting, Drake Hotel, Chicago, October 22, 1943; IUA/HBW presidential speech files.

31. Hawkins, Banding Together, 196–201.

32. George F. Heighway, quoting C. C. Little from the American Alumni Council in 1926, "An Alumni Fund Survey," 3; IUA/C213/308/Indiana University Foundation, 1943–44.

33. William Lowe Bryan sent Wheeler a letter of congratulations: "It was a good day for I.U. when you came as a student. It was another good day for I.U. when you came to found the Foundation" (WLB to Wheeler, November 8, 1944; quoted in Jane Wheeler Boling, "Lawrence Wheeler (1898–1952) Memoir," June 9, 1998, www .indiana.edu/~iirg/WHEELER/wheeler .html).

34. Donald C. Danielson, a former field secretary to the IU Alumni Association shortly after the war, testified, "Whatever success I enjoyed was directly linked to my mentor, Lawrence Wheeler" (quoted in Boling, "Lawrence Wheeler").

35. HBW to Indiana University Alumnus, April 3, 1944; IUA/C213/308/Indiana University Foundation, 1943–44.

36. Minutes of the Directors' Meeting of the Indiana University Foundation, December 12, 1944; IUA/C213/308/Indiana University Foundation, 1944–45.

37. Wheeler to HBW, February 6, 1946; IUA/C213/308/Indiana University Foundation, 1945–46.

38. BL, 375–76.

39. Adams's work toward a degree was interrupted by World War I. After the war he returned to IU and took enough credits to graduate in 1923, but he never applied for his degree. Adams received an honor-

ary master of laws degree in December 1942.

40. William Lowe Bryan to James S. Adams, December 6, 1944; IUA/C75/1/ Bryan, William & Charlotte Lowe, 1930–1944. On July 1, 1944, Bryan wrote to Wells, "Every day of these last seven years I have rejoiced that you are President of Indiana University." Wells replied, "The burdens of these seven years have been made lighter by your unfailing support and help," adding that he was fortunate indeed (WLB to HBW, July 1, 1944; HBW to WLB, July 1, 1944; IUA/C75/1/Bryan, William & Charlotte Lowe, 1930–1944).

41. See Schlesinger, *Act of Creation.* In addition to Wells, IU political scientist Edward Buehrig was present at the San Francisco conference as a member of the International Organization Section of the Postwar Planning Division of the State Department (Buehrig, "Political Science at Indiana University," 11n17).

42. BL, 378. He notes that Givens was "an honored Indiana University graduate."

43. Ibid., 379.

9. RENOUNCING PREJUDICE
The source of the epigraph is HBW, "Remarks on Layman Sunday, at the First Methodist Church, Bloomington, Indiana," 10:30 AM, March 5, 1944; IUA/ HBW presidential speech files.

1. Cothran, "The Attitude of Negro Students Toward Indiana University," 107–108. Blacks were excluded from ROTC with the canard that they all had flat feet.

2. IUA/C213/24/Anders, 1937–1945.

3. See Arsenault, *The Sound of Freedom: Marian Anderson, the Lincoln Memorial, and the Concert That Awakened America.*

4. "Resolutions presented to IU through Pres. Wells," Inter-Racial Commission, February 1942; IUA/C213/414/ Negro 1941–42.

5. Memos to Biddle, Clevenger, Shoemaker, and Smith, February 10, 1942; IUA/C213/414/Negro, 1941–42.

6. BL, 216.

7. Zora Clevenger to HBW, February 11, 1942; IUA/C213/414/Negro, 1941–42.

8. BL, 216–17. This account remains the only source of this story.

9. Walter C. Bailey to HBW, April 13, 1942; IUA/C213/414/Negro, 1941–42.

10. C. E. Edmondson to Walter C. Bailey, April 30, 1942; IUA/C213/414/Negro, 1941–42.

11. Charles W. Stewart to HBW, April 22, 1942; IUA/C213/414/Negro, 1941–42.

12. HBW to Stewart, May 5, 1942; IUA/C213/414/Negro, 1941–42.

13. Memo, "Negro Housing, 1941–42," IUA/C213/414/Negro, 1941–42.

14. Freyer, "The House That IU Built," 42.

15. Ibid., 42–43. For the story of Lincoln Hall, see BL, 218. In 1942, "Indiana University leased Kappa Alpha Psi house at 425 North Dunn from Mr. Dargan and completely redecorated it and made it available for housing of negro women. At the same time it leased the Dillon house at 426 East Tenth and provided accommodations for negro men. Both houses were under University rules and counselors were provided in each" (Harold W. Jordan, "War Housing on Bloomington Campus, July 1, 1942 to June 30, 1943," 4; IUA/C213/329/War Training Program, 1943–1944). The following year, housing for black men was "very slight," and so black women stayed in Kappa Alpha Psi and the Dillon house. Page 3 of following report from July 1, 1943 to June 30, 1944 (ibid.).

16. A series of brief memos was exchanged between Bartley and Wells following the performance. Wells laconically remarked, "maybe we should move Walter forward a little" in the auditorium. Walter Whitworth to Ross Bartley, n.d.; Bartley

to HBW, January 1943; Whitworth, "Marian Anderson Corrects a Flaw"; HBW to Bartley, January 25, 1943; IUA/C213/24/Anders, 1937–1945.

17. 1943 *Arbutus*, 153.

18. Sanders, "Leslie Pinckney Hill."

19. Beck, *Some Aspects of Race Relations at Indiana University*, 39.

20. IUMP, 83.

21. Beck, *Some Aspects of Race Relations at Indiana University*, 41.

22. I Corinthians 12:26–27.

23. Robson, "Open Letter on Race Hatred." See also Shapiro, *White Violence and Black Response*.

24. HBW, "Remarks on Layman Sunday, at the First Methodist Church, Bloomington, Indiana," 10:30 AM, March 5, 1944; IUA/HBW presidential speech files.

25. See Jaynes and Williams, *A Common Destiny*, 66–71.

26. Herbold, "Never a Level Playing Field."

27. HBW note; IUA/C213/414/Negro, 1944–45.

28. HBW to Prof. George W. Starr, School of Business, August 2, 1945; IUA/C213/414/Negro, 1945–46.

29. HBW to Robert W. Staums, field secretary, NAACP Indianapolis, August 22, 1945; IUA/C213/414/Negro, 1945–46.

30. Plew worked at the IMU for thirty-six years, retiring in 1983. He cut Wells's hair many times. After Plew retired, Wells went to Plew's barbershop on West Eleventh Street, and when Wells lost mobility, Plew came to his residence on East Tenth Street. John Plew, interview by James Capshew, January 28, 2005, WBP files; Beck, *Some Aspects of Race Relations*, 52–53; Leonard, "Tiny Barbershop Closing Its Door."

31. George Taliaferro, interview by James Capshew, March 27, 2003, WBP files. See also Knight, *Taliaferro*.

32. See Graham and Cody, *Getting Open*; and Gray, *Net Prophet*.

10. POSTWAR WORLD, HOME AND ABROAD

The source of the epigraph is MacClintock, "Wellsian Indiana for 25 Years," 13, 23.

1. Cohen, *The Shaping of American Higher Education*; Geiger, *Research and Relevant Knowledge*.

2. IUMP, 89.

3. Of the approximately 8 million veterans who used the benefits to 1951, 2.3 million attended colleges and universities.

4. "On the Campus."

5. IUMP, 46.

6. Ibid., 199.

7. Ibid.

8. Ibid., 201ff.

9. "On the Campus."

10. IUMP, 205.

11. Ibid., 213.

12. Quoted in ibid., 206.

13. Ibid., 209.

14. Ibid., 210–11.

15. Ibid., 211.

16. Ibid., 211–12.

17. Clark claimed, "No president of a major university was more conversant with what was actually going on in what appeared to be great confusion in crisis-construction" (ibid., 212).

18. Ibid., 213.

19. Ibid., 213.

20. Ibid., 225.

21. HBW, oral history interview by Bonnie Williams, March 19, 1992, Wylie House Collections. See also Capshew, "Home Design for Indiana University."

22. IUMP, 150, 180–81, 512.

23. Ibid., 17.

24. In this era, pervasive sex discrimination prevented the rise of gifted females, so nearly all deans, vice presidents, and other high-level administrators were male.

25. BL, 126.

26. Davis, *The Adventures of an Ultra-Crepidarian,* 351.

27. IUMP, 89.

28. Ibid.

29. Ibid., 103.

30. Skinner, "My Years at Indiana."

31. See Capshew, "Engineering Behavior."

32. Skinner, "Baby in a Box."

33. Skinner, *Walden Two.* See also Rutherford, *Beyond the Box.*

34. Thompson ran the composition program for the English Department. A colleague once described him as a "kindly, easy, gentle man, with a nice tough streak in him." Campbell, "The Department of English in the 1920's and 1930's," 124.

35. Quoted in BL, 284.

36. Ibid., 285.

37. Ibid., 287.

38. Quoted in ibid., 287.

39. Ibid., 289–90.

40. Quoted in ibid., 294.

41. Ibid., 296.

42. Quoted in ibid., 297.

43. Quoted in ibid., 300.

44. Ibid., 299.

45. Holmstedt, *The Indiana Conference of Higher Education,* 2.

46. Ibid., 3, 12–13.

47. It operated without a formal constitution until 1955 (ibid., 13).

48. Wells, "The Role of the University in a Democratic Society," Indiana Conference of Higher Education, November 7, 1947, 21; IUA/HBW presidential speech files; quoted in Holmstedt, *The Indiana Conference of Higher Education,* 29.

49. After many years of informal cooperation between member schools under the auspices of the Indiana Conference of Higher Education (ICHE), the Indiana Plan evolved and was presented formally in 1960. It restated its charter as a voluntary association comprising all thirty-three private, public, and church-related colleges and universities in the state. One

of its goals was to maintain a balance of 50 percent public and 50 percent private undergraduate enrollments, which it succeeded in doing from its founding in 1945. One valuable aspect of the group was to provide "the means for a common discussion and solution of the state's problems in higher education with the elimination of the frictions that so often exist." The two state universities, Indiana and Purdue, agreed not to create a branch campus or extension center without gaining the approval of any private institution serving the area (Holmstedt, *The Indiana Conference of Higher Education,* 82).

50. Peter Fraenkel in Brancolini, *The Vision of Herman B Wells.*

51. IUA/C75/50–52.

52. Under the Soviets, the University of Berlin was referred to as the University Unter den Linden, owing to its location on that broad boulevard. In 1949 it was renamed Humboldt University, in honor of its founder, Wilhelm von Humboldt, and his brother, Alexander von Humboldt.

53. BL, 314–15.

54. Lockridge, *The Shade of the Raintree,* 14, 451. In July 1947, Wells wrote a congratulatory note to Lockridge, adding his hope, "you may be one of the stalwarts in the maintenance of the great Hoosier literary tradition." Lockridge, who spent seven years crafting the novel, replied that he hoped his book would become "a permanent part of the Hoosier literary landscape." He closed with praise for Wells's work in "making a great university greater with each passing year." HBW to Ross Lockridge, Jr., July 26, 1947; Ross Lockridge, Jr., to HBW, August 23, 1947; IUA/C213/358/Lockridge, Ross 1938–1948.

55. The recollection of Helen Heady, who also remembered that her father, Austin Heady, came to the house and got rid of the poison, and poured the rest of the bottle in a nearby alley. It produced black

vapors. (Helen Heady, interview by James Capshew, October 2006; WBP files).

56. "Granville Wells."

57. John Hastings, oral history interview by Thomas Clark and Dorothy Collins, November 19, 1970; IUA/70-014.

58. Wells recalled later, "I was somewhat skeptical about the feasibility of the whole enterprise.... [I]t would be a very difficult project to initiate but I would take it to Clay" (Tent, *The Free University of Berlin*, 95).

59. Ibid.

60. Quoted in ibid.

61. Ibid., 95–96.

62. Ibid., 96.

63. Quoted in ibid.

64. Ibid., 94.

65. HBW to Marjorie Jean Smith, January 16, 1948; IUA/C75/50.

66. Quoted in Brancolini, *The Vision of Herman B Wells*.

67. BL, 245–46.

68. "Minutes of the Board of Director's Meeting," June 13, 1947; Wheeler to Wells, February 11, 1948; IUA/C213/308/Indiana University Foundation, 1947–48.

69. "Schedule of Investments," June 30, 1947; IUA/C213/308/Indiana University Foundation, 1947–48.

70. "Minutes of IU Foundation Board of Director's Meeting," June 13, 1948; IUA/C213/308/Indiana University Foundation, 1948–49.

71. "Minutes of the Meeting of the Indiana University Foundation Board of Directors," October 2, 1948; IUA/C213/308/Indiana University Foundation, 1948–49.

72. "Outline of Projects Book: What the Foundation Has Done Since June 1936" [October 1948]; IUA/C213/308/Indiana University Foundation, 1948–49.

73. Michaelmas, "Indiana, Our Indiana."

74. Wheeler to Alumnus, November 30, 1948; IUA/C213/308/Indiana University Foundation, 1948–49.

75. "Minutes of the Meeting of the Indiana University Foundation Board of Directors," June 4, 1949; IUA/C213/308/Indiana University Foundation, 1948–49.

76. According to American Alumni Council figures. HBW to Paul J. DeVault, November 3, 1949; IUA/C213/308/Indiana University Foundation, 1949–50.

77. Wells and Biddle talked about it as early as 1944 (HBW to Biddle, May 13, 1944; Biddle to HBW, May 19, 1944; IUA/C75/1/Biddle).

78. Cited in Savonius-Wroth, "Indiana University Press," 1.

79. Bernard Perry to Stith Thompson, December 10, 1949; Perry to HBW, January 4, 1950; Thompson to HBW, January 14, 1950; HBW to Perry, February 20, 1950 IUA/C213/565/University Press and Literary Quarterly, 1945–1953.

80. IDS, March 1950.

81. "II Report to the Faculty – Progress," Indiana University Press, April 1952; IUA/C213/565/University Press and Literary Quarterly, 1945–1953. The 1952 Pulitzer Prize in history went to R. Carlyle Buley, for *The Old Northwest*; the author had been a member of the history faculty since 1925.

82. Shalucha, "People Want to Become Self-Sufficient Gardeners"; "Garden Program Attracts National Attention."

83. Hargis and Williams, "Public Radio from Indiana University."

11. MUSIC APPRECIATION

The source of the epigraph is Long, "All's Wells That Ends Well."

1. Logan, *The Indiana University School of Music*, 23–25.

2. Ibid., 33ff.

3. It was one of three original buildings on the new 1885 campus. See Lahrman and Miller, *The History of Mitchell Hall, 1885–1986*.

4. Logan, *The Indiana University School of Music*, 27, 47–48, 111.

5. Dean Payne, Wells's chief assistant for faculty personnel, was of the opinion that, among the old guard, only Merrill should be asked to serve longer, even though he thought that Merrill's talents "were less those of a modern academic executive and more those of a sensitive artist." IUMP, 7.

6. Logan, *The Indiana University School of Music*, 99–100. Also described by Newell Long in "All's Wells That Ends Well." Wells was also heavily involved in recruiting Samuel T. Burns as professor of public school music in the summer of 1938. Logan, *The Indiana University School of Music*, 100; IUMP, 14.

7. Clemens, "An Historical Study of the Philosophies of Indiana University School of Music Administrators from 1910 to 1973," 71.

8. *Indiana University Bulletin*, 1939–40.

9. Logan, *The Indiana University School of Music*, 107–109.

10. Ibid., 109–110.

11. Ibid., 110–11.

12. IUMP, 483–84.

13. Logan, *The Indiana University School of Music*, 113.

14. Ibid., 114.

15. Ibid.

16. HBW to Ward Biddle, June 12, 1942, quoted in IUMP, 476.

17. HBW remarks in program of the Metropolitan Opera Association, 1946; IUA/C213/365/Metropolitan Opera Association, 1942–1962.

18. Logan, *The Indiana University School of Music*, 125–26.

19. From his younger days in the Jamestown Boys' Band to his college years in the Indiana University Band, Wells had made music. Not a particularly gifted player, Wells relished the exhilarating camaraderie and public exposure that came with band membership. The IU band provided a way to exercise his nascent entrepreneurial skills. As an undergraduate, he took music appreciation courses under Jack Geiger, a mainstay of the music school, who attracted many students with his jolly humor, even singing some of the parts of opera records he played for his classes (BL, 44).

20. Logan, *The Indiana University School of Music*, 133; italics original.

21. Ibid. The original source of the quotation is Bain, *Indiana University School of Music*, 5; of course, Bain was reconstructing the past to emphasize the historical inevitability of the rise of the music school during his twenty-five-year administration.

22. Logan speculates that Wells perhaps only developed the interest in music performance, as opposed to academic music, as a consequence of his recruiting visit to Texas in 1947 (133). My contention is that Wells's interest had been well developed and expressed before then. More accurately, Wells did not have a clear idea of how music might fit into the larger plans for IU when he hired Sanders in 1938, right before planning got underway for the IU Auditorium (née Hall of Music).

23. Logan, *The Indiana University School of Music*, 135.

24. Clemens, "An Historical Study," 149–51.

25. Logan, *The Indiana University School of Music*, 127.

26. Ibid., 154.

27. Ibid.

28. Ibid., 155.

29. Ibid., 118.

30. Clemens, "An Historical Study," 150.

31. Logan, *The Indiana University School of Music*, details the treatment of composer and pianist Anis Fuleihan (171–74).

32. Bain, *Indiana University School of Music*, 151.

33. Ibid., 149.

34. Baker received a master's degree in 1954, and returned as a faculty member in 1966 (Logan, *The Indiana University School of Music*, 175–76).

35. Eugene Weinberg, interview by Donald J. Gray, March 16, 2006; IUA/ Emeriti House oral histories.

36. 1956 Indiana University *Arbutus*, 144.

37. IUMP, 189, 499.

38. Ibid., 500.

39. Ibid., 500–501.

40. Ibid., 501.

41. Ibid., 502.

42. Tobias et al., eds., *Opera for All Seasons*.

43. BL, 258.

12. THE MAN BEHIND KINSEY

The source of the epigraph is IUMP, 285.

1. Gathorne-Hardy, *Alfred C. Kinsey*, 262.

2. Ibid., 249.

3. Christenson, *Kinsey*, 139.

4. Pomeroy, *Dr. Kinsey and the Institute for Sex Research*, 239.

5. Christenson, *Kinsey*, 139.

6. Pomeroy, *Dr. Kinsey and the Institute for Sex Research*, 239. Wells himself followed the practice of "plowing back" into the university any outside speaking fees or remuneration he received (HBW, oral history interview by James H. Jones, December 3, 1971, IUA/71-054.).

7. IUMP, 256.

8. Ibid., 257–59. By 1950, the male volume had sold more than three hundred thousand copies (266).

9. Ibid., 267.

10. Ibid., 268.

11. HBW, oral history interview by James H. Jones, December 3, 1971, IUA/ 71-054.

12. IUMP, 248.

13. There is no credible evidence that Wells ever dated. In the late 1990s, Wells told one of his nursing assistants, Liz

Egan, a story about his undergraduate crush on a nameless waitress who worked in a restaurant on Kirkwood across the street from the Sigma Nu house. He admired her from afar, and never communicated with her. She left a short time later (Liz Egan, personal communication, June 7, 2000).

14. Near the end of his life, he employed multiple houseboys, and there was one female, nonresidential helper in that group.

15. In an opinion piece (*Indianapolis Star*, 28 December 2000), Steve Sanders, defending the right to ask questions about Wells's sexual orientation, suggested: "It is perhaps ironic that as coy and discreet as he was about himself, Wells revered scholarship, and surely understood that biography in particular requires objective and complete assessment of its subject. Wells may not have told. But he would have defended the right to ask." Blaise Cronin, Dean of the IU School of Library and Information Science, reacted to Sanders's posing the question that Wells might have been gay, saying: "Some things are plausible; others are blindingly obvious. Wells's sexual orientation (active or passive) belonged to the latter category. I, of course have no first hand evidence to prove my assertion, but only a deaf and blind cultural anthropologist would have failed to pick up the secondary clues" (Cronin, "Gay Pride and Prejudice," 49–50).

16. Hesburgh, who took a vow of celibacy when he was ordained as a Catholic priest, reflected, "The vow of celibacy probably seems inhibiting or even unnatural to many, and it certainly is not a common calling. But for me, it has been, again, a liberating experience. Since I didn't belong to anyone, I belonged to everyone" (Hesburgh with Reedy, *God, Country, Notre Dame*, xi).

17. Wells, "Kinsey's 'Sexual Behavior in the Human Female' Receives Widespread Public Attention."

18. Wells kept on defending Kinsey and the Institute to the very end of his life. In 1998, the Indiana General Assembly threatened to withdraw funding from the Kinsey Institute after the new wave of Kinsey biographies appeared. In a letter to Governor Frank O'Bannon urging him to reject the proposed legislation, Wells recalled the heyday of controversy over the Kinsey studies fifty years before: "I told the Trustees that, as a public university, we must protect scientific research, regardless of how controversial it may be to particular individuals, groups or segments of society. I felt this principle was inviolate since no state university can thrive if it is beholden to special interests.... Today, more than a half-century after that initial conversation with our Trustees, my feelings have never been stronger" (HBW to Frank O'Bannon, January 27, 1998; IUA/ Accession 2006/010 HBW Chancellors records/Kinsey Institute-Letter to General Assembly, 1998.

13. A METROPOLIS OF BOOKS

The source of the epigraph is HBW, "Dedication Convocation of the Lilly Library," October 3, 1960; IUA/HBW presidential speech files.

1. Alexander, a 1901 graduate of IU, had worked his way through school as a library "stack boy." After graduation he became the reference librarian. In 1905 he left for Swarthmore College, where president Joseph Swain selected him as registrar, and later dean, before his return to IU in 1921. He died in 1943, shortly following his retirement.

2. Wells cited Miller as IU's first professionally trained head librarian in BL, 259.

3. In a November 1943 letter to Walter Jessup, Wells talks about releasing money from departmental control and using it under the direction of the Graduate School (and Dean Payne) to purchase scientific equipment and library materials (IUMP, 358).

4. *Indianapolis News,* December 5, 1941.

5. A shrewd judge of character, Wells realized IU needed self-motivated leaders, and was comfortable sharing the spotlight with colleagues.

6. IUMP, 181.

7. Perry to HBW, June 18, 1954; quoted in Savonius-Wroth, "Indiana University Press."

8. IDS, March 20, 1959; see also "Report on Indiana University Press, February 26, 1960; IUA/C213/566/University Press, 1953–1961.

9. Savonius-Wroth, "Indiana University Press."

10. Ibid. See also Keys and Galliher, *Confronting the Drug Control Establishment.*

11. Savonius-Wroth, "Indiana University Press."

12. IUMP, 515–17.

13. Madison, *Eli Lilly,* 6–37.

14. See Madison, *Eli Lilly.*

15. Silver, *J. K. Lilly Jr.,* 7.

16. Ibid., 8.

17. Randall, *Dukedom,* 352.

18. Byrd, "Introduction," 6–8.

19. Byrd, "Introduction," 9. See also IUMP, 517.

20. Randall, *Dukedom,* 353.

21. Some thought the severe lines of the structure resembled a mausoleum.

22. HBW, "Dedication Convocation of the Lilly Library," October 3, 1960; IUA/ HBW presidential speech files, 5.

23. IUMP, 307–308.

24. Ibid., 188.

25. Quotation in ibid., 521.

26. *IU Library Annual Report, 1937–38.* For 1936–37, in a nationwide ranking of forty-two university libraries, IU was thirtieth. Miller reported 2.3 million items in the university holdings in 1957 (IUMP, 517). In 1962, the total collections grew

to 4,053,488 (*IU Library Annual Report, 1961–62*).

27. Quoted in I U M P, 194.

28. Ibid., 194–95.

29. Ibid., 544, 625.

30. Dorothy C. Collins, H W S, 12.

14. EXPANDING THE UNIVERSITY'S UNIVERSE

The source of the epigraph is B L, 352. The founder of Methodism, John Wesley, said, "The world is my parish," which underlined the missionary nature of his religious movement.

1. Indiana University Foundation, Annual Report, 1949–50; I U A/C213/308/Indiana University Foundation, 1949–50.

2. HBW to J. A. Franklin, treasurer, November 21, 1950; I U A/C213/308/Indiana University Foundation, 1950–51.

3. Schwarb, *The Little 500*.

4. Wilcox to State Chairman, July 25, 1951; I U A/C213/308/Indiana University Foundation, 1951–52.

5. Minutes of the Meeting of the I U F Board of Directors, October 26, 1951; I U A/C213/308/Indiana University Foundation, 1951–52.

6. Minutes of the Meeting of the I U F Board of Directors, May 9, 1952; I U A/C213/308/Indiana University Foundation, 1951–52.

7. Heighway to Members of the Board of Directors, April 19, 1952; I U A/C213/308/Indiana University Foundation, Board of Directors Meeting, May 9, 1952.

8. HBW to Wilcox, May 20, 1952; I U A/C213/308/Indiana University Foundation, Board of Directors Meeting, May 9, 1952.

9. Wilcox to Board of Directors, August 18, 1952; I U A/C213/308/Indiana University Foundation, 1952–53. Later, Beck Chapel, funded in part by the donation of Frank O. Beck, campus chaplain, was completed in 1956.

10. *Indiana University Foundation 50th Anniversary Report*, 8.

11. Day, *The Development of Chemistry at Indiana University*, 463–71; I U M P, 449–45. Day cites bizarre stories falsely attributing the funding of Ballantine Hall to income from the sales of Crest toothpaste. See also Hunt, "Oral History."

12. Wells, *A Man, an Institution, and an Era*.

13. "Dr. Herman B Wells," 4–6.

14. The site of the President's House was selected in 1915, but Bryan deferred to other university needs and did not approve construction until 1923. Completed in July 1924, Bryan insisted on contributing $10,000 toward its construction (Myers, *History of Indiana University*, 251, 260).

15. Bryan and Bryan, *Last Words*, 7.

16. Phil Amerson, Wells's pastor at the First United Methodist Church, said, "With the first university, Jefferson put a library at the center. At I U, Wells put a chapel, suggesting that Jefferson might have had it right by assuming the intellect is at the heart of the university, but not entirely right" (quoted in Pete, "Funeral to Celebrate Wells' Life."

17. Wells recounted, "The meetings also would give insights into as yet not generally discernable intellectual, political, and economic currents abroad in the world. This was very exciting for me. To a small-town lad from Indiana it opened undreamed-of vistas" (B L, 369).

18. Ibid., 370–71.

19. HBW, "Remarks at Andrew Carnegie Commemorative Luncheon," New York, November 19, 1954; I U A/HBW presidential speech files. Republished in Wells, *Being Lucky Postscript*, 44–47.

20. Ibid., 45–46. See also McPherson, *Temples of Knowledge*.

21. HBW, "Remarks at Andrew Carnegie Commemorative Luncheon," 46.

22. Ibid.

23. Ibid., 47.

24. The group existed under the name Committee of Thirteen until 1951, when its name was changed to Council of Ten.

25. BL, 137–38.

26. Wells, "A Case Study on Interinstitutional Cooperation," 356.

27. The Big Ten's formal name was the Western Collegiate Athletic Association.

28. Wells, "A Case Study on Interinstitutional Cooperation," 356–58.

29. Wells, "A Case Study on Interinstitutional Cooperation," 356. See also HBW, memo, "A Case Study on Interinstitutional Cooperation," January 22, 1968; Howard University/Board of Trustees Records/Dr. Herman B Wells."

30. Wells, "A Case Study on Interinstitutional Cooperation," 356. See also Nissan and Burlingame, "Collaboration Among Institutions."

31. Orlando Taylor, interview by James Capshew, September 21, 2005, WBP files.

32. As black studies was becoming institutionalized in a new Department of Afro-American Studies, Taylor was appointed dean of Afro-American Affairs in 1969, but his appointment was rescinded after he became involved in a campus controversy (see chapter 17). See Wynkoop, *Dissent in the Heartland*.

33. Logan, *Howard University*, 537.

34. The modern ceremonial Indiana University Mace, derived from medieval sources and used as a symbol of authority, was another tradition instituted under the Wells administration. It was a gift of the local chapter of Phi Delta Theta in 1949.

35. See Moskowitz and Feeney, "Civil Rights Trailblazer Atkins Dies at 69."

36. Schoch, *Leo R. Dowling International Center*.

37. Ibid., 3.

38. Thomas House was eventually torn down to make way for Forest Residence Hall.

39. Foreign enrollments increased to 1,442 in 1970 and nearly 2,000 in 1980 while the center continued its operations. Dowling retired in 1977 and died in 1986; in 1992 the facility was renamed the Leo R. Dowling International Center. "In his 34 years of service to IU international students, it is said that Leo Dowling entertained every international student in his home at least once" (Schoch, *Leo R. Dowling International Center*, 5–6).

40. BL, 246.

41. O'Meara, "A Short History of the IU-NIDA Partnership"; BL, 245–48.

42. Walter Laves (1902–83) first met Wells during World War II in Washington, where he worked for the Bureau of the Budget and Wells was on assignment at the State Department. They met again serving on the U.S National Commission for UNESCO, of which Laves was chairman and Wells was vice-chairman in 1953–54. Laves was an IU faculty member from 1954 until his retirement in 1972 (BL, 380, 382).

43. O'Meara, "A Short History of the IU-NIDA Partnership," 3.

44. Ibid.

45. Quoted in ibid., 4.

46. Sutton was president of Indiana University from 1968 to 1971.

47. Ryan was president of Indiana University from 1971 to 1987.

48. Wells, "Widening Horizons," 140.

49. Byrum Carter, interview by Donald J. Gray; IUA/Emeriti House oral histories.

50. Laves became a member of IU's Department of Government (now Political Science) in 1954.

51. Educational Policies Commission, *Manpower and Education*.

52. Macleod, Review of *Manpower and Education*, 174.

53. BL, 386. The paper was later published as Lewis, Pinnell, and Wells,

"Needs, Resources, and Priorities in Higher Education Planning."

54. Educational Policies Commission, *Higher Education in a Decade of Decision.*

55. BL, 387.

56. Educational Policies Commission, *Higher Education in a Decade of Decision,* 98–99.

57. Ibid., 104.

58. Ibid., 105.

59. HBW to Sec State John Foster Dulles, June 19, 1957; IUA/C213/553/United Nations General Assembly, 1957–58.

60. HBW to Tom Spies, August 8, 1957; IUA/C213/553/United Nations General Assembly, 1957–58.

61. Brokenburr, an African American, sent a note of congratulations to Wells, offering his assistance (Brokenburr to HBW, [n.d.]; IUA/C213/553/United Nations-Letters of Congratulations).

62. "Report on the Twelfth Session of the General Assembly of the United Nations."

63. BL, 330.

64. See Walter A. McDougall, *The Heavens and the Earth.*

65. Ransel, *The Russian and East European Institute at Indiana University,* 2.

66. Quoted in ibid., 4.

67. Ibid.

68. Lombardi, "Indiana University," 103.

69. See ibid. for a sketch of international education at IU through the early 1980s.

70. Thomson and Laves, *Cultural Relations,* 127.

71. Scaife was president of the Board of Trustees of the University of Pittsburgh, and a fellow at Yale University. He died shortly after the trip. See BL, 340ff.

72. *Report on Higher Education in the Soviet Union.* See also "Crusading Educator."

73. *Report on Higher Education in the Soviet Union,* 23–24.

15. PASSING THE PRESIDENTIAL TORCH

The source of the epigraph is Cook, *The Book of Positive Quotations,* 20.

1. Edward E. Edwards and HBW, oral history interview by Thomas Clark and Dorothy Collins, August 5, 1974, IUA/74-011.

2. Around the same time, Wells began telling a story that his upcoming resignation, after twenty-five years in the position, was part of a plan he had made in 1938 with the trustees. This alleged agreement with the trustees is not supported by primary sources. Of course, it could have been made orally or informally in some other way. It seems plausible for 1938 because there was a general feeling that William Lowe Bryan had remained too long in the presidency when he retired after thirty-five years at age seventy-six. With the advent of a university retirement plan in 1937, mandatory retirement for administrators was set at sixty-five. Perhaps the story was an easy way to avoid talking about other issues.

3. Hennessy, *Herman B Wells,* 26–27.

4. Wells, "Widening Horizons," 140.

5. *Bloomington Herald-Telephone,* April 27, 1960; Wilson and Brondfield, *The Big Ten,* 298–316; Hammel and Klingelhoffer, *Glory of Old IU*; Byrd and Moore, *Varsity Sports at Indiana University.*

6. John Mee to Bill Orwing, March 7, 1961; IUA/C213/53/Athletics-Department Correspondence, 1960–61.

7. One of Wells's secretaries remembered that the NCAA sanctions were "one of the most disappointing events" of his presidency, and "weighed heavily" on his mind. But Wells "did not publicly reprimand any member of the Athletic Department and no one lost his job," which was "a testament to his sincere belief in the integrity of the Athletic Department" (Hennessy, *Herman B Wells,* 45, 53).

8. *Bloomington Herald-Telephone,* January 17, 1961.

9. Garrison, Letter to the Editor; HBW to Ben [Garrison], January 24, 1961; Roger Buck to HBW, January 21, 1961; IUA/C213/600/Willbern, Glen D., 1938–1961.

10. IUA/C213/600/Willbern, Glen D., 1938–1961.

11. Wells, "The Early History of Indiana University."

12. Ibid., 115.

13. Ibid., 121–22.

14. Ibid., 126.

15. Ibid.

16. Quotation from HBW, oral history interview by Bonnie Williams, March 19, 1992, Wylie House Collections. See also *Wylie House Museum.*

17. A similar award was created by Wells's successor, Elvis J. Stahr, in 1966, to honor seniors who have excelled academically while serving as student leaders. Three to five seniors annually receive the Elvis J. Stahr Distinguished Senior Award.

18. "Wells Receives Local NAACP's Annual Award."

19. Hesburgh and Wells held compatible views on the power of universities in building civil communities and worked tirelessly to advance the cause of higher education, both in their own institutions as well as for the commonwealth. Their unselfish leadership of the Hoosier state's consortium of universities, both public and private, made Indiana a national model of cooperation. They also shared elements of an ascetic, if not quite monkish, personal style in their bachelorhood and lack of ostentation. See Hesburgh with Reedy, *God, Country, Notre Dame.*

20. HBW, Commencement speech, June 1962; IUA/HBW presidential speech files.

21. Ibid.

22. Ibid.

23. "Wells Gets a Surprise Honor."

24. John W. Ashton, recommendation for Wells [May 1962?]; IUA/C212/7/Honorary Degrees Committee 1961–1962.

25. IUA/C212/7/Honorary Degrees Committee 1961–1962.

26. "Wells Gets a Surprise Honor."

16. EDUCATION AND WORLD AFFAIRS

The source of the epigraph is Thomson and Laves, *Cultural Relations,* 195.

1. Committee on the University and World Affairs, *The University and World Affairs,* 77.

2. Henry Heald to HBW, December 15, 1960, quoted in Hertko, "The Internationalization of American Higher Education," 28.

3. Ibid., 29.

4. Ibid., 30–33.

5. Ibid., 33.

6. Report of the Task Force to the Carnegie Corporation, the Rockefeller Foundation, and the Ford Foundation, "A New Agency in the Field of Education and World Affairs," October 16, 1961, cited in Hertko, "The Internationalization of American Higher Education," 35.

7. Hertko, "The Internationalization of American Higher Education," 38.

8. Ibid., 41.

9. Ibid., 41–43.

10. "Certificate of Incorporation of Education and World Affairs," September 14, 1962, cited in Hertko, "The Internationalization of American Higher Education," 44.

11. Ibid.

12. BL, 356.

13. Education and World Affairs, *The University Looks Abroad,* 222.

14. Ibid., 356–58. See also Hertko, "The Internationalization of American Higher Education," 51–60.

15. BL, 436–37; Sibley, "State University."

16. "Crusading Educator."

17. Wells, *The Legislature and Higher Education in New York State.*

18. Sibley, "State University," 13.

19. Hertko, "The Internationalization of American Higher Education," 67.

20. Ibid., 69–70.

21. Ibid., 88, 100.

22. HBW to John Gardner, January 28, 1968, cited in Hertko, "The Internationalization of American Higher Education," 125.

23. Hertko, "The Internationalization of American Higher Education," 154–56. Wells devotes a chapter to his experiences in EWA in BL (352–62), and provides a gloss on its activities and personalities.

24. BL, 362.

25. IUMP, 546–48.

26. Ibid., 548.

27. See BL, 476–77.

28. M. H. Farzad, personal communication, August 3, 2010.

29. Ibid.

17. BACK TO BASICS

The source of the first epigraph is from Wells, "Message to the University Community," reprinted in BL, 466. The second epigraph is emblazoned above a plaque of the names of donors to the IU Foundation located in the Indiana Memorial Union; its original source is obscure.

1. Elvis J. Stahr, "Resignation from the Presidency of the University," to IU Trustees, July 6, 1968; IUA/C218/Board of Trustees Minutes/July 6, 1968.

2. IUMP, 563.

3. Wynkoop, *Dissent in the Heartland,* 125.

4. Ibid., 121.

5. Ibid., 122–23.

6. BL, 361, 427.

7. IUMP, 235.

8. Wynkoop, *Dissent in the Heartland,* 6.

9. *Indiana Daily Student,* May 19, 1961, 1, as quoted in Wynkoop, *Dissent in the Heartland,* 6.

10. HBW, "State of the University Address," October 10, 1968, 2; IUA/HBW presidential speech files.

11. Ibid.

12. Ibid.

13. Ibid., 8.

14. HBW, "Message to the University Community," in BL, 466–76.

15. BL, 191.

16. HBW, "Message to the University Community," in BL, 466.

17. Ibid.

18. Ibid., 467–69.

19. Ibid., 469–71.

20. Ibid., 471–73. The Bloomington Faculty Council approved a classified-research policy for the first time in 1971.

21. Ibid., 473–74.

22. Ibid., 475.

23. Ibid., 476. In a rare display of personal pride, Wells wrote, "I am very proud of the document" and had it reprinted in an appendix (BL, 191).

24. Wynkoop, *Dissent in the Heartland,* 72.

25. BL, 428.

26. William E. Scott, in "Remembering Herman B Wells."

27. Wynkoop, *Dissent in the Heartland,* 82.

28. Ibid., 83.

29. Ibid., 86–87, 133.

30. John R. Krueger, in "Remembering Herman B Wells."

31. Ken Ritchie, in "Remembering Herman B Wells."

32. Krampetz and Vicinus, *Disorientation: Like It Is at IU.* Comprising graduate students and faculty, the New University Conference was formed in March 1968 and was disbanded in 1972. At its height in 1970–71, it had two thousand paid members with chapters on sixty campuses. See Pincus and Ehrlich, "The New University Conference."

33. Krampetz and Vicinus, *Disorientation: Like It Is at IU.*

34. After the death of his wife, Jean, Sutton remarried in March 1971. He died in April 1972 as a result of a car accident.

35. IUA/C74/2/Nobel Peace Prize Nomination.

36. Nothing further is known about the discussion that took place among the Nobel Committee members since the Nobel archives are closed for fifty years after the date of the event.

37. *Indiana University Foundation 50th Anniversary Report*, 9.

38. Ibid., 10–11.

39. BL, 173.

40. Waldman with Klemkosky, *The First One Hundred Years of Education for Business*.

41. Charlotte Pitcher to Owen D. Nichols, May 24, 1973; Dorothy Collins to James E. Cheek, June 18, 1973; HBW to Owen D. Nichols, August 10, 1973; Howard University Archives/Board of Trustees Records/Dr. Herman B. [*sic*] Wells (Laws).

42. Leonard, "For the Legacy of Herman B Wells, the Sky Is the Limit."

43. IUA/Ref Files/Wells, Herman B – Minor Planet.

44. Wells incorporated the tribute in BL, 25–28.

18. BEING PLUCKY

The source of the epigraph is from Peckham, *Indiana*, 146.

1. Clark, *Indiana University*.

2. IUMP, 652.

3. BL, ix.

4. The phrasing is indebted to Eric Sandweiss, personal communication, November 28, 2010.

5. Warriner, "The Veterans of World War II at Indiana University."

6. IUMP, xxi.

7. Gallman, "Herman as Machiavelli."

8. Peckham, *Indiana*, 188–89.

9. See Capshew, "Boone County Days."

10. BL, 9. Gallman thought Wells was a splendid example of a "Victorian optimist" in his ultimate faith in mankind's progress. "Fundamentally it was the belief that our species could and would become ever more civilized, that the future would be better than the past, that a kind of vaguely defined perfectibility was within reach," Gallman mused (John Gallman, personal communication, February 26, 2009). Marked by the reign of Queen Victoria of England from the 1830s to her death in 1901, Victorian-era attitudes and values were common for decades after.

11. Nicholson, *A Hoosier Chronicle*, 606.

12. BL, 9.

13. Ibid., 21, 25.

14. Ibid., 25.

15. Ibid., 26–27.

16. Ibid., 22. For a more complete account, see Capshew, "Boone County Days."

17. BL, 26.

18. Ibid., 18.

19. In early January 1937, a prostatic examination was conducted on Wells by W. F. Martin, M.D., at Battle Creek Sanitarium. Martin reported, "He had mumps and orchitis with partial atrophy of the right testicle which has remained very sensitive and any pressure or manipulation causes pain." If the pain "annoys him seriously and continues," the doctor advised removal of the testicle, adding, "I am sure it is non-functioning and of no value" (Battle Creek Sanitarium to HBW, January 6, 1937; IUA/C75/2/Health).

20. BL, 21.

21. The address was first published by Wells as "How to Succeed as a University President Without Really Trying." The speech was included in chapter 9 of BL, 140–53. Shepard Mead's bestselling humor book, *How to Succeed in Business Without Really Trying: A Dastard's Guide to Fame and Fortune* (1952) skewered 1950s

corporate America. In 1961, it inspired a Broadway musical of the same name, which received a Pulitzer Prize for Drama in 1962.

22. BL, 35.

23. The Travelers' Century Club website, www.travelerscenturyclub.org.

24. Vignettes of some of the world leaders Wells had met were eventually published in Wells, *Being Lucky Postscript*.

25. BL, xiii.

26. Pittman, "Herman B Wells."

27. "Wells"; "Herman B Wells."

28. "Books Reveal Legendary Lives of Hovde, Wells"; Royalty, "Purdue's 'Beer-Drinking' Educator"; Smith, "Folklore Shrouds Ex-I.U. President"; Fancher, "Wells Spent Life 'Being Lucky.'"

29. Pittman, "Herman B Wells."

30. Green, "Brief Biographical Sketch"; Sheridan, "Chancellor Wells' Memoirs"; "Wells Attributes Success to 'Being Lucky.'"

31. *Being Lucky* has remained in print to the present day.

32. Evans, "Reader Is the 'Lucky' One."

33. Horner, review of *Being Lucky*.

34. Henry, review of *Being Lucky*.

35. Perkins, review of *Being Lucky*.

36. Neufeldt, review of *Being Lucky*.

37. Fancher, "A Wells Album," 39.

38. Sauvain, "History: Part One."

39. Ibid.

40. Ibid.

41. Ibid.

42. IUA/Accession 2006/010 Box 44.

43. Financial Report, September 30, 1983; Executive Director's Annual Report to Members, September 1983; IUA/Accession 2006/010 Box 44.

44. Andrews, "Wells Could Lose $1 Million."

45. IUA/Accession 2006/010 Box 44.

46. Wells, "Preface to the 1992 Reprinting of *Being Lucky*," BL, xvi.

19. AN ICON AGING IN PLACE

The source of the epigraph is chapter 2 of Charles Dickens, *Barnaby Rudge* (1841).

1. Joan Bennett, in "Remembering Herman B Wells."

2. Mary Gaither, interview by James Capshew, October 20, 2005; WBP files.

3. Kenneth Gros Louis, personal communication, March 9, 2010.

4. Pinnell, "The Foundation."

5. Wells, "The Campaign for Indiana."

6. "The Eighties and Beyond."

7. Gilbert, "Indictments Near in IU Foundation Probe."

8. When Pinnell became president in 1983, he discovered the existence of a secret "cash advance" account that provided no-interest loans to top IU Foundation executives for personal use. Several years earlier, President Bill Armstrong had borrowed $18,000; Vice President of Finance James Elliott, $49,000; and Director of Real Estate Richard Beard, $27,000. Pinnell requested the executives pay back the money (which they did), and quietly abolished the unaudited account. In spring 1985, the Federal Bureau of Investigation launched an investigation. The agency had jurisdiction because the Foundation was a conduit for federal research grants won by faculty. The executives involved were interviewed by the FBI, and in late September 1988, after more than three years, a federal grand jury indicted Armstrong, Elliott, and Beardon on felony conversion charges for the use of Foundation money for their own benefit and for lying to investigators. By the following summer, all of the charges were dismissed on various technical grounds. See Gilbert, "Indictments Near in IU Foundation Probe," "Foundation Execs Charged," "IU Foundation Officials Greet Court Ruling with Optimism," and "Beard Case Closed – All Charges Dropped."

9. The only other time Wells consented to have his name attached to a facility or program was in 1991, when the Herman B Wells Center for Pediatric Research at IU's Riley Hospital for Children in Indianapolis was opened.

10. Wells, *Being Lucky Postscript.*

11. Brancolini, *The Vision of Herman B Wells.*

12. IU Foundation, *Herman B Wells Scholars Program.*

13. Until 1958, the first year of dental school could be completed on the Bloomington campus. Maesaka's father, Howard Maesaka, was a 1926 graduate of the IU School of Dentistry and practiced dentistry in Wahiawa, Hawai'i, and was acquainted with Wells and Claude Rich. Howard arranged for Bert Kobayashi to work as a Wells houseboy. Bert became the first of six Hawai'ian houseboys in succession (Ray Maesaka to James H. Capshew, May 10, 1991; JHC files).

14. Ray Maesaka to James H. Capshew, January 31, 1991; JHC files.

15. Capshew, *Students in Residence.*

16. Sauvain, "History: Part One," 6.

17. Ibid.

18. Andrews, "Wells Could Lose $1 Million."

19. IUA/Accession 2006/010 Box 44.

20. Sauvain, "History: Part One," 6.

21. See Sauvain, "History: Part Two."

22. Sauvain, "History: Part Two," 3.

23. Invitation and program of Meadowood's fifteenth anniversary. HBW/Accession 2006/010 Box 44.

24. Ibid.

25. Capshew, *Students in Residence.*

26. HWS.

27. Dottie Collins, HWS, 13.

28. Tom Ehrlich, HWS, 18; Tom Ehrlich, personal communication, January 26, 2009.

29. Eugene Brancolini, interview by James Capshew, October 9, 2008; WBP files.

30. Ibid.

31. Ibid.

32. Brancolini, *The Vision of Herman B Wells.*

33. Kearney, "Main Air Studio at WFHB." See also IDS, February 21, 1994; *Bloomington Herald-Times,* December 17, 1995; Howley, "Talking about Public Affairs Programming," and *Community Media.*

34. Wright, "Wells Adds Another Sagamore to His Honors."

20. A PEACEFUL PASSING

The source of the first epigraph is Hammarskjöld, *Markings,* 159. The source of the second epigraph is from Martone, "Country Roads Lined with Running Fences," 132.

1. IDS, March 8, 2000; update 9 March 2000; Wright, "Wells in Good Health."

2. Lalwani, "Friends, Family Remember Wells." Brand, in *A Celebration of Life,* 9. Brand told the same story at the Herman B Wells Centennial Celebration, June 7, 2002.

3. Nathan Zapf, quoted in Schuckel, "An Indiana Treasure."

4. Ibid.

5. "Chancellor Herman B Wells: We Were 'Lucky' to Have Known Him," IU Office of Communications and Marketing website, March 19, 2000, http://newsinfo.iu.edu/OCM/releases/wellsrem.htm.

6. Clarke, "A Day like No Other."

7. Pete, "Losing a Legend."

8. "Herman B Wells, 1902–2000."

9. Newman, "Herman B Wells."

10. "Indiana's Education Giant."

11. Schuckel, "An Indiana Treasure."

12. Ibid., A2.

13. Eskovitz, "Sigma Nu Honors Herman B."

14. Philip Amerson, interview with James Capshew, September 19, 2000; WBP files.

15. Ibid.

16. First United Methodist Church, Ushering plan for Wells funeral, [March 2000].

17. Order of Worship, Celebration of the Life of Herman B Wells, 1902–2000, March 22, 2000, 11:00 AM, First United Methodist Church, Bloomington, Indiana 47402; WBP files.

18. Philip Amerson, "Words of Christian Hope," funeral for Herman B Wells, March 22, 2000; WBP files.

19. Order of Worship.

20. *A Celebration of a Life.*

21. James H. Capshew, Donald J. Gray, and Henry H. H. Remak, "Chancellor Herman B Wells (June 2, 1902–March 18, 2000)," BFC Circular B32–2000. Reprinted in the appendix.

22. Kibbler, "The Life of a Legend."

23. Quoted in Will, "Dementia Takes Spirit before Body."

21. KEEPING THE
MEMORY GREEN

The source of the epigraph is chapter 22 of E. M. Forster, *Howards End* (1910).

1. York and Bland, "Sculpture of Wells in the Works."

2. Horn, "Statue of Herman Wells Dedicated."

3. York and Bland, "Sculpture of Wells in the Works."

4. Horn, "Statue of Herman Wells Dedicated."

5. *The Wells Archive.*

6. Bantin and Capshew, *The Wells Archive: Exploring the World of Higher Education.*

7. The painting hangs in the stairway off the hotel lobby of the Indiana Memorial Union.

8. The weekend following the Wells Archive symposium, another, very different event was dedicated to the memory of Wells. The Forty-second Monroe County Fall Festival offered a tribute to the late chancellor, a longtime supporter. The fes-tival, first held in 1935, was an expression of town pride and unity for Ellettsville, a village about seven miles west of Bloomington. Combining elements of a county fair and a Chautauqua meeting, it featured "varied exhibits, spectacular parades with brass bands and notable dignitaries, elaborate queen coronations, educational and religious programs, children's contests, family reunions, and wholesome entertainment, all presented absolutely free." The printed program's cover art featured a photograph of Jack's Defeat Creek, a well-known Ellettsville landmark, and the Christian-inflected motto for the year, "To God Be the Glory." Inside was a tribute to Wells, noting that he first become involved in the celebration in 1937, as Acting President, when he arranged for IU's Marching Hundred band to play. In 1951, he presented loving cups to the oldest man and woman at the festival. He had a part in subsequent festivals over the years. ("Dr. Herman B Wells," 4–6.)

9. Meunier, "One Year after His Death."

10. Schedule card, IUAM, Fall 2001–Spring 2002; WBP files.

11. Berry, "A Collector's Legacy."

12. Ibid.

13. The model, about six feet in length, resided for many years in the back patio of Wells's next-door neighbors, Cecil and Inez Harlos, at 1331 East Tenth Street, now the headquarters of the Wells Scholars Program.

14. Quoted in Trivedi, "Art in Everyday Life." See also Capshew, "Home Design for Indiana University."

15. The organizing group included Brian Kearney, James Capshew, Laura Plummer, Catherine Gray, and Michael Nelson.

16. "The Naming Ceremony for the Herman B Wells Library, Friday, June 17, 2005, 4 p.m., Library South Lawn"; IUA/Ref File: Buildings – IU Bloomington

Library (1969). D. Brady Egan, an undergraduate, reported that fellows students now say that they are going to "spend the evening with Herman" when they trek to the library (personal communication, December 28, 2010).

17. Hinnefeld, "Faculty Ask for Review of Herbert."

18. Acting Dean of the Libraries Patricia A. Steele, Remarks on Wells bust unveiling, October 19, 2007; WBP archives.

EPILOGUE

The source of the first epigraph is Francis Bacon, "Of Great Place," in *Essays* (1625). The source of the second epigraph is Otto Fenichel, quoted in Jacoby, *The Repression of Psychoanalysis*, 61.

1. Reprinted in the Appendix.

2. Devereux, *Re-Visioning the Earth*, 82.

3. Brancolini, *The Vision of Herman B Wells*.

Bibliography

Acheson, Dean. *Present at the Creation: My Years in the State Department.* New York: Norton, 1969.

Alexander, William A. "The Indiana University Library," in *History of Indiana University,* vol. 2, *1902–1937: The Bryan Administration,* Burton Dorr Myers, 597–611. Bloomington: Indiana University, 1952.

Anderson, Virginia. *The Auditorium at Indiana University: 50th Anniversary.* Bloomington: IU Marketing Services, 1991.

Andrews, Greg. "Wells Could Lose $1 Million over Loan for Meadowood." *Indiana Daily Student,* November 20, 1986.

Angell, Robert Cooley. *The Campus: A Study of Contemporary Undergraduate Life in the American University.* New York: Appleton, 1928.

Armstrong, Byron K. "The Colored Population of Bloomington." A.B. thesis, Indiana University, 1913.

Arndt, Richard T. *The First Resort of Kings: American Cultural Diplomacy in the Twentieth Century.* Washington, D.C.: Potomac Books, 2005.

Arsenault, Raymond. *The Sound of Freedom: Marian Anderson, the Lincoln Memorial, and the Concert That Awakened America.* New York: Bloomsbury Press, 2009.

Austin, Douglas V., and David D. Austin. "The Indiana Bankers Association: A Century of Progress and Change." *The Hoosier Banker* 81, no. 11 (1997): 6–21.

Backman, Earl L., ed. *Approaches to International Education.* New York: Macmillan, 1984.

Baden, Linda J., and Theodore R. Bowie. *Indiana University Art Museum, 1941–1982.* Bloomington: Indiana University Art Museum, 1982.

Bain, Wilfred C. *Indiana University School of Music: The Bain Regime, 1947–1973.* Bloomington, Ind.: Privately published, 1980.

———. *Indiana University Opera Theatre, 1948–1973.* Bloomington, Ind.: Privately published, [1990].

Bantin, Philip C., and James H. Capshew, eds. *The Wells Archive: Exploring the World of Higher Education.* Bloomington: Indiana University Libraries, 2000.

Beck, Daisy Woodward. *Once over Lightly: An Indiana University Story.* Bloomington, Ind.: n.p., 1961.

Beck, Frank O. *Some Aspects of Race Relations at Indiana University, My Alma Mater.* Bloomington, Ind.: Privately published, 1959.

Bell, Janet Cheatham. *The Time and Place That Gave Me Life.* Bloomington: Indiana University Press, 2007.

Berger, Ruth. "The IU Cyclotron as a Scientific Instrument, or, What the Social

Construction Was Constructed From." Unpublished manuscript.

Berry, S. L. "A Collector's Legacy." *Indianapolis Star*, October 28, 2001, I1.

Blake, I. George. *Paul V. McNutt: Portrait of a Hoosier Statesman*. Indianapolis: Central Publishing, 1966.

Bledstein, Burton J. *The Culture of Professionalism: The Middle Class and the Development of Higher Education in America*. Norton: New York, 1976.

"Books Reveal Legendary Lives of Hovde, Wells." *Indianapolis Star*, July 20, 1980.

Bossard, James H. S., and J. Frederic Dewhurst. *University Education for Business: A Study of Existing Needs and Practices*. Philadelphia: University of Pennsylvania Press, 1931.

Bostwick, Mary E. "Wells Takes Oath as Head of Indiana U." *Indianapolis Star*, December 2, 1938, 1, 3.

Bowen, Howard R. *Investment in Learning: The Individual and Social Value of American Higher Education*. San Francisco: Jossey-Bass, 1977.

Brancolini, Eugene, dir. *The Vision of Herman B Wells*. Bloomington, Ind.: WTIU, 1993.

Brennan, Eryn S. "'From Tree to the Trade': The Showers Brothers Factory." M.A. thesis, University of Virginia, 2006.

Bridges, Brian K., and Michell L. McClure. "A Home to Call Their Own: A History of the Neal-Marshall African American Culture Center." Unpublished manuscript.

Brown, Tamara L., Gregory S. Parks, and Clarenda M. Phillips, eds. *African American Fraternities and Sororities: The Legacy and the Vision*. Lexington: University Press of Kentucky, 2005.

"Bryan Lauds Ideals and Principles of Successor." *Bloomington Star*, December 2, 1938.

Bryan, William Lowe. *Farewells*. Bloomington: Indiana University, 1938.

Bryan, William Lowe, and Charlotte Lowe Bryan. *Last Words*. Bloomington: Indiana University Bookstore, 1951.

———. *Plato the Teacher*. New York: Scribner's, 1897.

Buehrig, Edward H. "Political Science at Indiana University: An Historical Essay." Bloomington: Political Science Department, Indiana University, 1983.

Burnham, John C. "Where Has Greatness Gone?" *Midwest Quarterly* 27 (1985–86): 129–48.

Byrd, Cecil K. "Introduction." In *The Lilly Library: The First Quarter Century, 1960–1985*, 3–17. Bloomington: Indiana University Lilly Library, 1985.

Byrd, Cecil K., and Ward W. Moore. *Varsity Sports at Indiana University: A Pictorial History*. Bloomington: Indiana University Press, 1999.

Cahill, David. *A History of Student Affairs at Indiana University (Emphasizing the Years 1961–1967)*. Bloomington, Ind.: n.p., 1967.

Campbell, JoAnn, ed. *The Greater Bloomington Chamber of Commerce: A History*. Bloomington, Ind.: n.p., 2003.

Campbell, Mary Elizabeth. "The Department of English in the 1920's and 1930's." In *The Department of English at Indiana University, 1868–1970*, edited by Donald J. Gray, 114–27. Bloomington: Indiana University Publications, [1971].

Capshew, James H. "Boone County Days." Unpublished manuscript.

———. "Bryan, William Lowe." *American National Biography* 3 (1999): 815–16.

———. "The Campus as a Pedagogical Agent: Herman Wells, Cultural Entrepreneurship, and the Benton Murals." *Indiana Magazine of History* 105 (2009): 179–97.

———. "Encounters with *Genius Loci*: Herman Wells at/and/of Indiana University." In "Iconic Leaders in Higher Education," edited by Roger L. Geiger.

Perspectives on the History of Higher Education 28 (2011): 193–222.

———. "Engineering Behavior: Project Pigeon, World War II, and the Conditioning of B. F. Skinner." *Technology and Culture* 34 (1993): 835–57.

———. "Herman B Wells: The Man Who Shaped Our World." *Bloom* 4, no. 1 (2009): 72–80.

———. "Herman B Wells, Indiana University, and the Prehistory of the Black Culture Center." Unpublished manuscript.

———. "Home Design for Indiana University: Herman B Wells and the Furnishing of the Campus." *Traces of Indiana and Midwestern History* 14, no. 3 (2002): 28–39.

———. "Indiana University as the 'Mother of College Presidents': Herman B Wells as Inheritor, Exemplar, and Agent." *Herman B Wells Distinguished Lecture Series* 9. Bloomington: Institute for Advanced Study, Indiana University, 2011.

———. "Indiana University in the Light of History." *Indiana Alumni Magazine* 57, no. 2 (1994). Unpaginated 1995 Historical Calendar supplement.

———. "The Legacy of the Laboratory (1888–1988): A History of the Department of Psychology at Indiana University." In *Psychology at Indiana University: A Centennial Review and Compendium,* edited by Eliot Hearst and James H. Capshew, 1–83. Bloomington: Indiana University Department of Psychology, 1988.

———. "Making Herman B Wells: Moral Development and Emotional Trauma in a Boone County Boyhood." *Indiana Magazine of History* 107 (2011): 361–76.

———. "The President, the Patron, and the Librarians: On the Origins of the Lilly Library." Unpublished manuscript.

———. "Professor Kinsey, President Wells, and Academic Freedom at Indiana University: Notes on the Early Years." Unpublished manuscript.

Capshew, James H., ed. *Students in Residence: At Home with Herman B Wells.* Bloomington, Ind: Privately printed, 1991.

Capshew, James H., Matthew H. Adamson, Patricia A. Buchanan, Narisara Murray, and Naoke Wake. "Kinsey's Biographers: A Historiographical Reconnaissance." *Journal of the History of Sexuality* 12, no. 3 (2003): 465–86.

Carmichael, Hoagy. *The Stardust Road.* New York: Rinehart, 1946. Reprint, Bloomington: Indiana University Press, 1983.

Carmichael, Hoagy, with Stephen Longstreet. *Sometimes I Wonder: The Story of Hoagy Carmichael.* New York: Farrar, Straus and Giroux, 1965.

Carmony, Donald F. *Indiana University: From Seminary Square to Dunn's Woods, 1820–1885.* Bloomington: Indiana University Publications, 1985.

Cartter, Allan M. *An Assessment of Quality in Graduate Education.* Washington, D.C.: American Council on Education, 1966.

Casey, Edward S. *Getting Back into Place: Toward a Renewed Understanding of the Place-World.* 2nd ed. Bloomington: Indiana University Press, 2009.

Catt, Patrick A. "From Opportunities to Obsolescence: The Postwar Management of the Indiana University Cyclotron, 1946–62." Unpublished manuscript.

Cattell, Jaques, ed. *American Men of Science.* 8th ed. Lancaster, Pa.: Science Press, 1938.

Cavanaugh, Robert E. *Indiana University Extension: Its Origin, Progress, Pitfalls, and Personalities.* Bloomington: IU Extension, 1961.

A Celebration of a Life: Remembering Herman B Wells. Bloomington: Indiana University Office of Publications, [2000].

"Centennial Celebration of the Opening of Indiana University." *Indiana University Alumni Quarterly* 11 (1924): 379–88.

Chamness, Ivy L. "Indiana University: Mother of College Presidents." *Indiana University Alumni Quarterly* 9 (1922): 46–49.

Chapman, M. Perry. *American Places: In Search of the Twenty-First Century Campus*. Westport, Conn.: ACE/Praeger, 2006.

Christenson, Cornelia V. *Kinsey: A Biography*. Bloomington: Indiana University Press, 1971.

Clark, Thomas D. *Indiana University, Midwestern Pioneer*. 4 vols. Bloomington: Indiana University Press, 1970–77.

Clark, William. *Academic Charisma and the Origins of the Research University*. Chicago: University of Chicago Press, 2006.

Clarke, Olivia. "A Day like No Other." *Indiana Daily Student*, March 31, 2000.

Clemens, James W. B. "An Historical Study of the Philosophies of Indiana University School of Music Administrators from 1910 to 1973." M.M.E. thesis, Indiana University, 1994.

Cohen, Arthur M. *The Shaping of American Higher Education: Emergence and Growth of the Contemporary System*. San Francisco: Jossey-Bass, 1998.

Cole, Jonathan R., Elinor G. Barber, and Stephen R. Graubard, eds. *The Research University in a Time of Discontent*. Baltimore: Johns Hopkins University Press, 1994.

Collins, Dorothy C., and Cecil K. Byrd. *Indiana University: A Pictorial History*. Bloomington: Indiana University Press, 1992.

Collins, Jim. "Level 5 Leadership: The Triumph of Humility and Fierce Resolve." *Harvard Business Review* 83, nos. 7/8 (2005): 136–46.

"Commencement 1924." *Indiana University Alumni Quarterly* 11 (1924): 355–78.

Committee on the University and World Affairs. *The University and World Affairs*. [New York]: Committee on the University and World Affairs, 1960.

Connell, Christopher. "Internationalizing the Campus: Profiles of Success at Colleges and Universities." NAFSA, 2003.

Cook, Gayle, and Diana Hawes. *Monroe County in Focus*. Bloomington, Ind.: Discovery Press, 1990.

Cook, John, comp. *The Book of Positive Quotations*. Minneapolis: Fairview Press, [1997].

Corn, Kevin J. "'Forward Be Our Watchword': Indiana Methodism and the Modern Middle Class." M.A. thesis, Indiana University, 1996.

Cothran, Tilman C. "The Attitude of Negro Students toward Indiana University." M.A. thesis, Indiana University, 1942.

Counts, Will, James H. Madison, and Scott R. Sanders. *Bloomington, Past and Present*. Bloomington: Indiana University Press, 2002.

Craig, Karen S., and Diana M. Hawes. *Bloomington Discovered*. Bloomington, Ind.: Discovery Press, 1980.

Cronin, Blaise. "Gay Pride and Prejudice." In *Bloomington Days: Town and Gown in Middle America*, 48–52. Bloomington, Ind.: AuthorHouse, 2006.

Cronon, E. David, and John W. Jenkins. *The University of Wisconsin: A History*, vol. 3, *Politics, Depression, and War, 1925–1945*. Madison: University of Wisconsin Press, 1994.

Crowley, Joseph N. *No Equal in the World: An Interpretation of the Academic Presidency*. Reno: University of Nevada Press, 1994.

Crump, William L. *The Story of Kappa Alpha Psi: A History of the Beginning and*

Development of a College Greek Letter Organization, 1911–1991. 4th ed. Philadelphia: Kappa Alpha Psi Fraternity, 1991.

"Crusading Educator: Herman Wells." *New York Times,* December 30, 1964, 13.

Curti, Merle. Review of *Indiana University, Midwestern Pioneer,* vol. 3, *Years of Fulfillment,* by Thomas D. Clark. *American Historical Review* 83 (1978): 1101.

Dalzell, Frederick. *Financing the Dream: The Federal Home Loan Bank of Indianapolis.* Indianapolis: FHLBI, 2007.

Darish, Patricia J. "African Art at the Indiana University Art Museum." *African Arts* 20, no. 3 (1987): 30–41.

Daugherty, Leo. "Six-Ton, $20,000 Mural History of State Decaying at Fair Grounds Awaiting Home Big Enough to Hold It." *Indianapolis Times,* February 8, 1938, 1.

———. "Suggestions for Preservation Of Murals Given by Lieber." *Indianapolis Times,* February 9, 1938, 3.

Davis, Harold T. *The Adventures of an Ultra-Crepidarian.* San Antonio, Tex.: n.p., 1962.

Day, Harry G. *The Development of Chemistry at Indiana University, 1829–1991.* Bloomington: Indiana University Department of Chemistry, 1992.

Devereux, Paul. *Re-Visioning the Earth: A Guide to Opening the Healing Channels between Mind and Nature.* New York: Fireside, 1996.

Diamond, Nancy. "'Time, Place, and Character': The American College and University Presidency in the Late Twentieth Century." *Perspectives on the History of Higher Education* 25 (2006): 157–81.

Dietrich, Barbara Kathleen. "Geographical Influences in the Development of Bloomington, Indiana." M.A. thesis, Indiana University, 1937.

Dober, Richard P. *Campus Architecture: Building in the Groves of Academe.* New York: McGraw-Hill, 1996.

Doss, Erika. *Benton, Pollock, and the Politics of Modernism: From Regionalism to Abstract Expressionism.* Chicago: University of Chicago Press, 1991.

"Dr. Herman B Wells, 1902–2000." In Forty-second Monroe County Fall Festival, September 21, 22, and 23, 2000, program, 4–6.

Durrell, Lawrence. *Justine.* New York: Dutton, 1957.

Dzuback, Mary Ann. *Robert M. Hutchins: Portrait of an Educator.* Chicago: University of Chicago Press, 1991.

Eaton, Quaintance. *Opera Caravan: Adventures of the Metropolitan on Tour, 1883–1956.* New York: Farrar, Straus and Giroux, 1957.

Education and World Affairs. *The University Looks Abroad: Approaches to World Affairs at Six American Universities.* New York: Walker, 1965.

———. *The Professional School and World Affairs.* Albuquerque: University of New Mexico Press, 1967.

Educational Policies Commission, NEA. *Manpower and Education: A Report by the Educational Policies Commission of the National Education Association and the American Association of School Administrators.* Washington, D.C.: National Education Association, 1956.

———. *Higher Education in a Decade of Decision.* Washington, D.C.: National Education Association, 1957.

Ehrlich, Thomas, with Juliet Frey. *The Courage to Inquire: Ideals and Realities in Higher Education.* Bloomington: Indiana University Press, 1995.

"The Eighties and Beyond: The Campaign for Indiana." In *1985–86 Annual Report, Indiana University Foundation,* 16–17.

Ellis, Edith Hennel. "The Trees on the I.U. Campus." *Indiana University Alumni Quarterly* 16 (1929): 328–31.

Eskovitz, Joel. "Sigma Nu Honors Herman B." *Indiana Daily Student,* March 22, 2000, 1, 14.

Evans, Jonathan. "Reader Is the 'Lucky' One." *Indiana Daily Student,* November 20, 1980, 11.

Fancher, John. "A Wells Album: Procedures May Change but Finding the Money Is Still the Aim." *Bloomington Herald-Telephone,* February 1, 1981, 39.

———. "Wells Spent Life 'Being Lucky.'" *Bloomington Herald-Telephone,* July 28, 1980.

Fass, Paula S. *The Damned and the Beautiful: American Youth in the 1920's.* New York: Oxford University Press, 1977.

Field, Oliver P. "Political Science at Indiana University, 1829–1951." *Studies Published by the Bureau of Government Research at Indiana University* 24 (1952).

Findley, Lisa R. "The Pedagogical Building." *Academe* 77, no. 4 (1991): 29–34.

Finkelstein, Lydia Brown. "Remembering Herman B Wells, 1902–2000." *Bloomington Herald-Times,* March 21–25, 2000.

"First Banking Exhibit," *The Hoosier Banker* 13, no. 12 (September 1928): 5.

Ford, Guy Stanton. *The Making of the University: An Unorthodox Report.* Minneapolis: University of Minnesota, 1940.

Foster, Kathleen, Nanette Esseck Brewer, and Margaret Contompasis. *Thomas Hart Benton and the Indiana Murals.* Bloomington: Indiana University Art Museum, 2000.

Frey, Juliet. *Islands of Green and Serenity: The Courtyards of Indiana University.* Bloomington, Ind.: Metropolitan, 1987.

Freyer, Megan. "The House That IU Built: Women Students, University Administration, and Housing, 1900–1970." B.A. Honors thesis, Indiana University, 2004.

Gaines, Thomas A. *The Campus as a Work of Art.* New York: Praeger, 1991.

Gallman, John. "Herman as Machiavelli." In *Herman Wells Stories: As Told by His Friends on His 90th Birthday,* edited by John Gallman, Rosann Green, Jim Weigand, and Doug Wilson, 23–24. Bloomington: Indiana University Press, 1992.

Gallman, John, Rosann Greene, Jim Weigand, and Doug Wilson, eds. *Herman Wells Stories: As Told by His Friends on His 90th Birthday.* Bloomington: Indiana University Press, 1992.

"Garden Program Attracts National Attention." *Indiana Alumni Magazine* 23 (May 1961): 14–16.

Gardner, Howard, and Emma Laskin. *Leading Minds: An Anatomy of Leadership.* New York: Basic Books, 1995.

Garrison, R. Benjamin. Letter to the Editor. *Bloomington Herald-Telephone,* January 20, 1961.

Gathorne-Hardy, Jonathan. *Alfred C. Kinsey: Sex the Measure of All Things: A Biography.* London: Chatto and Windus, 1998. Reprint, Bloomington: Indiana University Press, 2000.

Gealt, Adelheid M. *A Transforming Vision: Thomas T. Solley (1924–2006) and the Indiana University Art Museum,* compiled by Linda J. Baden. Bloomington: Indiana University Art Museum, 2006.

Geiger, Roger L. *To Advance Knowledge: The Growth of American Research Universities, 1900–1940.* New York: Oxford University Press, 1986.

———. *Knowledge and Money: Research Universities and the Paradox of the Marketplace.* Stanford, Calif.: Stanford University Press, 2004.

———. *Research and Relevant Knowledge: American Research Universities since World War II.* Piscataway, N.J.: Transaction Publishers, 2004.

Geiger, Roger L., David B. Potts, and W. Bruce Leslie. "Exploring Our Professional Backyards: Toward Writing Recent History of American Colleges and Universities." *History of Higher Education Annual* 20 (2000): 79–91.

Gieryn, Thomas F. "A Space for Place in Sociology." *Annual Review of Sociology* 26 (2000): 463–96.

———. "Truth-Spots." *Herman B Wells Distinguished Lecture Series* 5. Bloomington: Institute for Advanced Study, Indiana University, 2005.

Gilbert, Richard. "Beard Case Closed – All Charges Dropped." *Bloomington Herald-Times*, June 21, 1989.

———. "Foundation Execs Charged." *Bloomington Herald-Telephone*, September 29, 1988.

———. "Indictments Near in IU Foundation Probe." *Bloomington Herald-Telephone*, September 27, 1988.

———. "IU Foundation Officials Greet Court Ruling with Optimism." *Bloomington Herald-Telephone*, May 7, 1989.

Gilliam, Frances V. Halsell. *A Time to Speak: A Brief History of Afro-Americans of Bloomington, Indiana 1865–1965.* Bloomington, Ind.: Pinus Strobus Press, 1985.

Goss, David A. "History of the Indiana University Division of Optometry." *Indiana Journal of Optometry* 6, no. 2 (2003): 28–74.

Goss, David A., et al. "History of the Indiana University School of Optometry." *Indiana Journal of Optometry* 7, no. 2 (2004): 22–72.

Graham, Hugh Davis, and Nancy Diamond. *The Rise of American Research Universities: Elites and Challengers in the Postwar Era.* Baltimore: Johns Hopkins University Press, 1997.

Graham, Tom, and Rachel Graham Cody. *Getting Open: The Unknown Story of Bill Garrett and the Integration of College Basketball.* New York: Atria Books, 2006.

"Granville Wells, Father of I.U. President, Succumbs." *Indianapolis Star*, March 21, 1948, 1.

Graubard, Stephen R. "The Research University: Notes toward a New History." In *The Research University in a Time of Discontent*, edited by E. G. Barber, J. R. Cole, and S. R. Graubard, 361–90. Baltimore: Johns Hopkins University Press, 1994.

Gray, Donald J., ed. *The Department of English at Indiana University Bloomington, 1868–1970.* Bloomington: Indiana University Publications, [1971].

Gray, Hetty. *Net Prophet: The Bill Garrett Story.* Fairland, Ind.: Sugar Creek Publishing, 2001.

Gray, Ralph D. *IUPUI: The Making of an Urban University.* Bloomington: Indiana University Press, 2003.

Green, James L. "Brief Biographical Sketch: Herman B Wells." Press release, IU News Bureau, October 1980.

Greenleaf, Robert K. *Servant Leadership: A Journey into the Nature of Legitimate Power and Greatness.* Mahwah, N.J.: Paulist Press, 1977.

Gumprecht, Blake. *The American College Town.* Amherst: University of Massachusetts Press, 2008.

Hackerd, Jeremy L. "The Complex History of the Date Classes Began at the State Seminary of Indiana." Indiana Historical Bureau, Historical Marker Site Report, 2008.

Hammarskjöld, Dag. *Markings.* New York: Knopf, 1976.

Hammel, Bob, and Kit Klingelhoffer. *Glory of Old IU: 100 Years of Indiana Athletics.* Champaign, Ill.: Sports Publishing, 1999.

Harding, Samuel Bannister, ed. *Indiana University, 1820–1904.* Bloomington: Indiana University, 1904.

Hargis, Tom, and Emily Williams. "Public Radio from Indiana University: A History of Service." In *WFIU: 50 Years*, 3–23. Bloomington, Ind.: WFIU, 2000.

Harvey, Robert O. *Land Uses in Bloomington, Indiana, 1818–1950. Indiana Business Studies* 33. Bloomington: Bureau of Business Research, Indiana University, 1951.

Hawkins, Hugh. *Between Harvard and America: The Educational Leadership of Charles W. Eliot.* New York: Oxford University Press, 1972.

———. *Banding Together: The Rise of National Associations in American Higher Education, 1887–1950.* Baltimore: Johns Hopkins University Press, 1992.

Hazelwood, Craig B. "Better Banks and Bankers." *The Hoosier Banker* 13 (October 1927): 5–10.

Heilbron, J. L., and Robert W. Seidel, *Lawrence and His Laboratory: A History of the Lawrence Berkeley Laboratory.* Berkeley: University of California Press, 1989.

Hennessy, Mildred J. *Herman B Wells: Memories of a Colleague.* Bloomington, Ind.: 1stBooks, 2003.

Henry, David D. Review of *Being Lucky. Change* 12, no. 8 (1980): 59–60.

Herbold, Hilary. "Never a Level Playing Field: Blacks and the GI Bill." *Journal of Blacks in Higher Education* 6 (Winter 1994–1995): 104–108.

"Herman B Wells, 1902–2000." *Indiana Daily Student,* March 20, 2000, 1–8.

"Herman B Wells: 'With a Little Bit of Luck.'" *IU Newspaper,* May 5, 1980, 1, 7.

Herold, Don. "Indiana." *College Humor* 18, no. 4 (1929).

Hershberg, James G. *James B. Conant: From Harvard to Hiroshima and the Making of the Nuclear Age.* New York: Knopf, 1993.

Hertko, Joyce Mary. "The Internationalization of American Higher Education During the 1960s: The Involvement of the Ford Foundation and the Carnegie Corporation in Education and World Affairs." Ph.D. diss., Indiana University, 1996.

Hesburgh, Theodore M., with Jerry Reedy. *God, Country, Notre Dame.* New York: Doubleday, 1990.

Hewett, W. T. *Cornell University: A History.* New York: University Publishing Society, 1905.

"The Hillel Foundation." *Indiana University Alumni Quarterly* 25 (1938): 516.

Himm, Katie, and Lana Ruegamer Eisenberg. *There Are Jews in Southern Indiana: The Bloomington Story.* Fort Wayne: Indiana Jewish Historical Society, 2009.

Hinnefeld, Steve. "Faculty Ask for Review of Herbert." *Bloomington Herald-Times,* November 30, 2005, A9.

"The History of Banking in Indiana." *The Hoosier Banker* 50th anniversary issue (April 1947): 31ff.

Hollinger, David. "Academic Culture at Michigan, 1938–1988: The Apotheosis of Pluralism." *Rackham Reports* (1989): 58–101.

Holloway, Hortense Dolores. "The Social Structure of the Negro Community in Bloomington." M.A. thesis, Indiana University, 1946.

Holmstedt, Raleigh W. *The Indiana Conference of Higher Education, 1945–1965.* Bloomington: School of Education, Indiana University, 1967.

Hood, W. Peter. "Educational and Experiential Patterns of College and University Presidents Who Graduated from Indiana University." Ed.D. diss., Indiana University, 1970.

Hood, W. Peter. "I.U. – Mother of College Presidents." *Indiana Alumni Magazine* 62, no. 9 (June 1970): 36–39.

"Hoosier Highways." *The Hoosier Banker* 15, nos. 5–8 (February–May 1930).

Hope, Henry R. "The Indiana University Art Museum." *Art Journal* 30, no. 2 (1970–71): 170–77.

Horn, David. "Statue of Herman Wells Dedicated: Sculpture Captures IU Legend's Personality." *Bloomington Herald-Times,* October 22, 2000.

Horner, John E. Review of *Being Lucky. Indiana Magazine of History* 77 (1981): 288–89.

Howley, Kevin. *Community Media: People, Places, and Communication Technolo-*

gies. New York: Cambridge University Press, 2005.

———. "Talking About Public Affairs Programming: WFHB and the Legacy of Listener-Sponsored Radio." *Historical Journal of Film, Radio and Television* 21 (2001): 399–415.

Hudson, Herman C., comp. *The Black Faculty at Indiana University Bloomington, 1970–93.* Bloomington, Ind.: n.p., 1994.

Hughes, R. M. *A Study of the Graduate Schools of America.* Oxford, Ohio: Miami University, 1925.

———. "Report of the Committee on Graduate Instruction." *Educational Record* 15 (1934): 192–234.

———. "A Study of University and College Presidents." *School and Society* 51 (1940): 317–20.

Hunt, Elizabeth. "Oral History: How Americans Got Their Straight, White Teeth." Ph.D. diss., University of Pennsylvania, 1998.

Hutton, Edward L. *The Life and Times of Edward L. Hutton.* Cincinnati, Ohio: E. L. Hutton, 1992.

Hyde, Lewis. *The Gift: Creativity and the Artist in the Modern World.* New York: Random House, 1979.

Hyneman, Charles S. "A Half Century of Political Science." *A&S The Review* 7, no. 1 (1964): 1–8.

Indiana University Foundation 50th Anniversary Report, 1985–86. Bloomington: Indiana University Foundation, 1986.

"Indiana's Education Giant." *Louisville Courier-Journal,* March 21, 2000, A6.

IU Foundation, *Herman B Wells Scholars Program, Questions and Answers.* Bloomington: n.d. [c. 1991].

IU Library Annual Report, 1937–38.

IU Library Annual Report, 1961–62.

Jacoby, Russell. *The Repression of Psychoanalysis: Otto Fenichel and the Political Freudians.* New York: Basic Books, 1983.

Jaspers, Karl. *Existential Elucidation.* Vol. 2 of *Philosophy,* translated by E. B. Ash-

ton. Chicago: University of Chicago Press, 1970.

Jaynes, Gerald David, and Robin Murphy Williams. *A Common Destiny: Blacks and American Society.* Washington, D.C.: National Academy Press, 1989.

Jones, James H. *Alfred C. Kinsey: A Public/Private Life.* New York: Norton, 1997.

Jordan, David Starr. *The Days of a Man.* 2 vols. New York: World Book Company, 1922.

Kearney, Brian. "Main Air Studio at WFHB Named in Honor of Dr. Wells." *Spotlight* [WFHB newsletter] 1 (Autumn 2000): 15.

Keith, Brian D. *Follow the Limestone: A Walking Tour of Indiana University.* Bloomington: Indiana Geological Survey and Bloomington/Monroe County Convention and Visitors Bureau, 2009.

Kellerman, Henry J. *Cultural Relations as an Instrument of U.S. Foreign Policy: The Educational Exchange Program between the United States and Germany 1945–1954.* Washington, D.C.: GPO, 1978.

Kerr, Clark. *The Uses of the University.* 5th ed. Cambridge, Mass.: Harvard University Press, 2001.

———. *The Gold and the Blue: A Personal Memoir of the University of California, 1949–1967.* 2 vols. Berkeley: University of California Press, 2001–2003.

Keys, David Patrick, and John F. Galliher. *Confronting the Drug Control Establishment : Alfred Lindesmith as a Public Intellectual.* Albany: State University of New York Press, 2000.

Kibbey, Hal. "Original IU Cyclotron Contributed to the American War Effort." Indiana University News Release, IU News Bureau, August 22, 1989.

Kibbler, Anne. "The Life of a Legend." *Indiana Alumni Magazine* 62, no. 5 (May/June 2000): 38–44.

Kish, Kelly A. "Reds among the Cream and Crimson? Accused Communist

Faculty Members at Indiana University." Unpublished manuscript.

———. "The Board of Aeons: Student Participation in University Governance at Indiana University, 1921–1962." Unpublished manuscript.

Klauder, Charles Z., and Herbert C. Wise. *College Architecture in America.* New York: Charles Scribner's Sons, 1929.

Knight, Dawn. *Taliaferro: Breaking Barriers from the NFL Draft to the Ivory Tower.* Bloomington: Indiana University Press, 2007.

Koelsch, William A. *Clark University, 1887–1987: A Narrative History.* Worcester, Mass.: Clark University Press, 1987.

Kohák, Erazim. *The Embers and the Stars: A Philosophical Inquiry into the Moral Sense of Nature.* Chicago: University of Chicago Press, 1984.

Kotlowski, Dean J. "Launching a Political Career: Paul V. McNutt and the American Legion, 1919–1932." *Indiana Magazine of History* 106 (2010): 119–57.

Krampetz, Norman, and Martha Vicinus, eds. *Disorientation: Like It Is at IU.* Bloomington: Indiana University Chapter, New University Conference, 1969.

Kuh, George D., and Elizabeth J. Whitt. *The Invisible Tapestry: Culture in American Colleges and Universities.* College Station, Tex.: Association for the Study of Higher Education, 1988.

Kunstler, James Howard. *The Geography of Nowhere: The Rise and Decline of America's Man-Made Landscape.* New York: Simon and Schuster, 1993.

Kuykendall, Rufus Calvin. "The Negro at Indiana." *The Vagabond* 4, no. 1 (1927): 26–28.

Lagemann, Ellen Condliffe. *The Politics of Knowledge: The Carnegie Corporation, Philanthropy, and Public Policy.* Chicago: University of Chicago Press, 1989.

Lahrman, Dolores M., and Delbert C. Miller. *The History of Mitchell Hall,*

1885–1986. Bloomington: Indiana University Archives, [1987].

Lalwani, Shelia. "Friends, Family Remember Wells." *Indiana Daily Student,* March 22, 2000.

Lampman, Robert J., ed. *Economists at Wisconsin; 1892–1992.* Madison: University of Wisconsin, Department of Economics, 1993.

Lane, N. Gary. *Geology at Indiana University, 1840–2000.* Bloomington: Indiana University Department of Geological Sciences, 2000.

Laney, James T. "The Moral Authority of the College or University President." *Educational Record* 65, no. 2 (1984): 17–19.

Laohavichien, Uthai. "The Problems and Prospects of Public Administration Education in Thailand." *Asian Journal of Public Administration* 6, no. 1 (1984): 46–60.

Laves, Walter H. C., and Charles A. Thomson. *UNESCO: Purpose, Progress, Prospects.* Bloomington: Indiana University Press, 1957.

Leonard, Mike. "For the Legacy of Herman B Wells, the Sky Is the Limit." *Bloomington Herald-Times,* March 30, 2000, C1–C2.

———. "Tiny Barbershop Closing Its Door." *Bloomington Herald-Times,* September 9, 2004, C1–C2.

Levine, David O. *The American College and the Culture of Aspiration, 1915–1940.* Ithaca, N.Y.: Cornell University Press, 1986.

Lewis, John P., William G. Pinnell, and Herman B Wells. "Needs, Resources, and Priorities in Higher Education Planning." *American Association of University Professors Bulletin* 42, no. 3 (September 1957): 431–42.

The Lilly Library: The First Quarter Century, 1960–1985. Bloomington: Lilly Library, Indiana University, Bloomington, 1985.

Link, William A. *William Friday: Power, Purpose, and American Higher Education*. Chapel Hill: University of North Carolina Press, 1997.

Lockridge, Larry. *The Shade of the Raintree: The Life and Death of Ross Lockridge, Jr., Author of* Raintree County. New York: Viking Penguin, 1994.

Logan, George M. *The Indiana University School of Music: A History*. Bloomington: Indiana University Press, 2000.

Logan, Rayford W. *Howard University: The First Hundred Years, 1867–1967*. New York: New York University Press, 1968.

Lombardi, John V. "Indiana University." In *Approaches to International Education*, edited by E. L. Backman, 103–17. New York: Macmillan, 1984.

Long, Newell H. "All's Wells That Ends Well." In *Herman Wells Stories: As Told by His Friends on His 90th Birthday*, edited by John Gallman, Rosann Green, Jim Weigand, and Doug Wilson, 38. Bloomington: Indiana University Press, 1992.

Longstreth, Richard, ed. *Cultural Landscapes: Balancing Nature and Heritage in Preservation Practice*. Minneapolis: University of Minnesota Press, 2008.

Lowell, Mildred H. "Indiana University Libraries, 1829–1942." Ph.D. diss., University of Chicago, 1957.

MacClintock, Lander. "Wellsian Indiana for 25 Years." *The Arts and Sciences Review, Indiana University Bulletin* 60, no. 6 (February 1962): 10–23.

Macfarlane, Alan. *Reflections on Cambridge*. New Delhi: Social Science Press, 2009.

Macleod, Robert B. Review of *Manpower and Education. Journal of Higher Education* 29 (1958): 174.

Madison, James H. *Eli Lilly: A Life, 1885–1977*. Indianapolis: Indiana Historical Society, 1989.

———. *The Indiana University Department of History, 1895–1995: A Centennial Year Sketch*. Bloomington: Indiana University Department of History, 1995.

Madison, James H., ed. *Wendell Willkie: Hoosier Internationalist*. Bloomington: Indiana University Press, 1992.

Martin, John Bartlow. *Indiana: An Interpretation*. New York: Alfred A. Knopf, 1947.

Martone, Michael. "Country Roads Lined with Running Fences: A Dozen Story Problems about the Place of Place." In *Home Again: Essays and Memoirs from Indiana*, edited by Tom Watson and Jim McGarrah, 127–32. Indianapolis: Indiana Historical Society, 2006.

Matthews, Henry. *Kirtland Cutter: Architect in the Land of Promise*. Seattle: University of Washington Press, 1998.

McCarthy, Charles. *The Wisconsin Idea*. New York: Macmillan, 1912.

McDaniel, Forba. "Annual Report of the Secretary." *The Hoosier Banker* 14, no. 12 (September 1929): 18ff; and 15, no. 1 (October 1929): 54ff.

McDougall, Walter A. *The Heavens and the Earth: A Political History of the Space Age*. New York: Basic Books, 1985.

McIlveen, Rose. "Happy Birthday Chancellor Wells." Indiana University News Release, June 3, 1983.

McMains, Howard F. "The Indiana Seminary Charter of 1820." *Indiana Magazine of History* 106 (2010): 356–80.

"McNutt Is 'Not in I.U. Picture,' Trustee Friend Says." *Indianapolis Sunday Star*, December 12, 1937.

McPherson, Alan. *Temples of Knowledge: Andrew Carnegie's Gift to Indiana*. Kewanna, Ind.: Hoosier's Nest Press, 2003.

Meunier, John. "One Year after His Death, Well's [sic] Impact, Absence Still Felt." *Bloomington Herald-Times*, March 18, 2001.

Michaelmas, William Henry Tecumseh. "Indiana, Our Indiana," *Bloomington Star-Courier*, 1948.

Miller, Delbert C. *One Hundred Years: The History of Sociology at Indiana University, 1885–1985*. Bloomington: Indiana University Department of Sociology, 1985.

Miller, Tim. *Thomas Hart Benton and the Indiana Murals: Visions of the Past, Lessons for the Future*. Videocassette. Bloomington: Indiana University Media Production, 2001.

Mincey, Sarah, and Burney Fischer. *The Woodland Campus. Indiana University–Bloomington: A Historic Walking Tour*. Bloomington: Indiana University School of Public and Environmental Affairs, 2009.

"Minority Groups and the Expression of Student Thought." In *Report of the Self-Survey Committee to the Board of Trustees of Indiana University*, 152–61. 1939.

Moffat, Georgabell Henley. "A History of the Indiana University Auditorium and the Cultural Tastes of the Community as Reflected by Attendance at Auditorium Events from 1941 to 1952." M.A. thesis, Indiana University, 1953.

"Monroe County Leads All Parts of State in Students Attending Indiana University in 1921–22." In *Historic Treasures*, compiled by Forest M. Hall, 48. Bloomington: Indiana University, 1922.

Moore, Leonard J. *Citizen Klansmen: The Ku Klux Klan in Indiana, 1921–1928*. Chapel Hill: University of North Carolina Press, 1991.

Moskowitz, Eric, and Mark Feeney. "Civil Rights Trailblazer Atkins Dies at 69." *Boston Globe*, June 28, 2008, A1.

Musgrave, Paul. "The Man before the Myth." *Indiana Alumni Magazine* 66, no. 6 (July/August 2004): 26–29.

———. "Fractional Reform: Herman Wells and Hoosier Bankers." B.A. Honors thesis, Indiana University, 2004.

———. "'A Primitive Method of Enforcing the Law': Vigilantism as a Response to Bank Crimes in Indiana, 1925–1933."

Indiana Magazine of History 102 (2006): 187–219.

Myers, Burton D. *Trustees and Officers of Indiana University, 1820 to 1950*. Bloomington: Indiana University, 1951.

———. *History of Indiana University*, vol. 2, *The Bryan Administration, 1902–1937*. Bloomington: Indiana University, 1952.

"The Naming Ceremony for the Herman B Wells Library, Friday, June 17, 2005, 4 p.m., Library South Lawn." Bloomington: Indiana University, 2005.

Neufeldt, Harvey. Review of *Being Lucky. Educational Studies* 12 (1981): 314–15.

Nevins, Allan. *The State Universities and Democracy*. Urbana: University of Illinois Press, 1962.

"Newsboy to College Head." *Newsweek*, April 4, 1938, 30–32.

Newman, Andy. "Herman B Wells, President of Indiana U. in a Crucial Era." *New York Times*, March 21, 2000, C31.

Nicholson, Meredith. *A Hoosier Chronicle*. Boston: Houghton Mifflin, 1912.

Nissan, Luana G., and Dwight F. Burlingame. "Collaboration Among Institutions: Strategies for Nonprofit Management Education Programs." Indianapolis: IUPUI Center on Philanthropy, 2002.

Norvelle, Lee. *The Road Taken*. Bloomington: Indiana University Foundation, 1980.

O'Meara, Patrick. "A Short History of the IU-Nida Partnership." Unpublished manuscript.

O'Meara, Patrick, Howard D. Mehlinger, and Roxana Ma Newman, eds. *Changing Perspectives on International Education*. Bloomington: Indiana University Press, 2001.

"On the Campus." *Indiana Alumni Magazine* 8, no. 7 (1946): 5–15.

Owen, Kent Christopher, and Susan Mitten Owen. *Greek-Lettered Hoosiers: One Hundred Fifty Years of Fraternities and Sororities at Indiana University and in*

Bloomington. Bloomington, Ind.: Privately printed, 1995.

"Paper Read by Bert Fesler at the Annual Meeting of the Alumni Association of Indiana University at Bloomington, Indiana, at the June 15, 1936, Meeting of the IU Alumni Association." *Indiana University Alumni Quarterly* 23 (1936): 423–34.

Payne, Fernandus. *Memories and Reflections.* Bloomington: Indiana University, 1974.

Peckham, Howard H. *Indiana: A History.* Urbana: University of Illinois Press, 1978.

———. *The Making of the University of Michigan.* Ann Arbor: University of Michigan Press, 1967.

Perkins, James A. Review of *Being Lucky. Journal of Higher Education* 52 (1981): 649–50.

Perley, Maie Clements. *Without My Gloves.* Philadelphia: Dorrance and Co., 1940.

Pete, Joseph S. "Funeral to Celebrate Wells' Life." *Indiana Daily Student,* March 22, 2000, 1.

———. "Losing a Legend." *Indiana Daily Student,* March 20, 2000, 1.

Pincus, Fred L., and Howard J. Ehrlich. "The New University Conference: A Study of Former Members." *Critical Sociology* 15, no. 2 (1988): 145–47.

Pinnell, W. George. "The Foundation Is Organized and Operated for the Benefit of Indiana University." In *1984 Annual Report, Indiana University Foundation,* 2.

Pittman, Bill. "Herman B Wells: A Man For A Lot Of Good Reasons." *Indianapolis News,* September 1, 1980.

Pomeroy, Wardell B. *Dr. Kinsey and the Institute for Sex Research.* New York: Harper and Row, 1972.

Pope, Alexander. *Epistle IV, to Richard Boyle, Earl of Burlington,* 1731.

Power, Richard L. *Planting Corn Belt Culture.* Indianapolis: Indiana Historical Society, 1953.

Poyser, Jim. "A Chat with Herman B. Wells." *Bloomington Voice,* February 16–23, 1994.

The Presidents' Homes, Indiana University. Bloomington: Indiana University Office of Publications and Office of Creative Services, 2009.

"Public Gazes at Klansman Parade and Ceremonies." *Indiana Daily Student,* November 7, 1922, 1ff.

Pyle, Ernie. "Ernie Eats a Big Dinner with a College President." *Scripps Howard News Service,* August 26, 1940. In *Images of Brown County,* 35–36. Indianapolis: The Museum Shop, 1980.

———. "It's in the Air." *Indiana Daily Student,* September 5, 1922.

———. "President Hermie Wells and 'This Job' He's Got." *Scripps Howard News Service,* August 27, 1940. In *Images of Brown County,* 37–39. Indianapolis: The Museum Shop, 1980.

Randall, David A. *Dukedom Large Enough.* New York: Random House, 1969.

Ransel, David L. *The Russian and East European Institute at Indiana University: Celebrating 50 Years, 1958–2008.* Bloomington: REEI, Indiana University, 2008.

Ravitch, Diane. *The Troubled Crusade: American Education, 1945–1980.* New York: Basic Books, 1983.

Relph, Edward. "A Pragmatic Sense of Place." *Environmental and Architectural Phenomenology* 20, no. 3 (2009): 24–31.

"Remembering Herman B Wells, 1902–2000." *Bloomington Herald-Times,* March 21–25, 2000.

Report on Higher Education in the Soviet Union. Pittsburgh, Pa.: University of Pittsburgh Press, 1958.

Report of the Self-Survey Committee to the Board of Trustees of Indiana University, 1939.

Report on the Twelfth Session of the General Assembly of the United Nations by Hon. A. S. J. Carnahan and Hon. Walter H.

Judd of the Committee on Foreign Affairs Pursuant to H.Res. 29. Washington, D.C.: GPO, February 18, 1958.

"Report Trustees Cable McNutt Offer to Take University Presidency." Bloomington Evening World, May 19, 1937.

Rueben, Julie A. The Making of the Modern University: Intellectual Transformation and the Marginalization of Morality. Chicago: University of Chicago Press, 1996.

Ridge, Martin. "Frederick Jackson Turner at Indiana University." Indiana Magazine of History 89 (1993): 210–29.

Riesman, David R. "The College Presidency." Educational Studies 13 (1982): 309–35.

Riker, Dorothy. The Hoosier Training Ground, Indiana in World War II. Bloomington: Indiana War History Commission, 1952.

Robinson, Harry G., III, and Hazel Ruth Edwards. The Long Walk: The Placemaking Legacy of Howard University. Washington, D.C.: Moorland-Spingarn Research Center, 1996.

Robinson, Joe Bright. "A Study of the Negroes in Bloomington and What Negro Periodicals They Read." M.A. thesis, Indiana University, 1951.

Robson, William N. "Open Letter on Race Hatred." In Radio Drama in Action: Twenty-Five Plays of a Changing World, edited by Eric Barnouw, 62–77. New York: Farrar and Rinehart, 1945.

Roehr, Eleanor L. Trustees and Officers of Indiana University, 1950 to 1982. Bloomington: Indiana University, 1983.

Roose, Kenneth D., and Charles J. Anderson. A Rating of Graduate Programs. Washington, D.C.: American Council on Education, 1970.

Rothblatt, Sheldon. "Consult the Genius of the Place." In The Modern University and Its Discontents: The Fate of Newman's Legacies in Britain and America, 50–105. Cambridge: Cambridge University Press, 1997.

———. The Modern University and Its Discontents: The Fate of Newman's Legacies in Britain and America. Cambridge: Cambridge University Press, 1997.

———. "A Note on The 'Integrity' of the University." In Aurora Torealis, edited by Marco Beretta, Karl Grandin and Svante Lindqvist, 277–97. Sagamore Beach, Mass.: Science History Publications, 2008.

Rothenberger, Katharine. "An Historical Study of the Position of Dean of Women at Indiana University." M.A. thesis, Indiana University, 1942.

Royalty, Dennis M. "Purdue's 'Beer-Drinking' Educator." Indianapolis Star, July 20, 1980.

Rudolph, Frederick. The American College and University: A History. New York: Knopf, 1962. Reprint, Athens: University of Georgia Press, 1990.

Ruther, Nancy L. Barely There, Powerfully Present: Thirty Years of U.S. Policy on International Higher Education. New York: Routledge Falmer, 2002.

Rutherford, Alexandra. Beyond the Box: B. F. Skinner's Technology of Behavior from Laboratory to Life, 1950s–1970s. Toronto: University of Toronto Press, 2009.

Ryan, John W. "The Mosaic of the College and University Presidency." Educational Record 65, no. 2 (1984): 20–22.

Sachar, Abram Leon. "Ten Years at Indiana." In D'Vorenu: Indiana Hillel Annual, 1948, edited by Norman Sklarewitz, Corrine Hutner, and Bernard Kogan, 5–6. Bloomington: B'nai B'rith Hillel Foundation at Indiana University, 1948.

Sanders, Mark A. "Leslie Pinckney Hill." In The Concise Oxford Companion to African American Literature, edited by William L. Andrews, Frances Smith Foster, and Trudier Harris, 199. Oxford: Oxford University Press, 2001.

Sanders, Scott Russell. *Staying Put: Making a Home in a Restless World*. Boston: Beacon Press, 1993.

Sauvain, Harry. "The History of Meadowood: Part One." *Meadowood Messenger,* April 2005, 1–7.

———. "The History of Meadowood: Part Two." *Meadowood Messenger,* May 2005, 1–6.

Savonius-Wroth, Celestina. "Indiana University Press." Unpublished manuscript.

Schlesinger, Stephen E. *Act of Creation: The Founding of the United Nations: A Story of Superpowers, Secret Agents, Wartime Allies and Enemies, and Their Quest for a Peaceful World*. Cambridge, Mass.: Perseus Books Group, 2004.

Schoch, Lynn A. *Leo R. Dowling International Center: Celebrating 50 Years*. Bloomington: Indiana University International Services, 2009.

———. "Denis Sinor and Central Eurasian Studies." *IU International* (Spring 2008): 9–13.

Schuckel, Kathleen. "An Indiana Treasure." *Indianapolis Star,* March 20, 2000, A1–A2.

Schuyler, David. "Frederick Law Olmsted and the Origins of Modern Campus Design." *Planning for Higher Education* 25, no. 2 (1996): 1–10.

Schwarb, John. *The Little 500: The Making of the World's Greatest College Weekend*. Bloomington: Indiana University Press, 1999.

Scott, John C. *The Story of Sigma Nu: A Narrative History of the Fraternity, 1869–1926*. Indianapolis: Sigma Nu Fraternity, 1936.

Scott, Will Braxton. "Race Consciousness and the Negro Student at Indiana University." Ed.D. diss., Indiana University, 1965.

Senour, Frank C. *Art for Your Sake*. [Bloomington]: [Indiana University], 1924.

Shalucha, B. "People Want to Become Self-Sufficient Gardeners: The Beginnings With Youth." *Acta Horticulturae* (ISHS) 105 (1981): 23–34.

Shapiro, Herbert. *White Violence and Black Response: From Reconstruction to Montgomery*. Amherst: University of Massachusetts Press, 1988.

Sheridan, Dan. "Chancellor Wells' Memoirs; 'Being Lucky' Part of IU Life." *Indiana Daily Student,* October 17, 1980, 1.

Sherratt, Gerald R. "The Long Journey," *The Delta of Sigma Nu Fraternity* 79, no. 3 (Spring 1962): 141–45.

Shils, Edward. "The Academic Ethos under Strain." *Minerva* 13 (1975): 1–37.

Shirley, Janet Carter. *The Indiana University Alumni Association: One Hundred and Fifty Years, 1854–2004*. Bloomington: Indiana University Office of Publications, 2004.

Shively, George. *Initiation*. New York: Harcourt, Brace and Company, 1925.

Sibley, John. "State University Found Hampered in Its Operations." *New York Times,* December 30, 1964, 1, 13.

Silver, Joel. *J. K. Lilly Jr., Bibliophile*. Bloomington: The Lilly Library, Indiana University, 1993.

Sinclair, Upton. *The Goose-Step: A Study of American Education*. Revised ed. Pasadena, Calif.: n.p., 1923.

Skinner, B. F. "Baby in a Box." *Ladies' Home Journal* 62 (October 1945): 30–31, 135–136, 138.

———. "My Years at Indiana." Paper prepared March 31, 1988, for the Indiana University Department of Psychology Centennial Celebration, April 1988.

———. *Walden Two*. New York: Macmillan, 1948.

Smith, Bruce M. "Folklore Shrouds Ex-I.U. President." *Indianapolis Star,* July 20, 1980.

Stanton, Maura. "Biography." In *Cries of Swimmers*, 60. Salt Lake City: University of Utah Press, 1984.

Steele, Selma N., Theodore L. Steele, and Wilbur D. Peat. *The House of the Singing*

Winds: The Life and Work of T. C. Steele. Indianapolis: Indiana Historical Society, 1966.

Stewart, John L. *Yesterday Was Tomorrow: The Autobiography of John L. Stewart.* Durham, N.C.: n.p., 1976.

Stoke, Harold W. *The American College President.* New York: Harper and Brothers, 1959.

Storr, Anthony. *Feet of Clay: Saints, Sinners, and Madmen: A Study of Gurus.* New York: Free Press, 1996.

Study Commission for Indiana Financial Institutions. *Report of the Study Commission for Indiana Financial Institutions.* Indianapolis: Wm. R. Burford, 1932.

Sudhalter, Richard M. *Stardust Melody: The Life and Music of Hoagy Carmichael.* New York: Oxford University Press, 2002.

Swain, Joseph. "Forty Years of Indiana." *Indiana University Alumni Quarterly* 7 (1920): 393–401.

Tent, James F. *The Free University of Berlin: A Political History.* Bloomington: Indiana University Press, 1988.

Thelin, John R. *Higher Education and Its Useful Past: Applied Research in Research and Planning.* Cambridge, Mass.: Schenkman, 1982.

———. *A History of American Higher Education.* Baltimore: Johns Hopkins University Press, 2004.

Thomas, David A. *Michigan State College: John Hannah and the Creation of a World University, 1926–1969.* East Lansing: Michigan State University Press, 2008.

Thompson, Stith. *A Folklorist's Progress: Reflections of a Scholar's Life.* Edited by John H. McDowell, Inta Gale Carpenter, Donald Braid, and Erika Peterson-Veatch. Special Publications of the Folklore Institute 5. Bloomington: Folklore Institute, Indiana University, 1996.

Thomson, Charles A., and Walter H. C. Laves. *Cultural Relations and U.S. Foreign Policy.* Bloomington: Indiana University Press, 1963.

Thornbrough, Emma Lou. *Since Emancipation: A Short History of Indiana Negroes, 1863–1963.* Indianapolis: Indiana Division American Negro Emancipation Centennial Authority, 1963.

———. *Indiana Blacks in the Twentieth Century.* Bloomington: Indiana University Press, 2000.

Thorpe, Charles, and Steven Shapin. "Who Was J. Robert Oppenheimer? Charisma and Complex Organization." *Social Studies of Science* 30 (2000): 545–90.

"To the Alumni and the Trustees." *The Vagabond* 2, no. 3 (1925): 44.

Tobias, Marianne Williams, George Calder, C. David Higgins, Nancy J. Guer, and Charles H. Webb, eds. *Opera for All Seasons: 60 Years of Indiana University Opera Theater.* Bloomington: Indiana University Press, 2009.

Toner, William M., and N. M. Davis. "Why a Commerce School?" *The Vagabond* 3, no. 2 (1926): 23–27.

Topping, Robert W. *The Hovde Years: A Biography of Frederick L. Hovde.* West Lafayette, Ind.: Purdue University Press, 1980.

———. *A Century and Beyond: The History of Purdue University.* West Lafayette, Ind.: Purdue University Press, 1988.

Trivedi, Riddhi. "Art in Everyday Life: A Glimpse into Herman B Wells' Art Collection." *Indiana Daily Student,* October 4, 2001.

Turner, Frederick Jackson. "Pioneer Ideals and the State University." *Indiana University Bulletin* 8 (June 15, 1910): 6–29.

Turner, Paul Venable. *Campus: An American Planning Tradition.* Cambridge, Mass.: MIT Press, 1984.

"The Union Building Should Have an Adequate Auditorium!" *The Vagabond* 1, no. 4–5 (1924): 9–10.

"Vale." *The Vagabond* 2, no. 4 (1925): 16–17.

Veatch, Henry. *Towards a History of the Indiana University Philosophy Department in Bloomington.* Bloomington: Indiana University Department of Philosophy, 1997.

Veblen, Thorstein. *The Higher Learning in America: A Memorandum on the Conduct of Universities by Business Men.* New York: B.W. Huebsch, 1918.

Waid, Frederic M. "Why Is Indiana the 'Mother of College Presidents'?" *Indiana Alumni Magazine* 1, no. 7 (1939): 12.

———. "Why Is Indiana the 'Mother of College Presidents'?" *Indiana Alumni Magazine* 1, no. 8 (1939): 12, 30–31.

Waldman, Joseph. *Things Remembered: A History of the Kelley School of Business.* DVD. Bloomington: Indiana University Kelley School of Business, 2003.

Waldman, Joseph M., with Andra Klemkosky. *The First One Hundred Years of Education for Business: 1902–2002.* Bloomington: Indiana University Kelley School of Business, 2002.

Walter, Eugene Victor. *Placeways: A Theory of the Human Environment.* Chapel Hill: University of North Carolina Press, 1988.

Warriner, David R. "The Veterans of World War II at Indiana University, 1944–1951." Ph.D. diss., Indiana University, 1978.

"The Watch Tower." *The Hoosier Banker* 13, no. 10 (July 1928): 10.

Weatherwax, Paul. *The Woodland Campus of Indiana University.* Bloomington: Indiana University Foundation, 1966 [revised 1974, 1985].

"Wells: Writing Book Was a Traumatic Experience." *Bloomington Herald-Telephone,* April 30, 1980.

Wells, H. B. "Service Charges for Small or So-called Country Banks." M.A. thesis, Indiana University, 1927.

———. "Service Charges for Small or So-called Country Banks." *The Hoosier Banker* 12, nos. 11–12 (August and September 1927): 1ff.

———. "Top Heavy Bank Supervision." *Banking* 27, no. 10 (April 1935): 13–15, 81.

Wells, Herman B. *Being Lucky: Reminiscences and Reflections.* Bloomington: Indiana University Press, 1980.

———. *Being Lucky Postscript.* Bloomington: Indiana University Foundation, 1986.

———. "The Campaign for Indiana." In *1984 Annual Report, Indiana University Foundation,* 20.

———. "A Case Study on Interinstitutional Cooperation." *Educational Record* 48 (1967): 355–62.

———. "How to Succeed as a University President Without Really Trying." *Educational Record* 45 (1964): 241–45.

———. "Kinsey's 'Sexual Behavior in the Human Female' Receives Wide-spread Public Attention." *Indiana Alumni Magazine* 16, no. 1 (October 1953): 8–9.

———. *The Legislature and Higher Education in New York State: A Report by the Legislature's Consultant on Higher Education.* New York: Academy for Educational Development, 1964.

———. *A Man, an Institution, and an Era.* New York: Newcomen Society in North America, 1952.

———. "Message to the University Community." *Indiana Daily Student,* November 1, 1968.

———. "Remarks at Andrew Carnegie Commemorative Luncheon." New York, November 19, 1954.

———. "The Role of the University in a Democratic Society." 1947.

———. "Widening Horizons." *Educational Record* 38 (1957): 136–40.

Wells, Herman G. [*sic*] "The Early History of Indiana University as Reflected in the Administration of Andrew Wylie, 1929–1851." *Filson Club History Quarterly* 36, no. 2 (1962): 113–27.

The Wells Archive: Exploring the World of Higher Education: An Event to Celebrate the Contributions of Herman B Wells to Higher Education. Video recording. Bloomington: Indiana University Radio and Television Services, 2000.

"Wells Attributes Success to 'Being Lucky.'" *IU Newspaper,* October 24, 1980.

"Wells Gets a Surprise Honor." *Bloomington Herald-Telephone,* June 4, 1962, 1.

"Wells Receives Local NAACP's Annual Award." *Indiana Daily Student,* May 18, 1962.

Westfall, Richard S. "Newton and His Biographer." In *Introspection in Biography: The Biographer's Quest for Self-Awareness,* edited by Samuel H. Baron and Carl Pletsch, 175–89. Hillsdale, N.J.: Analytic Press, 1985.

Whitworth, Walter. "Marian Anderson Corrects a Flaw." *Indianapolis News,* January 15, 1943.

Will, George. "Dementia Takes Spirit before Body." *Bloomington Herald-Times,* July 16, 2006.

Williams, William Carlos. "Kenneth Burke." *The Dial* 87 (1929): 6–8.

Wilson, Kenneth L. (Tug), and Jerry Brondfield. *The Big Ten.* Englewood Cliffs, N.J.: Prentice-Hall, 1967.

Wilson, Robin, and Roger E. Wyman. *The Committee on Institutional Cooperation: A Twenty Year History, 1958–1978.* N.p.: CIC, n.d.

Witlwarmer, Elisha. "T. C. Steele, Artist and Gentleman." *The Vagabond* 1, no. 4–5 (1924): 15–18.

Woodburn, James A. "Since the Beginning: A Retrospect." *Indiana University Alumni Quarterly* 11 (1924): 297–320.

———. *History of Indiana University,* vol. 1, *1820–1902.* Bloomington: Indiana University, 1940.

Wright, Mike. "Wells Adds Another Sagamore to His Honors." *Bloomington Herald-Times,* June 11, 1997.

———. "Wells in Good Health at 97, Despite IU Posting, Rumors." *Bloomington Herald-Times,* March 9, 2000, 1.

Wylie, Theophilus A. *Indiana University, Its History from 1820, When Founded, to 1890.* Indianapolis: Wm. B. Burford, 1890.

Wylie House Museum: Bringing History Home. Bloomington: Indiana University Libraries, [2010].

Wynkoop, Mary Ann. *Dissent in the Heartland: The Sixties at Indiana University.* Bloomington: Indiana University Press, 2002.

Yokley, Raytha L. "The Negro Community in Bloomington." M.A. thesis, Indiana University, 1941.

York, Julie, and Terrence Bland. "Sculpture of Wells in the Works." *South Bend Tribune,* March 22, 2000.

Zirker, Joan. "The Way it Was: IU in 1945." *Arts and Sciences* 10, no. 1 (1987): 5–10.

Zook, George F., and others. *Higher Education for American Democracy: A Report of the President's Commission on Higher Education.* Washington, D.C.: GPO, 1947.

Index

JAMES H. CAPSHEW is a historian of science and learning at Indiana University, where he teaches courses in the history of the modern university, the social role of the scientist, and neuropsychological pathography, among other subjects. Fascinated by individuals' navigation of their institutional lives and cultural contexts in twentieth-century America, his research has two main foci: the scientific profession of psychology and the ethos of higher education. He is author of *Psychologists on the March: Science, Practice, and Professional Identity in America, 1929–1969* as well as numerous scholarly articles, and has served as editor of the journal *History of Psychology* and as editor for psychology of the *New Dictionary of Scientific Biography.*

This book was designed by Jamison Cockerham at Indiana University Press, set in type by Cathy Bailey, and printed by Sheridan Books, Inc.

The typefaces are Arno, designed by Robert Slimbach in 2007, Optima, designed by Hermann Zapf in 1955, and Electra, designed by William A. Dwiggins in 1935. All were issued by Adobe Systems.